Entrepreneurship
2000

Entrepreneurship
2000

Edited by
Donald L. Sexton
Ewing Marion Kauffman Foundation
Center for Entrepreneurial Leadership Inc.

and

Raymond W. Smilor
Ewing Marion Kauffman Foundation
Center for Entrepreneurial Leadership Inc.

Upstart
Publishing Company
a division of Dearborn Publishing Group, Inc.
Chicago, Illinois

Publisher and Acquisition Editor: Jere L. Calmes
Editorial Assistant: Becky Rasmussen
Production Manager: Karen Billipp

Copyright © 1997 by The Center for Entrepreneurial Leadership Inc. at The Ewing Marion Kauffman Foundation

Published by Upstart Publishing Company,
a division of Dearborn Publishing Group, Inc.

Printed in the United States of America
96 97 98 10 9 8 7 6 5 4 3 2 1

Library of Congress Cataloging-in-Publication Data
    Entrepreneurship / edited by Donald L. Sexton and Raymond W. Smilor.
       p.   cm.
    Papers presented at a conference.
    Included bibliographical references and index.
    ISBN 1-57410-064-5
    1. Entrepreneurship--Congresses. 2. New business enterprises--Management--Congresses. I. Sexton, Donald L. II. Smilor, Raymond W.
Hb615.S725 1996   96-43653
338'.04--dc20   CIP

35521741

Contents

Section I: Financing Growth

Section II: Growth Strategies

Section III: Entrepreneurship Education

Section IV: Broader Dimensions of Entrepreneurship

Section V: Research Applications, Issues, and Needs

List of Figures and Tables

Figures

Tables

Foreword

Once a man's mind is stretched by imagination,
it never returns to its original dimension.
—Oliver Wendell Holmes

IMBEDDED IN THE WORLD OF ENTREPRENEURSHIP are the concepts of growth and change. Since the initial conference on the state of the art in entrepreneurship in 1980 and the publication of *The Encyclopedia of Entrepreneurship* (1982), the field, like the topic, has encountered significant growth and change. The second and third conferences in 1985 and 1990 reflected this change as described in *The Art and Science of Entrepreneurship* (1986) and *The State of the Art of Entrepreneurship* (1992). This book, *Entrepreneurship 2000*, the fourth in the series reviews changes since 1990 and projects research needs and issues to the year 2000.

In 1980, the field was in its infancy and was best described by a quote made by Thomas Jefferson at the embarkation of a new country: "The price of ignorance is too great to pay." Sexton hoped that the first state-of-the-art entrepreneurship book would soon become obsolete as the field advanced also reflects this understanding. In the same book, Vesper noted that the decline in U.S. industrial performance had inspired federal research support for studies of innovation processes which included those of entrepreneurship. From Vesper's note of industrial decline in 1980, the world of entrepreneurship has changed dramatically.

In the second conference and book, *The Art and Science of Entrepreneurship* (1986), Kevin Farrell of *Venture* magazine stated, "By almost any measure, the 1980s are shaping up as the most entrepreneurial decade in U.S. history." Donald Burr, CEO of People Express, stated, "We are on the edge of a new golden age that will make previous [entrepreneurial] efforts look small." Further, these changes were identified as permanent: "The entrepreneurial revolution, recent though it is not a passing phenomenon but a permanent change in the economic landscape."

By the third conference and book (1992), the entrepreneurial revolution was in full swing. Wilson Harrell, former publisher of *Inc.* magazine, identified the changes in the nation's economy and the impact of fast growth entrepreneurial firms by stating, "If it weren't for the entrepreneurs, we would be in a depression that would make 1929 seem like a boom.... It is only the entrepreneurs who are running these new fast growing businesses who have made the difference between boom and bust!" John Hughes, President of the Coleman Foundation, summarized the impact of entrepreneurship by saying, "Entrepreneurship has been the wave of the past, is certainly the wave of the present, and will continue to be the wave of the future."

The wave has continued. Currently, in a climate of corporate downsizing, new business starts are at an all-time high. New jobs are being generated by fast-growth firms that are much in excess of the jobs lost by larger firms and employment is at an all-time high. The wave of entrepreneurship has become a tidal wave.

The task now, for both researchers and practitioners, is to work together to build a partnership and develop an infrastructure that will enable dynamic change to continue and support the rapid growth phenomenon called entrepreneurship.

And like any field, the ability to study and to understand has grown as entrepreneurship research matures and builds on earlier foundations.

—**Rollie Tillman**
Chairman, Kenan Institute of Private Enterprise

Preface

The Practices of Entrepreneurship

What do entrepreneurs do? What defines entrepreneurial behavior? What makes an entrepreneur entrepreneurial? To me, these are the questions that are or ought to be at the heart of entrepreneurship research. If they are, then entrepreneurship research becomes an effort to understand and explain the scope and nature of human achievement. And what we learn contributes to shaping an academic discipline with meaning, dignity, and excitement.

Peter Drucker (1985) has observed that entrepreneurship is a practice. It is a doing; it requires that one act. I think he is right. But what practices uniquely characterize the entrepreneur? If the definition of an entrepreneur focuses on what he or she does, then, for me, the entrepreneur is a person who

- ❖ pursues opportunity
- ❖ acts with passion for a purpose
- ❖ lives proactively
- ❖ builds teams
- ❖ enjoys the journey to create lasting value

Pursues Opportunity

Entrepreneurs recognize and pursue opportunities. An idea is always at the center of an opportunity, but not all ideas are opportunities. Research needs to tell us more about the difference between an idea and an opportunity, and when and how an entrepreneur knows the difference. Clearly, an opportunity is customer-driven. It is rooted in meeting a real need in the marketplace, solving a real problem, or filling a real niche within a reasonable time. Thus, there is a "window" to every opportunity. But we need to understand better how the timing of a product or service adds real value for the customer.

Usually, the entrepreneur pursues the opportunity with minimal or limited resources. Howard Stevenson and the entrepreneurship faculty at the Harvard Business School have thus defined entrepreneurship as "the pursuit of opportunity beyond the resources one currently controls" (Stevenson and Gumpert, 1985). This ability to make progress with limited resources is one of the elements of the entrepreneurial process that is both fascinating and still mysterious to entrepreneurship researchers. We know that entrepreneurs do this, but we still don't know enough about their uncanny knack to leverage limited resources.

Part of this is certainly based on the entrepreneur's ability to innovate. As Drucker (1985) points out, "Innovation is the specific function of entrepreneurship.... It is the means by which the entrepreneur either creates new wealth-producing resources or endows existing resources with enhanced potential for creating wealth." Innovation apparently requires a prepared mind. Simon (1985) argues that the most creative and innovative individuals develop "chunks" of knowledge. These are sets of patterns and relationships that develop over time that allow one to see solutions to problems—to make connections between events and actions. And yet, there are many examples of young entrepreneurs, à la Michael Dell, who innovate without those "chunks." So something else must be at work as well.

One concept that requires further exploration is "bisociation"—a phenomenon historian Arthur Koestler (1990) observed in the creative process. Bisociation is the ability to relate two seemingly unrelated things to produce that "ah-ha" sensation in the marketplace. Michael Dell combined computers and mail order to launch Dell Computer Corporation; Fred Smith related mail and overnight delivery to start Federal Express; and Debbie Fields linked cookies and information technology to build Mrs. Fields Cookies.

I'm reminded of the story of the Texas rancher who's visiting with a Missouri farmer. Their conversation soon gets to the size of the property that each owns, and the Texas rancher asks the Missouri farmer to tell him how big his farm is. The farmer points and says, "Well, if you go from the edge of my house, over to the oak tree, then cut across to that creek, then go up the hill to the stone wall, then come around to that big rock over there, then circle over to the barn and then back to the edge of my house, that's my farm." The Texas rancher, looking rather proud, says, "Well, in Texas, I can get in my car at dawn, travel all day long, and at nightfall, I'm still not at the other end of my property." To which, the farmer replied, "You know, I used to own a car like that!"

For the entrepreneur, pursuing an opportunity is often like riding a roller coaster. One must endure constant and unseen ups and downs, turns and twists. The ability to deal with the unexpected and handle the unknown—to tolerate ambiguity—is part and parcel of the entrepreneurial process. Not knowing whether one can make payroll or facing the loss of a primary customer or needing to find capital for growth and survival puts physical and emotional strains on the entrepreneur. The person who needs routine, who expects assurances, who counts on guarantees is likely to find the entrepreneurial process an extremely disquieting experience. This difference toward ambiguity was demonstrated in a very funny film of a few years ago, *The Inlaws*, which matched an orderly, conservative, strictly by-the-book dentist with a unconventional, off-the-wall, make-it-up-as-you-go-along government agent. The two found themselves in a life-threatening situation in which they faced a crazed South American dictator. Just before meeting the dictator, the dentist asked, "What should we do?" The agent told him, "Go with the flow." To which the dentist replied, "What flow?" One had a comfort with ambiguity; the other was distraught over it. How do we, as researchers, understand this tolerance for ambiguity better?

Acts With Passion for a Purpose

Perhaps the most observed phenomenon of the entrepreneurial process is the passion of the entrepreneur. To me, passion is the enthusiasm, joy, and zeal that come from the energetic and unflagging pursuit of a worthy, challenging, and uplifting purpose. In the entrepreneur, it is described as drive—the determined, optimistic, and persistent desire to succeed at one's own venture. It is the "fire in the belly" that makes the improbable possible. It is the well-spring of the entrepreneur's Ripkinesque stick-to-itiveness to always, always show up for the game.

But what is passion? What is its common cause? Where does it come from? Passion is intrinsic. Its locus is inside each one of us. So it does not have to be—in fact, cannot be—instilled or motivated into somebody else. It must only be given the freedom and opportunity to emerge. A sausage manufacturer in Kansas City beams when talking about the quality and taste of his sausage; a software developer in Austin, Texas, radiates when describing her product; and a young designer of CD-ROMs in San Diego glows when showing off his latest innovation. Each has found his or her own passion that gives purpose to what they do. In the epistle dedicatory of *Man and Superman* (1903), George Bernard Shaw provided an essential insight when he said, "This is the true joy in life—the being used for a purpose recognized by yourself as a mighty one."

Passion can take an unconventional but very practical form in entrepreneurial ventures. Jack Stack, chairman and CEO of Springfield ReManufacturing Corporation in Springfield, Missouri, and the other 119 employee owners of the company, translated their passion into a clear, concise, and convincing purpose for SRC when they took over a company in desperate straits in 1983. Faced with an 89 : 1 debt-to-equity ratio, a labor-versus-management mindset, and an environment of uncertainty and doubt, they told each other in their mission statement, "Don't run out of cash and don't destroy from within." (Stack, 1992) They never have. Their shared passion has built a culture of ownership, education, open information about all financials, teamwork, and performance that has made SRC a $100 million per year company and one of the 100 best companies to work for in America.

Lives Proactively

It's one thing to have purpose and passion; it's another to do something about them. Entrepreneurship ultimately depends on performance. Entrepreneurs who perform demonstrate Steven Covey's first habit of highly effective people—to be proactive. Proactivity, according to Covey (1989), means that our behavior is a function of our decisions, not our conditions. We have the initiative and responsibility to make things happen. Reactive people are driven by their circumstances; they make excuses about what prevents them from doing something. Proactive people are "response-able." Rather than let a situation determine how they would act, proactive people act to change their situation.

Imagine that you are in the following situation. You are walking up a timbered mountainside with a group of other people. Suddenly and unexpectedly, a huge firestorm erupts in the forest and begins to sweep uphill toward you. The flames are a hundred feet high and a hundred yards deep. An inferno engulfs the entire side of the mountain below you. The heat is so intense that whole trees explode into burning torches in an instant. You and the others turn and begin to run up the steep mountainside. It is a race for your lives—reaching the crest of the mountain means safety. But the fire is faster than you are. You know that you cannot outrun the fire, that you cannot reach the top of the mountain before the fire reaches you. What do you do?

This situation actually happened. In his profound and deeply moving book, *Young Men and Fire*, Norman MacLean (1992) recounts the great Mann Gulch fire of August 1949. Sixteen smoke jumpers from the U.S. Forest Service were trapped on the side of a mountain when the blow-up occurred. As they started their race for life, Wag Dodge, the head of the crew, did something remarkable; he invented an escape fire—he actually started his own fire in the face of the inferno, stepped into the burnt out area, and then let the firestorm roar over him. He was proactive in the extreme.

He tried to get the others to join him, but each refused and continued running up the hill, all but two to their deaths. Dodge acted to change the situation, rather than let the situation dictate his response. That's what entrepreneurs do.

There's a lesson here too about the nature of risk-taking in the entrepreneurial process. Maclean points out that Dodge's action took "as much guts as logic." In other words, both are necessary. But I would suggest that they are viewed quite differently by those inside and by those outside the entrepreneurial process. What we see often depends on where we're standing.

Entrepreneurs are usually referred to as risk-takers. But I don't think this is quite accurate, if we mean by that the gambler who is willing to bet everything on one roll of the dice and then prays that it comes up seven or eleven. A better analogy would be the chess player, who may make a bold move, but also understands the parameters of the game and anticipates the possible countermoves. In this sense, the entrepreneur prefers the odds to be stacked in his or her favor. More importantly, the entrepreneur seeks to secure those odds by acquiring superior knowledge or a key advantage about the domain in which the risk is taking place. For example, Ewing Kauffman, when he was deciding to quit his lucrative job as a salesman for a pharmaceutical firm to start his own company, first went to his three best customers and asked them if they would continue to buy from him if he provided the same quality at the same price. When each agreed to do so, he launched Marion Laboratories (Morgan, 1995).

Consequently, entrepreneurs tend to see the logic rather than the guts of their actions. They are willing to take calculated risks because they have come to terns with the possible ramifications of their actions, and thus feels comfortable with the uncertainty—that is, the riskiness—of the situation.

At the same time, the opportunity to act can never be entirely separated from the opportunity to fail. Thus, the person on the outside of the entrepreneurial process tends to see the guts rather than the logic of entrepreneurship. To the person on the outside, the entrepreneur can appear to be taking enormous risk, to be making a leap of faith into unknown territory. The perception of risk is thus at the very heart of what entrepreneurship is all about because it is so entwined with the element of change and action. If we ask ourselves, what is it that entrepreneurs do? Then one answer is that they act to create and manage change. And research needs to provide better insight into how and why this occurs.

Builds Teams

Every entrepreneur must develop and/or acquire the skill and expertise to run an enterprise. This skill development is not a well-understood process. It involves the practical but essential ability to manage change both personally and organizationally. Personal know-how involves skills such as leading, communicating, listening, and negotiating. Organizational know-how involves marketing, finance, accounting, production, and manufacturing.

Successful entrepreneurship requires quantitative information and qualitative insights. One springs from data, the other from experience; one relies on numbers, the other on judgment; one demands objectivity, the other personal involvement and commitment.

As an enterprise grows, entrepreneurs learn that they can't do everything themselves. Consequently, team building becomes a critical way to acquire know-how by complementing and extending the skills of the lead entrepreneur. As Kourilsky (1995) points out, the entrepreneurial development team usually has an extremely strong affinity for the entrepreneur and a commitment to the integrity of the entrepreneur's business vision. The team engages in entrepreneurially innovative and proactive applications of its group skills to scale up the venture's resources, processes, and performance.

For the entrepreneur, team building requires more than the ability to bring in complementary skills or additional expertise. It demands that one learn how to tolerate strength in others. For me, therein lies the crux of successful or failed team building. Ironically, there is a paradox at work here. The entrepreneur must confront his or her fear of letting go, of being out of complete control. Holding on too tightly to anything actually risks losing everything. So the practical issue for the entrepreneur is to learn how to let go but hold on at the same time. What can research tell us about this?

One response has been that the entrepreneur can motivate others to do his or her bidding. I doubt that one can actually motivate others. But one can inspire others! The key, as explained by Slaughter (1996), is that one must recruit and retain self-motivated individuals, and then give them the freedom and opportunity to achieve not only the company's goals but their own. We need to understand better how entrepreneurs do this.

Another dimension to team building—the creation and utilization of fluid, ad hoc teams—is also essential to entrepreneurial success. Aldrich and Zimmer (1986) showed that entrepreneurship is facilitated or constrained by linkages between entrepreneurs, resources, and opportunities and by the social relationships through which entrepreneurs obtain information, resources, and social support. Thus, entrepreneurship is embedded in networks of continuing social relations. The more extensive, complex, and diverse the web of relationships, the more the entrepreneur is likely to have access to opportunities, the greater the chance of solving problems expeditiously, and ultimately the greater the chance of success for the venture. The fewer, less dense, and more homogeneous the web of relationships, the less likely it is for a new venture to succeed. The networking dimension is especially important to understand to learn how entrepreneurs leverage human, financial, and technological resources.

Enjoys the Journey

Why would anyone choose the life of an entrepreneur? Why would anyone consciously want to work long hours for low pay, perhaps give up the security (perceived or real) of employment in government, a large corporation, or even a university, willingly walk the tightrope of success and failure, and tolerate constant ambiguity by wondering where the next investment will come from or how to make payroll?

One reason is certainly a desire for control. Entrepreneurs like to be in charge of their own destinies, to do their own thing. They seek independence, which is often expressed in being one's own boss. But the decision to take the entrepreneurial road, I think, goes deeper than this. From my observation, people become entrepreneurs because it can be such an effective way to leave a legacy—to be able to point to a significant accomplishment done well. Thus, entrepreneurship is intertwined with human achievement.

One's legacy, it seems to me, is the outcome of the convergence of competence and character—the coming together of how we do something with who we are. Competence demands performance. It involves one's ability to do something well; it marks achievement. Character reflects the degree to which one demonstrates integrity and honorable conduct.

Legacy was evidenced in the final principle that Ewing Kauffman and his 3,400 associates at Marion Laboratories developed as part of their credo for the firm, which they called "Foundations for an Uncommon Company." They wrote, believed in, and lived the following:

> We have a responsibility for excellence and innovation. We do all that we do to the very best of our ability and with the strongest enthusiasm we can generate. It is the very nature of our business to do things that have never been done before and for which there are always reasons they cannot be done. Success for us requires the ability and the spirit to find a pathway through any obstacle, even when no pathway is visible at the start.

If entrepreneurship research can illuminate why and how entrepreneurs, even in the midst of the surprises and vicissitudes of venture creation, manage to enjoy the journey, then it will provide real insight into the scope and nature of human achievement. And in the final analysis, that is what genuinely meaningful research ought to do.

—Raymond W. Smilor

REFERENCES

Aldrich, H. and C. Zimmer. 1986. Entrepreneurship Through Social Networks. In D.L. Sexton and R.W. Smilor (eds.): *The Art and Science of Entrepreneurship*. Cambridge, MA: Ballinger, 3-23.

Covey, S.R. 1989. *The Seven Habits of Highly Effective People: Powerful Lessons in Personal Change*. New York: Simon and Schuster.

Drucker, P. 1985. *Entrepreneurship and Innovation: Practice and Principles*. New York: HarperBusiness.

Koestler, A. 1990. *The Act of Creation*. New York: Viking.

Kourilsky, M. 1995. *Entrepreneurship Education: Opportunity in Search of Curriculum*. Kansas City, MO: Center for Entrepreneurial Leadership.

MacLean, N. 1992. *Young Men and Fire*. Chicago: University of Chicago Press.

Morgan, A. 1995. *Prescription for Success: The Life and Values of Ewing Marion Kauffman*. Kansas City, MO: Andrews and McMeel.

Simon, H.A. 1985. What we know about the creative process. In R.L. Kuhn (ed.): *Frontiers in Creative and Innovative Management*. Cambridge, MA: Ballinger, 3-22.

Slaughter, Michie P. 1996. Seven keys to shaping the entrepreneurial organization. In R.W. Smilor and D.L. Sexton (eds.): *Leadership and Entrepreneurship: Personal and Organizational Development in Entrepreneurial Ventures*. Westport, CN: Quorum Books, 99-110.

Stack, J. 1992. *The Great Game of Business*. New York: Doubleday.

Stevenson, H., and Gumpert, D. 1985. The heart of entrepreneurship. Cambridge, MA: *Harvard Business Review* (March-April).

Acknowledgments

THIS BOOK, LIKE ANY ENTREPRENEURIAL ADVENTURE, is the result of a dedicated entrepreneurial team. The vision for this book was provided by Ewing Marion Kauffman when he endowed the Ewing Marion Kauffman Foundation and with it, the Center for Entrepreneurial Leadership Inc. His philosophy was to share the rewards with those who contributed to the results and to give something back to the community. This book, following Mr. K's vision, is our attempt to share with the academic and business community the fruits of our labor in the area of research. Our gift is the starting level of knowledge to future researchers and practitioners, with the charge that they expand on what has been provided to them and, in turn, give it back to their predecessors in the profession. It is hoped that we have presented what we know, hypothesized about what we don't know, and suggested what we need to know.

This book started with senior researchers in the field identifying the current research needs as well as the scholars who were most knowledgeable in each specific area. Four of the researchers in this book contributed to all three of the previous books. They are David Brophy, Arnold Cooper, Jeffry Timmons, and Bill Wetzel. Their contributions as well as their friendship has enhanced both the book and our lifetimes.

This book could not have survived the initial start up without the support of Michie Slaughter, President of the Center for Entrepreneurial Leadership Inc., as well as his understanding of the time and effort necessary to bring it to the community. Nor could it have passed through the transitions in complexity of the venture without the efforts of Barbara Anderson, Victoria Hall, and Patsy Neblock. They organized the conference, gathered the manuscript, and worked tirelessly in addressing the changes and requests of the editor.

Thanks also to our editor, David Prout, to Karen Billipp, our designer and project manager, to Becky Rasmussen, editorial assistant, and everyone else at Upstart Publishing for their efforts to make the manuscript more readable.

We especially thank Jere Calmes, publisher of Upstart Publishing, for working with us for the second time on a state-of-the-art book.

We also appreciate the contribution of the foreword by Rollie Tillman, former director of the Kenan Institute and a long-time respected professional and friend.

We thank our entrepreneurial partners in life, Carol and Judy, for sharing their time with us so that we could complete this book.

Finally, each of us wishes to thank his coeditor for making this, our second state-of-the-art joint venture, a professional and personal rewarding effort.

—**Donald L. Sexton**
—**Raymond W. Smilor**

Upstart Publishing Company would like to extend their gratitude to the 1996 Upstart Editorial Advisory Board, consisting of the following members:

Gerald Hills, University of Illinois, Chicago

Robert D. Hisrich, Case Western Reserve University

Frank Hoy, University of Texas, El Paso

Donald F. Kuratko, Ball State University

Dale Meyer, University of Colorado

Donald L. Sexton, Ewing Marion Kauffman Foundation

George T. Solomon, George Washington University

Harold P. Welsch, DePaul University

About the Contributors, Sponsors, and Editors

The Contributors

Zoltan F. Acs is the Harry Y. Wright Professor of Economics and Finance in the Robert G. Merrick School of Business at the University of Baltimore, and Associate Director of the Center for International Business Education and Research (CIBER), College of Business and Management, at the University of Maryland.

Howard E. Aldrich is the Kenan Professor of Sociology, Director of the Sociology Graduate Studies Program, and Adjunct Professor of Business, at the University of North Carolina, Chapel Hill.

Ted Baker is a graduate student in the Sociology Department at the University of North Carolina at Chapel Hill.

David J. Brophy is Professor of the Finance Faculty at the University of Michigan School of Business Administration and Director of the UM Office for the Study of Private Equity Finance.

John Sibley Butler is Professor of Management and Sociology at the University of Texas at Austin. He holds the Dallas TACA Centennial Professorship in Liberal Arts (Sociology) and the Arthur James Douglass Centennial Professorship in Entrepreneurship and Small Business (Management).

Bill Bygrave is the Frederic C. Hamilton Professor for Free Enterprise and Director of the Center for Entrepreneurial Studies at Babson College.

Arnold C. Cooper is the Louis A. Weil, Jr., Professor of Management at the Krannert Graduate School of Management, Purdue University.

Jeffrey G. Covin is the Hal and John Smith Chair of Entrepreneurship and Small Business Management at the School of Management, Georgia Institute of Technology.

Catherine M. Daily is Assistant Professor of Management in the Krannert Graduate School of Management, Purdue University.

William J. Dennis, Jr., is Senior Research Fellow at the NFIB Education Foundation in Washington, DC.

John Freear is Professor of Accounting and Finance and Associate Dean at the Whittemore School of Business and Economics at the University of New Hampshire.

Patricia G. Greene is the New Jersey Professor of Entrepreneurship and Small Business at Rutgers University.

Ramona K. Z. Heck is the J. Thomas Clark Professor of Entrepreneurship and Personal Enterprise at Cornell University.

Robert D. Hisrich is the A. Malachi Mixon III Chair and Professor of Entrepreneurial Studies at Weatherhead School of Management, Case Western Reserve University.

Frank Hoy is Dean of the College of Business Administration and Texas Commerce Bank Professor of Business at the University of Texas at El Paso.

Bruce A. Kirchhoff is Distinguished Professor of Entrepreneurship and Director of the Technological Entrepreneurship Program at New Jersey Institute of Technology.

Marilyn Kourilsky is Vice President at the Ewing Marion Kauffman Foundation Center for Entrepreneurial Leadership.

Ian C. MacMillan is Executive Director of the Sol C. Snider Entrepreneurial Center and George W. Taylor Professor of Entrepreneurial Studies.

Patricia McDougall is Associate Professor of Management at the Georgia Institute of Technology.

Ben Oviatt is Associate Professor of Management at Georgia State University.

J. William Petty is Professor of Finance and holds the W. W. Caruth Chair of Entrepreneurship at Baylor University.

Bruce D. Phillips is Director of the Office of Economic Research of the U.S. Small Business Administration.

Michie P. Slaughter is President and Chairman of the Center for Entrepreneurial Leadership Inc., at the Ewing Marion Kauffman Foundation.

Dennis P. Slevin is Professor of Business Administration at the Katz Graduate School of Business, University of Pittsburgh.

Jeffrey E. Sohl is Associate Professor of Management Science in the Department of Decision Sciences and Director of the Center for Venture Research at the Whittemore School of Business and Economics at the University of New Hampshire.

Jeffry A. Timmons is the Franklin W. Olin Distinguished Professor of Entrepreneurship at Babson College.

Nancy Upton holds the Ben Williams Chair in Entrepreneurship and is Director of the John F. Baugh Center for Entrepreneurship at Baylor University.

S. Venkataraman is the Warren H. Bruggeman '46 and Pauline Urban Bruggeman Distinguished Chair at Rensselaer Polytechnic Institute.

William E. Wetzel, Jr. is Director Emeritus of the Center for Venture Research. Before his retirement, he served as the Forbes Professor of Management at the Whittemore School of Business and Economics and Director of the Center for Venture Research, University of New Hampshire.

Dennis R. Young is Governing Director of the Mandel Center for Nonprofit Organizations, Mandel Professor of Nonprofit Management, and Adjunct Professor of Economics at Case Western Reserve University.

John E. Young is the Albert Franklin Black Professor of Entrepreneurship at the University of New Mexico's Robert O. Anderson School of Management.

About the Sponsor

The Center for Entrepreneurial Leadership Inc., was established in 1992 by a truly remarkable entrepreneur, Ewing Marion Kauffman. Mr. Kauffman built a pharmaceutical firm into a major health care company with more than $1 billion in sales at the time of its merger with Merrell Dow. The Center, in Kansas City, Missouri, is an independent 501(c)(3) not-for-profit educational organization funded by the Ewing Marion Kauffman Foundation. It pursues a vision of accelerating entrepreneurship in America.

About the Editors

Donald L. Sexton, Ph.D., is the director of the National Center for Entrepreneurship Research at the Ewing Marion Kauffman Foundation's Center for Entrepreneurial Leadership Inc., Kansas City, Missouri.

Dr. Sexton has had two careers ... one in business and one in academia. He spent 18 years in industry, 10 years in engineering and operations research, and 8 years as a turn-around manager. He managed four firms from losses to profitable operations. During his 17 years in academia, he taught at two major universities. At Baylor University he held the Caruth Chair in Entrepreneurship, where he established entrepreneurship majors at both the undergraduate and graduate levels, and the Center for Entrepreneurship. At the Ohio State University, he held the William H. Davis Chair in the American Free Enterprise System.

He has published seven textbooks and numerous articles, has lectured widely, and has assisted in the establishment of entrepreneurship programs at many universities throughout the United States and in 14 foreign countries. He has been recognized for his achievements by the Small Business Administration, the National Federation of Independent Business, the Freedom Foundation, and the Association of Collegiate Entrepreneurs.

Dr. Sexton holds a B.S. in Math/Physics from Wilmington College and an M.B.A. and Ph.D. from the Ohio State University. He is listed in *Who's Who in America* and *Who's Who in Finance and Industry*.

Raymond W. Smilor, Ph.D., is vice president, Center for Entrepreneurial Leadership Inc., Ewing Marion Kauffman Foundation, Kansas City, Missouri. He was the first chairholder of the Marion Merrell Dow Chaired Professorship in Entrepreneurship at the Henry W. Bloch School of Business and Public Administration at the University of Missouri–Kansas City.

Dr. Smilor has published extensively, with refereed articles appearing in several journals. He is the author or editor of 10 books including *Financing and Managing Fast-Growth Companies: The Venture Capital Process* (Lexington, 1985), *The Art and Science of Entrepreneurship* (Ballinger, 1987), *The New Business Incubator* (Lexington, 1986), *Customer-Driven Marketing: Lessons from Entrepreneurial Technology Companies* (Lexington, 1989), *Technology Transfer in Consortia and Strategic Alliances* (Rowman and Littlefield, 1992), and *Leadership and Entrepreneurship* (Quorum Books, 1996). His works have been translated into a number of languages including Japanese, French, and Italian. Because of his teaching, research, publications, and community initiatives in the area of entrepreneurship over the years, he was selected as one of the Entrepreneurs Of The Year® in 1990 for his activities in support of entrepreneurship, and inducted into the Entrepreneur Of The Year Institute®.

Dr. Smilor has lectured internationally and has been recognized for teaching innovation and excellence in both graduate and executive development programs. He earned his Ph.D. in U.S. history at the University of Texas at Austin.

Introduction

I find the great thing in this world is not so much where we stand,
as in what direction we are moving.
—Oliver Wendell Holmes

IN 1980, A SMALL GROUP OF RESEARCHERS joined together in an effort to assess the state of the art of research in an emerging academic area called entrepreneurship. Although these pioneers felt that this new emerging area had significant potential for economic and academic development, few realized that they were looking at the leading edge of a revolution.

Fifteen years later, the realities of the new revolution are now clearly evident in the United States. According to the U.S. Department of Labor Non-Farm Employment Data, the American economy generated over 27 million new jobs between 1980 and 1995. Virtually all of the new jobs between 1980 and 1990 came from new and smaller firms. In addition, the 1994 edition of the *Small Business Administration's Handbook of Small Business Data* estimated that 65 to 70 percent of the new jobs from 1990 to 1995 would be generated by new and smaller firms. Further, Dun and Bradstreet reported in 1995 that new businesses number in the 1.2 to 1.5 million range with 740,000 new business incorporations.

Researchers in 1980 did not anticipate that in 15 years entrepreneurship classes would be taught in 800 to 1,000 universities or that seven out of 10 high school students would want to have their own businesses in their adult years. Likewise, no one would have predicted that, in December 1993, the General Assembly of the United Nations would unanimously pass a resolution recognizing entrepreneurship as a major social and economic force and urge member countries to create programs and implement policies to encourage as well as to support entrepreneurship among their populations.

Finally, the researchers did not expect that changes in the American economy due to the downsizing of larger corporations would result in changes in employment from almost one in four workers holding jobs in major corporations a few years ago, to less than one in ten now.

The state of the art in academic research has also changed since 1980. As reported in the first entrepreneurship book (Kent et al., 1982), the field was in its embryonic stage. Little was known about the subject and myths about entrepreneurship based on opinions, not on rigorous research or facts, abounded. Business failures were the topic of the day and some people believed that half of all new businesses failed in the first year and 90 percent failed in five years. Given this data, one might have accepted the general academic opinion at the time that entrepreneurship was not an area worthy of academic pursuit. Other misleading opinions popular in this era included the notion that venture capitalists stole businesses from entrepreneurs and that private venture capital angels were mythical creatures. Many more curious conclusions were all made without any input from entrepreneurs or quality-based research. Further, starting a business was the key factor, and few people talked about transitions in growth or changes in business complexity. However, there was a growing excitement about the potential of this field.

Five years later, the second conference and book (Sexton and Smilor, 1985), revealed that entrepreneurial research was beginning to develop and concerns for more rigorous investigation using validated test instruments and longitudinal studies of performance were addressed. Suggestions of the need for development of comprehensive theoretical frameworks were made in an effort to relate research to performance. The emphasis was leaning more toward understanding the factors that contribute to growth in an effort to answer the question, Why do some firms perform better than others? Although major breakthroughs were few, the attitude was one of considerable excitement about the future of entrepreneurial research.

By the third conference and book (Sexton and Kasarda, 1990), the excitement and optimism was matched with a maturing awareness of the size and complexity of the field. More importantly, the research community began to:

❖ Realize what it did not know.

❖ Structure its research to permit it to explore the basic shortcomings in its knowledge and build a full understanding of the field.

❖ Conduct its explorations in a more careful manner so that the results were extendible and not confounded by uncontrollable or unknown variables.

Academics, as well as practitioners, have a responsibility to destroy myths and develop truth in their respective areas. Toward this end, this book addresses issues that will help academics more fully understand the cause-and-effect relationships that contribute to business growth and success and explores the entrepreneurial issues that are so directly involved in the current economic revolution. In addition, it is absolutely essential that researchers effectively communicate their findings about the benefits of entrepreneurship to public policy reform that will encourage entrepreneurial efforts to create jobs and improve the well-being of our society.

The chapters in this book represent the most important topics in the field today and substantiate the need for continued effort as the entrepreneurship revolution thrusts into the 21st century. The chapters fall into the following five categories:

Section I   Financing Growth

Section II   Growth Strategies

Section III   Entrepreneurship Education

Section IV   Broader Dimensions of Entrepreneurship

Section V   Research Applications, Issues, and Needs

The work presented reflects a desire to communicate the research efforts to a broader audience of the academic, practitioner and public policy communities. The broadening of the field is represented by topics not found in earlier state-of-the-art books as well as an increased depth of understanding throughout the area. The field of entrepreneurship or the entrepreneurial revolution is being realized for the contribution it has made to our students, our lives, and our economic community.

There should be no doubt that entrepreneurship, with its recognized impact on job creation, national output of products and services, and contribution to the overall growth and vitality of our economy, is a subject deserving much thought and study by academic institutions. It should also be evident that efforts to provide clear, comprehensive, and objective data and expand the research capacity for entrepreneurship are important investments in our nation's economic future.

Financing Growth

The chapters in this section cover the topics of financing growth, venture capital, informal venture capital, and harvesting the value of the firm.

Brophy suggests that as we have learned more about growth capital financing, it has become even more important. The area has received increased attention among investors, entrepreneurs, and public policymakers and should prove to be attractive to researchers over the next five years. Addressing the financing needs of fast-growth firms, he suggests, must be a top priority item of U.S. public policy and private sector development. He also suggests that the recent research interest in the field has been encouraged by the availability of the CRISP and COMPUSTAT tapes, the development of other financial information databases, and changes in investment regulations, such as ERISA, SBIC, and SCOR.

Timmons and Bygrave revisit the research in the formal venture capital market via a review of projections about the area in the last state-of-the-art book. Their conclusion: The industry structure has changed significantly in each of the three previous reviews since 1980. Since 1990, the industry has seen significant growth, increased competition, a shake out, and large firms becoming larger, with the result that today the industry has never been healthier. Research in this area has tended to be conducted in areas of concern to the firms. Topics related to value-added, differentiation, investment decision-making, valuing, and harvesting are current topics of concern.

Freear, Sohl, and Wetzel report that the informal venture capital market is substantially larger than the institutional venture capital market. It is larger by a factor of three to five with regard to investments and 10 to 15 times larger in the number of ventures financed. They also caution that these estimates are difficult to verify due to the invisible nature of the angel market. This is one of the major impediments to research in this area, which is not surprising since angel capital providers are a diverse and dispersed population of high-net-worth investors who place a high value on anonymity. There are no directories of business angels, and no public records of the estimated 1 to 1.5 million investor families or their investment transactions. Despite these difficulties, the expansion of the informal venture capital markets in the United States, United Kingdom, and Europe make for promising opportunities for research in this area.

Petty examines a topic that is often the dream of many entrepreneurs, the harvesting of the value invested in the firm. Harvesting is more than merely selling and leaving the business. It is capturing value, reducing risks, and creating future options for the entrepreneur. Petty suggests that a preoccupation with starting and growing the business has resulted in a lack of research on this topic. This is understandable since one cannot harvest what has not been created. Yet, few events in the lifetime of the entrepreneur, and for the firm itself, are more significant than the harvest. Through a review of the fundamental approaches of harvesting and what is known about the process, Petty concludes:

❖ The entrepreneur's appreciation of the harvest process is intertwined with his or her personal goals and objectives.

❖ Decisions made in the present have significant impact on the value of the firm at harvest.

❖ Regardless of personal preferences, a time will come when the entrepreneur will need to harvest the venture.

Growth Strategies

Growth emerged as a distinguishing factor between entrepreneurship and small business in the mid-1980s. This issue has become even more important as the impact of rapid growth firms has been recognized in the United States economy. The following topics on growth research and their contributors were selected based on input from top researchers in the field.

Covin and Slevin propose that businesses today are facing extraordinary challenging environments marked by increased complexity and the need for more rapid and dynamic transitions to different strategic postures and more viable organizational forms. Following the premise that growth poses a challenge to management that requires dealing with chaos, complexity, and contradiction, a lack of resolution of these problems may lead to failure among seemingly successful, high-growth firms. The authors offer two major themes inherent in managing growth and complexity: 1) Complexity is here to stay, and 2) transitions are central to growth. They also point out that entrepreneurs must develop new skills that will allow them to manage the transitions needed to achieve the high-growth status.

Cooper and Daily report on entrepreneurial teams and their contribution in growth-oriented firms. They suggest that entrepreneurial teams are the heart of any new venture, yet there is little empirical research examining how teams are formed, how they function and how they influence organizational performance. Theoretical frameworks from other disciplines can also be drawn upon in examining entrepreneurial teams, such as work on small group behavior, organizational rules, organizational decision-making, and human capital. Unfortunately, most research in this area has been anecdotal and lacking in a theoretical base. Hence, research has not made much progress in five years. However, with the importance of this area to fast-growth firms and the current lack of research on the subject, there are many opportunities for future research that will enhance our understanding of entrepreneurial teams.

Venkataraman and MacMillan make the suggestion that the choice in organizational mode in new business development is critical to the long term development of the firm. The authors report that firms grow through three different modes: internal development, purchase of other firms, or through some type of cooperative arrangement. A review of the literature indicates that not all modes are available to the newer firms due to aspects of newness risk. There is a dire need for high-quality empirical research in this area, and the key research challenge is to make theoretical constructs operative and to obtain quality data for the testing of these constructs.

Kirchoff and Acs report that the dynamics of births and deaths of firms is a major source of growth in economic activity, realignment of competitive market shares, and increases in productivity. They also submit that births and deaths of firms are not indelibly linked as in human life. Research on the births of firms has been hampered by a shortage of long-term databases that include information on ownership data. The firm deaths area of research has been plagued by inconsistencies in the definitions of death, failure, determinations, or discontinuances. Currently, the two most prominent definitions are either bankruptcy or a cession of operation with a loss to one or more creditors. In essence, according to the authors, two questions still remain:

❖ Why do some businesses fail?

❖ Which ones will fail and which ones will survive?

Entrepreneurship Education

The purpose of academic research is to develop and test an hypothesis in such a way that the data is accurate and reliable, the sample is large enough to be extrapolated to a larger population, and the analysis is conducted in such a way which allow findings to accurately depict the results. Without these considerations, the results may be little more than unsubstantiated opinions.

In this section, the chapters address the very important audiences of teaching and learning entrepreneurship. Namely, elementary and secondary school students, university students, and practicing entrepreneurs.

Kourilsky and Carlson revisit the area of entrepreneurship education at the elementary and high school level by reviewing the development and dissemination of curricula intended for these levels. The impetus of this effort is drawn from a 1994 Gallup Poll that found:

❖ Seven out of 10 students surveyed want to start a business.

❖ Four out of five high school students believe that entrepreneurship should be taught in the schools.

❖ Nearly 9 out of 10 students rate their knowledge of entrepreneurship as "very poor to fair."

These findings leave no doubt that a need exists for entrepreneurship education at the elementary and high school level. The challenge is one of developing curricula and disseminating the information to meet the existing demand. The authors caution that before disseminating a curriculum, it must undergo a four-step evaluation process of effectiveness, responsiveness, transferability, and dissemination.

Young draws a distinction between entrepreneurial knowledge and entrepreneurial learning. He suggests that entrepreneurial knowledge is transmitted primarily to students while entrepreneurial learning is the process used by practicing entrepreneurs to solve problems or enhance their skill levels. He suggests that entrepreneurship education and entrepreneurial learning may be emerging as two distinct but strongly related subfields. Research in the field is limited and most of the research has been directed toward what to teach, how to teach it and how to measure the outcome. On the other hand, a wide body of literature exists on cognitive learning styles. The key, according to the author, is to relate the broad-based learning theories and concepts to the narrower topic of entrepreneurial learning. He also suggests combining both the teaching aspects for students and the learning styles of entrepreneurs for a more effective approach to this topic.

Broader Dimensions of Entrepreneurship

As knowledge about entrepreneurship expands and as the field grows, research activities expand to recognize that entrepreneurship encompasses a broad area of many aspects and dimensions. In this section, the state-of-the-art chapters examine family business, racial and ethnic businesses, international business, and entrepreneurship in the not-for-profit sector.

Upton and Heck examine a long-standing form of entrepreneurship that has only become a topic of research in the last decade—family business. The issues facing research in this area are similar to those of the broader issue of entrepreneurship in the early 1980s, namely, a struggle for definitional clarity and a lack of adequate databases to support deductive and exploratory research needed to test theories. Currently, research is narrow in scope and focused primarily on transitions. Few studies are comparative and even fewer have been replicated. Estimates of the number of family-owned or family-controlled firms range from 1.7 to 2.0 million, including many Fortune 500 companies. Given that family business research must take into consideration both the family and the growth of the firm, this is an area with significant research opportunities.

Butler and Greene examine the process by which ethnic and racial groups develop, manage, and maintain business enterprises. By tracing the history of entrepreneurship and ethnicity, they conclude that the community dimension is both important and inherent in the business creation process. They also indicate that research findings related to economic behaviors are enhanced by a consideration of race, ethnicity, and religion. Further, they feel that the study of ethnic or minority entrepreneurship needs to draw from a broader base of methodology which emphasizes theoretical grounding not only of the research question but of the appropriate population and sample selection as well. The authors challenge research in this area with the question: Why do ethnic entrepreneurs have different economic outcomes if their businesses are founded through similar processes and with some similarity in resource input?

McDougall and Oviatt suggest that entrepreneurship and international business have been the two most explosive fields of study in U.S. business schools within the last decade. They further report that international entrepreneurship is at the intersection of these two growing areas of interest. According to the authors, international entrepreneurship is not an academic discipline. Rather, it is an arena in which many disciplines apply and extend their theories to discover and explain facts about entrepreneurship across national borders. Given the recent changes in global competition, the downsizing and outsourcing of larger corporate organizations, the availability of experienced personnel, the increasing numbers of new firm starts, and the growth occurring in emerging firms, it appears that this is an area fertile for research.

Hisrich and Young address a new topic in the area of entrepreneurship. To many, entrepreneurship is intricately tied to growth in sales, profits, or some other measurable asset. To the authors, entrepreneurship in the not-for-profit sector does not fit the classic entrepreneurship domain. Yet, as they argue, developing new products and services, modernizing production operations, searching for innovative changes and obtaining funding are actions that are often used to describe entrepreneurial firms. They report that the literature on nonprofit sector innovation and entrepreneurship is wide ranging, scattered in its foci, and relatively thin. Nonetheless, the research builds on much wider literature of innovation and entrepreneurship in the economy as a whole and reveals a number of solvent themes that suggest further explanation and research that can help guide nonprofit managerial practice.

Research Applications, Issues, and Needs

Academics have been criticized for the lack of relevance of their research to a broader audience. In each of the previous state-of-the-art books, academics have issued the call for reaching out to broader audiences and especially to the research community and public policymakers. In this section, issues of relevance, databases, research methods, and research needs are discussed.

Hoy notes the calls for relevance in entrepreneurship issues in the three previous state-of-the-art books and evaluates the relevance of the research to the stakeholder. He suggests that there are four primary stakeholder groups, namely, colleagues, students, practitioners, and public policy formulators. The answer to whether entrepreneurship research is being communicated to these stakeholders is "not much." The author states that while the awareness of entrepreneurship research has increased among the stakeholder groups, external stakeholders continue to be uninformed of entrepreneurship research findings or skeptical of the contributions. He proposes two courses of action:

❖ Entrepreneurship researchers should use language that communicates clearly to the stakeholder.

❖ Researchers need to use new media to transmit their findings to a wider audiences.

Phillips and Dennis review the major databases available for analysis of formation, growth, and validity of smaller firms. Their review was based on the availability of data in the database as it relates to firm or owner characteristics, financial information, employment and wages, and timeliness. On this basis they discuss the pros and cons of the major existing databases in the public and private sectors and the parameters of other databases currently in development. They express concern that reductions in federal expenditures in this area may have a significant negative impact on the quality, quantity, and timeliness of the data. They are also concerned that existing databases are highly fragmented, follow varying formats, employ assorted definitions, have different and generally unrelated foci, and have a utility that may rapidly change and negate the value of the database altogether. Yet the amount of data on firms is expected to increase as people recognize the importance of entrepreneurship. Clearly, a step in the right direction.

Aldrich and Baker review the development and utilization of acceptable research methods from the perspectives of normal science, multiple paradigms, and pragmatism in an effort to determine how much progress has been made in the field. They conclude that the field lacks an institutionalized set of programs teaching a consistent paradigm to new scholars. This, they suggest, is in part due to the fact that recruits to the field are trained by established academics from a variety of disciplines and are exposed to a wide range of standards and methods. Using a research classification scheme similar to that used in earlier state-of-the-art reviews, they conclude that research designs and methodologies have not changed much in the last five years. Further, they feel that attempts to establish rules or admonitions are not effective and that the field will be shaped by those who produce research that interests and attracts others to build on their work.

Sexton, in the final chapter, reviews the research progress in the area of entrepreneurship, assesses the current state-of-the-art, and summarizes and prioritizes the research issues raised by the authors. It is through quality academic research that the body of knowledge of this exciting field can be advanced and transmitted to the appropriate audiences.

This book represents the fourth of a series of books published at five-year intervals since 1980 that assess the state-of-the-art in entrepreneurship research. The field has grown considerably over the last 15 years, not only in the research area but as a significant contributor to the economic development and growth of the nation.

Entrepreneurship—with its recognized impact on job creation, national output of products and services, and contribution to the overall growth and vitality of our economy—should be the subject of much thought and study. Efforts to provide clear, comprehensive, and objective data and expand the research capacity for entrepreneurship are important investments in our nation's economic future.

—**Michie P. Slaughter**

SECTION I

Financing Growth

Financing Growth

FINANCING THE ADDITIONAL FUNDS needed is a problem for all firms that grow faster than the rate that can be achieved through internally generated funds. The state of the art of knowledge about the availability, requirements, and techniques of gathering financial resources to pursue growth opportunities has expanded exponentially since the early 1980s. Much more is now known about matching the type and level of funding to the strategic plans of the business and matching the type, amount, and requirements of funding with the appropriate funding institutions.

Just as achieving growth carries with it all the problems of starting a business plus a whole lot more, the same happens in the financing area. A firm without growth plans most likely will not encounter many areas discussed in this section, namely, the informal venture capital market (private investors), the formal venture capital market, mezzanine financing, and the initial public offering market. Further, firms that do not grow do not achieve the magnitude necessary, and therefore do not have the opportunity, to utilize a number of methods to "cash out" or "harvest" their investment in the business.

The venture capital industry was fragmented and had few standard policies and procedures in the early 1980s. Now it is a well-developed industry that has pushed the operational envelope through better understanding of techniques and methodologies as well as more efficient utilization of technological advancements.

Although the private investor's desire for anonymity has restricted access to these investors, the ability of some to serve as a gatekeeper or matchmaker has increased the number, dollar amount, and efficiency of these investments. By some accounts, private investments exceed those of the better recognized venture capital firms by a magnitude of three to five times.

It is interesting to note that while funds invested by private individuals are provided primarily by entrepreneurs who have "cashed out," or taken their investments from their firms, this section includes the state of the art in "harvesting" the business for the first time.

Brophy opens this section with an overview of the state of the art in research in financing growth. Timmons and Bygrave discuss projections about the venture capital market field made in 1990 and look at the problems expected in the next five years. As they indicate, an active initial public offering market has increased activity in the venture capital field by allowing the firms to cash out on their older investments and raise new and larger funds for new investments. On the negative side, the growth in the stock market has been such that over the last year, investors have found greater returns in the stock market than in the venture capital markets and with less riskier investments.

Freear, Sohl, and Wetzel examine changes in the informal venture capital or private investor area, especially the aspects of forming investor/entrepreneur matchmaking institutions or mega-funds/mega-groups of private investors with similar investment criteria.

The last chapter in this section by Petty provides insights into what is known and what is not known about taking out the entrepreneur's value in the firm.

CHAPTER 1

Financing the Growth of Entrepreneurial Firms

DAVID J. BROPHY

ENTREPRENEURS AND FINANCIERS, and the researchers who study them, have come to recognize that the internal and external growth capital financing of entrepreneurial ventures, and of the companies that they spawn, is a key aspect of the entrepreneurship process and that it must be understood from both the demand and supply sides. This has led to a sharpened focus on finance among entrepreneurs and financiers of all types, and an increase in the amount of research being devoted to the financing of entrepreneurial, emerging growth firms during those parts of their lives in which their securities are not publicly traded. While students of corporate strategy and management continue to lead in entrepreneurship research, increasingly researchers from economics, finance, and law have found it rewarding to pursue theoretical and empirical studies of entrepreneurial phenomena, in particular the financing of entrepreneurial companies. The assets of such companies are intangible and consist primarily of growth options; complex security contracts are used to mitigate the risks that reflect the lack of marketability of their securities about which information is costly and difficult to obtain.

This development is a very positive one for entrepreneurship research, inasmuch as it brings new categories of researchers to the field, broadening and deepening the set of intellectual resources, information, and publication outlets brought to bear upon entrepreneurial research. In this chapter, we review the themes that have emerged as a result of this recent increase in interest in the financing of entrepreneurial growth firms and propose a research agenda for the immediate future.

Nature of the Financing Problem

The general problem in financing the growth of a business is usually considered by researchers from the viewpoint of the firm which seeks to raise the capital involved. The inherent assumptions are that financial markets will supply a complete variety of financing types (e.g., simple or complex parcels of debt or equity) and that it is up to the firm's owner/managers to choose an optimum combination of personal investment, reinvested earnings, external debt and external equity, with relative accessibility and cost of capital determining the optimum mix. For established firms with collateral and with a track record in an established industry, the supply assumption may hold. However, the problem involved in financing the growth of entrepreneurial firms is best seen in the context of emerging, "fast growth" firms while they are still private firms, closely held by owner/managers and initial investors. As discussed below, the supply assumptions may not always hold for such firms, causing systematic market mismatches at particular stages of life of the fast-growth-oriented firm.

Fast-growth-oriented companies represent most of the power of the small business sector to create wealth, income, and jobs. Research indicates that the bulk of the job creation within the small business sector is generated by fewer than five percent of the total number of the firms in that sector (Hall, 1995). Other research speaks to the increased interest in new firm formation and development by individuals as an alternative to employment with larger firms (Harrison, 1994). Still other evidence shows the wealth creation capacity of such firms through initial public offerings, strategic partnering, and sale of such companies to larger firms (Barry et al., 1990). Encouraging emerging fast-growth companies offers the United States potential for technological innovation, improved quality of life, and strong economic growth. Providing access to finance for such firms in their development and growth stages is central to improving these prospects and must be a top priority item of U.S. public policy and private-sector development. It is important to expand the base of what we really know about the processes involved in this financing. As a result, it offers an important challenge to the community of scholars interested in research on entrepreneurship.

In the extreme, the most interesting and perhaps most important "growth capital financing" case is often that of the entrepreneurial firm which has the potential for fast growth, predicated on outstanding growth options, which is knowledge-based and technologically driven, and which is derived from productive use of primarily intangible assets in a rapidly developing field with no well-documented operating history. Such characteristics are reflected in a great many of the "cutting edge," emerging growth companies, in the United States and other countries, which are competing and operating interdependently in a global economy. These are the firms upon which we count to discover and to develop today's market niches into tomorrow's leading manufacturing, retail, and service industries. Capabilities and techniques designed to accommodate the needs of such firms and to realize their wealth-creating capabilities are easily adapted to the needs of less complicated entrepreneurial firms of all sizes, e.g., those in well-established markets with assets acceptable as loan collateral and with more modest growth aspirations. These characteristics have been cited by many in the financial community—including banks, nonbank lenders, venture capital funds, and investment bankers—as representing inherent unacceptable risk and are good reasons for avoiding this type of investment. The diseconomies of small parcel finance are also cited as a negative factor: given the modest amounts of capital involved and the disproportionate amount of fixed cost, "due diligence," and monitoring costs involved for modest expected returns (on average), many investors and intermediaries eschew the opportunity to get involved.

Camp and Sexton (1992) studied venture capital disbursement trends between 1980 and 1990, a period characterized by exceptional returns from 1980 to 1983 and very low returns for the remainder of the decade. Following the high returns through 1983, increased capital flowed into the industry, increasing competition for investment opportunities, driving up deal prices, and setting up lower investment returns. The authors document the sharp decline in inflows of new capital to venture capital funds following 1985, the shift away from early-stage to later-stage investment, and the changes in the industry placements for initial or first-round investments away from technology-based deals.

This combination of a perceived unacceptable risk/return relationship and investment diseconomies pose special problems for firms of varying types of ownership, many of which carry an extra burden of prejudgment with them as they approach the financial community. These include women-owned and minority-owned firms and family businesses, franchises, and microbusinesses whether they are "lifestyle" or "job substitution" small businesses or firms seeking to achieve their fast-growth potential. If the United States is to realize the maximum nationwide benefits of strong fast-growth companies, public policy and private sector initiative must enable and encourage the refined development of the financial system to effectively serve the needs of small businesses in general and, in particular, that subset of the universe of firms with fast-growth potential. Relevant research can make a important contribution toward this end.

The private, closely held entrepreneurial company progresses by idiosyncratic development through roughly defined life stages from start-up through emerging growth to stable self-sufficiency and maturity. Through most of this emergent development, the firm is dependent upon financial support from the initial subscription of "founders' investment" and by successive rounds of external private equity and debt funding to supplement internal cash flows reinvested in the business. At some appropriate point, as a consequence of development, financial supporters may be able to "harvest" their investment through the firm's initial public offering, leveraged buyout, or merger/acquisition. In this journey through the critical events and life stages—with financing involved at virtually every stage and event—the agency, contracting, investment valuation, structuring, and pricing issues reach their highest levels of importance and require solutions. This aspect of the problem has begun to attract the attention of leading researchers from the fields cited above.

Investment in a publicly traded company with a resilient liquid market may be reasonably reversed at any time by sale of the stock, whereas an investment in a private or thinly traded public market either has no liquidity or involves a large "haircut" in disposing of the investment position. In the absence of a reasonable exit through sale, contractual financing arrangements are the key to investment because they define the rights, responsibilities, and implications for all parties. While the basic issue with any company is whether the intended customer will buy the product investment contracts protect all parties against agency risk. Agency risk is borne by one party who depends upon another person (the agent) to act with his or her interest in mind. The risk may run both ways in a private investment contract.

As discussed below, there is a strong demand for private equity finance from firms other than small to midsize, emerging, fast-growth-oriented company (i.e., the typical venture capital-type company). Increasingly, larger firms with longer track records in more stable, lower-growth industries are in demand of private equity finance to fund growth opportunities in industry consolidation through acquisitions, debt restructuring and reduction, mezzanine financing before going public or selling out, and financing through private placement after becoming a public company. So strong is this demand, and so profitable the terms of trade for institutional investors' net of the risk involved, that many such investors have dedicated funds to this type of investment in combination with or in lieu of investment in venture capital. Much of the following discussion centers on the development of the private equity finance market in response to the demand to finance the growth of entrepreneurial firms.

The Evolving Research Environment

The environment for research on financing entrepreneurial firms has gradually improved during the post-World War II period. Anecdotal case study data and information—characteristic of the pre-1978 years—have been supplemented by broader and deeper sources, increasingly in the form of databases suitable for cross-sectional and longitudinal analyses. The increased availability of information in "researchable" form has drawn the attention of researchers who wish to test theories and techniques in this newly accessible context. For purposes of this paper, it is worth reviewing the development of available information on venture capital and private equity finance over the years, as well as some of the research that has provided important insights and understanding about this market.

With the formation by the community of venture capital investment funds of the National Venture Capital Association (NVCA) in 1973, an annual investment survey of member NVCA firms was initiated, with selected data being released for publication by the association. The motivation behind the association was political (to effectively lobby Congress on behalf of the industry on matters of taxation and regulation and to let the public know how important growth-company development and financing is to America) and educational (to provide training programs for new entrants to the business). The publication of investment data encouraged many academic researchers to directly survey venture capital firms in the hopes of developing interesting information useful for research in entrepreneurship. In some cases, this direct approach was very successful (MacMillan et al., 1985), but overall results were spotty, as firm partners became unwilling to disclose details for "uncontrolled" publication and as the cost of compliance with "academic" surveys were viewed as a burden.

Venture Economics, Inc., contracted with NVCA to administer surveys and to release information through the quarterly *Venture Capital Journal* and through a set of special reports generated from the data and sold commercially either as tabulated data or as special analyses of various types. In time, Securities Data Company of New York (now owned by Thompson Corporation) purchased Venture Economics, Inc., thus acquiring ownership of *Venture Capital Journal*. Owning the journal along with related publications, including *Going Public: The IPO Reporter*, *Private Placements*, and *Mergers and Acquisitions*, effectively concentrated the source of useful data on private and public transactions in one company, which still controls the nature and form of data released to subscribers and purchasers. At least two other firms, VentureOne and The Private Equity Analyst now gather similar data independent of Venture Economics, Inc., and market, through subscription, both general venture capital market information and very specific analyses of venture capital and private equity partnerships and their investments. Furthermore, the *Asian Venture Capital Journal*, *European Venture Capital Journal*, and *Canadian Venture Capital Journal* regularly publish information on their markets in a global context.

Another pool of information on venture capital and private equity finance is kept by institutional limited partners and by the small number of highly influential financial advisors who provide advice on this market to institutional and high net worth individuals and families. These advisors (referred to in the market as "gatekeepers"), have the ability to analyze the quarterly reports of their client firms and to follow the market by means of their own databases supplemented by what they can purchase from the commercial vendors cited above. They may manage the private equity fund positions of many such investors and may oversee investment in as many as 100 to 200 operating investment funds. Because they monitor and receive information on so many portfolios, they have unique insight regarding the investment terms and performance of large numbers of the private equity finance market transactions. This information has great value in monitoring and evaluating fund management performance and suitability for new investment at the margin. Except under very tight confidentiality conditions, this information is not made publicly available.

Through associative relationships, institutional limited partners are able to exchange data among themselves on the performance of their investment portfolios as well as to compare the way various general partners value investee firms for quarterly reporting purposes. This repository of data rarely if ever finds its way to publication, except in those instances in which selected information might be helpful in arguing the case of venture capital and private equity finance in public policy debates. Nonetheless, a certain amount of information has made its way to the public, albeit carefully controlled in its form and content. One such avenue is through the prospectus filed with the Securities and Exchange Commission (SEC) at the time of public offering of a portfolio company. From information released through these means, we are able to learn a lot about how the market is developing and to make increasingly clear interpretations of developments we observe. Gradually, useful data is making its way to the academic and research community, and researchers are converting it into articles that enhance our understanding of the financing of entrepreneurial firms of whatever size, stage of life, and risk category. Several of these pieces of research are discussed in the balance of this section.

This recent research interest has been encouraged by several motivating and enabling factors. Having ground to a fine research powder the University of Chicago Center for Research on Securities Prices (CRSP) data on publicly traded securities since the late 1960s, scholars in finance, economics, and law have begun to discover the world of private equity finance and venture capital, a world that has many more transactions in it per unit of time than the world of publicly traded securities but one that has been systematically unobserved and underserved by academic research.

In the mid-1970s and into the early 1980s, as corporate restructurings proliferated and the financial community employed "highly leveraged transactions" in corporate buyouts, mergers, acquisitions, and aggressive takeovers, finance scholars employed agency theory to explain the capital structure characteristics that resulted from such transactions and even to rationalize the use of extremely high leverage ratios. Agency theory is most important in explaining the illiquid private equity/debt financing transaction, representing the basis upon which the covenants used in leases, bank loans, and venture capital/private equity finance deal contracts are established. Following the 1986 tax legislation that removed the main tax advantages of such transactions and the contemporaneous banking regulatory changes that virtually prohibited further bank involvement in high-leverage transactions, research in finance, and in law and economics began to apply agency theory to financial contracting in general—and discovered venture capital and private equity finance as a fruitful field of application. This has led to increased research interest in the contractual mechanisms that bind together entrepreneurs (i.e., the owner/manager team), investors (both individual and institutional), and financial intermediaries (the venture capitalist, the "angel," the commercial banker, and the investment banker, either separately or in combination). As a result, greater insight is being gained regarding ways in which the inherent riskiness and "small-parcel diseconomies" issues may be mitigated for potential sources of growth capital, with a resulting improvement in accessibility to financial markets for entrepreneurial fast-growth firms. Whatever its source and motivation, as more information comes forth, the higher become the prospects for more participants to understand the market and to increase its accessibility and efficiency.

The Private Equity Finance Market and Its Components

The most significant change in the market for growth capital for entrepreneurial firms since 1980 has been the development of a clearly defined private equity finance market, an "umbrella" market definition that includes both the organized and informal (i.e., "angel") venture capital markets and pools of capital dedicated to nonventure capital private equity placements. The importance of this development derives from the fact that private equity finance has now become a recognized and accepted investment plan asset category for institutional investors, such as public and private pension funds, corporate strategic partnerships, insurance companies and endowment funds. The result is a large, growing and stable flow of institutional capital toward the provision of equity capital for private firms that are in the process of formation, early growth, expansion, restructuring, and acquiring private finance for these purposes even after "going public." Assets in this category also include strategic direct investments (e.g., oil and gas properties and timberland resources) as well as venture capital and nonventure capital private placement funds.

Comprehensive research on this market is contained in the recently released Board of Governors of the Federal Reserve study titled *The Economics of Private Equity Finance* (Fenn et al., 1995). The study estimates that private equity finance market totaled $100 billion in committed capital at the end of 1994. Of that total, an estimated $30 billion was in venture capital, with $70 billion devoted to nonventure capital investment. The components of this market consist of the set of private transactions between investors (individual and institutional) and investee firms. Some investor firms may be classified as "venture capital," i.e., start-up through expansion-stage investments in firms such as technology-based companies considered inherently risky. Others may be classified as "nonventure capital," i.e., mezzanine, restructuring, turnaround, or special situation acquisition investments in inherently low-risk "mundane" firms and industries. In these situations, professional investment managers, structured as general partners of limited partnership investment pools, play the role of intermediary. Private equity finance is one-sixth the size of outstanding bank debt and is estimated to be the fastest growing component of corporate finance. Of its two components, faster growth is being realized by the nonventure capital portion. This indicates the growing demand for mezzanine finance, that is, finance prior to or as a supplement to the funds raised through initial public offerings. It also reflects the demand for private placement equity and debt capital (under SEC rule 144a) for publicly traded companies.

The growth of this market extends the influence of institutional investors marginally further into the governance of public companies to the extent that public companies employ private equity finance. More significantly, their influence on the governance of private companies is substantially increased as such companies employ more institutional funds. The general partners of private equity investment funds represent the wishes of their institutional limited partners. They are active investors and aggressively seek to influence the governance of their investee firms. The implications of this influence are important: the "institutional activist" approach to corporate governance of large corporations is a well-known phenomenon in recent years. This tendency on the part of institutions to exert their strength on the performance of corporations may well extend through private equity finance funds to companies as they grow, restructure, and renew themselves. The open question which should interest researchers is the effect that increasing institutionalization and centralization of influence through finance will have on the market for developing growth-oriented firms, which has been more atomistic at the microeconomic level and more driven toward "creative destruction" by entrepreneurial impulse and drive.

This development was presaged by Bygrave and Timmons in *Venture Capital at the Crossroads* (1992), in which they presented an overview of research and information developed through roughly 1989 and argued that venture capital appeared to be shifting away from seed and early-stage investment and going toward later-stage mezzanine investments as the "investment stage of choice." Their main thesis was that the "venture" seemed to have gone out of venture capital and that both institutional investors and general partners of venture funds appeared to prefer to avoid seed and early stage investing in favor of later-stage mezzanine and restructuring (leveraged buyout) investment. This observation in part reflected the cyclicality of the venture capital business, which mirrors differences in the levels of opportunities existing at any time between "start-up" deals, later-stage deals, and restructuring deals. In part, however, it reflected a secular trend that has been borne out in the years since publication of the book.

The motivation of institutional investors' interest in private equity finance is based upon the positive relationship between return on investment and risk they enjoy by adding private equity finance to their several portfolios. In a study of return/risk measures of various investment categories, Schilit (1993) compared the performance of venture capital funds, stocks and bonds of more mature business-es, and other investment opportunities. His conclusion was that, while venture capital returns were twice those of publicly held common stock, the standard devi-ation of venture capital returns were three times those of publicly traded stock. On its face, this would seem to conform to the conventional wisdom regarding the risk/return characteristics of venture capital investment. When viewed as individ-ual investments (with no allowance for portfolio effect), this risk/return profile augers poorly for the availability and cost of equity capital for entrepreneurial growth companies and for institutional interest in the asset class. As shown below, however, combining these investments in portfolios and the portfolios into larger portfolios (i.e., into "funds of funds") enhances the return/risk relationship and provides increased access to institutional funds for financing the growth of entre-preneurial firms.

The basis upon which the "fund of funds" concept is built is demonstrated in a paper by Brophy and Gunther (1988). Using a comparison of publicly traded small business investment companies (SBICs) and high-growth-oriented mutual funds, the authors demonstrated that the portfolio of SBIC investment funds provided an above-market rate of return, total diversification of unsystematic risk, and a below-market systematic risk (as measured by the beta coefficient). The SBICs were used as a proxy for limited partnership venture capital (LPVC) funds, inasmuch as there are no publicly traded LPVCs. The point is that portfolio theory provides institu-tional investors an investment which provides above-market returns with below-market risk through investment in a portfolio of venture capital investments. Scott (1994) extends the "fund of funds" logic by analyzing private equity finance as an asset class within the institutional investment total portfolio. He argues that alter-native private equity finance investments behave more like commodities than like financial assets, and some are more appropriate than others as vehicles for passive investment at the institutional level. Short-selling constraints of private funds with no public market, and price effects of consumer demand may make commodities overpriced from an investment standpoint and may require active management. While use of futures contracts may overcome these problems, institutional investors exert their influence over private equity finance through their very substantial influence on the general partners of the funds through which they invest.

Research over the past five years has produced increased insight regarding the financial economic logic and operating characteristics of the venture capital and private equity finance fund. The most impressive insight has been the way in which private-sector efforts, driven by market-expanding motivations, have pressured changes in investment regulations (specifically the Investment Advisor's Act of 1940, ERISA) to make possible the shaping of the limited partnership as an ideal practical vehicle for the intermediation of venture capital and private equity finance. This is an outstanding example of how private-sector pressure on an aspect of public policy can work to eliminate the perverse side effects of an otherwise positive set of regulations and law.

A more recent example of institutional change is the 1992 revision of the regulations governing SBICs. These entities are now permitted to adopt the limited partnership form, acquire funding from institutional investors, and to receive federal government funding in the form of preferred stock rather than debt. This enables SBICs to make equity investments without the burden of making current interest payments on their borrowings from the government as under the prior regulations. While a number of new SBICs have been chartered under the new rules, there is little research to date on investment performance.

Commercial banks are expanding their role as financiers of entrepreneurial firms. Following a prolonged period in the aftermath of the recession of the late 1980s during which bank credit to business was very tight, banks have begun to structure special credit programs for small and midsize firms, especially fast-growth-oriented companies. The use of credit scoring and other computer-based methods of analysis and monitoring is making this market quite attractive for banks. Furthermore, banks, through their holding companies and SBICs, have been actively involved in the private equity finance market. Although they have concentrated in the nonventure capital part of the market, banks are beginning to seek the higher expected returns that come with investments in earlier stages of investment. While lending and investment to smaller emerging growth-oriented companies has been considered beyond bankers' risk tolerance in the past, the combination of these securities into portfolios—as well as the securitization and sale in selected cases—has heightened the interest of banks in this market.

Several recent articles provide excellent reviews of the emerging body of information and research concerning venture capital and private equity finance in general. Based upon information and familiarity with the venture capital process, Sahlman (1988) presented an insightful analysis of the contractual arrangements that bind institutional investors via the limited partnership to the general partner and the fund to the investee firm. In this paper, he showed how the limited partnership form of organization mitigates most of the governance issues and risk in the venture capital and private equity finance fund. He also demonstrates that "real option" theory—an emerging concept in finance—is the theoretical and practical underpinning of the process of "staged" venture capital and private equity finance investments. In a later and related article, Sahlman (1990) expanded the breadth of his study to explain the comprehensive system of governance that binds together the "players" in the venture capital process. He gives a useful overview of the contracting technologies developed by venture capital professionals in order to combine the interests of the three parties involved in the venture capital investment process: the investor (individual or institutional), the intermediary (direct investor or venture capital fund, e.g., a C corporation or limited partnership), and the investee firm. This article has served to stimulate other research, particularly the work of Lerner (1994), as discussed below.

In a comprehensive review paper, Barry (1994) shows how recent research has utilized existing databases and produced new ones. This new data has supported the development by researchers of models and empirical evidence regarding the process of screening venture capital investments, the use of venture capital syndicates, staging of venture capital investment, and the participation of venture capitalists in initial public offerings. Barry states that much has been learned about contract technology which permits venture capitalists to manage their dual roles as agent with respect to their limited partner investors and as principal with respect to their investment position in portfolio companies. He also concludes that, while researchers have determined what venture capitalists do, there is still much debate about how and, indeed, whether venture capital finance adds value—i.e., "more than money"—to the entrepreneurial firm. These papers provide a useful background for the present review of research on financing the growth of entrepreneurial firms.

The investment decision-making process within a venture capital limited partnership has been modeled and described by Fried and Hisrich (1994). Based upon case study research, this paper concluded that the process is designed to reduce the risk of adverse selection on the part of the investor. A multistage process includes origination of a set of investment opportunities, an investment screen specific to the investors' criteria, a generic screen relative to competition, valuation, and negotiations leading to closing. This valuable process provides benefits to both the supply side and demand side of the market.

Lerner (1994) demonstrates and explains the syndication of venture capital investment. Using a sample consisting of 271 biotechnology firms, Lerner finds three rationales for syndication. Syndication is commonplace, even in first rounds—with venture capitalists of similar levels of experience. In later rounds, funds tend to syndicate to their peer funds and to venture capital funds with less experience. Syndicate members tend to maintain their percentage stake of total investment during subsequent rounds of funding.

Valuation, Structuring, and Pricing the Growth Capital Investment

A difficult aspect of the growth financing process is the valuation of the private firm. In cases where the predominant assets of the firm are physical, general purpose and have liquid secondary markets, objective measures and comparable private and public transactions are available. For the most part, the nonventure capital investments referred to above as part of private equity finance have these characteristics and experience lower costs of capital than do venture capital investments. Where the firm is unique, where its values are in growth options and its assets are intangible and human resource-based, the valuation is more likely to be subjective and based upon negotiation. The venture capital deals referred to above more generally have these characteristics and, as noted, typically a higher cost of capital.

Valuation in the private growth capital financing process is mutually derived by investor and investee firm. The total firm valuation estimates of entrepreneur and investor are typically revealed in the pricing of the financing deal, that is, the amount of the firm's equity to be exchanged for the money to be invested. The valuation is typically predicated upon a comparison with similar firms or upon a discounted analysis of projected cash flows. Hypothetically, the values determined by either method should be approximately equal. In a study of transaction for which both projected cash flows and transaction prices of comparable companies were available, Kaplan and Ruback (1996) concluded that valuations obtained through these two methods were mutually consistent for the cases involved.

An important related problem is the appropriate discount rate to use in the discounted cash flow (DCF) approach to valuation. Because of the difficulty of observing comparable cases, estimates are required. The issues involved in this approach are well laid out by Painter (1995), who demonstrates how a weighted average cost of capital may be calculated for a private firm. While publicly traded comparable firms may be used as benchmarks, marketability discounts are extremely important. This topic is central to the valuation of assets with marketability constraints and is well treated in an article by Longstaff (1995).

In the simplest investment structuring arrangement, dollars are offered for ordinary voting common shares in the investee company, with the percentage of the total common stock exchanged reflecting both the economic interest and the voting power acquired in exchange for the money. Under this arrangement, for example, a 50.1 percent interest receives both dominant economic interest and voting control in most matters. To have a supermajority vote (e.g., in matters requiring 60 percent approval), the party would also obtain 60 percent of the economic interest, whether or not the parties to the investment felt that to be fair. While the use of plain vanilla common stock structuring is simple, it is inadequate where complex capital structure issues are involved.

Most financing of entrepreneurial growth companies are structured to offset the complexity of the investment. Norton and Tenenbaum (1993) discuss alternate means of structuring private equity deals and show the effects of venture capitalist characteristics on the structure of the venture capital deal. They demonstrate the use of common and convertible preferred stock and debt of various types, indicating how financing structures differ by investment stage and by characteristics of the venture capital firm involved. They conclude that smaller less diversified investors used common stock predominantly, while larger more diversified funds routinely used convertible preferred stock, regardless of the perceived risk of the investment.

Barney et al. (1994) investigated the factors that determine the nature of formal contractual relations between venture capitalist and entrepreneur. They concluded that covenants were constructed to cover managerial and market opportunism. They are put in place when these events are considered likely to occur, when there are obstacles to monitoring, and when returns to starting a new firm are large. Formal covenants are less likely to exist where the management team has worked together for a long time and where the team has a substantial portion of its net worth invested in the firm.

Lerner (1995) studied the "oversight" role of venture capitalists through board memberships and concluded that oversight was more intense when perceived need was greater. Venture capitalist representation on boards increased relative to nonventure capitalist members around the time of CEO turnover. Gompers (1995) studied the complex investment structures employed when agency and monitoring costs are present. Expected agency costs increase in cases where assets are less tangible, where growth options are important, and where asset specificity predominates. When venture investors concentrate investments in early-stage high-technology investments, information asymmetries are highest. Decreases in industry ratios of tangible assets to total assets, higher market to book ratios, and greater R&D intensities lead to more frequent monitoring and more complex investment structures. Venture capitalists gather information on a frequent basis and maintain the option to discontinue funding projects that have little probability of going public.

Financing Entrepreneurial Growth Through Public Equity Market

The public marketplace offers a twin benefit to entrepreneurial, fast-growth companies and to nonventure capital companies (as defined above). The initial public offering (IPO) is considered an event that certifies the value of the firm and provides an opportunity for liquidity for those investors who have held essentially illiquid securities for a period of four to seven years. Also, the public market provides continued access to capital for the company as it continues to grow. While the public market has been very hospitable to fast-growth firms over the past five years, a major obstacle for the fast-growth company has always been the cost of going public, the reporting and disclosure costs involved and the stock price volatility risk entailed in being a public company.

An important recent study by Aggarwal and Rivoli (1991) highlights this concern. With respect to the risk of a premature public issue, the study shows that "best efforts" issues (representative in the extreme of smaller unseasoned company issues) are three times more expensive than "firm commitments." Even within firm commitments, the economies of scale are impressive: a typical small-firm commitment issue of $2.5 million will cost 32 percent of proceeds, whereas a large issue of $25 million will cost 16 percent of proceeds. The costs are defined to include direct cash expenses such as legal and accounting fees, the investment bank's commission, and the costs resulting from what the authors call "the investment banker's practice of pricing initial public offerings below their market values." Some speculate that the high fees charged by service providers reflect the risk of lawsuit in the event that investors are dissatisfied with the performance of the firm after the IPO. Discussions of this cost come under the heading of "tort reform" in the current national debate.

There is yet another significant cost that is especially important for the emerging fast-growth company which goes public prematurely: the post-offering open market valuation of the company's stock will be subject to wide market volatility, often tying future financing tightly to the market condition of the stock. Some evidence (Brophy and Verga, 1988) suggests that venture capital-backed companies receive better terms in the process of initial public offerings, which may be yet another source of "value added" for the fast-growth company that engages financing through a venture capital fund.

The process of going public is an effective quality filter, with the filter admittedly more refined in some periods than in others. In general, it is the companies that hold the potential for sustainable fast growth which have successful initial public offerings. This potential generally must be evidenced by a number of years of operating results before the IPO route makes economic sense. As shown above, the costs of small public issues can eat up a third or more of the issue's proceeds. From that perspective, a public offering is usually not considered appropriate for small businesses and entrepreneurial firms unless and until they have proven themselves in a technical, operational, and financial way. In general, various sources of private equity finance are employed before a public offering is contemplated.

Nonetheless, some firms do go public early and some survive to tell about it. Furthermore, not every firm going public is backed by a formal venture capital firm of the type discussed above. In 1993, for example, only 11.3 percent of the market (measured by dollar volume) represented venture-backed deals, a decline from 18 percent in 1992. For some firms, going directly to the public market without the benefit of institutional venture capital is appropriate and preferred. While the legal and regulatory requirements of the SEC and state blue-sky laws are impressive and costly, there are market access programs that reduce the cost of such financing, e.g., the SCOR program discussed below.

The SEC for some time has been sensitive to the regressive cost of entering the public market for smaller firms with smaller-size issues. The Regulation "A" offering has been used extensively and has provided many firms with a toehold in the public market, followed subsequently by a regular-size stock offering. With the emergence of NASDAQ and particularly the NASDAQ Small Capitalization Stock Market, the viability and attractiveness of being publicly traded has been increased for many firms.

Recently the SEC has approved the use of Small Capitalization Offering Registrations (SCOR) by firms that wish to raise a limited amount of funds with a public offering which clears the SEC and may be sold on an interstate basis. The advantage to the issuing company is that the company itself may issue the offering without employing an underwriting firm. Aftermarket liquidity through permissible exchanges of the shares may be available, subject to state blue-sky securities regulations. The offering has characteristics similar to both a private placement and a standard public offering. For smaller issues offered to people known or local to the company, the lower costs and increased flexibility are a big advantage for the issuing company.

Along with SCOR offerings, companies may directly issue private placement securities. Private placements include smaller packages of restricted stock sold to individual investors, as well as the larger packages of equity or debt with equity kickers for which the growing company is eligible once it has passed the operating break-even point. Changes in federal and state securities regulations have recently opened the door for expanded use of private placements for corporate issuers of all sizes. The introduction of SEC Rule 144a permits private placement investors to sell the securities so acquired either privately or publicly without any holding period restriction. Under Rule 144a, investors had to hold the securities for at least two years, making the investment essentially a "buy and hold" decision. Along with Rule 144a, the Small Corporate Offering Registration Form (SCOR Form U-7), now adopted by most states, make the limited public offering and the private placement market a potentially useful route to growth capital for emerging fast-growth companies.

Companies wishing to raise smaller amounts of money (say $2 million or less) now have available to them the ability to sell SCOR offerings as well as syndicated private placements of equity, debt, or hybrid securities. Both approaches are less expensive than the "best efforts" or small "firm commitment" IPOs discussed above, and can be viewed as an alternative to a registered offering or as a substitute for or complement to venture capital or "angel" financing.

However, institutional acceptance is quite important to the growth of the private placement market. The liquidity of these offerings is enhanced by the existence of several trading mechanisms. NASDAQ has introduced a trading and quotation system for unregistered equity and debt securities. The Pacific Coast Stock Exchange is conducting a three-year pilot program in the listing and trading of SCOR offerings. Other systems are likely to be provided by private sector companies and should be encouraged and enabled by public policy. The liquidity provided by such systems, along with the ratings systems being put in place by Standard and Poors and the National Association of Insurance Commissioners, will contribute to the strengthening of the market. To encourage the pooling of such securities and the efficient investment of funds in them, revision of the Investment Advisors' Act of 1940 may be helpful. The Act currently limits investment pools exempt from the Act to those with fewer than 100 persons. Enlarging this number would result in larger pools being formed without the substantial regulatory costs involved.

Small businesses and entrepreneurial firms are able to sell securities directly to individual investors under state exemptions from securities laws and under SEC Rule 504; to this extent, the current regulatory system probably meets their needs. However, as the need for funds increases and the securities sales process becomes more complex, the role of the broker/dealer becomes important to an effective system of sale and resale. A key to the accessibility of small business and entrepreneurial companies to public markets for their securities is the role of the broker/dealer. Appropriately trained and knowledgeable broker/dealer intermediaries are needed to lead the placement of the securities involved here. At present, most of the SCOR securities are marketed directly by issuing companies. The ones marketed by broker/dealers have been much more successful to date. Under federal and state broker/dealer laws and regulations, there is a need to provide for an effective license at an intermediate level between the one needed to run a "Wall Street" investment banking house and the simple "finders" license issued at the state level. This would improve the market for SCORs, for angel financing, and for venture capital investments in general.

These evolving alternative and complementary sources of funding for emerging fast-growth companies will expand and make more complete the market for emerging company finance. This is happening at the same time that the traditional mainstays of this market are recovering from their recent doldrums. The venture capital industry is showing double-digit returns again and is a leading part of the institutional plan-asset allocation for the foreseeable future. The small-capitalization public stock market is performing very well in the United States and in other countries and is attracting both institutional and "retail" support. These market components are quite cyclical, and the newly developed facilities discussed here will undoubtedly be cyclical as well. The expansion of alternative sources of capital will help the emerging companies that have such an important role to play in the economy of today and the next century. Whether SCORs turn out to be popular, useful, or flawed will be determined by the marketplace. The point is that they represent the design of a vehicle intended to reduce or remove an obstacle to financing small firms and entrepreneurial fast-growth companies at an early stage of life.

Lerner (1994) examined the timing of IPOs and private financings by venture capitalists. Venture capital funds generate the bulk of their capital gains from IPOs. Lerner's analysis of a sample of biotechnology firms indicates that firms go public when valuations are high and raise private equity finance when valuations are cyclically low. Lerner concludes that seasoned venture capitalist are good at hitting valuation peaks in the public market.

Jain and Kini (1995), studied venture capital participation and the post-issue operating performance of IPO firms. They found that the post-IPO financial performance of venture capital-backed firms was superior to that of non-venture backed firms. They argue that the market recognizes the value of monitoring by venture capitalists as reflected by high values at the time of IPO and beyond. Helwege and Liang (1996) investigated patterns of financing following the initial public offering, hypothesizing the well-known capital structure "pecking theory" (initial capital, followed by retained earnings, with debt used up to a ratio supported by the equity; new equity sold when debt ratios reach their limits) would prevail, inasmuch as the firm now had access to public markets for the sale of external equity. The authors conclude that firm management did not follow the pecking order, availing themselves of debt built upon retained earnings rather than systematically issuing additional public shares.

Greatest Research Need: Financing in the Early Stages

Financing the seed, start-up, and early-stage capital needs of a fast-growth potential company is challenging because it combines both the inherent risk and diseconomies of small parcel finance characteristics discussed above. With some exceptions, institutional equity investors and lenders have systematically steered clear of investment at this stage of company development. They have been encouraged in this by their institutional sources of funds, most of which have preferred the opportunity to invest in companies that, while exhibiting lower growth potential, showed lower inherent risk and employed larger amounts of capital, i.e., did not suffer the "small parcel" diseconomies. As discussed below, the bulk of financing at this stage of growth is provided by founders, family members, friends, and angel investors—individuals who may have a personal or professional interest in the founders or the project. Financing from these informal sources, along with conserving cash through "bootstrapping," represent the principal method by which emerging firms—and especially technology-based firms—raise their initial capital and sustain themselves in the earliest periods of their growth.

Bhide (1992) studied a sample of 100 firms in 1989 drawn from *Inc.* magazine's top-500 list of highly successful U.S. growth companies and concluded that "boot-strapping" is attractive to owner/managers because it provides greater flexibility than does institutional venture capital investment. He states that 80 percent of the sur-veyed firms were financed at startup through the founders' personal funds, with $10,000 as the median amount. Of the "bootstrappers," only 20 percent raised fol-low-on funds through the issue of external equity in the five or more years they had been in business up to the time of the survey. The rest of the firms used retained earn-ings or debt for follow-on funding, thus conserving valuable equity. In a review of firms that have "gone public" between 1970 and 1995 (Brophy, 1996), only 30 per-cent received private equity funding from the organized venture capital market prior to IPO, thus lending credibility to the notion that alternative sources of funding other than the "organized venture capital industry" exist for emerging fast-growth companies.

In an important study of emerging fast-growth companies' funding by stage of development, Freear and Wetzel (1990) found that independent individuals were the major source of funds at the seed or R&D stage of growth companies' development, providing 48 percent of the funds. Individuals were significant providers of funds in the company start-up stage as well, accounting for 20 percent of the total funding. In subsequent stages participation by founders and independent individuals declined sharply as a percentage of total capital raised. Owner/managers tend to participate in equity through options, and individuals who invest at later stages do so typically in situations where the size of the financing round is considerably smaller ($100,000 to $200,000) than would be found at this stage of development in a fast-growth com-pany ($1 to $6 million).

Wetzel and others have designed "angel networks" through which investment opportunities may be disseminated. While practical difficulties may have limited the effectiveness of these systems to date, clarification of legal and regulatory issues can serve to open up this avenue to equity capital in the future. The Securities and Exchange Commission, in permitting Small Capitalization Offering Registrations for small offerings of equity capital by the issuing firm's management, has taken steps in this direction. State Securities Commissions still have the right to qualify these offerings under state blue-sky laws. States that wish to facilitate the process may offer exemptions from state laws in favor of SEC registration. In fact, the SEC is cooperating fully in encouraging the marketing of securities—even young speculative issues—via Internet. Cooperation between federal and state legislators and regulators in developing a "seamless" securities regulation system in the United State will add greatly to the efficiency of the market for small offerings of equity-based securities. Research in this area is very much needed as a guide to private practice and public policy.

In *The 1995 National Census of Early-Stage Capital Financing*, information is presented on the funding experiences of a set of venture capital funds that invest in seed and early-stage investments (Meyer et al., 1995). The 180 funds polled in the Census were selected because they state in their promotional literature that they will consider seed and early-stage investment deals. Because of this liberal definition, they are felt to comprise the universe of funds in the United States that engage in this stage investment. The survey has been conducted biannually since 1989 and the response rate was lower in 1995 than in previous years (36 firms versus 67 in 1993). Interviews with nonrespondents led the authors of the Census report to conclude that the declining response rate reflects a decline in available capital and investment activity by the funds, i.e., a reduction of effective supply of seed and early-stage capital through organized supply channels.

The funds are equally divided among private capital-based, public capital-based, and combinations of private and public capital. Private funds are capitalized by institutional investors, while public funds obtain their capital principally from state governments; combinations are from both of these sources. Private funds report return on investment equal to industry standards of 15 to 20 percent over the 1989 to 1994 holding period, while public funds report returns lower than private funds but higher than the S&P 500, and short- and long-term U.S. Government debt yields over the same period. The lower performance of public funds reflects the limitations on investment imposed on them by state constitutions. In many cases, these funds can make loans, grants, or provisions of property (e.g., labs and buildings) but cannot make equity investments: equity investments in private companies are considered "gifts" and, as such, are unconstitutional in some states. In some instances, states are constitutionally incapable of investing in the very companies using state and locally sponsored incubator facilities intended to help young companies develop and grow. Research might be focused profitably upon the value of an interconnected layering of federal, private-sector, and state and local efforts to improve the environment for the growth of entrepreneurial firms and improving their access to growth capital.

In a comparative study of angel-backed firms and venture capitalist-backed firms, Fiet (1995) concludes that angels rely on the entrepreneurs to protect their investment against market risk. Angels are more concerned with agency risk than with market risk, that is, they are more concerned with picking the right person(s) in whom to invest. Venture capitalists are more concerned with market risk, since they know how to handle agency risk via investment contracting and monitoring. Fiet suggests that this pattern may lead to market segmentation. This segmentation idea is supported by Ehrlich et al. (1994), who report that, although venture capitalists impose higher standards of performance, they provide more information and assistance than individual investors. The authors conclude that a formalized venture capital approach may be needed by entrepreneurs with strong technical backgrounds and limited managerial experience, while entrepreneurs with stronger managerial experience may prefer individual investors who impose fewer changes upon the managerial team.

Since at least the Sherman Antitrust Act of 1890, a political tradition has developed in the United States of using public policy to provide a "level playing field" for small business in general and, in recent decades, for smaller businesses by type of ownership (e.g., minority- and women-owned). This philosophy was first applied to finance through the Reconstruction Finance Corporation in the 1930s and through the Small Business Administration since the early 1950s. Controversy has surrounded these programs continuously, with proponents claiming that they overcome "financial market failures," i.e., the failure of financial markets to adequately serve small business, and opponents arguing that they lead to "government failure", i.e., interference by government with the natural market processes of choice and exclusion.

A Research Agenda: Where Next?

The study of growth capital financing for entrepreneurial firms should prove very attractive to researchers over the next five years. Its importance has never been greater, nor has it ever received as much attention among investors, entrepreneurs, and public policymakers. Furthermore, it is global in its setting and its implications.

On the demand side, entrepreneurs must become smarter in finance, more knowledgeable in the sources of funds, and sharper in negotiating investment terms. This is both a research opportunity and a teaching opportunity for our universities and business schools. Entrepreneurs must understand the basic economics of their businesses in order to make more compelling cases to bankers and equity investors. Research that builds cogent practical models of various types of firms and industries will be of great help in raising the level of economic and financial understanding among entrepreneurs.

Researchers are positioned to learn more about the institutional practices and characteristics of private equity finance providers of all types. This includes learning more about the institutional investor, whose understanding of venture capital, private equity finance and emerging growth companies has received little research attention to date. By the same token, the place of bank credit and bank-based private equity finance in our modern setting demands research attention.

New organizational arrangements should be tested in order to reduce the inherent riskiness of seed and early-stage investment, the most critically important aspect of the private equity finance process. It is important to improve the access to and reduce the cost of start-up and early-stage finance.

The major opportunity for finance students in this field is the exploration of effective methods of valuation of the private firm and the valuation of the investment, structured to mitigate risk and reduce the cost of capital. This is a challenge, but may be addressed by comparing companies in the years just prior to going public with the performance of the firm in the years just after it has gone public. This research will go far to reducing the cost of capital for early-stage companies.

As always, we must continue to learn more about the angel investors, the major sources of growth capital finance for entrepreneurial firms. We must learn more about their financial characteristics and about the institutional arrangements that will facilitate their activities.

REFERENCES

Aggarwal, R., and P. Rivoli. 1991. Evaluating the costs of raising capital through an initial public offering. *Journal of Business Venturing* 6(5):351-361.

Barney, J.B., L. Busenitz, J. Fiet, and D. Moesel. 1994. The relationship between venture capitalists and managers in new firms: Determinants of contractual covenants. *Managerial Finance* 20(1):19-30.

Barry, C.B., C. Muscarella, J. Peavey, and M. Vetsuypens. 1990. The role of venture capital in the creation of public companies. *Journal of Financial Economics* 27:447-473.

Barry, C.B. 1994. New directions in research on venture capital finance. *Financial Management* 23(3):3-15.

Beltz, C.A. (ed.). 1994. *Financing Entrepreneurs*. Washington, DC: AEI Press.

Bhide, A. 1992. Bootstrap finance: The art of start-ups. *Harvard Business Review*, November-December, 109-117.

Brophy, D.J. 1996. "Financing the emerging growth company in the 21st century." Prospects for Small Business and Entrepreneurship in the 21st Century. Washington, DC: White House Conference on Small Business (forthcoming).

Brophy, D.J., and M.W. Gunther. 1988. Publicly traded venture capital funds: Implications for institutional "fund of funds" investors. *Journal of Business Venturing* 3(summer):187-206.

Brophy, D.J., and J.A. Verga. 1988. More than money? The influence of venture capitalists on initial public offerings. Paper presented at the Babson Entrepreneurship Research Conference, Calgary.

Bruno, A.V., and T.T. Tyebjee. 1985. The entrepreneur's search for capital. *Journal of Business Venturing*, 1(1):61-74.

Bruno, A.V., E.F. MacQuarrie, and C.G. Torgrimson. 1992. The evolution of new technology ventures over 20 years: Patterns of failure, merger and survival. *Journal of Business Venturing* 7(4):291-302.

Bygrave, W.D., and J.A. Timmons. 1992. *Venture Capital at the Crossroads*. Cambridge, MA: Harvard Business School Press.

Camp, S.M., and D.L. Sexton. 1992. Trends in venture capital investment: Implications for high technology firms. *Journal of Small Business Management* 30(3):11-19.

Ehrlich, S.B., A.F. DeNoble, T. Moore, and R.R. Weaver. 1994. After the cash arrives: A comparative study of venture capital and private investor involvement in entrepreneurial firms. *Journal of Business Venturing* 9(1):67-82.

Fiet, J.O. 1995. Risk avoidance strategies in venture capital markets. *Journal of Management Studies* 32(4):551-574.

Fried, V., and R. Hisrich. 1994. Toward a model of venture capital activity. *Financial Management* 23(3):28-37.

Freear, J., and W.E. Wetzel, Jr. 1990. Who bankrolls high-tech entrepreneurs? *Journal of Business Venturing* 5(2):77-89.

Gompers, P. 1995. Optimal investing, monitoring and the staging of venture capital. *Journal of Finance* 50(5):1461-1489.

Fenn, G.W., N. Liang, and S. Prowse. 1995. *The Economics of the Private Equity Finance Market*. Wasington, DC: Board of Governors of the Federal Reserve System.

Harrison, B. 1994. *Lean and Mean—The Changing Landscape of Corporate Power in the Age of Flexibility*. New York: Basic Books.

Hall, C. 1995. The entrepreneurial engine. Presented at OECD Workshop on SMEs: Employment, innovation and growth. Washington, DC: June 16 to 17.

Helwege, J., and N. Liang. 1996. Financing growth after the IPO. *Journal of Applied Corporate Finance* 8(4):73-83.

Jain, B.A., and O. Kini. 1995. Venture capital participation and the post-issue operating performance of IPO firms. *Managerial and Decision Economics* 16:593-606.

Kaplan, S.N., and R.S. Ruback. 1996. The market pricing of cash flow forecasts: Discounted cash flows versus the method of comparables. *Journal of Applied Corporate Finance* 8(4):45-60.

Kazanjian, R.A., and R. Drazin. 1990. A stage-contingent model of design and growth for technology based new ventures. *Journal of Business Venturing* 5(3):137-150.

Keeley, R.H., and L.A. Turki. 1992. "Risk/return profiles of new ventures: An empirical study." Unpublished manuscript.

Lerner, J. 1994. Venture capitalists and the decision to go public. *Journal of Financial Economics* 35:293-316.

Lerner, J. 1995. Venture capital and the oversight of private firms. *Journal of Finance* 50(1):301-318.

Longstaff, F.A. 1995. How much can marketability affect security values? *Journal of Finance,* 50(5):1767-1774.

MacMillan, I.C., R. Siegel, and P.N. Subba Narishma. 1985. Criteria used by venture capitalists to evaluate new venture proposals. *Journal of Business Venturing* 1(1):61-74.

Meyer, R., R. Radosevitch, E. Carayannis, M. David, and J. Butler. 1995. *The National Census of Early-Stage Capital Financing.* Albuquerque, NM: Orion Associates.

Miles, M., J. Roberts, D. Machi, and R. Hopkins. 1994. Sizing the investment markets: A look at the major components of public and private markets. *Real Estate Finance* 11(1):39-49.

Norton, E., and B. Tenenbaum. 1993. The effects of venture capitalists characteristics on the structure of the venture capital deal. *Journal of Small Business Management* 31(4):32-41.

Painter, M.J. 1995. Taking a WACC at private companies. *CA Magazine* 128(10):35-36.

Sahlman, W.A. 1988. Aspects of financial contracting in venture capital. *Journal of Applied Corporate Finance* 1(2):23-36.

Sahlman, W.A. 1990. The structure and governance of venture capital organizations. *Journal of Financial Economics* 27:473-521.

Scott, J.H., Jr. 1994. Managing asset classes. *Financial Analysts Journal* 50(1):62-69.

Siegel, R., E. Siegel, and I.C. MacMillan. 1993. Characteristics distinguishing high-growth ventures. *Journal of Business Venturing* 8(2):169-179.

Schilit, K. 1993. A comparative analysis of performance of venture capital funds, stocks and bonds, and other investment opportunities. *International Review of Strategic Management* 4:301-320.

Wetzel, W.E., Jr. 1987. The informal venture capital market: Aspects of scale and market efficiency. *Journal of Business Venturing* 2(4):299-314.

CHAPTER 2

Venture Capital: Reflections and Projections

JEFFRY A. TIMMONS
AND
WILLIAM D. BYGRAVE

A T THE 1990 STATE-OF-THE-ART CONFERENCE it was concluded that the classical venture capital area would be replaced by a new era of merchant capitalists, which would change the entire field of venture capital (Bygrave and Timmons, 1992; Timmons and Sapienza, 1992). Now, in 1996, it is time to reflect on the state of the art in entrepreneurship research as it existed in the venture capital industry five years ago, review the current status of the field, project where the field might be in the next five years, and identify the research issues and opportunities that need to be addressed to move the field forward.

The questions now being asked, as the state of the art in entrepreneurship research is revisited once again with reflections on the findings and predictions of research made five years ago, are:

❖ What is the state of venture capital today?

❖ How have the predictions of 1990 fared?

❖ Where is venture capital headed?

❖ What are the critical issues facing the industry today and in the next century?

❖ What research issues need to be addressed to enhance our understanding of the field and to assist both venture capitalists and entrepreneurs as they move into the next millennium?

The State of the Art in 1990

The state of the art of research in venture capital has changed significantly since Brophy (1986) remarked that the development of the venture capital field had been broadened and moved "ratchet-like" to a permanently higher level of significance in our economic and research interests. By 1992, the venture capital industry changed from "ratchet-like" to explosive growth, had become global, and had seen many structural changes, all during a period of intensified competition. The explosive growth brought about an increase in venture capital firms to 674, with annual commitments of $2.4 billion, annual disbursements of $3.3 billion, and an average firm size of $49.5 million (Timmons and Sapienza, 1992).

Spectacular as it was, the growth of venture capital in the United States was small compared with growth worldwide. The U.S. pool of venture capital had grown just under 40 percent from 1986 to 1989. During the same period it had grown over 10 percent in Europe, Japan, and elsewhere. While in 1989, the United States still dominated the number of venture capital firms, the average European venture capitalist managed 14 percent more capital than the average U.S. firm.

The dramatic growth in the United States and abroad was interwoven with fundamental changes in the structure of the industry. Venture capital firms had been splintered into groups of small, medium, and "mega" funds specializing by stage of financing, product, technology, region, and customer type. Also, by 1989 private venture capitalist firms were dominating the percent of capital under management and the top ten of a total of 95 venture capital firms (14 percent) controlled 59 percent of the capital. In essence, the industry became one of "boutiques" and "department stores" with a vast array of choices in between.

The changes in the industry structure necessary to support the explosive growth also served to create fierce competition within the industry and to drive down its profitability. According to Bygrave (1992) the overall rates of return for venture capital had dropped to about 5 percent in 1988.

Predictions for the 1990s versus Reality

At the heart of the analysis of the industry during the 1980s were the flows of capital, returns on investment, and changes in investing strategies and patterns. The industry had experienced a radical transformation during the previous decade in the areas of new capital commitments (Figure 2.1, p. 31) and venture capital investments (Figure 2.2, p. 32). As indicated earlier, there was concern over the profitability of the industry and the determinants of the industry. Profitability at that time is shown in Figure 2.3 on p. 33. This analysis captured the aftermath of the 1980s change in the industry as it grew tenfold to over $30 billion under management.

FIGURE 2.1
USA Venture Capital New Capital Commitments
1969 through 1990

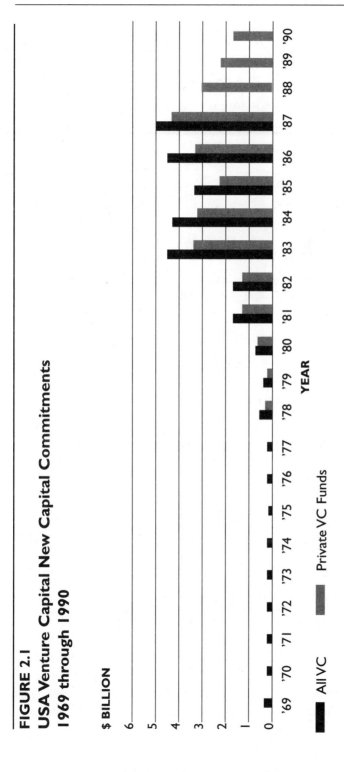

Source: Venture Economics, Inc.
(Numbers after 1987 were reported for only independent private funds.)

FIGURE 2.2
USA Venture Capital Investment
by Year 1979 through 1989

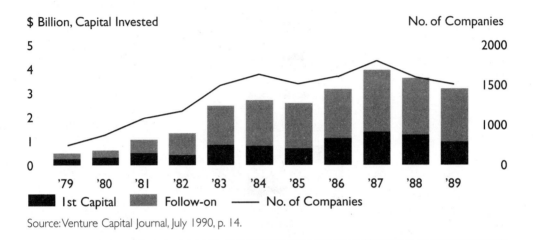

Source: Venture Capital Journal, July 1990, p. 14.

The following ten predictions were made for the industry in 1990:

1. Market mechanisms will cull under-performing firms from the industry. The U.S. shake-out will end by the mid-1990s, with about 40 or so top performers earning returns higher than 20 percent.

2. The U.S. industry, with $45 to $50 billion under management, will rank third behind Europe and Japan, in that order.

3. A shake-out will begin in the European venture capital industry, mirroring what happened in the United States approximately five years earlier.

4. A new technology wave (parallel to the microprocessor and the biotechnology era of the 1970s) will precipitate a surge of interest in start-up and early-stage investing.

5. The 1980s style of merchant capital will steadily lose ground to creative financial strategies and alternative sources of capital.

6. Increasingly savvy entrepreneurs will seek funding primarily from the 50 to 75 venture capital firms with reputations for value-added skills who are committed to structuring deals in ways that equitably share risks and rewards with management.

7. Mergers with strategic partners, such as those pioneered by biotechnology companies, will become the harvest choice because of the unpredictability of IPO markets.

FIGURE 2.3
Determinants of Venture Capital Industry Profitability

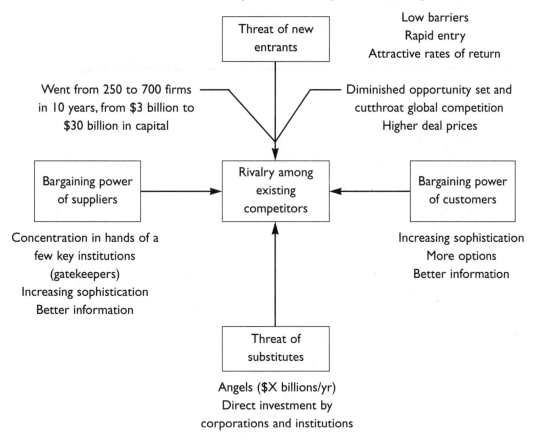

Source: M. Porter, W. Sahlman, and H. Stevenson, presentation to the National Venture Capital Association, May 1989.

8. As more and more seed-stage companies are built with the intent of merging with giant corporations rather than going public, the concentration will be on building R&D assets rather than generating quick profits.

9. A unique form of venture capital will emerge in former Eastern block nations, especially Germany and the Soviet Union, with extensive links to Western venture capital and investment banking.

10. Competition for deals, capital, and venture capital know-how will become global.

How have these predictions fared? Most of the trends and directions of the last state-of-the-art book are becoming or are reality. The industry shake-out has occurred and, in subtle ways, continues. For example, in the number of firms managing venture capital declined from 637 in 1993 to 591 in 1994, a one-year drop of 7 percent (*Venture Capital Annual Review,* 1994). Further, only 80 groups were raising new funds in 1994, compared with 143 in the 1983–84 period (*Venture Capital Yearbook,* 1995). In addition, the shake-out in Europe was occurring as predicted. Merchant capital is alive and well in the United States and seems to be here to stay. Continued specialization and differentiation of investing strategies, and understandably, a penchant for earlier rather than later exits continues. The robust IPO markets from 1991 to 1996 has closed the venture capital-backed IPO gap that was fretted about in the previous state-of-the-art review and has had a significant beneficial impact on both exit liquidity and returns.

In 1994, commitments by limited partners exceeded $4 billion for the first time since 1987 (Figure 2.4, p. 35). Although this is only about half of the commitments in the peak years of the early and mid-1980s, in real dollars, it is still robust by historical standards. By early 1996 a familiar concern of too much money chasing too few deals, had recurred in the industry. For venture capitalists this meant that valuations were getting much too high while entrepreneurs were feeling that valuations were much too low and had a long way to go! The 1990 prediction of "a new technology wave" driving the next generation of deals seems to be on schedule in the information technology area revolution and especially the Internet. While the generic risk of another bout of the "capital market myopia" (Sahlman and Stevenson, 1986) that characterized the Winchester hard-disk drive industry from 1983 to 1986 as a result of an overabundance of capital and an over-eagerness to invest is lower now, the Netscape saga is a healthy reminder that there may be a perpetual capacity in the capital markets for such myopia to recur. The generation of investors who learned the painful lessons of hard-disk drives is not all the same group of investors who are leading the charge on Internet deals.

What about the prediction of a disappearing act of "classic venture capital"? The fundamental pattern has not changed significantly. Meyer et al. (1995) reported the total capital under management of just over $1 billion, or about 2.5 percent of the industry's total. Reports by *Venture Capital Journal* and others suggest a slight increase in seed and start-up investing compared with the dormant days of the late 1980s. Yet the industry preference for larger funds, larger deals, less risk, later stage investing, and earlier exiting continues. This is evident in Table 2.1 on p. 36, which illustrates how follow-on funds have grown larger and larger. Seventy-seven mega-funds, each

FIGURE 2.4

USA Venture Capital Commitments

to Independent Private Funds 1969 through 1995

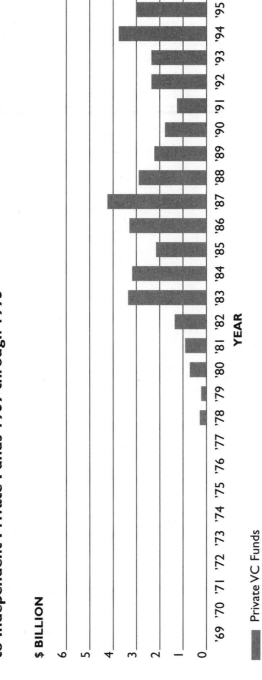

$ BILLION

 Private VC Funds

Source: Venture Economics, Inc.

(Numbers after 1987 were reported for only independent private funds.)

exceeding $100 million in committed capital, accounted for 62.5 percent of the capital under management in the industry at the end of 1994. And despite the stellar results of 1994 and 1995, raising a second, third, or fourth fund appears to be getting more difficult and less fun for all but the superstar performers.

TABLE 2.1
Venture Capital Funds Raised 1994 to 1995 (to date)

Fund	Size in Millions
Summit Ventures IV, L.P.	$ 500
Global Private Equity Fund II, L.P.	313
Olympus Growth Fund II, L.P.	268
APA Excelsior IV, L.P.	265
Sprout Capital VII, L.P.	250
New Enterprise Associates VI, L.P.	230
Kleiner Perkins Caufield & Byers VII, L.P.	225
Oak Investment Partners VI, L.P.	225
Weston Presidio Capital II, L.P.	225
Frontenac VI, L.P.	218
Norwest Equity Partners V, L.P.	200
Mayfield VIII, L.P.	185
Greylock Equity Limited Partnership	175
William Blair Capital Partners V, L.P.	157
Institutional Venture Partners VI, L.P.	140
U.S. Venture Partners IV, L.P.	135
Morgan Stanley Venture Capital Fund II, L.P.	126
Grotech Capital Partners IV, L.P.	126

From Asset Alternatives, Inc.

The earlier prediction that the pools of venture capital in Japan and Europe would exceed those in the United States, even if definitions were agreed on, does not appear to be happening. The emergence of unique forms of venture capital in the former Eastern Bloc nations has already occurred, and its spread does appear to be global as anticipated.

Finally, after contrasting investing strategies of the classic venture capitalists in the 1960s and 1970s and the new brand of "merchant capital," the following seven venture capital investing strategies were suggested for the 1990s:

1. Concentrate on the quality of the management and the market potential of their portfolio companies.

2. Seek a more active role of the lead investor.

3. Focus on where they, as general partners, can bring the most know-how, wisdom, and contacts.

4. Devise creative harvesting alternatives to IPOs. Strategic partnering, which has proven its viability in biotech, is one such alternative.

5. Raise additional funds only on the basis of superior investment opportunities, not on the basis of available money.

6. Devise creative deal structures that ensure equitable incentives for investors and management.

7. Establish linkages to the global venture capital network via alliances, joint-ventures, reciprocal investing, co-investing, and exchange of people.

At mid-decade there appears to be an increasing number of funds that are crafting strategies sympathetic with these principles. And in numerous instances there appears to be a revival of the value-added investing practices that have distinguished the industry for so long. This pattern is expected to continue as a competitive necessity.

The Current State of Venture Capital

The venture capital industry in early 1996 can be characterized as in Figure 2.5, p. 38. Compared with the state of venture capital in 1991 (see Figure 2.3, p. 33), there has been a dramatic overall improvement. Between 1983 and 1984, 143 groups were raising funds, compared with just 80 in 1994, and only the most experienced and proven were succeeding. The industry shake-out has led to a more stabilized and consolidated situation. Pension funds are back investing, and both their commitments and disbursements to portfolio companies by venture capitalists are back up to the $4 billion level, versus $1.271 billion in 1991 (see Figure 2.4, p. 35). Returns have also improved back to the 20 percent plus range (Table 2.2, p. 39), thanks in large part to the robust IPO markets. Yet it is also apparent, given these averages, that many funds are not achieving returns in the 20 percent per annum range. It appears there will continue to be exits of these under-performing funds from the industry.

Competition has increased as well. One indication of the increase in competition for deals is the decline in mean time to close the deal. During the quieter days from 1990 to 1992, due diligence on a start-up company might have taken six months or more to complete. By late 1995 one deal got to a handshake in 45 days by two of the

FIGURE 2.5
Venture Capital Industry, A Porterian View, 1996

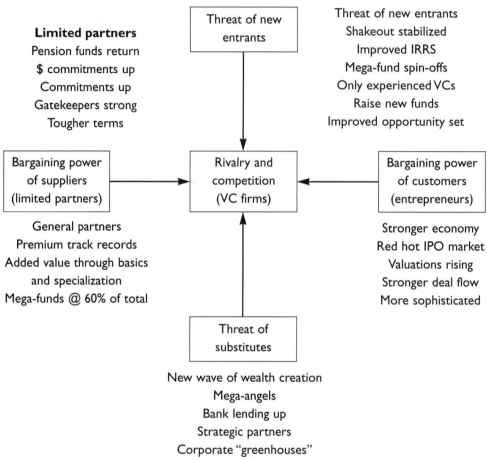

Source: Adapted from M. Porter, W. Sahlman, and H. Stevenson, presentation to the National Venture Capital Association, May 1989.

most experienced and highest performing funds. One price for this renewed activity is increasingly tougher requirements by the limited partners.

Competition is coming from beyond the industry in ways never before seen. The new wave of wealth creation beginning in the 1970s and 1980s has created a new generation of "mega-angels" with average investments in the $250,000 to $1 million and more range. A Boston financial information entrepreneur whose successful harvests has enabled him to create a $30 million private equity pool is now competing

TABLE 2.2
Venture Capital Industry Composite
Holding Period Returns as of 12/31/94
Annualized Holding Period IRR as of 12/31/93

Portfolio of	I Year	3 Year	5 Year	10 Year	20 Year
1969–94	15.7	15.6	13.7	10.0	11.5
1969–90	16.2	16.0	13.8	10.0	11.6
1980–90	16.2	16.0	13.9	10.0	
1981–90	16.5	15.3	13.2	9.7	
1982–90	16.5	15.4	13.3	9.8	
1983–90	16.6	15.6	13.4	10.1	
1984–90	17.5	16.6	14.3	10.7	
1985–90	18.5	17.5	15.5		
1986–90	19.1	18.2	15.8		
1987–90	22.9	19.9	16.9		
1988–90	22.8	20.8	17.7		
1989–90	25.9	20.8	16.4		

From Venture Economics Investor Services

successfully with leading venture funds for start-up deals. Their entrepreneurial experience and knowledge in technology and market areas is perceived by potential investees as superior to that of the most credible venture funds. Coupled with less capital-intensive information age and Internet ventures, this is a significant alternative source of equity capital and value-added know-how.

Corporate America is also becoming another competitor to traditional venture capital. America Online has created a "Greenhouse" for upstart ventures that can benefit from a strategic alliance and capital via the Internet. Creative deal structures with built-in buyouts are tempting some entrepreneurs to forgo an unlimited upside for more certainty and a known attractive payoff. Even management consulting groups have joined the fray. They believe their value-added advantage is in bringing their strategic consulting skills to the venture. This is more prevalent in later-stage deals and turnarounds.

Entrepreneurs continue to benefit from this renewed competition. Valuations for both IPOs and private equity deals are nearly 50 percent higher than 1990, and many observers are suggesting that 1996 may surpass the record-breaking 1995.

With inflation under control and the banks decidedly back lending aggressively, the private capital markets are the most favorable since the heydays of the early 1980s.

Eight Industry Paradoxes

The industry has never been healthier. A new breed of talented fund managers has been attracted to the industry. It is one of the career opportunities of choice among the M.B.A. graduates and experienced executives alike. Yet the industry faces a new set of paradoxical conditions it has not previously experienced. Each has significant strategic and competitive implications for general and limited partners alike, as well as intriguing research opportunities. Consider the following paradoxes and potential research questions:

1. *Gatekeepers are getting stronger and stronger but add less and less value to the venture capital process.* The intrusion of gatekeepers into the value chain of the venture capital investing process is a unique entrepreneurial event in and of itself. People still ask the question, What value do gatekeepers add to the process? Yet even more firms enter the gatekeeper game.

2. *Average deal size continues to increase, yet the information superhighway age ventures are often started with relatively little capital.* One 1994 start-up completed its first year with just $90,000 of seed capital from friends and relatives. During that time the firm had developed its on-line system, signed up leading investment banks, consulting and accounting firms as customers, was receiving positive press, and had several offers for financing from both leading venture capitalists and private investors.

3. *As venture capital becomes more accessible and more abundant, it becomes a less important source of financing to increasing numbers of entrepreneurs.* The pool of angel investors is growing rapidly and continues to dwarf formal venture capital. The more knowledgeable and sophisticated 1990s entrepreneurs are quick to spot opportunities to invest in early-stage companies that traditionally have been the easier deals for the venture capital industry.

4. *As opportunity sets and deal flows grow larger and larger, the competition for the best deals become greater.* Bidding auctions are now commonplace for larger private equity deals. Management teams have become more sophisticated in managing and orchestrating fund raising in the private equity capital markets and are contributing to the increased competition among suppliers of capital for attractive ventures.

5. *As the industry pursues more specialized and focused technology and market strategies, more general venture capital investing skills, i.e., know-how, competencies, and networks, become more—not less—important.* This is an irony for the 1990s.

6. *Institutional investors and pension funds are becoming more important as a source of capital but are the worst fit for classic venture capital funds.* Since the 1990 state-of-the-art review, this pattern appears to have worsened. Why is this so? As limited partners have become increasingly demanding and restrictive in their covenants with general partners, and insist on tighter fee structures with higher thresholds and preferential returns, the pressure toward raising larger funds doing later stage deals has intensified. The economics of classic venture capital are more difficult to reconcile with these demands.

7. *While the industry is as strong as it has ever been, more funds are vulnerable to more competitive threats than ever before.* As noted earlier, competition has never been greater, nor has the industry been healthier.

8. *Creating wealth requires that the founding general partners relinquish wealth.* For the first time major partnerships have disintegrated. While these are extremely complex and delicate situations, one pattern has emerged: when there is no succession plan and less sharing of the carried-interest among new and younger partners, the partnership is doomed to cessation.

Recent Research (1991 to 1996)

As the industry has become more competitive, venture capital firms have been paying more attention to their competitive advantages. One key dimension of strategy is differentiation. For some firms an important way to differentiate themselves is the concept of value added besides money. Sapienza (1992) investigated when venture capitalists add value besides money to their investments and found a positive correlation between value added and venture performance. However, when Rosenstein et al. (1993) studied the boards of venture-capital-backed high-tech firms, they found that, in general, CEOs did not value the advice of their venture capitalist board members more than that of other outside board members, except when their lead investor was a member of a top-20 venture capital firm. The difference between the findings of Sapienza and Rosenstein et al. can be explained by the samples because Elango et al. (1995) found that while some venture capital firms spend a lot of time advising early-stage portfolio companies, many others do not.

In a study that relates to the process of value adding, Sapienza and Korsgaard (1995) employed procedural justice theory to study whether the way in which entrepreneurs share information with their venture capitalists impacts those investors' propensity to trust the entrepreneur and the ongoing relationship with the entrepreneur's company. They found that timely feedback was related to greater trust in the entrepreneur, greater commitment to the entrepreneur's decisions, and less monitoring by the venture capitalist. However, these factors had no significant impact on intention to reinvest.

If the notion of value added makes a difference, it should be possible to measure the financial value of value added by looking at the return on investment. The authors know of no attempt to examine this thought other than an internal study of the portfolio of TA Associates (Landry, 1992). The paper indicated that TA Associates had earned its greatest returns on portfolio companies where the firm had spent the least time advising the entrepreneur, and vice versa. From this it was concluded that the most important value added came during the investment evaluation and selection process, not after the investment had been consummated.

At least one venture capital firm is bringing the notion of value added to strategic clusters of its portfolio companies. According to Moukheiber (1996), Kleiner Perkins Caufield & Byers, has created a Western-style *keiretsu* of portfolio companies with products and services for the Internet. Kleiner's partners are consciously tying together pieces of their portfolio companies with products for the World Wide Web. Since those partners serve on investee boards, it seems to offer fertile ground for research studies of interlocking directorships.

Venture capital firms also differentiate themselves by specialization. Ooghe et al. (1991) used data published by the European Venture Capital Association to demonstrate that venture capital in each European country has unique characteristics, and that European venture capital has different characteristics than its American counterpart. Subsequently, Manigart (1994) used the founding statistics for venture capital firms in the United Kingdom, France, and the Netherlands to make a test of organizational ecology theory. In the United States, Gupta and Sapienza (1992) looked at the determinants of venture capital firms' preferences regarding the industry diversity and geographic scope of their investments. In another study, Elango et al. (1995) examined four potential sources of differences among venture capital firms, namely, venture stage of interest, amount of assistance provided by the venture capitalist, size of the venture capital firm, and geographic location.

Research into the venture capital investment decision-making process has been a continuing topic. Recent work has focused on the process of evaluation of the business plan. For example, Hall and Hofer (1993) examined venture capitalists' decision criteria in new venture evaluation by using verbal protocols. They found that important criteria were the fit with firm's investing guidelines, and the long-term growth and profitability of the industry segment in which the firm will operate. They also found that the quality of the entrepreneur was not a key factor. Likewise, Zacharakis and Meyer (1995), using social judgment theory to gain insights into how venture capitalists screen business plans, found that the product and the market potential ranked higher than the entrepreneur as an evaluation criteria. While their findings are useful for entrepreneurs writing business plans, they do not get to the heart of venture capital decision-making, which is how venture capitalists decide whether or not to invest in ventures that get beyond the initial reading of the business plan. In the same vein, Fiet (1995) applied finance and sociology theories to study how venture capitalists rely on informants to help them evaluate potential investments. His research suggests that certain types of informants may be more effective in facilitating the entrepreneur's search for venture capital.

Valuing and harvesting of venture capital investments has been relatively neglected as an academic research area in the United States in recent years, even though it is central to understanding the industry. Keeley and Turki (1995) developed a venture capital price index to estimate private company values at any time between market transactions. They constructed a stock price index for venture capital transactions using a pilot sample of 1,041 transactions from 274 companies. One interesting aspect of harvesting is what to do with the "living dead," which, simply put, are portfolio companies that have done neither well enough to be IPO candidates nor poorly enough to be classified as "losers." Ruhnka et al. (1992) examined the strategies used to deal with the living dead, which comprised 21 percent of 3,418 companies in portfolios of 80 venture capital firms.

Concern about harvesting venture capital-backed companies stimulated the European Foundation for Entrepreneurship Research (EFER) and the European Venture Capital Association (EVCA) to organize a conference on Realizing Enterprise Value: IPOs, Trade Sales, Buybacks, MBOs, and Harvests held at the London Business School in December 1992. One of the important findings of the research was that exits were more problematical in Europe than America because Europe lacked an equivalent to the NASDAQ stock market. One recommendation was that Europe should pursue a Pan-European stock market. Subsequently, one of the editors of the book, Jos Peeters, managing director of Capricorn Venture Partners and past president of EVCA, led an effort that culminated in the formation of the European Association of Securities Dealers Automated Quotation (EASDAQ), which, it is expected, will become operational in the second half of 1996 (Bygrave et al., 1994).

Future Research Opportunities

This area will continue to be a fertile field of researchers interested in policy, strategy, and the improvement of practice. Roughly 90 percent of all research published in this area has been completed within the last ten years. As the industry continues to expand and evolve into the broader concept of private equity and growth capital, research opportunities will grow. In addition, course development in entrepreneurial finance can also benefit from further research on everything from valuations to IPOs to deal structuring and other topics, such as those noted below.

A wide range of issues offer rich opportunities for research. These would include those previously mentioned plus a host of topics in several general areas. What are the most effective strategic alliances? What are the trends and impact of strategic alliances between venture capitalists and midsize companies? What are the current syndication parameters for venture capital investments? Are there means of improving the process? What are the pros and cons and trends for syndication?

Internal Venture Capital Operations

General partner succession and fund perpetuity are becoming major concerns in the venture capital area. What are the effective ways of handling this problem area? What are the problems and pitfalls, and how do they impact on the process? What are the problems and benefits of interlocking portfolio companies? What are the most efficient ways of achieving this "bundling" process?

Information either to increase knowledge in a specific area or in the due diligence process is an important aspect of all venture capital firms. Are there ways to improve the effectiveness of this process?

Personnel Issues

Are there more effective measures to enhance performances other than existing covenants, overrides, and partnership considerations? Have the existing approaches been effective, and how can they be improved?

Industry Competitiveness

What is the expected impact of alternatives to venture capital, e.g., America Online and mega-angels of the industry? What is the competitive impact of second-tier markets in the industry? How does a firm develop and demonstrate a strategy on a value-added differentiation? Can a firm develop a differentiation based on governance of the portfolio companies, intellectual property, or licensing and technology transfer capabilities? How do the competencies of venture capital differ from other forms of capital?

Public Policy Issues

What government policies and recommendations help or hinder venture capital operations? What are their cost-benefit impacts on the industry? What impact has the industry had on job creation, capital formation, and economic development of the country?

Concluding Comments

There are abundant opportunities for venture capital research that can combine topics of interest to both practitioners and scholars. However, it appears that the more relevant the research is to practitioners, the more difficult it is to conduct that research because venture capitalists are notoriously inaccessible to academic researchers. The industry is small in terms of the number of firms and professionals and so active that the growth of research has become an onerous burden for the industry. There is a burnout from too many questionnaires and too many organizations attempting to collect data, principally for commercial purposes.

We end with a caveat. The venture capital industry is heterogeneous. Hence, it is very important for researchers in this field to report the characteristics of the firms being studied. Recently, some of the manuscripts submitted to leading journals have omitted descriptive statistics that reviewers must have before they can evaluate the work. This is a trend that should be discouraged.

REFERENCES

Brophy, D.J. 1986. Venture capital research. In D.L. Sexton and R.W. Smilor (eds.): *The Art and Science of Entrepreneurship*. Cambridge, MA: Ballinger Publishing, 119-144.

Bygrave, W.D. 1992. Venture capital returns in the 1980's. In D.L. Sexton and J.D. Kasarda (eds.): *The State of the Art of Entrepreneurship*. Boston: PWS-Kent, 438-461.

Bygrave, W.D., M. Hay, and J.B. Peeters, (eds.). 1994. *Realizing Investment Value*. London: Financial Times/Pitman.

Bygrave, W.D., and J.A. Timmons 1992. *Venture Capital at the Crossroads*. Cambridge, MA: Harvard Business School Press.

Elango, B., V.H. Fried, R.D. Hisrich, and A. Polonchek. 1995. How venture capital firms differ. *Journal of Business Venturing* 10(2):157-170.

Fiet, J.O. 1995. Reliance upon informants in the venture capital industry. *Journal of Business Venturing* 10(3):195-223.

Gupta, A.K., and H.J. Sapienza. 1992. Determinants of venture capital firms' preferences regarding the industry diversity and geographic scope of their investments. *Journal of Business Venturing* 7(5):347-362

Hall, J., and C.W. Hofer. 1993. Venture capitalists' decision criteria in new venture evaluation. *Journal of Business Venturing* 8(1):25-42.

Keeley, R.H., and L.A. Turki. 1995. A venture capital price index. In W.D. Bygrave et al. (eds.): *Frontiers of Entrepreneurship Research 1995*. Wellesley, MA: Babson College, 381-393.

Landry, K. 1992. Analysis of portfolio returns: TA Associates, presented at the Annual Meeting of the European Venture Capital Association, Madrid, Spain.

Manigart, S. 1994. The founding rate of venture capital firms in three European countries (1970–1990). *Journal of Business Venturing* 9(6):525-541.

Meyer, R., M. David, J. Butler, E. Caragannis, and R. Radoevich. 1995. The 1995 National Census of Early Stage Capital Financing. Orion Technical Associates, Inc., Albuquerque, NM.

Moukheiber, Z. 1996. Kleiner's web. *Forbes*, March 25, 1996, 40-42.

Ooghe, H., S. Manigart, and Y. Fassin. 1991. Growth patterns of the European venture capital industry. *Journal of Business Venturing* 6(6):381-404.

Rosenstein, J.R., A.V. Bruno, W.D. Bygrave, and N.A. Taylor. 1993. The CEO, venture capitalists, and the board. *Journal of Business Venturing* 8(2):99-113.

Ruhnka, J.C., H.D. Feldman, and T.J. Dean. 1992. The "living dead" phenomenon on venture capital investments. *Journal of Business Venturing* 7(2):137-155.

Sahlman, W.A., and H H. Stevenson. 1986. Capital market myopia. *Journal of Business Venturing* 1(1):7-30.

Sapienza, H.J. 1992. When do venture capitalists add value? *Journal of Business Venturing* 7(1):9-27.

Sapienza, H.J., and M.A. Korsgaard. 1995. Performance feedback, decision making processes, and venture capitalists support of new ventures. In W.D. Bygrave et al. (eds.): *Frontiers of Entrepreneurship Research*. Wellesley, MA: Babson College, 452-464.

Timmons, J.A., and H.J. Sapienza. 1992. Venture capital: The decade ahead. In D.L. Sexton and J.D. Kasarda (eds.): *The State of the Art of Entrepreneurship*. Boston: PWS-Kent, 402-437.

Venture Capital Annual Review. 1994. Boston: Venture Economics Publishing.

Venture Capital Yearbook. 1995. New York: Venture Economics Publishing.

Zacharakis, A.L., and A.D. Meyer. 1995. The venture capitalist decision: Understanding process versus outcome. In W.D. Bygrave et al. (eds.): *Frontiers of Entrepreneurship Research*. Wellesley, MA: Babson College, 465-478.

CHAPTER 3

The Informal Venture Capital Market: Milestones Passed and the Road Ahead

JOHN FREEAR,

JEFFREY E. SOHL,

AND WILLIAM E. WETZEL, JR.

S INCE THE 1990 STATE OF THE ART in Entrepreneurship Research Conference, the informal venture capital market has attracted substantial attention. The reasons are not hard to find. The United States and the major global economies are in the process of mutating from industrial/manufacturing economies to entrepreneurial economies driven by information and accelerating technological change. In the United States, from 1979 to 1995, while Fortune 500 payrolls declined by over 4 million jobs, the entrepreneurial economy generated over 24 million jobs. About 75 percent of these jobs were created by fewer than 10 percent of small firms. Job-generating businesses are started and driven by entrepreneurs. For entrepreneurs, size is a transient characteristic. Innovation, risk, growth, and the creation of wealth for entrepreneurs and investors distinguish entrepreneurial ventures from other small businesses. One economist observed that our country's ace in the hole is our ability to spawn a lot of high-growth entrepreneurial ventures.

Access to seed and start-up capital is the principal financial obstacle to the vitality of entrepreneurial economies. Informal venture investors, business angels, are the primary source of early-stage external equity financing for entrepreneurial ventures (Freear and Wetzel, 1992). From the 1960s to the early 1990s, the U.S. economy spawned a growing choir of angels—self-made high net worth investors in entrepreneurial ventures. For example, in 1984, 40 percent of the Forbes 400 Richest People in America were entirely self-made, i.e., first-generation money. By 1994, 80 percent of the Forbes 400 were self-made.

The transition to an entrepreneurial economy has profound implications for investors, the equity capital markets, and public policy designed to promote job growth, deficit reduction, and global competitiveness. The invisible and demonstrably inefficient informal venture capital market will attract even greater attention during the next five years. For example, access to "patient capital" emerged from the 1995 White House Conference on Small Business as the most critical obstacle to the vitality of emerging high-growth ventures. The need was defined more precisely as seed and start-up capital on the order of $250,000 to $1 million, well below the interest thresholds of most venture capital funds, but well within the range of typical private equity investor financing.

Research into the informal venture capital markets has kept pace with the growth in professional and public policy interest in business angels and the role they play in entrepreneurial economies. However, access to quality data remains the biggest single obstacle to research in this field. Again, the reasons are not hard to find. The invisible angel capital market serves a diverse and dispersed population of high net worth investors who place a high value upon anonymity. There are no directories of business angels, and no public records of their investment transactions.

The discussion that follows updates the material published in *The State of the Art of Entrepreneurship* (Sexton and Kasarda, 1992). The concluding section of Chapter 18, "Towards the Year 2000: A Research Agenda" summarized eight agenda items as follows:

1. More attention will be paid to measures of the scale of the angel market, but convincing results will remain elusive owing to lack of data and, to a lesser degree, lack of commonly accepted definitions of angels.

2. More research is needed into the ABCs of angels—their attitudes, behavior, and characteristics. This research should shed light on questions about the existence of categories of angels, i.e., subsets of angels that display common characteristics.

3. The reliability of data collection techniques need improvement. Identifying a representative sample of the entire angel population is a challenge that remains unmet. Research to date has been based on convenience samples. Longitudinal research is another unmet challenge.

4. Future research will address the efficiency of the private equity markets that serve emerging high-growth ventures. Public policy issues will drive much of this work.

5. More attention will be given to the development of explanatory and predictive theories for empirical testing.

6. Attention will be paid to the interface between the early-stage private equity market (the angel market) and institutional sectors of the capital markets,

in particular venture capital funds, investment banks, and capital market intermediaries.

7. Research into the international dimensions of the angel market will gain increasing relevance and attention.

8. The significance of patient capital in an entrepreneurial economy will lead to research that focuses on public policy issues that affect the availability of seed and start-up equity financing for emerging high-growth ventures.

In the following discussion, the authors provide an overview of the research that has been completed since 1990. Topic categories have been employed as a means of organizing the discussion. However, the topics are not mutually exclusive. Decisions to include a particular piece of research in a particular category are admittedly somewhat arbitrary. Every attempt has been made to provide a representative sample of the most significant research. The authors accept responsibility for all errors of interpretation, emphasis and oversight.

Milestones Passed

How Large is the Informal Venture Capital Market?

New insights into the scale of the informal venture capital market are limited. The new data support the 1990 and earlier inferences that the informal venture capital market is substantially larger than the institutional venture capital market. Conservative estimates suggest that angel investments exceed venture capital fund investments by a factor of three to five and that the number of ventures bankrolled by angels exceeds the number of ventures financed by venture capital funds by a factor of ten to fifteen. Verification of these estimates is hampered by the invisible nature of the angel market.

Pre-1990 estimates of the scale of the U.S. informal venture capital market include Gaston (1989a), Gaston and Bell (1988), and the Congressional Office of Technology Assessment (1984). Gaston estimated that 720,000 private equity investors make 489,000 equity capital investments per year, valued at an estimated $32.7 billion. When an additional investment of $22.9 billion of debt capital is included in the total, Gaston and Bell estimated that the informal market supplies annual informal capital of $55.6 billion. In 1984, the Congressional Office of Technology Assessment estimated the total number of firms financed annually by private investors at 87,300, or 42 times larger than the number financed by professional venture capital funds. They estimated that $55 billion per year is invested by this group compared with $3 billion invested by professional investors.

Ou's (1993) work provides more recent estimates of the scale of the private equity market. Using the 1989 Consumer Finance Survey, Ou updated his earlier study of holdings of privately held business assets by American families and devoted one section to "Informal Investors and Their Investment." According to Ou, an informal investor is any individual who provides risk capital directly to a business for the purpose of asset appreciation and who is minimally involved in the day-to-day operation of the business at the time of the investment. He excluded nonpecuniary motivation, such as helping a son or a daughter start a business or helping a friend in need of capital. Based on this definition, Ou estimates that the total number of informal investor families in the United States is in the range of 1 to 1.5 million.

Harrison and Mason (1992a) point out that there is little comparative information on the size of the informal venture capital pool in the United Kingdom or other European economies, despite recent recognition that the apparent underdevelopment of this market in the United Kingdom represents a major barrier to the development and growth of new ventures. Harrison and Mason found that informal investors are playing an important role in venture financing in the United Kingdom in three ways:

1. They make small-scale investments in new and early-stage ventures, where the equity gap is most significant.

2. They are more permissive in their financing decisions than the formal venture capital industry in terms of having lower rejection rates, longer exit horizons, and lower target rates of return.

3. They invest locally and can thereby close the regional equity gap arising from the overconcentration of venture capital investment in the core southeast region in the United Kingdom

Harrison and Mason (1992a) and Mason and Harrison (1993a) estimated that there are approximately 50,000 private investors in the United Kingdom. Their ballpark estimate of capital invested by these individuals is about $3 to $7.5 billion per annum compared with an annual investment of around $1.5 billion by the formal venture capital industry. Their survey evidence indicated that informal investors have up to three times as much capital available for investment as they have already invested.

Angel Typologies

For a cross-country comparison of "typical" angel profiles, see Kelly and Hay (1996a). Research conducted in the United States (Gaston and Bell, 1988; Wetzel, 1981), United Kingdom (Harrison and Mason, 1992a; Mason et al., 1993; Stevenson and Coveney, 1994), Canada (Riding and Short, 1989) and Sweden (Landstrom, 1993a) portrays a "typical" angel investor as:

❖ a middle-aged male

❖ with a reasonable net income and net worth

❖ and previous start-up experience

❖ who makes one investment a year, usually close to home

❖ and prefers to invest in high-technology and manufacturing ventures

❖ with an expectation to sell out in three to five years

Despite many common traits, the diversity of the angel population has been recognized for some time. Only recently have attempts been made to define categories of angels with common characteristics. Gaston (1989b) subdivided angels into what he perceived to be the ten most important individual categories and went on to provide a market profile for each subtype.

In a survey covering nearly 500 British angels, Stevenson and Coveney (1994) developed an angel typology based on entrepreneurial backgrounds and levels of investment. Their study described six types of angels:

❖ *Virgin Angels:* Individuals with funds available who are looking to make their first investment but have yet to find a suitable proposal.

❖ *Latent Angels:* Rich individuals who have made angel investments but not in the past three years, principally because of a lack of locally-based proposals.

❖ *Wealth Maximizing Angels:* Rich individuals and experienced businessmen who invest in several business for financial gain.

❖ *Entrepreneur Angels:* Very rich, very entrepreneurial individuals who back a number of businesses for both the fun of it and as a better option than the stock market.

❖ *Income-Seeking Angels:* Less affluent individuals who invest some funds in a business to generate an income or even a job for themselves.

❖ *Corporate Angels:* Companies that make regular large angel-type investments, often for majority stakes.

Stevenson and Coveney concluded that the angel market in Britain is relatively untapped and may be much larger than previously estimated. They found that the large majority (70 percent) of angels would have liked to have made more investments had they come across suitable opportunities, and that 76 percent expected to increase their investment activities over the next five years. A significant number of angels (29 percent) was most attracted to the fun and satisfaction of investing. They propose that their angel typology can be used to target distinct types and to predict their investment strategies.

Freear et al. (1994a) examined high net worth individuals, without regard to their investment histories or their propensity to invest in entrepreneurial ventures, and partitioned their sample into three groups: 1) business angels with experience in investing in entrepreneurial ventures, 2) interested potential investors with no venture investment history, and 3) uninterested potential investors. All three groups shared similar views about the economic significance of the entrepreneur and entrepreneurs' problems securing equity capital. Where the interested potential investor and business angel clearly differ is on the scale of their commitment and their motivation for investing. The potential investor will commit a smaller dollar amount to any one venture, is more inclined to participate with other investors, and is more apt to see venture investing as a diversification strategy than the seasoned business angel.

Sullivan (1991) contrasted entrepreneur and nonentrepreneur investors. She observed that past informal investment research suggests that a large proportion of informal investors is likely to be successful entrepreneurs and that a separate stream of research suggests that entrepreneurs exhibit certain distinguishing characteristics. She integrated these two streams by comparing entrepreneurs and nonentrepreneurs within a sample of informal investors. She drew two concepts from studies of entrepreneurial attributes: risk propensity and the desire for control and independence. From informal investment research, she drew on aspects of the investment process and the concept of empathy. Sullivan found that the 150 entrepreneurs in her sample differed from the 60 nonentrepreneurs in several ways. Entrepreneurs perceived their downside risk to be less. They did not participate in the firm to a greater degree, but were more independent in investment style. They expressed greater interest in supporting new businesses and were more likely to invest in early-stage ventures. They also tended to make more investments than nonentrepreneurs.

Kelly and Hay (1996b) examined a specific subsegment of the informal venture capital market in the United Kingdom, namely, investors who have made at least three private investments (so-called serial investors) and explored the linkage between investor characteristics, investment activity and performance. Two distinct groups emerged: one that invested on their own all the time and another that invested with others almost exclusively. Kelly and Hay's analysis of actual investment behavior revealed the following patterns:

❖ Serial investors in the United Kingdom coinvest to a much greater degree than previously thought.

❖ Investments are made in a variety of industrial sectors, and in a majority of instances, in industries where the investor and/or syndicate partner has limited direct previous experience.

❖ Familiarity with the business concept appears to be a necessary, but insufficient prerequisite to the decision to invest.

❖ Agency risk is managed, to some extent, by backing entrepreneurs who are known personally to the investor, another syndicate member, and/or to the referrer of the deal.

❖ When serial investors choose to invest with others, they display a greater propensity to back unknown entrepreneurs. When the performance linkage is made, prior knowledge of the entrepreneur emerges as a discriminating factor. For all but one of the investments where a loss was realized or performance had fallen short of expectations, investors or syndicate partners did not have prior personal knowledge of the entrepreneur.

❖ In view of the time required to undertake various postinvestment activities including monitoring, portfolio size appears to be limited to four or five investments at any one time.

In the United Kingdom, public policy has concentrated largely on supporting means for bringing investors and entrepreneurs together in a timely and efficient manner. Based on their work, Kelly and Hay recommend that facilitating the formation of syndicates is a public policy initiative worth exploring.

Mason and Harrison (1995) found that informal investments, especially larger deals, may involve syndicates of business angels. Often a key individual brings the syndicate together by referring the deal to friends, business associates, or relatives. They refer to this type of angel as an "archangel." They also found that some financial intermediaries are now playing this archangel role and call this new type of player in the informal venture capital market the "institutional archangel."

Landstrom (1995) identified two distinct strategies used by Swedish investors in making investment decisions. Specialist investors choose to limit their activity to areas related to their particular market and/or technical expertise. Compared with investors who sought portfolio diversification in terms of industry and/or stage of development, specialists examined fewer proposals and exhibited a higher propensity to invest than explicitly diversified investors. Otherwise, the two groups exhibited similar proposal evaluation criteria. Landstrom (1993a) also found two extreme categories of informal investors in Sweden. One extreme was representative of many informal investors in the United Kingdom. They could be characterized as infrequent and less sophisticated investors, who invest small amounts of money and behave as rather passive investors. The other extreme was more representative of informal investors in the United States. They seemed to be more professional and active in their informal investments. Informal investors in Sweden displayed some similarities with their U.S. counterparts but worked less actively with their portfolio firms.

Post Investment Relationships—The Value-Added Issue

Since the 1990 State of the Art of Entrepreneurship Research Conference, further light has been shed on postinvestment relationships between angels and the entrepreneurs they finance. Freear and Wetzel (1992) reported on working relationships between entrepreneurs in new technology-based firms and their angel and venture capital fund backers. In 75 percent of the angel-backed firms, at least one private investor held a seat on the board of directors. Venture capital funds were represented on the boards of over 90 percent of venture capital backed firms. For both groups, board representation was the most common role, followed in frequency by a consulting relationship—65 percent for individual investors and 57 percent for venture capital funds.

Entrepreneurs were asked to rate their working relationships with private investors and venture capital funds on a five-point scale that ranged from very productive to very counterproductive. For both types of investors, three-quarters of the entrepreneurs rated their relationships as either very productive or moderately productive. The data suggest that entrepreneurs typically derive value from their individual investors that is above and beyond the provision of equity funding.

Mason and Harrison (1992) compared the roles of venture capitalists and informal investors in entrepreneurial companies in the United Kingdom. Using data from ventures that had raised capital from venture capital funds and informal investors, Mason and Harrison presented a profile of the contribution made by each in over 19 aspects of venture operation. Their analysis suggested that the two groups of investors make contributions to broadly similar ranges of function, with financial issues and an advisory role being the most important. However, on most dimensions, informal investors were more likely to be reported as making no greater contribution than venture capitalists. However, informal investors were more likely to be credited with making a helpful contribution to a number of strategic and operational areas. According to Mason and Harrison, differences of emphasis within an overall similar ranking of the most important areas in which an external investor contribution is made (with venture capitalists usually overemphasizing monitoring and control functions and informal investors usually overemphasizing market development issues) suggest that the primary differences between the two investor groups in terms of their attitude toward and contribution to their investee ventures is qualitative rather than quantitative, and is based on differences in style and viewpoint.

Ehrlich et al. (1994) asked a group of southern California entrepreneurs to assess the characteristics of their relationships with their primary investors. They then contrasted results between entrepreneurial firms that had received venture capital funding versus private investor funding. Differences were examined along the following lines:

❖ Levels of investor involvement in entrepreneurial firms.

❖ Reporting and operational controls placed on the firm.

❖ Types of expertise sought by the entrepreneur.

The study found that entrepreneurs perceive that both venture capitalists and private investors are involved in similar sets of activities, such as interfacing with the investor group, obtaining alternative sources of equity funding, monitoring financial and operational performance, serving as a sounding board for the entrepreneurial team, and formulating business strategy. Entrepreneurs indicated that they had more difficulty in achieving performance targets set by venture capital firms. Venture capital firms required entrepreneurs to report to them on a more frequent basis and to supply a higher amount of verbal feedback.

The Ehrlich et al. study found that entrepreneurs seek expertise through their investors generally in the areas of staffing and financial management. However, venture capitalists provide assistance in selecting the venture's management team significantly more often than private investors. They suggest that entrepreneurs with strong managerial experience may prefer private investors because they are less likely to alter the makeup of the managerial team. However, entrepreneurs with technical backgrounds may find that a venture capital firm provides valuable help in accessing and attracting top management personnel with relevant experience.

Ehrlich et al. conclude that there are important differences between venture capitalists and private investors in terms of the value-added benefits they bring to entrepreneurial firms. Thus, in searching for capital, an overzealous founder may find that the long-term costs can far exceed the short-term benefits if there is a mismatch between the relevant parties. From whom the entrepreneur gets his or her money is just as important as how much capital is obtained.

Financial Theory and the Informal Venture Capital Market

The development of a body of research goes through several overlapping stages. In the first, researchers establish the existence of an area worthy of study. In the second, researchers collect, assimilate, interpret, and disseminate empirical evidence about the subject, its context, and its relationship to other areas. In the third stage, researchers seek to transform their interpretation of evidence into explanatory and predictive theories, drawing on their knowledge base in related fields. The study of the informal venture capital markets has moved through the first and second stages and is beginning to penetrate the third stage. Concepts and models drawn from the field of finance that await application to the informal venture capital market include efficient capital market assumptions and the application of portfolio management theory to the informal venture capital market, particularly the relevance of utility theory to the decision models of private equity investors, the assessment and management of business risk (unsystematic risk) and of agency risk inherent in private equity transactions, the implications of information asymmetries, social embeddedness theory, signaling theory, and option pricing models.

Norton (1990) and Norton and Tennenbaum (1993a and 1993b) were among the first to point out the application of theoretical issues developed in the field of finance to the venture capital markets. Since 1990, progress has been made in the empirical testing of informal venture capital market hypotheses drawn from financial theory. Truly significant progress awaits the availability of larger and more representative databases.

Fiet (1995a) studied the use of informants in the venture capital industry. He found that the more a business angel or a venture capital firm is concerned with market or agency risk, the less likely he will be to use informal network informants. Market risk arises from unforeseen competitive circumstances, whereas agency risk results from the separate and possibly divergent interests of investors and their informants. Venture capital firm investors consult formal network sources more frequently than do business angels.

In a comparison of risk avoidance strategies employed by business angels and venture capital firm investors, Fiet (1995b) found that differences in their approaches to evaluating risk lead them to hold predictably different views of the dangers of market and agency risk. Business angels tend to rely upon the entrepreneur to protect them from losses due to market risk. Consequently, they are more concerned with agency risk than market risk. Venture capital funds are more concerned with market risk because they have learned to protect themselves contractually from agency risk using boilerplate contractual terms and conditions. A likely result of their different approaches to avoiding risk is a segmentation of venture capital markets with important implications for both entrepreneurs and future research.

Whether or not coinvestors trust each other is an underlying issue in network reliance. Fiet (1991) found that business angels rely more upon themselves for investment information than upon their network of other business angels, supporting predictions from transactions cost theory. The opposite was found among venture capital firms, supporting theories of social embeddedness. The degree of reliance was a function of the amount of network experience. Experience generated trust, which controlled opportunism.

Landstrom (1993b) looked at agency theory and its application to small firms in the Swedish venture capital market. One basic assumption of his study was that agency theory can provide an essential framework to explain the interaction between informal and formal venture capitalists and their portfolio firms. Five hypotheses were generated from agency theory and tested on 62 firms backed by informal venture capitalists and 145 firms backed by formal venture capitalists. Landstrom concluded that agency theory fails to provide a satisfactory framework to explain either the informal venture capitalist's, or the formal venture capitalist's relationships to their portfolio firms. More exploratory research must be done to develop a theory of finance applicable to small firms' situations.

Mason and Harrison (1992) point out that developments in the supply of capital in the 1980s have reduced the size of the equity gap in the United Kingdom. However, such developments have not adequately met the need for smaller amounts of venture capital, especially for firms seeking to raise seed and start-up capital. They argue that informal venture capital provides a promising solution to closing the equity gap. However, its potential is limited by inefficiencies in the operation of the informal venture capital market. Mason and Harrison propose a number of policy initiatives to overcome these inefficiencies. One immediate step that could be taken to stimulate the flow of informal venture capital to potential investee businesses is the establishment of a network of locally or regionally based and managed business introduction services. In view of the economics of operating such services, which are unlikely to be capable of operating on a nonsubsidized for-profit basis, government intervention is required if the development of the informal risk capital market is to occur.

Sullivan and Miller (1990) used a set of hypothetical scenarios to determine whether or not informal investors were strictly wealth maximizers. Two hypotheses were derived from a synthesis of theory of finance and past informal research. Their results revealed a strong positive correlation between risk and return. However, informal investors could not be described as wealth maximizers, as classical theory of finance assumes. The latter finding is consistent with the conclusions of a number of studies of informal risk capital, as well as the "minority opinion" in finance theory pointing to an investor with multiple objectives and varying individual preferences.

International Informal Venture Capital Research

Since 1990, academic, professional, and public policy interest in the informal venture capital markets has seen startling growth in the international arena. The creation in 1991 of the International Informal Venture Capital Research Network (IIVCRN) is indicative of the growth of international interest in the informal venture capital markets. IIVCRN was established as a result of research collaboration among Professors Freear, Sohl, and Wetzel (Center for Venture Research, University of New Hampshire, U.S.A.), Colin Mason (University of Southampton, U.K.) and Richard Harrison (Ulster Business School, U.K.).

The IIVCRN is an informal association of researchers and practitioners who are active in the field of informal venture capital. Its objectives are to provide a forum for bringing together researchers and practitioners to exchange information and ideas, to promote the importance of informal venture capital among the research community, and to disseminate research findings to practitioners and those concerned with public policy. The group's activities include a newsletter (edited by Colin Mason), an annual research workshop, collaborative research, and collaborative publications. IIVCRN intends to remain an informal association open to all active researchers in the field of informal venture capital. Countries represented include the United States, United Kingdom, Canada, Sweden, Finland, and Denmark.

Mason cited four main impressions that can be drawn from the contents of the 1994 IIVCRN newsletter. First, it highlights the impressive strides that the small core of active researchers who comprise the IIVCRN have made in enhancing our understanding of the informal venture capital market. Second, it indicates the variety of new issues that are being examined. Third, the promotion of the informal venture capital market is now high on the policy agendas of many countries and members of the Network are playing influential roles in policy debates, and initiative formulation as well as through hands-on involvement in practical initiatives. Finally, it is particularly striking to note the impressive growth in informal research activity and initiatives in Europe since the launch of IIVCRN in 1991. Since the 1994 newsletter, studies of the informal venture capital market, many prompted by public policy debates, have been initiated in South Africa, Australia, Japan, New Zealand, the Philippines, and the Netherlands.

Public Policy and the Informal Venture Capital Markets

The global movement toward entrepreneurial economies, economies equipped to cope with accelerating rates of change and heightened uncertainty in virtually all aspects of human life, has attracted the attention of those in a position to shape public policy in the United States and overseas. In the United States, the driving issues include job creation, deficit reduction, and global competitiveness. According to Wetzel (1995), seven pernicious and pervasive misconceptions about the process that have been unfolding over the last 30 years must be dispelled before effective public policy can be designed. He maintains that differences in the political agendas of fast-track entrepreneurial companies and more traditional small businesses are most vivid in the area of capital formation. The capital formation challenge confronting the United States is not adequate credit for small business, but adequate high-risk, patient, value-added equity capital for entrepreneurs. The following misconceptions, and his perceptions of the underlying reality, are discussed by Wetzel:

1. Small business is the job-generating engine in the United States.

2. Access to credit is the major financial obstacle to job creation.

3. Most venture capital comes from the venture capital funds listed in *Pratt's Guide to Venture Capital Sources.*

4. All venture investors are equally venturesome.

5. Every good deal gets funded.

6. Limited access to credit is the most serious financial obstacle confronting high-growth established firms.

7. Capital gains taxes are a tax on the wealthy.

Following the 1995 White House Conference on Small Business, the Office of Advocacy of the Small Business Administration, working with the Securities and Exchange Commission, undertook the task of creating a National Angel Network. The SBA initiative is an effort to develop a new capital market designed to accomplish the following objectives:

✤ Increase opportunities for qualified private equity investors to participate in the rewards and risks of financing emerging growth companies.

✤ Provide entrepreneurs with expanded access to the private equity markets.

✤ Reduce the cost of raising private equity capital through the use of standard interstate disclosure documents and policies.

✤ Reduce the costs of raising private equity capital through legislative and regulatory provisions that limit the liability of professional service providers.

✤ Employ controlled access to the Internet as the vehicle for a new capital market.

✤ Accomplish the above while maintaining an appropriate balance between venture promotion and investor protection.

These objectives are designed to create a more efficient private equity market—a market populated by fully informed buyers and sellers and involving minimum transactions costs. In free-enterprise economies, efficient markets allocate scarce resources to their most productive uses.

In the view of a number of independent observers, the United Kingdom has led the way in terms of policy initiatives to promote informal venture capital activity. On behalf of the Small Firms Policy Branch of the Department of Trade and Industry (DTI), Mason and Harrison (1995) have undertaken a final review and evaluation of five U.K. informal investment demonstration projects. In October 1991, the government provided pump-priming funding to five Training and Enterprise Councils (TECs) for projects intended to stimulate locally or regionally based informal investment projects built around business introduction services. Mason and Harrison's report is not yet available for general dissemination.

In their survey of British business angels, Stevenson and Coveney (1994) claim that reputable Business Introduction Agencies attract some of the richer, more active angels in Britain and that the agencies are only scratching the tip of a potentially sizable iceberg. They also claim that as these agencies address some of the factors identified as restricting investment, they could play a much more vital role in encouraging an enterprise culture in Britain, particularly if they were linked together by a national network based on proven principles of best practice.

In a report commissioned by Advent, Ltd., a leading London-based venture capital company specializing in the provision of equity finance for technology-based firms, Hay and Abbott (1994) conclude that a strong case can be made for providing tax incentives to encourage the formation and growth of U.K.-based new technology-based firms (NTBFs). They note that classic venture capital (hands-on provision of relatively small amounts of finance, business advice, and management input to potentially world-scale NTBFs in their seed, start-up, and early stages of development) has made a significant contribution toward the creation of jobs, national wealth, and higher standards of living for those economies in which it has been practiced (especially the United States). Despite noting in their opening paragraph that for generations, rich individuals and families have provided risk capital for the purpose of starting, or expanding, business enterprises, Hay and Abbott confine their description, analysis, and comments to the formal venture capital industry. The contribution of their model and conclusions to the public policy debate justifies the inclusion of their work in this paper.

The Lumme et al. (1996) study of Finnish angels contains several general observations about Finnish entrepreneurs and informal investors that are relevant to public policy discussions. They maintain that for an increase in informal venture capital activity to occur, several requirements must be met. A basic requirement is the belief that there are sufficient ventures with high growth potential and that the operational environment of these ventures is sound. There should also be a change in entrepreneurs' attitudes toward venture capital. A company's decision to look for outside equity should not be taken as a sign of weakness. Entrepreneurs must be willing to provide information about their ventures, share ownership, and allow equity investors to participate in strategic decisions.

Lumme and colleagues make the following recommendations:

❖ Establish business introduction services to improve the flow and quality of information between businesses seeking finance and business angels.

❖ Develop cooperation between venture capitalists and business angels.

❖ Promote syndication among business angels.

❖ Develop indirect models to encourage investments in unquoted companies.

❖ Provide taxation and guaranty incentives.

Harrison and Mason (1995) developed a typology of angel networks and used their typology to address a number of issues involving business angel networks. The paper argues for a continued commitment to not-for-profit (public-sector-supported) initiatives to close the investment size and regional gaps that exist in the United Kingdom.

Manigart and Struyf (1995) examined the financing of high-tech start-ups in Belgium. They found that private individuals and nonfinancial corporations were willing to bear the highest risk, as they were willing to invest at the start-up phase. Private investors were difficult to locate. Venture capital funds were the most important suppliers of capital for the growth phase of the firms in their sample.

Informal Venture Capital—Market Mechanisms

It has been recognized for some time that the economics of the institutional venture capital market preclude that market from effectively serving the need for relatively small amounts of seed and start-up capital for promising high-growth ventures. In their study of the financial histories of new technology-based firms (NTBFs) founded in New England, Freear and Wetzel (1992) concluded that private individuals and venture capital funds play complementary rather than competing roles in the financing of NTBFs. This complementary relationship has two dimensions—size and stage. First, at all stages, venture capital funds tend to invest substantially more dollars per round than private individuals. Size differences became more pronounced as the stage of the financing advanced. Second, private investors exhibited a significantly higher propensity to invest at the seed and start-up stages than other investors, suggesting that private investors may have longer exit horizons and, possibly, less risk aversion. In a very real sense, private investors operate the farm system where high-growth ventures are launched. For an overview of the private investor market for venture capital, see Freear et al. (1994b).

Over the last 15 years, a variety of experimental efforts have been undertaken to increase the efficiency of the angel market. Most of the experimental efforts to improve the effectiveness of the early-stage equity markets have taken the form of so-called venture capital networks or business introduction services. Descriptions and analyses of projects undertaken in the United States and Europe can be found in a recent book edited by Harrison and Mason (1996). In the opening paragraph of their preface, Harrison and Mason attribute these efforts to the existence of a continuing finance gap for small firms that has been the subject of on-going debate in many countries. The gap is particularly identified with a shortage of equity capital and is experienced most sharply by certain types of firm (notably high-tech ventures) at particular stages of development (especially those looking for seed and start-up capital) and in specific regions (outside the major national financial centers).

In Harrison and Mason's view, the book reflects the interpenetration of academic research and policy formulation. Its publication is testimony to the ability of academic research to help shape and influence the direction and outcome of public policy in the United Kingdom, United States, Canada, Sweden, and Denmark. The book is the first formal output of the International Informal Venture Capital Research Network.

Contributors to Harrison and Mason's book conclude their chapters with a set of "Implications for Practice," such as:

❖ An adequate flow of quality investment opportunities is necessary to attract investors; without some measures of quality control over the nature of businesses registering with the service, investor dissatisfaction is likely.

❖ The confidentiality of investor data is essential.

❖ Without an operating budget large enough to hire full-time staff and support on-going marketing efforts, the level of service offered will not be sufficient to attract investors and entrepreneurs.

❖ Attraction of sponsorship funding, contributions in kind, and endorsements from professional and financial intermediaries is vital.

❖ It takes time, money, and committed personnel to build a network's reputation and establish a track record of success. Successful networks share a number of characteristics: they are adequately financed, based in or close to major population centers, close to centers of formal venture capital activity, and have been in existence long enough to build up confidence in the network.

❖ Informal investing is, in part, a personal process, and purely impersonal (computer-based) and centralized (national) match-making services may fail to meet the needs of the market.

❖ The informal market for risk capital is not a national marketplace but a local and personal market. The importance of the local aspect as a spur to investment is vital and should be translated into the establishment of local investment associations, networks, or syndicates.

❖ It is important to have a large enough operating area for a service to ensure that a viable number of investor and entrepreneur registrations are obtained.

❖ Business introduction services attract both active and virgin angels; local/regional business introduction services attract both local and nonlocal investors.

❖ Investors' forums are an effective matching mechanism; however, because not all investors are able to attend, they should be used in conjunction with other mechanisms. The use of alternative technologies, such as teleconferencing, CD-ROM, and videos should also be considered.

❖ Charging success fees raises both image problems and practical difficulties.

❖ Evaluation of business introduction services should consider the wider benefits to businesses: advice and counseling, the hands-on involvement of investors, feedback from investors who decided not to invest, and the leverage effect on other sources of finance. A business introduction service should be run by an organization with the highest professional standing and without vested interests.

Among the above Implications for Practice are references to investor forums and the use of multimedia technology, including teleconferencing. Using trained students in a simulated business forum teleconference, Bracker et al. (1994) attempted to determine whether teleconferenced business forums are a viable medium to enhance the bringing together of informal investors and entrepreneurs where distance is a significant barrier to communication. In this first of its kind study, the authors, acknowledging that much work still needs to be done, conclude that the results of their work are promising. Their study has potentially significant implications that may foster greater entrepreneurial development in regions of the country presently devoid of or limited in entrepreneurial and informal investor activity. Their work has moved us closer to providing another vehicle for more efficient utilization of resources.

Little or no information is available on the actual rates of return on informal venture investors portfolios or on the timing and method of exit. In another first of its kind study, Lumme et al. (1996) surveyed 38 active business angels in Finland who had made a total of 155 investments; 20 of these investors had made 49 exits. Two issues are addressed. First, evidence is presented on investment performance and the timing and method of exit. Second, the paper explores differences between those investors with a successful track record of exits and those with an unsuccessful track record. Differences are identified in terms of motivation for investing, volume, and sources of information on investment opportunities, prior relationship with investee businesses, perception of value added, and employment background. The authors caution that their conclusions should only be regarded as suggestive in view of the small numbers involved.

Brophy and Chambers (1991) examined the impact of symposia that bring together entrepreneurs and private investors. They found that the University of Michigan's Growth Capital Symposium appeared to be involving firms that subsequently attracted private placement capital, both formal and informal venture capital.

Mason et al. (1996) provide a case study of VentureNet—a computer-based national network enabling business angels seeking investments to find entrepreneurs seeking equity finance quickly and efficiently. VentureNet was established by Enterprise Support Group, Ltd., a private-sector company established in 1988 and was the subject of a management buyout in 1992 from 3i plc, the United Kingdom's leading venture capital company. Because of the attitudes of existing players, combined with the opportunities created by the Internet, VentureNet has decided that it will no longer rely upon intermediaries to make contact with investors and businesses and will, instead, seek clients directly. It still intends to involve intermediary organizations in the follow-up stages of the matching process.

The Road Ahead

Driven by the emergence of entrepreneurial economies in the United States and abroad, interest in the informal venture capital market is certain to accelerate in the years ahead. Although much has been accomplished, there are substantial contributions still to be made to increase our understanding of the early-stage equity financing market. The market mechanisms surrounding the informal venture capital market should provide fruitful lines of inquiry, regarding:

1. Characteristics of an effective market for early-stage equity financing for entrepreneurs.

2. Scale of the informal venture capital market from a demand as well as a supply point of view.

3. Size of the population of virgin angels.

4. Techniques for tapping the know-how and the capital of virgin angels.

5. Characteristics of the interface between the market for business angel financing and other capital market institutions including, in particular, venture capital funds.

Theoretical foundations need to be refined, especially (a) the contribution of, for example, utility theory and agency theory to the understanding of decision models employed by business angels and (b) empirical tests of the theoretical underpinnings of the informal venture capital markets.

Angel characteristics need to be more fully developed, including:

❖ Characteristics of investment opportunities that are most effective in overcoming business angels' propensity to invest close to home.

❖ Better evidence defining the ABCs (attitudes, behavior, and characteristics) of business angels.

❖ Characteristics that define useful subsets of angels.

To address many of these issues, two initiatives will assist in refining and uncovering some of the subtleties of the informal venture capital market: (a) creating informal venture capital databases that are substantial enough to support rigorous research and (b) creating longitudinal investor, entrepreneur, and market databases from efforts to establish national angel markets.

Developing a more informed knowledge base of investment strategies will involve:

❖ Acquiring further insights into the range and quality of postinvestment relationships between business angels and the entrepreneurs they finance.

❖ Evaluating the performance of the venture investment portfolios of business angels, including realized rates of return, nonfinancial returns, holding periods and exit strategies.

❖ Discovering information on the pricing and terms and conditions of informal venture capital deals.

Research on the following issues will provide insight for public policy decisions, particularly, the role public policy can play in overcoming early-stage equity financing obstacles confronted by entrepreneurs and the influence of tax strategies on the flow of informal venture capital.

Looking ahead, the most promising opportunities for informal venture capital research are expected to flow from international efforts to create new early-stage equity capital markets for entrepreneurs. The next five years are certain to generate both more and higher quality informal venture capital research than the last five years.

REFERENCES

Bracker, J.S., G.H. Van Clouse, and R.A. Thacker. 1994. Teleconferencing business forums: An approach to linking entrepreneurs and potential investors. *Entrepreneurship and Regional Development* 6(3):259-274.

Brophy, D.J., and B.R. Chambers. 1991. The growth capital symposium: An intervention into the market for growth capital. In N.C. Churchill et al. (eds.): *Frontiers of Entrepreneurship Research*. Wellesley, MA: Babson College, 422-434.

Center for Venture Research, University of New Hampshire. 1995. *Innovation, Technology and the Information Revolution: Creating New Capital Markets for Emerging Ventures.* White paper prepared for the SEC Government/Business Forum on Small Business Capital Formation, Providence, RI, September 13-14.

Congressional Office of Technology Assessment. 1984. *Technology, Innovation and Regional Economic Development.* Washington, DC: US Congress Office of Technology Assessment, OTA-STI-238.

Ehrlich, S.A., A.F. De Noble, T. Moore, and R.R. Weaver. 1994. After the cash arrives: A comparative study of venture capital and private investor involvement in entrepreneurial firms. *Journal of Business Venturing* 9(1):67-82.

Fiet, J.O. 1991. Network reliance by venture capital firms and business angels: An empirical and theoretical test. In N.C. Churchill et al. (eds.): *Frontiers of Entrepreneurship Research.* Wellesley, MA: Babson College, 445-455.

Fiet, J.O. 1995a. Reliance upon informants in the venture capital industry. *Journal of Business Venturing* 10(3):195-223.

Fiet, J. 1995b. Risk avoidance strategies in venture capital markets. *Journal of Management Studies* 3(4):551-574.

Freear, J., J.E. Sohl, and W.E. Wetzel. 1992. The investment attitudes behavior and characteristics of high net worth individuals. In N.C. Churchill et al. (eds.): *Frontiers of Entrepreneurship Research.* Wellesley, MA: Babson College, 374-387.

Freear, J., and W.E. Wetzel. 1992. The informal venture capital market in the 1990s. In D.L. Sexton and J.D. Kasarda (eds.): *State of the Art of Entrepreneurship.* Boston: PWS-Kent, 462-486.

Freear, J., J.E. Sohl, and W.E. Wetzel. 1993. Angel profiles: A longitudinal study. In N.C. Churchill et al. (eds.): *Frontiers of Entrepreneurship Research.* Wellesley, MA: Babson College, 557-558.

Freear, J., J.E. Sohl, and W.E. Wetzel. 1994a. Angels and non-angels: Are there differences? *Journal of Business Venturing* 9(2):109-123.

Freear, J., J.E. Sohl, and W.E. Wetzel. 1994b. The private investor market for venture capital. *The Financier* 1(2):7-14.

Freear, J., J.E. Sohl, and W.E. Wetzel. 1996. Technology due diligence: What angels consider important. Presented at the Babson College/Kauffman Foundation Entrepreneurship Research Conference, University of Washington, March 20-23.

Gaston, R., and S. Bell. 1988. The informal supply of capital. Unpublished report prepared for the US Small Business Administration, Applied Economics Group.

Gaston, R.J. 1989a. The scale of the informal capital markets. *Small Business Economics* 1:223-230.

Gaston, R.J. 1989b. *Finding Private Venture Capital for Your Firm.* New York: John Wiley and Sons, 48-78.

Harrison, R.T. and C.M. Mason. 1992a. The roles of investors in entrepreneurial companies: A comparison of informal investors and venture capitalists. In N.C. Churchill et. al. (eds.): *Frontiers of Entrepreneurship Research.* Wellesley, MA: Babson College, 388-404.

Harrison, R.T., and C.M. Mason. 1992b. International perspectives on the supply of informal venture capital. *Journal of Business Venturing* 7(6):459-475.

Harrison, R.T., and C.M. Mason. 1992c. The roles of investors in entrepreneurial companies: A comparison of informal investors and venture capitalists. In N.C. Churchill et al. (eds.): *Frontiers of Entrepreneurship Research.* Wellesley, MA: Babson College, 388-404.

Harrison, R.T., and C.M. Mason. 1993. Finance for the growing business: The role of informal investment. *National Westminster Bank Quarterly Review,* May 1993, 17-29.

Harrison, R.T., and C.M. Mason. 1995. Informal venture capital investment activity through business introduction services: Is there still a role for public policy? In W.D. Bygrave et al. (eds.): *Frontiers of Entrepreneurship Research.* Wellesley, MA: Babson College, 479-493.

Harrison, R.T., and C.M. Mason. 1996. *Informal Venture Capital: Evaluating the Impact of Business Introduction Services.* London: Woodhead-Faulkner, 248-272.

Hay, M., and S. Abbott. 1994. *Investing for the Future—Promoting Seed, Startup, and Early Stage Venture Capital Funding of New Technology-Based Firms in the UK.* London Business School and Advent Ltd., 1-72.

Kelly, P., and M. Hay. 1996a. *Informal Venture Capital.* Teaching note, London Business School, 1-23.

Kelly, P., and M. Hay. 1996b. Serial investors: An exploratory study. Presented at the Babson College/Kauffman Foundation Entrepreneurship Research Conference, University of Washington, 1-14.

Landstrom, H. 1993. Informal risk capital in Sweden and some international comparisons. *Journal of Business Venturing* 8(16):525-540.

Landstrom, H. 1993. Agency theory and its application to small firms: Evidence from the Swedish venture capital market. *Journal of Small Business Finance* 2(3):203-218.

Landstrom, H. 1995. A pilot study on the investment decision-making of informal investors in Sweden. *Journal of Small Business Management* 10(4):67-76.

Lumme, A., C. M. Mason, and M. Suomi. 1996. The returns from informal venture capital investments: Some evidence from Finland. Presented at the Babson College/Kauffman Foundation Entrepreneurship Research Conference, University of Washington, March 20-23.

Manigart, S., and C. Struyf. 1995. Financing high-technology start-ups in Belgium. Presented at the Babson College/Kauffman Foundation Entrepreneurship Research Conference, London Business School, April 9-12.

Mason, C., and R. Harrison. 1992. The supply of equity finance in the UK: A strategy for closing the equity gap. *Entrepreneurship and Regional Development* 4:357-380.

Mason, C., and R.T. Harrison. 1993a. Promoting informal venture capital: An evaluation of a British initiative. In N.C. Churchill et al. (eds.): *Frontiers of Entrepreneurship Research.* Wellesley, MA: Babson College, 525-537.

Mason, C., and R.T. Harrison. 1993b. Strategies for expanding the informal venture capital market. *International Small Business Journal* 11(4):23-28.

Mason, C., R.T. Harrison, and J. Chaloner. 1993. Informal risk capital in the UK: A study of investor characteristics, investment preferences, and investment decision-making. Venture Finance Working Paper No. 2, Southampton, UK: Urban Policy Research Unit, University of Southampton.

Mason, C., and R.T. Harrison. 1995. Institutional archangels: New players in the UK's informal venture capital market. Unpublished paper.

Mason, C., R.T. Harrison, and J. List. 1996. VentureNet: A new approach to the promotion of informal venture capital investments. Presented at the Babson College/Kauffman Foundation Entrepreneurship Research Conference, University of Washington, March 20-23.

Meeks, F., and K. Lewis. 1995. Blue chips in your own backyard. *Forbes,* April 24, 166-172.

Norton, E. 1990. An overview of venture capital finance. Unpublished working paper, Fairleigh Dickinson University.

Norton, E., and B. Tennenbaum. 1993a. Specialization versus diversification as a venture capital investment strategy. *Journal of Business Venturing* 8(5):431-442.

Norton, E., and B. Tennenbaum. 1993b. The effects of venture capitalists' characteristics on the structure of the venture capital deal. *Journal of Small Business Management* 31(4):32-41.

Ou, C. 1993. Holdings of privately-held business assets by American families: Findings from the 1989 consumer finance survey. Unpublished paper presented at the Fifth Small Business Financial Research Symposium, California State University, Long Beach, Long Beach, CA, April 29, 1-18.

Riding, A., and D. Short. 1989. Informal investors in the Ottawa-Carleton region: Experiences and expectations. *Entrepreneurship and Regional Development* 1:99-112.

Sexton, D.L., and J.D. Kasarda. (eds.). 1992. *The State of the Art of Entrepreneurship.* Boston: PWS-Kent Publishing Company, 1-607.

Stevenson, H., and P. Coveney. 1994. *Survey of Business Angels: Fallacies Corrected and Six Distinct Types of Angels Identified.* Templeton College, Oxford, and Venture Capital Report, Ltd., Henley on Thames, UK, October 1-10.

Sullivan, M.K. 1991. Entrepreneurs as informal investors: Are there distinguishing characteristics? In N.C. Churchill et al. (eds.): *Frontiers of Entrepreneurship Research.* Wellesley, MA: Babson College, 456-468.

Sullivan, M.K., and A. Miller. 1990. Applying theory of finance to informal risk capital research: promise and problems. In N.C. Churchill et al. (eds.): *Frontiers of Entrepreneurship Research.* Wellesley, MA: Babson College, 296-310.

Wetzel, W. 1981. Informal risk capital in New England. In K.H. Vesper et al. (eds.): *Frontiers of Entrepreneurship Research*. Wellesley, MA: Babson College, 217-245.

Wetzel, W.E., and J. Freear. 1993. Promoting informal venture capital in the US: Reflections on the history of Venture Capital Network. In R.T. Harrison and C.M. Mason (eds.): *Informal Venture Capital: Information, Networks and Public Policy*. Hempel Hempstead, U.K.: Woodhead-Faulkner, 61-72.

Wetzel, W. 1995. Economic policy in an entrepreneurial world. *Venture Capital Journal* 35(4):52-54.

CHAPTER 4

Harvesting Firm Value:
Process and Results

J. WILLIAM PETTY

FOR MOST WITHIN THE ACADEMIC COMMUNITY, entrepreneurship has come to be viewed as a process involving the relentless pursuit of a potential investment opportunity without regard to resources currently owned (Stevenson and Gumpert, 1985; Stevenson and Sahlman, 1987). The objective of this pursuit depends in part on the nature of the opportunity itself. For micro-firms, the goal is mostly to provide a "preferred" lifestyle. For mega-firms, or entrepreneurial firms, on the other hand, the objective is to create economic value. Although micro- and mega-firms have some similarities, there are real differences between them, an important one being the opportunity for the mega-firm to harvest a terminal value from the investment that is not present for the micro-firm. Thus mega-firms are of primary interest to us within the context of harvesting a venture.

Most of the academic literature in entrepreneurship has concentrated on the earlier stages of the entrepreneurship process, namely, identifying and exploiting an opportunity. Little attention has been given to exiting or what has come to be called *harvesting the business*, which is the focus of this chapter.

Harvesting an entrepreneurial firm is the approach taken by the owners and investors to realize terminal after-tax cash flows on their investment. It defines how they will extract some or all of the economic value (cash flows) from the investment. Also, from the entrepreneur's perspective, the issue of harvesting is about more than money, involving personal and nonfinancial aspects of the harvest as well. Even an entrepreneur who realizes an acceptable value for a firm may come away disappointed with the overall outcome of the harvest.

How Important Is Harvesting?

There is little in the way of hard evidence as to the exact significance of the harvest; that is, it cannot be said precisely how much of the value realized from a venture is attributable to a successfully implemented harvest strategy. However, from intuition alone, one would expect that few events in the life of the entrepreneur, and for the firm itself, are more significant than the harvest.

In one sense, the harvest is not as important as successfully identifying an opportunity or even growing the firm. These two phases of the entrepreneurial process are without question the primary value-creating activities. However, *the availability and effectiveness of the exit ultimately determines the value to be realized from the venture.* While value must first be created, it must then be realized for any real benefit. Thus, the terminal liquidity, or lack thereof, provided by the harvest will ultimately determine the value received from the venture. The inability to harvest at a *fair* value would be much like buying a stock, watching its value increase over time, but not being allowed to capture the value by selling the stock. However, the stock analogy fails to capture the complexity of the harvest relative to selling a publicly traded stock.

The significance of the problem may also be viewed from a macro perspective by considering the large number of family-owned firms that will be faced with the prospects of the harvest. It has been estimated that 18 percent of the financial assets held by U.S. households, or $2.4 trillion, is invested in privately held firms, mostly family-owned businesses—$300 billion more than these same households have invested in publicly traded companies (Paré, 1990). Many of these privately owned firms were founded by entrepreneurs in the 1950s and 1960s who are or soon will be contemplating and executing a harvest or exit strategy. The same situation also exists in Europe. As many as 17,000 European companies received equity venture capital during the past decade (Batchelor, 1992). Most of those investments have yet to be harvested.

The harvest is also of prime importance to outside investors. These investors typically have a priori expectations about their investment that include either taking the firm public or being acquired by other investors (Freear et al., 1990). Investors, be they professional venture capitalists or private informal investors, have an obvious vested interest in the exit mechanism used to liquidate their investment. While not having the same personal significance for the firm's investors as it does for the entrepreneur, the effectiveness of the harvest affects the amount and timing of the after-tax cash flows to be received, which in turn determines the eventual return earned on the investment. From experience, they realize that time can exact a fierce penalty on the rate or return. A successful entrepreneurial venture returns at least 40 percent compounded annually to investors over a holding period of four to five years. To achieve such a return requires a terminal cash-flow multiple of 5.4 times the original investment. However, the same yield over 10 years requires 28.9 times the original investment. Thus, an investment in a high-risk venture that is unrealized after 10 years is thought to be long past its "sell-by" date in all but a few rare instances. Consequently, venture capitalists are reluctant to make an investment without having some idea as to how an exit will be arranged.

In short, the opportunity to exit successfully from a venture is thought to be a significant factor in the entrepreneurial process, both for the entrepreneur and for any investors providing risk capital.

In examining the literature on harvesting the venture, there are four areas of interest:

1. Developing a strategy.

2. The value-creating process.

3. The process of the harvest.

4. The European experience in harvesting.

When Does the Harvest Begin?

The typical prescription for developing a harvest strategy is simple: *Now, not later.* Timmons (1994) suggests that entrepreneurs build a great company but do not forget the harvest, he also advises that entrepreneurs should keep harvest options open and think of harvesting as a vehicle for reducing risk and for creating future entrepreneurial choices and options. Thus, crafting a harvest strategy is viewed as something to be done early on and as an ongoing process along with growing the business, even well before the impending need or desire to harvest.

Given the conventional wisdom of the need for a harvest strategy even before the event, a natural question would be, Do entrepreneurs ever follow this advice? To answer this question, one must rely on limited empirical evidence. Holmburg (1991) surveyed CEOs at computer software firms that went public between 1980 and 1990. He found that 15 percent had a written harvest strategy as part of the original business plan; 5 percent developed a formal exit strategy subsequent to preparing the business plan; 40 percent had given some thought to the harvest; and the final 40 percent did not give any consideration to the harvest beforehand (Figure 4.1, p. 74). Similar results were found in another study where 40 percent of the CEOs surveyed did not consider the harvest at the outset of the venture (Hyatt, 1990). Thus, it can be concluded—based on our limited information—that roughly 60 percent give some advance thought to the harvest, either informally or formally. However, only 20 percent appear serious in their efforts.

FIGURE 4.1
Developing the Harvest Strategy

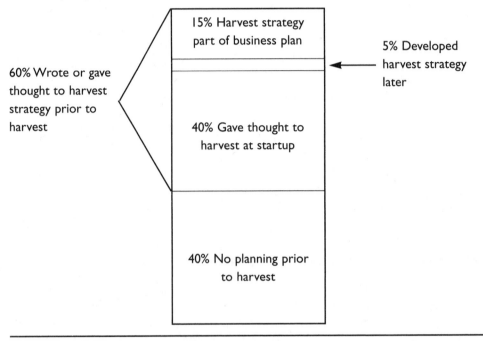

You Cannot Harvest What You Have Not Created

Valuing a firm when the stock is not traded in the marketplace is difficult in the best of circumstances. But even worse is forecasting the value of a startup some five or 10 years into the future. Financial contracting requires some estimate of the venture's terminal value and an assumed horizon date for the harvest (Sahlman and Summer, 1988). The problem is one of assigning value to an asset for which the greatest amount of incomplete and conflicting information exists. To be even more precise, founders and early-stage investors are in reality purchasing an option on the future cash flows to be exercised if the firm does well; the option characteristics are especially apparent when staged commitments are allowed.

The possible approaches for determining a company's value are legion. However, most investors in entrepreneurial firms rely on some multiple of earnings, be it net income, operating income, or earnings before interest, taxes, depreciation, and amortization (EBITDA). For instance, a multiple of EBITDA plus the firm's cash is often used to estimate firm value. Outstanding debt is subtracted to determine the value of the equity. This approach, while simple, begs an important question: What *should* determine harvest value? Two basic perspectives can be used in answering the question: either the accountant's "map of the territory" or the economist's. An accountant would say that earnings drive firm value—the larger the earnings, the greater the firm value. The economist's map of firm value, on the other hand, is based on the present value of future cash flows.

To the extent that a willing buyer is prepared to pay some multiple of earnings for a firm, value—at least from all appearances—is based on earnings. But there is little in the way of an economic rationale or any empirical evidence to suggest that a firm's value is closely linked to earnings (Brennan, 1995). Instead, many believe that value ought to be determined by finding the present value of future cash flows discounted at the opportunity cost of funds for the given level of risk (Copeland et al., 1994). Nevertheless, the conventional wisdom that earnings matter continues to carry the day for most investors.

The issue of valuation as it relates to the harvest strategy is important; one cannot structure the deal without some notion of what the harvest value will be. However, the issue can be expressed more fundamentally by asking, Will economic value be created with the capital that is being invested in the venture? Given that a start-up company is not traded publicly, one cannot depend on the capital markets for that information. Even so, firm value can correctly be represented as the capital invested in the business plus any value created by earning economic rates of return that exceed the cost of capital; or stated negatively, firm value is equal to the capital invested, less the value destroyed by earning rates of return less than the firm's opportunity cost of funds.

As a firm moves in time toward the harvest, there are two questions that are of primary importance. First, are the current owners and managers effectively creating firm value? The answer to this question can be answered easily from historical financial data by estimating the economic value added (EVA) over time. The economic value added from a firm's operations in year t (EVA$_t$) could be estimated as follows (Stewart, 1991):

$$\text{EVA}_t = (\text{return on capital}_t - \text{cost of capital}_t) \times \text{invested capital}_t$$

where return on capital is measured as *economic* income divided by the amount of capital (cash) invested in the company over its life, and cost of capital is the investors' opportunity cost of funds—a concept almost totally alien to most entrepreneurs. This single measurement of economic value added, which is seldom considered by large companies (much less smaller companies), can tell us a great deal about the value-creating ability of a company, an issue of import if there is to be any value to harvest.

The second and related question is, Could new owners do more with the company than the founders? If so, then the firm would have greater value in the hands of new owners. That is, growing a venture to the point of diminishing returns and then selling it to others better able to carry it to the next level is a proven way to create value. How this incremental value will be shared between the old and the new owners largely depends on the relative strengths of each party in the negotiations, i.e., who wants the deal the most.

With the foregoing as a backdrop, the next step is to examine the actual harvesting process.

The Harvesting Process

For the most part, designing a harvest strategy is limited to one of several options. The more common ways to harvest include the following:

❖ Restructuring the company's goals and strategies in order to increase the cash flows extracted from the business by the owners and investors.

❖ Being acquired by or merged into another, usually larger, company.

❖ Private sale for cash, debt, and/or equity to: (1) another company or group of investors; (2) management, frequently through a leveraged management buyout; (3) employees, usually in the form of an employee stock option plan; or (4) family members.

❖ Public stock offering.

How do entrepreneurs view these options? Again drawing on Holmburg's (1991) study of the computer software CEOs who took their firms public, each respondent was asked to reflect back to the start-up stage of the company and to rank the probability at that time that the firm would use one of four alternative harvest strategies at some point in the future. The options included an initial public offering, being acquired by a larger company, merging with another firm, and a leveraged buyout by employees. Somewhat of a surprise, 65 percent of the CEOs considered an initial public offering as their most likely choice; 30 percent assigned the highest probability to being acquired by a larger company, and the remaining 5 percent thought a leveraged buyout by employees would occur. These results are supported by another recent survey of 100 CEOs where more than half planned on going public from the initial start-up phase (Hyatt, 1990). The discussion that follows briefly explains several of the above options.

Increasing the Firm's Free Cash Flows

A firm's free cash flows represent the amount of cash that can be distributed to its investors—debt and equity—after all operating needs have been met. Specifically,

$$\text{Free cash flows} = \text{operating profits after tax} + \text{depreciation} - \text{investments required to grow the firm}$$

In a firm's early years, everything goes into growing the company. All available cash is devoted to growth, which means that the last term in the above equation is large. For most growth firms, the free cash flows are significantly negative in the early years. As a firm and its industry matures, the opportunity to grow declines, which can result in sizable amounts of free cash flows.

Many of the fights in the 1980s between management and corporate raiders occurred in mature industries, such as oil and steel, over the use of the firm's cash flows. Management was using them to invest in unrelated businesses, usually with dismal results, while the raiders thought the newly acquired firms should not have been acquired because the result was a loss of focus. So the raiders attempted to take over these widely diversified businesses in an attempt to return them to their core businesses—and to return the cash flows to the investors. A substantial part of the academic literature in this area focused on this debate (e.g., Donaldson, 1994; Bhide, 1989).

Within the context of harvesting, the concern is not so much about the battle over the use of the free cash flows as it is in converting them into a way of harvesting an entrepreneurial firm. Specifically, at some point, an entrepreneur and any investors in the venture may decide to slow or even discontinue the company's sales growth rate. Rather than reinvesting all the cash flows back into the company, the owners begin cashing out of their investment. Only the amount of cash is retained that is necessary to maintain current markets—there is no effort to grow the present markets or expand into new markets. The free cash flows can then be harvested without affecting current operations. For many ventures, this event may occur as a natural consequence of maturing markets where competition has removed any growth opportunities that earn returns greater than the firm's cost of capital. The mistake at this point is for the entrepreneur not to harvest. Thus, restricting a company's growth is a viable strategy for harvesting the venture, but it requires some time to accomplish.

Increasing the firm's free cash flows has two potential advantages. First, the owners can retain the ownership of the company if they are not ready to sell. Second, the strategy is not dependent on finding an interested buyer and going through the often time-consuming and energy-draining experience of negotiating the sale, nor does the owner face the exciting, but at times frustrating, process of a public stock offering.

There are, however, some disadvantages as well. In harvesting the business, the desire is to maximize the after-tax cash flows going to the company's owners and investors. If the firm simply distributes the cash flows as dividends, the income will be taxed both as corporate income and again as personal dividend income to the stockholders. There are ways, within limits, to avoid this problem, but it may not provide the entrepreneur as much discretionary cash flow as an outright sale. Another disadvantage of this strategy is the chance that the firm may not be able to sustain its competitive advantage while simultaneously harvesting the venture. If so, the end result may be an unintended liquidation. Finally, for the entrepreneur who is simply tired of the day-to-day operations, harvesting the venture by siphoning off the free cash flows over time may be asking for too much in the way of patience. Unless there are other individuals within the company who are qualified to provide the needed managerial leadership, then the strategy may be too emotionally draining.

Merging or Being Acquired

In terms of mergers and acquisitions, the literature has mostly been concerned with the rationale and success of acquiring or merging with another company, especially in an unrelated business (Weston et al., 1990). The predominant question has been, What can management accomplish through corporate diversification that the owners cannot achieve through their own diversification and with a lot more ease?

The 1980s came to be known the decade of the deals and as a time of hostile takeovers, which to many instinctively felt wasteful and harmful. But not all was bad about the 1980s. The decade's merger and acquisition (M&A) activity allowed the shareholders of a significant number of privately held companies to realize the value "locked-up" in their companies via a market-based transaction. In other words, the M&A activity of the 1980s allowed many entrepreneurs the opportunity to harvest their investment that might not have otherwise been possible.

The financial issues related to selling a firm are basically the same with any exit strategy, namely, how to value the company for the purpose of the sale and how to structure the payment. However, financial matters, while not insignificant by any means, are not the only issues of importance when it comes to selling the firm and may not even be the primary concern.

To gain some understanding into this process, Petty et al. (1994) collected a sample of acquisition transactions of privately held companies reported in *Mergerstat Review* between 1984 and 1990. The sample was limited to acquisitions valued between $5 million and $100 million. Also, 278 venture-backed companies that were acquired between the years of 1987 and 1990 were identified through the *Venture Economics* database, which included the names of venture capitalists who had participated in the financing. With this combined listing, background information about the buyer and seller and about the acquisition itself was collected from the Dow Jones News Retrieval Service.

The issues addressed in the study fell into one of three areas: 1) the decision to sell, 2) the selling process, and 3) the post sale. Using these issues as guidelines, phone interviews were conducted of a limited sample of the entrepreneurs—efforts to interview venture capitalists were essentially unsuccessful. Some of the conclusions reached from the interviews were as follows:

1. Some of the entrepreneurs were significantly disappointed with the acquisition process and the final outcome. They came to realize that the firm served as the base for much of what they did, both in and out of the business arena. This sentiment existed more with owners of the low-tech firms, especially service firms, than with the high-tech companies.

2. The most prevalent reason for selling the company related to estate planning and the opportunity to diversify their investments. A second reason for the sale related to the need for financing growth, which the firm or the owner did not have the capacity to provide.

3. The harvest did provide the long-sought-after liquidity, but some entrepreneurs found managing money more difficult, and less enjoyable, than they had expected and less rewarding than operating their own company.

4. The disillusionment of selling the firm was particularly evident when the entrepreneur continued in the management of the company but under the supervision of the acquiring owners. The differences in corporate culture became a significant problem for both companies involved in the transaction, but more so for the selling entrepreneur.

5. A number of the selling owners were disappointed in the advising they received from the "experts." After the fact, they wish they had talked to other entrepreneurs who had been through the experience of a company sale.

6. Most entrepreneurs relied on their staff and advisors to determine a fair price for their company. Thus, they would talk in terms of cash flows and earnings, most often the capitalization or multiple of the earnings or cash flows, and seldom the present value of future cash flows. However, most of the entrepreneurs felt they had a sense of what they would accept for the firm, and that instinct had a greater influence than did the supporting computations. Most often, the price was not a serious issue.

7. There is considerable downside risk if the acquisition is not consummated. During the negotiations, management's focus and attention shifts from company operations to consummating the sale. Members of the existing management team may be promised promotions after the acquisition, which are not fulfilled after the negotiations fail. Hence, there is a real risk of losing part of the management team and certainly taking several months to regain the firm's focus.

In addition to selling the firm or being acquired by independent purchasers or acquires, the harvest strategy can be accomplished by selling to the firm's own management or its employees, as described in the following two sections.

Management Buyout

As already observed, the 1980s will long be remembered—not so favorably by some managers and employees—for the unfriendly takeovers and corporate restructurings, involving corporate raiders and takeover artists, such as Carl Icahn and T. Boone Pickens. These paragons—or parasites some might say—popularized financial engineering, in which an attempt to buy a company is made for the purpose of restructuring it and selling it off in pieces to the highest bidder. To finance the deal, heavy amounts of debt are incurred, with as much as 90 percent of the financing coming from high-yield debt, thus the name *leveraged buyout*. If the leveraged buyout is performed not by outsiders but by the firm's own management, we have a *management buyout* (MBO).

The MBO has been used by some to thwart outside raiders and by others to refocus current management's vision. The evidence is clear that MBOs can contribute significantly to a firm's operating performance by increasing management's focus and intensity and that the benefits accruing from MBOs are not short-term in duration. (See Kaplan, 1989 and 1991 for an analysis of the operating effects of large-firm MBOs, and Wright et al., 1992b, for smaller-firm MBOs.)

Given the empirical evidence of increased efficiencies produced from an MBO and the proven longevity of these benefits, an MBO should be considered a potentially viable means for transferring firm ownership—both for large and small businesses. In like manner, an MBO can serve as a possible means for harvesting a venture. While the managers within many entrepreneurial businesses frequently have a strong interest and incentive to buy the business, they often lack the financial capacity to do so. An MBO can resolve this intractability. It simply means that they must be prepared to live in a glass house and with the unforgiving nature of debt financing.

If an MBO is used to consummate the sale, not only is the new owner exposed to financial risk, so is the selling owner. Also, to the extent that the entrepreneur accepts debt in consideration for the company, there is a potential complication to be resolved. The deal must then be structured to minimize potential agency problems. Specifically, if the new owners have placed little if any of their own money in the deal, they may be inclined to take risks that are not in the best interest of the selling entrepreneur; they simply have nothing to lose if the company fails. Also, if the terms of the deal include an earnout where the final amount of the payment depends in part on the subsequent profit performance of the company, the buying owners have an incentive to do things that lower the firm's profits during the earnout period. Thus, the entrepreneur needs to take great care in structuring the deal; otherwise, there will most likely be disappointment with the outcome.

In addition to their recent popularity in the United States, management buyouts have come to be used in Europe as well. In Europe, the venture capital industry has had a significant role in MBOs, especially for smaller firms. Wright et al. (1992a) evaluated a sample of 182 venture-backed MBOs and found the same improvement in operating efficiencies and longevity as did researchers in the United States. Also, European managers who undertake MBOs typically anticipate their exit to be in the form of a public offering, but almost invariably the firm is sold to a third party. This last finding will become clearer at a later point in the chapter.

Employee Stock Ownership Plan

Employee stock ownership plans (ESOPs) were designed to increase productivity by linking employee compensation to company performance and by giving employees a role in management through their voting rights as shareholders. The research to date suggests that ESOPs have indeed been effective toward these ends. For instance, using both Tobin's (Tobin, 1969) and accounting performance variables, Park and Song (1995) found that average performance significantly increases after establishing or expanding an ESOP (see also Beatty, 1995). There are also tax advantages with ESOPs that are not available with other retirement plans.

In response to the above benefits, owners of small and midsize firms have been the primary users of ESOPs when they are ready to sell (Englander, 1993). The opportunity for employees to invest in employer stock and the significant tax savings not available with other retirement plans—for employers and employees alike—makes the ESOP potentially attractive as a way to harvest the venture (Beatty, 1995).

A *leveraged* ESOP particularly fits the needs of an entrepreneur wanting to harvest a venture. This type of ESOP borrows money to buy the company's stock. By having access to borrowed money, the leveraged ESOP can make large purchases of the stock at one time, conceivably purchasing the entire company. Figure 4.2, p. 82, presents a flow chart of the sequence of events when a leveraged ESOP is used to provide an employee retirement plan and, in conjunction, to allow the present owners to sell their stock. The firm first establishes an ESOP and guarantees any debt borrowed by the ESOP for the purpose of buying the company's stock. Next, the ESOP borrows money from a lender, and the cash is used to buy the owner's stock. The shares are held by a trust, and the company makes annual tax-deductible contributions to the trust so it can pay off the loan. As the loan is paid off, shares are released and allocated to the employees.

FIGURE 4.2
The Harvest: Using the Leveraged ESOP

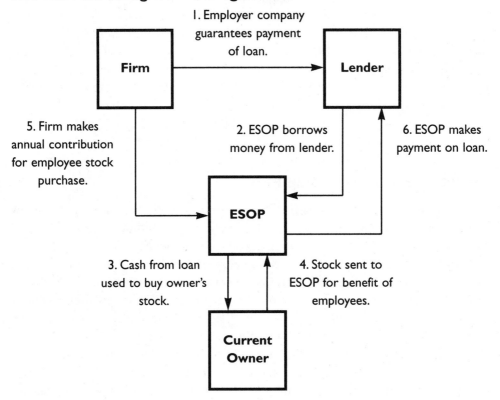

Adapted from D.R. Garner, R.R. Owen, and R.P. Conway, *The Ernst & Young Guide to Raising Capital*, New York: John Wiley & Sons, 1991, p. 282.

While an ESOP benefits the owner by providing a market for selling stock, it also carries with it some tax advantages that make the approach attractive to owner and employee alike. Some of the benefits are as follows:

1. If the ESOP owns at least 30 percent of the firm after purchasing the shares, the seller can avoid current tax on the gain by using the proceeds to buy other securities.

2. If the ESOP owns more than 50 percent of the company, those who lend money to the ESOP are taxed on only 50 percent of the income received from such loans. Thus, the lender can afford to offer a lower interest rate, usually about $1\frac{1}{2}$ percentage points below a company's normal borrowing cost.

3. The dividends that a business pays on the stock held by the ESOP are allowed as a tax-deductible expense; that is, the dividends are treated like interest expense when it comes to taxes.

Despite the advantages ESOPs offer, they are not appropriate for all companies. If the entrepreneur does not want the employees to have control of the company, then an ESOP is not an option. Also, the ESOP must cover all employees, and the owners are required to disclose certain information about the company, such as its performance, and its key executives' salaries, which for some entrepreneurs is not palatable. Finally, using an ESOP can place the employees in double jeopardy, where both their jobs and their retirement funds depend on the success of a single business. Even so, an ESOP has considerable potential when crafting a harvest strategy.

The next section looks at the option for harvesting the venture that most would love to attain, but few do.

Initial Public Offerings

An initial public offering (IPO) is not in and of itself a primary means for harvesting a venture. While founders and the shareholders clearly benefit from an IPO, its principal purpose in most situations is to facilitate the raising of future capital. Simply put, publicly traded stock provides for greater liquidity, which allows the company to raise capital on more favorable terms than if it were privately held. These perceptions are borne out in Holmburg's (1991) study, where he asked the CEOs of firms that had gone public to indicate the level of importance of some 17 different possible motivations for the public offering. The items receiving the highest percentage of "very important" responses are as follows:

Raise capital for growth	85%
Raise capital to increase working capital	65%
Facilitate acquiring another firm	40%
Establish a market value for the firm	35%
Enhance the firm's ability to raise capital	35%

For all practical purposes, the CEOs clearly considered financing future growth as the primary impetus for going public. Without a strong IPO market, young high-growth firms would have limited access to the public capital markets, but equally bad, they would have less access to private investors who rely on the IPO market to harvest their investment. However, at the same time, the IPO market is beneficial to the founding entrepreneur in the form of increased liquidity and the enhancement of future options, both of which reduce the investor's risk exposure. So it may not be a pure harvest in the same way of other approaches where cash is received, but the investor captures some of the same advantages accruing to the firm.

Understanding the IPO Process

The IPO process can be one of the most exhilarating, but also frustrating and exhausting, experiences an entrepreneur will encounter (Sutton and Beneddetto, 1990). Managements of large companies, much less small ones, do not like being exposed to the vicissitudes of the capital markets and to the world of investment bankers.

In a survey of the *Inc.* magazine's top 100 firms, the CEOs who had participated in public offerings indicated they spent 33 hours per week on the offering for $4\frac{1}{2}$ months (Brokaw, 1993). The cost of the IPO process seemed excessive and exorbitant to many. They found themselves not being understood and having little influence in the decisions being made. Disillusionment with the investment bankers, and much of the entire process itself frequently occurred. At some point, the owners wondered where they had lost control of the process, a feeling generally held by most entrepreneurs involved in a public offering.

The chronology of a public offering is relatively straightforward, namely:

❖ The management decides to go public.

❖ An investment banker is selected to serve as the underwriter, who in turn brings together a group of investment houses to help sell the shares.

❖ A prospectus is prepared.

❖ The managers, along with the investment banker, go on the road to tell the firm's story to the brokers who will be selling the stock.

❖ On the day before the offering is released to the public, the decision is made about the actual offering price.

❖ All the work, which by now has been months, comes to fruition in a single event—offering the stock to the public and waiting for the consequence.

During this process, the firm's owners and managers are answering such questions as:

❖ What do we need to do in advance of going public?

❖ What are the legal requirements?

❖ Who should be responsible for the different activities and how should we structure our team to make it all happen?

❖ How do we choose an investment banker?

❖ How do we determine an appropriate price for the offering?

❖ How is life different after we are a public company?

While the foregoing issues are important, they do not represent the complete story. The missing element is the shift in power that occurs during the process. When the chain of events begin, the company's management is in control. They can dictate whether or not to go public and who the investment banker will be. However, after the prospectus has been prepared and the road show is underway, the firm's management, including the entrepreneur, is no longer the primary decision-maker. Now the investment banker has control of the decisions. Finally, the marketplace, in complement with the investment banker, begins to take over, and ultimately it is the market that dictates the final outcome.

In addition to the issue of who controls the events and decisions in the IPO process, one other matter is important—understanding the investment banker's motivations in the IPO process. Stated differently, who is the investor banker's primary customer here? Clearly, the issuing firm is rewarding the underwriter for the services being performed through the fees paid and a participation in the deal. But the economics for helping with an IPO may not be as rewarding for the investment banker as other activities, such as involvement with corporate acquisitions. The investment bank is also selling the securities to its customers on the other side of the trade. Thus, it becomes unclear as to what is driving the pricing decision by the investment banker (Sahlman, 1988). This potential agency problem may be one of the reasons for the up-front underpricing of IPOs (Welch, 1996).

While the process of going public may prove frustrating and exasperating, the eventual outcome frequently is not. In a survey of firms listed on the French *Second Marché* (secondary market), most CEOs were very satisfied with their decision (Desroches and Belletante, 1992). The firm owners thought the external image of the firm was improved in the eyes of the suppliers, customers, and others after the offering, along with an increased effectiveness in the level of communications, strategy, and other internal management-related aspects. They disliked, however, the fluctuations in the firm's share price, which they did not believe reflected firm performance. Similar results were observed by Desroches and Jog (1989) in a study of 194 firms that went public in Canada. They concluded that CEOs do not convey a significant loss of control and actually welcome the more structured decision-making which resulted from going public. Although they did not like the valuation of their shares by the marketplace, their conclusion was that going public does imply significant and positive changes to the status of the firm, management structure, and the entrepreneur.

While the Canadians were overwhelmingly pleased with the outcome of going public, they like the French, disliked the feeling of powerlessness about the firm's stock price and the belief that the market price does not reflect the true value of the firm. This view is one that is held by managers across the board, without respect to firm size. The perception is that the capital markets are myopic; that management is under pressure for short-term performance and can no longer look to the shareholder's long-term best interests (Jones et al., 1992).

While there are certainly anomalies, as explained in the next section, there is absolutely no empirical evidence that the capital markets are short-sighted, while management can see more clearly into the long-term future. If anything, it is management that is myopic, not the markets (Miller, 1994).

Understanding the IPO Market

If contemplating a public offering, management needs to have an understanding of the basic nature and peculiarities of the new-issues market. In this area, there is no lack of empirical work about the outcomes of new offerings. Specifically, three anomalies have been found:

1. There is a large amount of empirical literature validating IPO underpricing, dating back 20 years—all finding that the distribution of initial returns to be highly skewed, with significant positive means (Ibbotson, 1975). The average first-day return of a new issue falls somewhere between 10 percent and 15 percent. These results are even more pronounced for smaller, younger companies going public than for their older, more established counterparts. For instance, the average initial return on IPOs with an offering price of less than $3.00 was found to be an amazing 42.8 percent, whereas the average initial return on IPOs with an offering price of $3.00 or more was only 8.6 percent (Chalk and Peavy, 1987). Moreover, underpricing persists in every country with a stock market, although the amount of underpricing is different from country to country (Loughran et al., 1994).

2. There are cycles in both the volume of new issues and the magnitude of first-day returns. The periods of high average initial returns are known as "hot issue" markets. (Hot issue markets were first identified by Ibbotson and Jaffe, 1975.) The cycles in underpricing allow one to predict next month's average initial return based upon the current month's average with a high degree of accuracy, i.e., the first-order autocorrelation of monthly average initial is 0.66. Likewise, high-volume months are almost always followed by high-volume months, where the autocorrelation is 0.89 (Ibbotson et al., 1994)

3. New issues tend to underperform for up to five years after the offering (Loughran, 1993). For IPOs during the period 1975 to 1984, the total return from the end of the first day of trading to three years later was 34.5 percent,

compared with the return on the NYSE of 61.9 percent (Ritter, 1991). Again these findings were even more pronounced for younger firms than for established firms. There is also reason to believe that the earnings per share of companies going public typically grows rapidly in the years before going public, but then actually declines in the first several years after the IPO (Jain and Kini, forthcoming)

Ibbotson et al. (1994) described the IPO market pricing as a puzzle to those who otherwise believe in efficient capital markets and argued that the anomalies are interrelated by periodic overoptimism by investors which causes many firms to rush to market, resulting in disappointing returns to long-term investors when the issuers fail to live up to overly optimistic expectations. They also found that firms that issue during low-volume periods typically experience neither high initial price run-ups nor subsequent long-run underperformance and that the patterns are much more pronounced for smaller, younger companies going public than for their older, more established counterparts. Their finding is consistent with evidence by Hanley and Ritter (1993) suggesting inefficiencies in markets for smaller-cap stocks.

In short, the IPO market has somewhat a personality of its own and one that acts a bit different from the rest of the capital markets—a fact that needs to be understood by an entrepreneur wanting to take a firm public.

A Venture Capital Perspective of IPOs

Many venture capitalists believe that an IPO produces a higher price than an outright sale. That belief is encouraged by the fact that the average valuation of IPOs between 1988 and 1992 was $106.9 million versus $37.4 million for private sales. But the companies floating IPOs are mostly stars or potential stars, whereas those that are sold include not only stars but also many mediocrities with no hope of going public.

The gains realized through IPOs were almost five times greater than the next most profitable method of harvesting the venture, according to a study of how 26 venture capital funds exited 442 investments from 1970 to 1982 (Soja and Reyes, 1990). That study found that 30 percent of the exits were through IPOs, 23 percent private sales, 6 percent company buyouts, 9 percent secondary sales, 6 percent liquidations and 26 percent write-offs.

A study of 77 high-tech companies backed by venture capital that had IPOs between 1979 and 1988 found that the times returns (amount returned ÷ amount invested) on the venture capital investment at the initial offering price was 22.5 times for the first round; 10 times for the second round; and 3.7 times for the third round (Bygrave and Stein, 1989). Four years after the IPO the times return was 62.7 times for the first round, 38.1 times for the second, and 13.5 times for the third.

The average compound annual rate of return for the first round of venture capital at the time of the IPO was 220 percent; four years after the IPO (about seven years after the first round of venture capital), it had declined to 57 percent. So although the times return increased from 22.5 times to 62.7 times, the rate of return declined because of the longer holding period—another indication of underpricing of new issues.

According to industry wisdom, venture capitalists financing seed and start-up high-technology companies are looking for compound annual returns of 50 percent or more; for second-stage financings they tend to look for 30 to 40 percent; while third-round investors may expect returns of 25 to 30 percent (Morris, 1985).

A rule of thumb is a return in five years of seven times the first venture capital (a compound rate of return of 48 percent). The evidence in the above studies gives some credence to these expected returns. However, in the latter 1980s, the returns of funds started in the 1980s fell far short of expectations, mainly owing to the public's loss of interest in speculative IPOs during the latter 1980s. As a result, many venture-backed companies were unable to go public. Thus, venture funds were unable to reap their expected harvests. The return of a "hot" IPO market in the 1990s has provided hopes of a return to the earlier years. However, based on limited evidence, the returns probably have only returned to the 15 to 20 percent range.

The European Experience with Harvesting

To understand the environment for harvesting in Europe, one can draw on the comprehensive work edited by Bygrave et al. (1994). In this study, realizing investment value is the result of collective efforts of a group of researchers who carefully examined the harvesting process across Europe.

The organized venture capital industry in Europe is little more than 12 years old, in contrast to 50 years for the U.S. industry. There were a few players in Europe before 1980, most notably the U.K. firm now named 3i, and at least one unsuccessful American-style venture capital firm that was set up in the 1960s. But it was during the entrepreneurial era of the 1980s that European venture capital grew explosively. From 1984 through 1992, the venture capital funds under management in Europe grew from ECU 3.6 billion to ECU 38.5 billion (EVCA, 1991–93). More recently, the total capital under management in Europe approximates that of the United States.

Unlike the United States, however, where entries and harvests have been roughly in balance, the amount of money being invested in portfolio companies by European venture capital funds far exceeds the amount being divested. For instance, over five years (1988 to 1992), ECU 21.2 billion was invested in portfolio companies but only ECU 9.4 billion was divested. Of course, some of that imbalance is because the total pool of venture capital continues to grow. But that is only a partial explanation because the amount of new funds raised has been declining since it peaked in 1989. If the 1990 to 1992 trend continues, a log jam of unrealized investments is building up.

By the end of 1992, most people within the European venture capital industry agreed that much of the investment-divestment imbalance was due to the relative scarcity of viable harvest options. For instance, of 158 MBOs completed in the period 1983 to 1985 in the United Kingdom, more than 70 percent had not been harvested successfully by June 1992 (Wright et al., 1992a). That lack of successful exits is particularly acute with smaller MBOs.

At the start of the 1990s, frustration on the part of venture capitalists in the United Kingdom and the Netherlands over the lack of exit options gave rise to a number of new initiatives designed to facilitate harvesting. Among them were proposals for a pan-European private secondary market for venture capital investments and for a local participation market for Dutch venture capital investment (Onians, 1993; Elbertse, 1993).

During the 1980s, a number of European countries set up second- and third-tier stock markets in order to facilitate IPOs by small companies that could not meet the requirements of the main markets. These markets include the Unlisted Securities Market (USM) in the United Kingdom, the *Second Marché* in France, and the Parallel Market in the Netherlands. A surge in venture capital in the United Kingdom, France, and the Netherlands coincided with a boom in these countries' secondary markets. However, despite these efforts to create equity markets for private firms, the results have been unsuccessful. For instance, the USM is to be closed at the end of 1996 to be replaced by the Alternative Investment Market (AIM). In addition, a pan-European exchange is being formed called the EASDAQ in an effort to create the equivalent of the NASDAQ in the United States. So at the present, Europe continues to lack a well-established market for IPOs.

Given the limited accessibility to the IPO market as an exit strategy, venture capitalists in Europe have primarily resorted to company sales as their exit mechanism of choice—41 percent of all exits in Europe come through the company being sold, compared with 10 percent exits through IPOs. Here too, however, the number of corporate sales has decreased in recent years. In the United Kingdom, the number of sales of MBOs averaged 39 per year from 1981 through 1988, but fell to 15 in 1989, 8 in 1990, and 3 in 1991. Fortunately, trade sales in other European nations have not been as severely affected. Even so, the European venture industry, along with the entrepreneurs in whose companies they have invested, is experiencing severe problems in realizing the value created through its investments.

Current State of Affairs and the Need for Research

Based on the prior research, several things can be said about harvesting with reasonable certitude:

❖ To harvest value, it must first be created. Whether a firm is high-tech or low-tech, small or large, economic value is created only by earning rates of return that exceed the investors' opportunity cost of the funds—including the owners'. Value is destroyed by earning rates of return that are less than the opportunity cost of the funds—again including the equity owners. Creating value and capturing the value are not the same thing. Without the opportunity to harvest, a firm's owners and investors will be denied a significant amount of the value that has been created over the firm's life.

❖ Harvesting is more than merely selling and leaving a business. It is about capturing value (cash flows), reducing risk, and creating future options

❖ There are four fundamental approaches to harvesting a venture: 1) Restructuring the company's goals and strategies in order to increase the cash flows extracted from the business by the owners and investors; 2) selling to outsiders, management, employees, and/or family members; 3) being acquired or merged into another business; or 4) issuing stock to the public.

❖ Investors providing high-risk capital—particularly venture capitalists—generally insist on an exit strategy as part of the terms of the deal. As a result, the accessibility to venture capital is driven by the availability of harvest options.

❖ Return distributions resulting from venture-backed harvests and IPOs are known.

❖ The window of opportunity for harvesting quickly opens and closes. That is, there are waves of IPOs and merger and acquisition opportunities.

Besides what is known about harvesting an entrepreneurial firm, there are also some impressions based on intuition and anecdotal evidence, including:

❖ Few events in the life of the entrepreneur, and for the firm itself, are more significant than the harvest.

❖ Some entrepreneurs are averse to thinking about the harvest, while others begin the venture to harvest it.

❖ The decision to harvest is frequently the result of an unexpected crisis rather than a well-conceived strategy.

Finally, some things are still not known about the harvest. The following questions are begging further research:

❖ How much difference does an effective harvest strategy make in releasing the value within the firm for the benefit of the owners and investors?

❖ What is the entrepreneur's perspective about the harvest? How do these expectations compare to the final outcome?

❖ How important is timing in the harvest? How does the entrepreneur know when to harvest?

❖ What can be done to increase the effectiveness of the harvest?

❖ How do the entrepreneur's personal preferences and situation affect the harvest?

❖ What can be done by the entrepreneur to enhance the probability of a successful harvest?

❖ A better understanding of the actual process of the harvest is needed. Some things are known about the outcomes but little about the process, e.g., 1) What are the catalysts that bring the entrepreneur and investors to the decision to harvest? 2) How do they make a choice as to the approach to be taken in harvesting? 3) What does the entrepreneur need to know before going through an IPO?

These questions and many others go unanswered. There is so much that could be done. The primary limitations are the researcher's own creativity and the limited availability of quality data. Gaining access to the needed information is no small matter in this area. Nevertheless, given some creativity and diligence, numerous research questions could be addressed, and the importance of the topic calls us to take up the challenge.

REFERENCES

Batchelor, C. 1992. Enterprise looks for a way out. *Financial Times*, December 22.

Beatty, A. 1995. The cash flow and informational effects of employee stock ownership plans. *Journal of Financial Economics* 38(2):211-230.

Bhide, A. 1989. The causes and consequences of hostile takeovers. *Journal of Applied Corporate Finance* 2(2):36-59.

Brennan, M.J. 1995. A perspective on accounting and stock prices. *Journal of Applied Corporate Finance* 8(1):43-52.

Brokaw, L. 1993. The first day of the rest of your life. *Inc.* 15(5):144.

Bygrave, W.D., and M. Stein. 1989. A time to buy and a time to sell: A study of venture capital investments in 77 companies that went public. In N. C. Churchill et al. (eds.): *Frontiers of Entrepreneurship Research*. Wellesley, MA: Babson College, 288-303.

Bygrave, W.D., M. Hay, and J.B. Peeters, (eds.). 1994. *Realizing Investment Value*. London: Pitman Publishing.

Chalk, A., and J. Peavy. 1987. Initial public offerings: Daily returns, offering types and the price effect. *Financial Analyst Journal* 27(4):65-69.

Copeland, T., T.T. Koller, and J. Murrin. 1994. *Valuation: Measuring and Managing the Value of Companies*. New York: John Wiley and Sons.

Desroches, J.J.-Y., and B. Belletante. 1992. The positive impact of going public on entrepreneurs and their firms: Evidence from listing on the "Second Marché" in France. In N.C. Churchill et al. (eds.): *Frontiers of Entrepreneurship Research*. Wellesley, MA: Babson College, 466-480.

Donaldson, G. 1994. *Corporate Restructuring: Managing the Change Process from Within*. Cambridge, MA: Harvard Business School Press.

Elbertse, E. 1993. Developing exit mechanism in your market. Presentation at European Venture Capital Association business seminar on exiting in Europe, Venice, February 11-12.

Englander, D.W. 1993. Cashing out through ESOPs. *Small Business Reports* 18(10):43-45.

European Venture Capital Association (EVCA). 1991–93. *Venture Capital in Europe: EVCA Yearbooks*. Zaveman, Belgium.

Freear, J., J.A. Sohl, and W.E. Wetzel. 1990. Raising venture capital: Entrepreneurs' views of the process. *Frontiers of Entrepreneurship Research*, 223-265.

Holmburg, S. 1991. Value creation and capture: Entrepreneurship harvest and IPO strategies. In N.C. Churchill et al. (eds.): *Frontiers of Entrepreneurship Research*. Wellesley, MA: Babson College, 191-204.

Hyatt, H. 1990. The dark side (of going public). *Inc.* 12(6):46-56.

Ibbotson, R.G. 1975. Price performance of common stock new issues. *Journal of Financial Economics* 2(3):235-272.

Ibbotson, R.G., and J.F. Jaffe. 1975. Hot issue markets. *Journal of Finance* 30(4):1027-1042.

Ibbotson, R.G., J.L. Sindelar, and J.R. Ritter. 1994. The market's problems with the pricing of initial public offerings. *Journal of Applied Corporate Finance* 7(1):66-74.

Ibbotson, R.G., J.L. Sindelar, and J.R. Ritter. 1993. Initial public offerings. *Journal of Applied Corporate Finance* 1(2):37-45.

Jain, B, and O. Kini. (Forthcoming). The post-issue operating performance of IPOs. *Journal of Finance*.

Jones, S., M.B. Cohen, and V.V. Coppola. 1992. Going public. Sahlman, W.A., and Stevenson, H.H. (eds.): *The Entrepreneurial Venture*. Cambridge, MA: Harvard Business School Publications.

Kaplan, S. 1989. The effects of management buy-outs on operating performance and value. *Journal of Financial Economics* 24:217-254.

Kaplan, S. 1991. The staying power of leverage buyouts. *Journal of Financial Economics* 29:287-313.

Loughran, T. 1993. NYSE vs. Nasdaq returns: Market microstructure or the poor performance of IPOs? *Journal of Financial Economics* 33:241-260.

Loughran, T., J. Ritter, and K. Rydqvist. 1994. Initial public offerings: International insights. *Pacific-Basin Finance Journal* 2(3):165-199.

Miller, M. 1994. Is American corporate governance fatally flawed? *Journal of Applied Corporate Finance* 6(4):32-39.

Morris, J.K. 1985. The pricing of a venture capital investment. In S.E. Pratt and J.K. Morris (eds.): *Pratt's Guide to Venture Capital Sources*, 9th edition. Wellesley Hills, MA: Venture Economics.

Onians, R., 1993. A european secondary market. Presented at EVCA business seminar on Exiting in Europe, Venice, February 11-12.

Paré, T.P. 1990. Passing on the family business. *Fortune* 127(9):50.

Park, S., and M.H. Song. 1995. Employee stock ownership plans, firm performance, and monitoring by outside blockholders. *Financial Management* 24(4):52-65.

Petty, J.W., B.E. Bygrave, and J.M. Shulman. 1994. Harvesting the entrepreneurial venture: A time for creating value. *Journal of Applied Corporate Finance* 7(9):48-58.

Ritter, J. 1991. The long-run performance of initial public offerings. *Journal of Finance* 46(3):3-27.

Sahlman, W.A. 1988. Aspects of financial contracting in venture capital. *Journal of Applied Corporate Finance* 1(4):23-36.

Sahlman, W.A. 1989. Teaching notes accompanying CML Group, Inc. *Going Public*. Cambridge, MA: Harvard Business School Publishing Division.

Soja, T.A. , and J.E. Reyes. 1990. *Investment Benchmarks: Venture Capital*. Needham, MA: Venture Economics.

Stevenson, H.E., and D.E. Gumpert. 1985. The heart of entrepreneurship. *Harvard Business Review* 63(2):85-94.

Stevenson, H.E., and W.A. Sahlman. 1987. Entrepreneurship: A process, not a person. Working paper 87-06, pp. 1-49.

Stewart, G.B., III. 1991. *The Quest for Value*. New York: HarperCollins, pp. 136-140.

Sutton, D.P, and M.W. Beneddetto. 1990. *Initial Public Offerings*. Chicago: Probus Publishing Company.

Timmons, J. 1994. *New Venture Creation*. Chicago: Irwin, p. 654.

Toben, J. 1969. A general equilibrium approach to monetary theory. *Journal of Money, Credit, and Banking* 1:15-29.

Welch, I. 1996. Equity offerings following the IPO: Theory and evidence. *Journal of Corporate Finance* 2:227-259.

Weston, J.F., K. Chung, and S. Hoag. 1990. Theories of mergers and tender offers. In *Mergers, Restructuring and Corporate Control*. Englewood-Cliffs, NJ: Prentice Hall, 190-222.

Wright, M., K. Robbie, Y. Romanet, S. Thompson, R. Joachimsson, J. Bruining, and A. Herst. 1992a. Realizations, longevity and the live-cycle of management buy-outs and buy-ins: A four-country study. Presented at the European Federation for Economic Research (EFER) Forum, London Business School, December 12-14.

Wright, M., S. Thompson, and K. Robbie. 1992b. Venture capital and management-led buy-outs: European evidence. *Journal of Business Venturing* 7(1):47-71.

Wright, M., S. Thompson, K. Robbie, and P. Wong. 1992c. Management buy-outs in the short and long term. In N.C. Churchill et al. (eds.): *Frontiers of Entrepreneurship Research*. Wellesley, MA: Babson College, 302-316.

Growth Strategies

Growth Strategies

G ROWTH IS THE VERY ESSENCE OF ENTREPRENEURSHIP. As the field has matured and become more sophisticated, growth has been the distinguishing factor between small business and entrepreneurship. Through the missionary efforts of Wilson Harrell (1992), the field has recognized that significant differences exist between the problems associated with starting a business and growing one. Harrell also pointed out that most assistance programs are developed for business starts, and these programs and their organizations have failed to recognize that programs designed to assist business starts have limited value for assisting business growth. Birch (1979) was one of the first to quantitatively identify the impact of fast-growth firms on the nation's economy, and Stevenson and Gumpert (1985) gave us the definition of entrepreneurship as a capacity for opportunity recognition and the ability to gather the resources necessary to pursue the opportunity.

A number of studies have attempted to quantify growth and to define rapid growth. Unfortunately, most of these studies have been based on qualitative data, specific time frames, large corporations, and subsectors of the *Inc. 500* studies. To date, a quantifiable growth rate for sustainable growth and/or rapid growth has not been developed. With the development and access to longitudinal databases, these needs are expected to be filled in the near future.

Knowing a growth rate is only an expression of what has happened in the firm. The real need is to know what actions or best practices have impacted on the growth of the firm so that researchers can predict growth before it actually occurs. Studies of this type will help move the field from a body of knowledge that helps us better train and educate students to one that has real-time practical applications for entrepreneurs trying to expand their businesses.

In this section, the state-of-the-art research is explored as it pertains to the problems of growth from the aspect of managing transitions as the business becomes more complex in the chapter by Covin and Slevin. Cooper and Daily examine the impact of management teams on the growth of firms, and Venkataram and Macmillan have suggested that the choice of organizational modes is an important factor in new business growth and development. Finally, Kirchoff and Acs discuss research activities that explore the problems and realities associated with debunking the myths of business starts and failures.

REFERENCES

Birch, D. 1979. *The Job Generation Process.* Unpublished report, prepared by the Massachusetts Institute of Technology Program on Neighborhood and Regional Change for the Economic Development Administration, U.S. Department of Commerce, Washington, DC

Harrel, W. 1992. Foreword. In D. Sexton and J. Kasarda (eds.): *The State of the Art of Entrepreneurship.* Boston: PWS-Kent, xiii-xiv.

Stevenson, H., and. D. Gumpert. 1985. *The Heart of Entrepreneurship. Harvard Business Review* (March-April):85-94.

CHAPTER 5

High Growth Transitions: Theoretical Perspectives and Suggested Directions

JEFFREY G. COVIN

AND

DENNIS P. SLEVIN

I N LOOKING AT THE TRENDS CHARACTERISTIC of today's business environment, one must be impressed with the tremendous amount of churning that exists in American industry. Companies seem to be in a continuous process of either high growth, downsizing, restructuring, and rebirth or some other dramatic change. Cases of successful adaptation to evolving markets and business contexts abound, as shown by the examples listed below:

❖ Dell Computer revenues were up 52 percent in 1995. They've grown from 2 billion dollars in 1992 to over 5 billion dollars in 1995. Michael S. Dell, the youngest CEO ever to bring his company into the Fortune 500, says that they have continuously changed their business model and strategy as they have grown.

❖ Comcast grew 144 percent in 1995 to a total of 3.3 billion dollars in sales. Brian L. Roberts, their young president, believes that Comcast's corporate strategy will enable the company to sustain this rapid growth trajectory throughout the decade.

❖ Lockheed Martin, formed by the merger of Lockheed and Martin Marietta, is a survivor in an industry that has undergone dramatic structural changes. Through redefining its strategic priorities away from defense business and toward the private sector and global competitiveness, Lockheed Martin was able to realize a 74 percent increase in sales in 1995.

❖ Seagate Technologies has used a strategy of vertical integration to achieve an average annual growth rate of 68 percent and outstanding earnings per share over the last ten years.

Nonetheless, while some companies are changing dramatically in positive directions, growing rapidly and making necessary transitions, others are having more negative experiences.

❖ Tenneco has been unsuccessful so far at implementing its plan to refocus on growth markets. Tenneco's revenues declined by 33 percent in 1995 and earnings fell well below Wall Street projections.

❖ Aetna Life and Casualty, despite its concerted efforts to address problems in the areas of environmental liability, property casualty losses, health care, and real estate, experienced a 26 percent reduction in revenues in 1995.

The anecdotal evidence is quite strong. Businesses today are facing extraordinarily challenging environments, marked by increased complexity and the need for more rapid and dramatic transitions to different strategic postures and more viable organizational forms. This trend is occurring in businesses across the organization size spectrum, from small entrepreneurial start-up companies to large, multibillion dollar corporations.

The purpose of this chapter is to present a model that represents a novel yet theoretically grounded framework for looking at issues such as complexity, transitions, and related variables in the context of high-growth small firms and new ventures. The following section describes the construct of complexity. The proposed complexity management model is then described, followed by a discussion of the advantages and benefits of this model. As a means to elucidate the specific requirements and foci of complexity management, several studies are reviewed which identify growth-related problem areas common to small businesses. A typology of problem resolution approaches for dealing with managerial complexity is then discussed, followed by a description of an empirically validated analytical framework that may prove useful in assessing both the need for and achievement of specific transitions along key organizational "competitiveness" dimensions. The final two sections of the chapter cover the implications of the proposed complexity management model for future research and managers, respectively.

The Construct of Complexity

At the risk of sounding redundant, it should be noted that complexity is not a simple construct. Nonetheless, in many writings the term "complexity" is used freely, often without definition, and with apparently little or no critical complaint from readers. It is one of those constructs that nearly everyone seems to understand at least at some root level without careful introspection. In a recent and well-done book concerning coping strategies for modern day management challenges, the term complexity is indicated in the index as appearing on 33 different pages (Price Waterhouse Change Integration Team, 1996); however, complexity is never once defined. This book's definitional oversight should not be criticized too harshly because it was not the authors' intent to spend substantial time defining constructs, but rather to present general prescriptions for dealing with "chaos, complexity, and contradiction." However, in a state-of-the-art essay, suggesting future directions for the field, it may be appropriate to step back and attempt some more precise definitions of complexity and related constructs.

In common parlance, something is viewed as complex when it is composed of two or more related parts. Thus, number of elemental parts and their relationships appear to be important to understanding the construct of complexity. Moreover, if one looks back at research concerning the manner in which human subjects process information, some additional insights into the nature of complexity emerge (e.g., Simon, 1979).

Specifically, substantial research was conducted in the 1950s and 1960s concerning the ways in which human subjects process patterned sequences of symbols (Leeuwenberg, 1969; Restle, 1970; Simon and Kotovsky, 1963; Vitz and Todd, 1969). Numerous theoretical presentations on this topic have been published in journals and books (e.g., Glanzer and Clark, 1962; Gregg, 1967; Klahr and Wallace, 1970; Laughery and Gregg, 1962; Simon and Sumner, 1968; Williams, 1972).

In the context of human information processing, complexity is often operationalized in terms of a sequence of symbols. Consider the following three sequences of letters from the alphabet:

1. A A A A A A A A A A A A
2. A B A B A B A B A B A B
3. A D J K B L O R Z C Q P

It seems intuitively clear that Sequence 1 above is simpler than Sequence 2, and that Sequence 3 is the most complex of the three. This conclusion relates to the relationship between the symbols. If a human information processor wished to learn one of the above sequences, he or she must either: memorize the sequence or discover the pattern and memorize it (Gregg, 1967).

So it appears clear that the relationship between the symbols is an indicator of the complexity of the sequence. In addition, the code length of the sequence also relates to complexity. If Sequence 3 above were twice as long as it is currently, one could conclude that it was, indeed, more complex. Thus, at the human information processing level, two constructs emerge as key to a definition of complexity: 1) number of related parts and 2) differences between the related parts.

A third component of complexity can be readily inferred from writings on this topic, that is, the factor of *uncertainty*. Often, uncertainty is used as a synonym for or at least a partial descriptor of complexity. In the sequence of symbols above, if at any point in the sequence, the human information processor finds the various letters changing in a random pattern, then he or she encounters what, indeed, might be called a complex situation.

Finally, based on writings on the topics of organizational structure and processes, it is clear that the concept of interdependence is central to the quest for understanding complexity. For example, Thompson (1967) views complexity to be a function of the type of interdependence that exists between organizational system subunits. He suggests that interdependence is amenable to operationalization along a Guttman-type scale in which pooled interdependence presents the simplest system, sequential interdependence a more complex system, and reciprocal interdependence the most complex system. Thompson (1967) argues that complexity implies more and deeper interdependencies. In other words, more points of contingency in the system.

Simon's (1962) arguments regarding complex systems are consistent with those of Thompson. Simon defines a complex system as one consisting of a large number of parts that interact in a nonsimple way. Further, Simon makes three specific points about the nature of complexity in his discussion. First, he suggests that complexity frequently takes the form of hierarchy, i.e., complex systems are often composed of subsystems that, in turn, may have additional subsystems. Second, he suggests that hierarchical systems may have the capability to evolve at a more rapid rate than non-hierarchical systems of similar size. Third, he suggests that hierarchical systems can be decomposed into the relevant subsystems (Simon, 1962). Thus, it seems that at both the organizational and general systems levels, there is a convergence of the manner in which the construct complexity might be applied.

Considering the above discussion, *complexity can be defined as the number of different heterogeneous elements in the system.* Complexity increases when the number of elements increases, the differences between those elements increase, the interdependencies between those elements increase, and the uncertainty of those elements increases.

The construct "complexity" can be applied at a variety of levels. One may suggest, without much argument, that the environment of business is increasing in complexity. Modern literature is replete with terms such as chaos, hypercompetition, high velocity, and paradox. At the organizational level, complexity has meaning as well. Higher structural complexity, for example, implies greater levels of organizational or task differentiation and integration (Lawrence and Lorsch, 1967). Finally, at the managerial level, complexity has substantial meaning which will be developed in more detail as a primary variable that small and/or entrepreneurial firms must deal with as they engage in transitions. In a double loop sense, as will be demonstrated below, complexity leads to transitions, and transitions lead to complexity.

Toward a Complexity Management Model

The complexity management model proposed in this paper is depicted in Figure 5.1 on p. 104. This model links constructs relating to growth, complexity, transitions, and organizational performance. The model has been derived from literature which focuses on:

1. How growth aspirations become realized.

2. How increased organization size contributes to managerial complexity.

3. How such complexity is then managed to achieve effective transitions to new organizational states and behavioral patterns.

4. How reconfigured organizational "gestalts," defined in terms of the transitioned organizational system elements and behavioral patterns, then contribute to superior profitability.

This section of the paper describes the theoretical derivation of each of these sections of the complexity management model.

FIGURE 5.1
A Complexity Management Model of Firm Growth

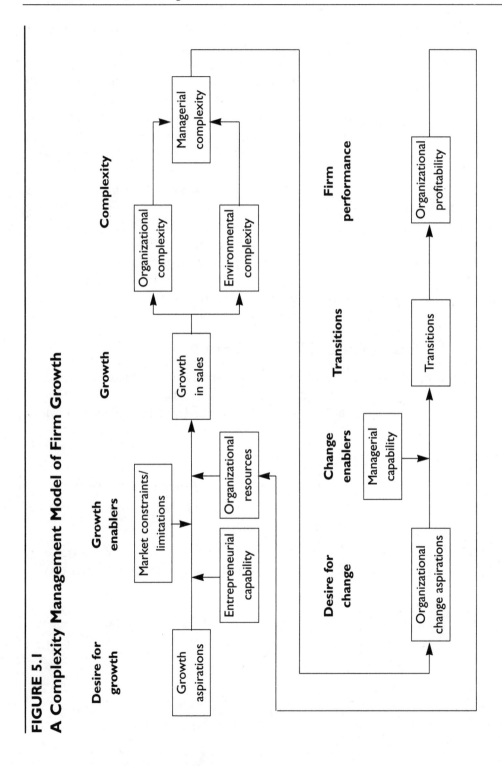

Determinants of Firm Growth

The left-hand side of the model—that is, the transformation of growth aspirations into sales growth—builds upon a firm growth model proposed by Sexton and Bowman-Upton (1991). They argue that growth is a function of a number of marketing and management-related factors. The marketing factors in Sexton and Bowman-Upton's model include the size of the served market niche (as a function of competitive and environmental factors), the expected duration of the market window of opportunity, and the product life cycle stage of the firm's product or product line. These factors are subsumed under the label "market constraints/limitations" in the current model. The management-related factors in Sexton and Bowman-Upton's model include the entrepreneur's (or principal strategic decision-maker's) propensity for growth, ability to manage growth, ability to identify subsequent product and/or market opportunities, and ability to exploit identified opportunities through future growth. "Growth aspirations" is the label used in the current model to describe the entrepreneur's (or principal decision-maker's) desire or propensity for growth. "Entrepreneurial capability" is the label used to describe the preceding "ability" factors in the current model.

In brief, Sexton and Bowman-Upton (1991) argue that the upper limit on realized sales growth will be determined by various market constraints. The size of the market niche served by the firm represents the volume of sales theoretically available to the firm. The actual sales generated within this niche will be constrained by the amount of time the firm has to serve this niche—i.e., the opportunity window—as well as by the rate of sales within this niche, as determined by a product's position in its life cycle. The extent to which the sales potential of a niche is realized will be a function of the desire for growth on the part of the principal strategic decision-makers in the firm. Desired growth levels can exceed the theoretical potential of the served niche, in which case desired growth will not be realized. However, when a desired growth level falls within the sales limit of the niche, this desired growth will be realized to the extent that the firm's managers are proficient in managing growth. In other words, ability to manage growth, broadly defined, is depicted in Sexton and Bowman-Upton's model as moderating the relationship between desire for growth and realized growth. Additional growth cycles in a firm are created as the principal strategic decision-makers recognize new growth opportunities and respond to these with appropriate product/market strategies.

The current growth model adopts the Sexton and Bowman-Upton model as key to depicting how growth aspirations are transformed into realized growth in sales. Market constraints/limitations and one's ability to promote current growth and recognize and exploit future growth opportunities (herein labeled "entrepreneurial capability") are clearly moderators of the relationship between growth aspirations and realized sales levels. However, the current model adds another variable as a moderator of this relationship. That is, the extent to which growth aspirations are achieved is anticipated to be affected by the type and amount of resources controlled or available to the firm. The label "organization resources" is defined broadly in the current model to include employees, financial resources, intellectual and other intangible assets (e.g., trademarks), plant and equipment, technological capabilities, organizational systems, and core competencies. This additional variable—really, a set of variables—is included in the model because an organization's resources determine that organization's ability to support growth. For example, the growth aspirations of an organization's managers may be high, but realized sales may be abysmal unless that organization possesses the resources needed to support the growth strategy. Thus, organizational resources operate as a moderator of the relationship between desired and realized sales independent of and in addition to market constraints/limitations and entrepreneurial capability.

The achievement of a particular level or growth rate of sales should not be viewed as evidence of long-term organizational viability. In fact, in their review of high-growth strategy research, Hoy et al. (1992) concluded that high firm growth rates may be minimally or even negatively correlated with firm profitability. As observed by Fombrun and Wally (1989), Adizes (1989), and many others, larger firms are not necessarily more viable firms because growth per se creates a host of problems which pose a challenge to management. This relationship between growth and ensuing complexities is discussed next.

Relationship Between Growth and Complexity

Many high-potential, high-growth firms have died because of an inability to manage the complexity that accompanies the growth process and a larger organization size. Hambrick and Crozier (1985), for example, have identified four recurring challenges facing the managers of rapid-growth firms—instant size, a sense of infallibility, internal turmoil, and extraordinary resource needs. Inadequacies in the management of each of these challenges may lead to failure among seemingly successful high-growth firms. Clifford (1975) described the challenge of growth and size management as one of managing complexity. He argued that companies often fail or, at a minimum, have their growth stalled if they cannot successfully manage complexity both internal and external to the organization.

Thus, growth leads to increased managerial complexity. For the purposes of this chapter, *managerial complexity will be defined as an indicator of the challenge faced by managers as a function of the number, variety, and interrelationships among tasks required to effectively and efficiently administer the operations of a firm.*

The sources of managerial complexity may originate within an organization's boundaries. For example, as organizations grow in size they often experience a need for greater task differentiation and integration (Lawrence and Lorsch, 1967). Responses to these needs are reflected in what Blau (1970) refers to as the vertical and horizontal complexity of the organization's structure. This structural complexity may reduce the administrative challenge faced by any particular manager in the organizational system. However, a greater number of heterogeneous parts of the system attributable to greater vertical and horizontal complexity increases the overall administrative challenge. Similarly, growth demands the creation of various organizational subsystems which may be unnecessary in many smaller firms (Chandler, 1962). Strategic planning systems, formalized management information systems, and human resource development systems, for example, tend to emerge in response to felt deficiencies in these areas subsequent to periods of growth. The creation and effective administration of these subsystems represent a challenge to firm managers which contributes to the overall stock of managerial complexity. The task of managers is to, in essence, ease the growing pains that naturally occur as greater size is realized (Flamholtz, 1986).

In short, growth leads to greater managerial complexity by requiring that managers establish business practices and organizational attributes commensurate with and supportive of their firms' size and scope of operations. Successful growth implies not only the realization of increased size but the creation of an organizational system which exhibits a high degree of internal fit among the "7-S" factors identified by McKinsey and Company (namely, the organization's strategy, structure, staff, style, systems, skills, and shared values) as essential to the effective implementation of large-scale change. As will be argued in a later section, growth requires a redefinition of type and state of elements in the organizational gestalt. Reducing the tension that builds within the gestalt as a consequence of a less-than-perfect fit among the organizational elements is a primary challenge to the managers of growing firms.

Growth may also lead to increased managerial complexity by changing the environmental contexts within which firms operate. Mintzberg (1979) argues that the environments of large firms are often more complex than those of smaller firms because larger organizations generally offer greater numbers of products and services, each having particular external institutional associations and linkages. Thus, even among two firms operating within the same industry, the larger of these firms will tend to interface at more points with its external environment. Such greater imbeddedness within an environmental context will often require more administrative attention on management's part since managerial complexity will increase as a function of the number, variety, and interrelationships among the linkages that exist between a firm and the parties in its operating environment.

The preceding paragraph argues that growth may change how an organization relates to its environment by changing the nature of the organization-environment interface. Growth may also contribute to changing environmental attributes. For example, as the market power of a firm increases with greater sales volume, competitors may alter their behaviors in response to or in anticipation of the growing firm's actions, thus changing the operating environment of this firm. Miller and Friesen (1984a) noted this effect when they observed that entrepreneurial actions on the part of individual firms are often emulated by industry rivals, thereby increasing the overall level of environmental dynamism. When the operating environment "reacts" to a firm's growth in such a manner, the environment becomes less predictable. This diminished predictability contributes to managerial complexity by increasing task uncertainty, which makes it more difficult for organizations to successfully navigate their environments over time.

Consistent with the preceding points, Figure 5.1, p. 104, depicts growth in sales as contributing to greater organizational and environmental complexity. Managerial complexity, in turn, can be modeled as a function of the level of organizational and environmental complexity required or faced by the firm. The key to dealing effectively with such growth-derived managerial complexity is an ability to recognize and resolve the problems associated with a redefined organizational context in which previously appropriate behavioral patterns and organizational system characteristics may no longer operate in the firm's best long-term interest. A more detailed description of this challenge is presented below.

Problem-Solving for Needed Transitions

The administrative challenge associated with managerial complexity is commonly described as a set of problems that must be resolved in order to effect needed transitions in the organizational system (e.g., Dodge et al., 1994; Scott and Bruce, 1987; Smith et al., 1985). The specific sets of problems likely to be encountered as organizations grow are well described in the literature. Kazanjian (1988), for example, empirically identified 18 "dominant problems" often faced by technology-based new ventures as they transition from smaller to larger organizational forms. Hambrick and Crozier (1985) observed four "fundamental challenges" in effectively managing rapid-growth firms. Conceptual "metamorphosis" models of small business growth like those presented by Churchill and Lewis (1983) and Mount et al. (1993) delineate many of the managerial "crises" that must be resolved to successfully transition to subsequent growth stages. (The specific growth-related problems described in these and other studies will be summarized later in this chapter.)

The resolution of problems created during the process or as a consequence of firm growth is the essence of effective transitioning to a more viably functioning organization. The realization of growth suggests that a firm has achieved a good "external fit" with its environment. That is, sales growth is appropriately interpreted as an indicator of a firm's effectiveness in responding to market needs. However, as argued by Miller (1992), firms with high degrees of external fit may be less attentive to maintaining needed complementarities among the components of their internal organizational systems. Similarly, Hedberg et al. (1976) have noted that some firms become so preoccupied with adapting to their environments that internal fit among the elements of their organizational systems is never achieved. Thus, the challenge of dealing with managerial complexity subsequent to firm growth can be described, in part, as one of reconfiguring the internal organizational system to achieve greater congruence among interdependent elements. Such congruence will ensure the efficiency of the system essential to long-term organizational viability. As noted previously, organizational growth does not guarantee organizational viability. Many firms reach their greatest size just before they die (Adizes, 1989).

Some of the changes needed to improve the functioning of an organization whose size has strained the capabilities of its structure and systems may be implemented without concern for the state of other elements and activities comprising the organizational gestalt. This will be the case when the object of a needed transition is "loosely coupled" to other components of the organizational system (Aldrich, 1979). As such, another part of the challenge of dealing with managerial complexity is recognizing the need to embrace new behavioral patterns or processes that could be defined as falling outside the domain of interdependent organizational system elements. Also, some growth-related problem areas may call for managerial actions that are not inherently of a "systems" nature. For example, strategic decision-making methods, when not formalized, may be regarded as indicative of how an organization operates but not a "system" element per se. Yet research suggests that effective approaches to strategic decision-making vary with the size of an organization (e.g., Miller and Friesen, 1984b). Therefore, a singular focus on the establishment or reestablishment of internal fit among organizational system elements is unlikely to adequately capture the scope of necessary problem-solving action as managers deal with their firms' growing pains.

The set of skills required to guide the transitioning of modes of operation and system elements to more viable states is referred to in the current model as "managerial capability." This capability is not simply the capacity to create growth, which was more accurately captured by the concept of entrepreneurial capability discussed earlier. Rather, the phrase "managerial capability" is intended to denote an ability to build the organization internally or strengthen the organizational system such that unnecessary tensions or incompatibilities among the organization's components are minimized and new, contextually appropriate behavioral patterns and processes are adopted.

Managerial capability affects the perception of transitions needed in the organization as well as the extent to which those needed transitions are achieved. Thus, while managerial complexity reflects the challenge faced by managers as a function of the number, variety, and interrelationships among tasks required to effectively and efficiently administer the operations of a firm, managerial capability represents the organization's ability to meet this challenge. The transitions purposefully achieved in an organization will be a function of the desire to enact organizational changes and the ability of managers to bring these changes about. Consistent with these points, Figure 5.1 (p. 104) shows managerial complexity as an antecedent of "organizational change aspirations," and managerial capability as a moderator of the relationship between these aspirations and realized transitions in organizational system elements and operations.

To summarize, it has been argued that the effective management of complexity necessitates the alleviation or elimination of various "problems" which are likely to emerge as organizations grow in size. Transitions in the state of internal organizational system elements are often required to address these problems, as is a redefinition of organizational behavioral patterns and processes. Managers must possess an ability to identify the causes of deficiencies in the efficient functioning of their organizations, redefine any dysfunctional practices or outmoded characteristics among the independently operating, loosely coupled elements in the organizational system (Aldrich, 1979), and reconfigure the interdependent elements in the system to create more cohesive organizational gestalts that promote long-term viability.

Relationship Between
Organizational Reconfiguration and Performance

Hanks (1990) offers a concise explanation of the problems growth can cause and how reconfigured organizational gestalts contribute to superior performance following periods of growth. Specifically, he argues that increased size and complexity place demands on firms that can often not be met with the structures and systems which were in place during the growth period. The essential managerial task is to create a new gestalt comprised of organizational attributes and systems interrelationships which are appropriate for the larger-size firm.

Of particular interest in Hanks' characterization of the need for reconfiguration is the implication that the desire for more *efficient* operations is the impetus behind post-growth internal structure and system changes. This notion of reconfiguring the organizational gestalt to create a more efficient system is, in fact, a common prescription for the management of growing organizations (e.g., Miller, 1992; Tushman and Romanelli, 1985). Accordingly, organizational profitability—a widely recognized efficiency criterion—is shown in Figure 5.1 to result from transitions among an organization's dysfunctional or incongruent behavioral patterns and system elements to more appropriate states. Organizational profitability, in turn, is shown to impact organizational resources.

Advantages and Contributions of the Current Model

In the interests of evaluating the merits of the current model, it is important to explicitly delineate its value added, emphasizing those areas in which the current model circumvents commonly recognized weaknesses inherent in many of the existing growth models. The following is a list of areas in which this model has particular advantages or otherwise makes contributions over existing theoretical perspectives on the growth phenomenon.

Not a Metamorphic Growth Model

A number of metamorphic growth models have been proposed over the years as theoretical lenses through which the growth process might be viewed and better understood. These models suggest a biological life-like progression of the organization through various life cycle stages over time. However, not all organizations progress through the same stages of growth nor exhibit similar characteristics in each stage. Further, questions as basic as how many stages of growth exist have not been adequately answered and, we believe, will never be satisfactorily answered given the diverse methodological approaches to empirically modeling the growth phenomenon. Sexton and Bowman-Upton (1991) offer a broad and useful critique of life cycle models. They warn of the hazards of drawing close analogies between natural phenomena and social phenomena. Certainly in a chaotic, hostile, and rapidly changing world, a model must be available to researchers that does not suggest some sort of orderly, predictable metamorphosis from one stage to another as organizational life progresses. Thus, the proposed model is neither metamorphic nor time-dependent but rather centered around the core construct of complexity and the transitions needed to ensure the sustained integrity of the organizational system. This theoretical lens provided by the model is more appropriate for the world of certain, yet discontinuous, change faced by growing firms.

Complexity, a Key Variable

As one looks at the literature on high-growth new ventures, a strong theme emerges concerning the importance of successfully managing the complexity that accompanies the realization of increased organization size. This complexity can occur in a wide range of variables and is difficult to describe in a constrained fashion. However, it is clearly a core topic of great relevance to high-growth new and small firms, and researchers in the future must face the challenge of understanding it and measuring it.

An Appropriate Model for Corporate Redefinition

In addition to the case of high-growth businesses, a tremendous amount of churning may occur across the business units of multidivisional corporations. Large diversified organizations may have some business units that are completely redefining themselves, others that are growing quite rapidly, and others that are declining precipitously. And such changes may all be occurring at the same time. The current model, or components therein, may be relevant as one attempts to better understand the process and challenges of large-scale organizational change. Moreover, the proposed model is, to a certain extent, a model of fit that broadly suggests how managers might reduce the tension that builds in the organizational system as a result of misfit between the current organizational gestalt and the firm's transition needs (Naman and Slevin, 1993). Thus, the proposed model could be useful in facilitating an understanding of why and how organizational gestalts may need to be reconfigured.

Modeled Transitions, Not Stages

A focus on transitions is increasingly recognized as essential to understanding the formation and growth of new businesses. The popular business press is replete with case examples of new ventures that experience extremely high growth and then die, and other new ventures that never quite get off the ground in spite of creative and highly promising strategies. The importance of understanding and managing high-growth transitions has recently been acknowledged by both the academic and practitioner communities. At the January 1995 Entrepreneurial Leadership Research Conference in San Diego (sponsored by the Center for Creative Leadership and the Center for Entrepreneurial Leadership at the Ewing Marion Kauffman Foundation), a group of academics and practitioners concluded that entrepreneurial transitions are one of the most important themes for future study. Transitions represent an important administrative challenge, and we must better understand how to conceive of and manage them.

In summary, the proposed complexity management model provides a novel and meaningful lens through which the growth process might be more fully understood. The intent is not to discredit the many fine theoretical contributions to the firm growth literature, but rather to encourage researchers and practitioners alike to step back and reflect on what is actually occurring in businesses as they grow in size and/or scope over time. The managerial challenge in these organizations is accurately described as one of dealing with increased complexity through the enactment of essential transitions within the organizational system. With this as a premise, the following suggestions for future research should facilitate understanding of the complexity management process. Before this is done, however, a more detailed discussion of the nature of the problems to be resolved in the management of complexity is warranted. This is the focus of the following section.

Growth-Related Problem Areas Contributing to Managerial Complexity

A cursory review and explanation of the relationship between firm growth and managerial complexity was presented in the prior overview of the complexity management model. However, in order to better understand the specific demands of the complexity management task, one needs to be aware of the types of problems commonly encountered by firms as they grow. Fortunately, a wealth of empirical and conceptual research has discussed these problems. In the interests of clarifying the nature of the complexity management task, a few representative writings on growth-related problems among small firms will be reviewed.

The Churchill and Lewis (1983) article identifies five stages of growth among small firms. Eight factors were identified as key management concerns or potential problem areas during the growth process. Four of these factors relate to the organization per se, and four of them relate to the business owner/entrepreneur. The four organization-focused concerns identified in Churchill and Lewis's article include:

1. Financial resources (e.g., cash and borrowing power).
2. Personnel resources (i.e., the number, depth, and quality of people in the organization).
3. System resources (defined in terms of the degree of sophistication of information and planning and control systems).
4. Business resources (e.g., customer relations, market share, supplier relations, manufacturing and distribution processes, technology, and reputation).

The four owner/entrepreneur-focused concerns described in Churchill and Lewis's article include the owner/entrepreneur's :

1. Personal and business goals.
2. "Operational abilities" relating to, for example, marketing and production.
3. Ability to manage others and willingness to delegate responsibility.
4. "Strategic abilities" relating to forward thinking and matching opportunities with initiatives and resources over time.

The preceding eight factors were observed to differ in importance across the five growth stages.

Similar to Churchill and Lewis (1983), Scott and Bruce (1987) proposed a five-stage model of small business growth. Scott and Bruce's model identifies the common "crises" faced by small firms as they strive to transition from one stage of growth to the next. Although the specifics of the Scott and Bruce model are too detailed to discuss here, the "most likely crises" associated with each stage-to-stage transition can be briefly identified (as labeled in the original article) as follows:

❖ *Inception-to-Survival Crises:* "The emphasis on profit" (i.e., need for a positive cash flow), "administrative demands" (i.e., need for increased formalization of systems), and "increased activity and its demands on time" (i.e., need to delegate supervisory tasks).

❖ *Survival-to-Growth Crises:* "Overtrading" (i.e., uncontrolled growth), "the increased complexity of expanded distribution" (i.e., need to adapt distribution systems to new geographic areas or types of customers), "change in the basis of competition" (i.e., increased emphasis on price-based competition, in conjunction with the creation of supporting competencies), and "pressures for information" (i.e., need to further formalize planning and control systems).

❖ *Growth-to-Expansion Crises:* "Entry of larger competitors" (i.e., need to choose strategies for defending or building market position in the face of formidable competition), and "the demands of expansion into new markets or products" (i.e., need to control and coordinate expanding and/or diversifying operations).

❖ *Expansion-to-Maturity Crises:* "The distance of top management from the action" (i.e., need to recognize that power and responsibility must be handed over to others throughout the organization) and "the need for external focus" (i.e., need for a proactive, anticipatory, and externally focused management style).

Research by Hambrick and Crozier (1985) identified four problem areas among rapidly growing firms. These problem areas were not described in the context of discrete stages. They include instant size, a sense of infallibility, internal turmoil, and extraordinary resource needs. Instant size was observed to create disaffection among firm employees and to render existing skills and systems inadequate. A sense of infallibility resulted from reflection on the firm's success and often led to a reluctance to change strategies or behaviors as conditions warranted. Internal turmoil arose, for example, from the influx of many new people into the organization, many of whom would not know each other nor the particular contributions expected of them. Finally, rapid-growth firms were often found to be cash starved and facing a "bare-bones existence" despite their apparent success. Thus, rapid growth placed extraordinary resource demands on the surveyed companies. Solutions to these problems were noted to include giving employees a financial stake in the firm, minimizing hierarchy, introducing "big company" processes as supplements to (rather than replacements of) existing approaches, reinforcing the original core vision of the firm, hiring and developing personnel needed for the future, and being able to envision and anticipate the firm in a larger organizational state.

Based on a small-sample field study of technology-based companies, Kazanjian (1988) developed a list of 18 "dominant problems" likely to be faced by such companies. He then conducted a larger survey research project to assess the perceived significance of these problems among technology-based new ventures in various stages of growth. Using data collected from this larger sample of companies, Kazanjian (1988) was able to identify, using factor analysis, six dimensions of dominant problems that characterize the growth process. These dimensions, along with the individual problem areas that best define them, were reported as follows:

❖ *Organizational Systems Problems:* Develop management information systems and cost controls; define organizational roles, responsibilities, and policies; develop financial systems and internal controls.

❖ *Sales/Marketing Problems:* Meet sales targets; attain profit and market-share goals; penetrate new geographic territories; provide product support and customer service.

❖ *People Problems:* Attract capable personnel; achieve management depth.

❖ *Production Problems:* Produce in volumes that meet demand; develop a network of reliable vendors and suppliers.

❖ *Strategic Positioning Problems:* Establish firm position in new product market segments; develop new product or technology application.

❖ *External Relations Problems:* Secure financial resources and backing; acquire key outside advisors, board members.

Finally, in a study of 645 small businesses, Dodge et al. (1994) observed that the following eight "internal" problem areas were repeatedly mentioned as impediments to growth: adequate capital, cash flow, facilities/equipment, inventory control, human resources, leadership/direction, organization structure, and accounting system. Additionally, the following eight "external" problem areas were reported as trouble spots by these firms' managers: customer contact, market knowledge, market planning, location, pricing, product considerations, competitors, and expansion. In contrast with much prior research, which has tended to view small firm growth problems as predominantly internal, Dodge and his colleagues found that small business managers tend to perceive their greatest problems as originating in their firms' externally oriented activities. Also noteworthy was the finding that small businesses face both situational problems, which tend to be specific to particular organizational life cycle stages, and core problems, which persist without substantive change in importance over the organizational life cycle.

Collectively, the preceding studies suggest several conclusions concerning the nature of the growth-related problems which contribute to managerial complexity.

1. Growth-related problems occur in all functional areas within the organization.

2. Growth-related problems may either originate from deficiencies within particular organizational elements or subsystems or from incompatibility between particular organizational elements or subsystems.

3. Growth-related problems may relate to both organizational and managerial inadequacies.

4. Resource deficiencies, broadly defined, seem to be at the root of many growth-related problems.

5. Growth-related problems may have their origins in phenomena either internal to or external to the organization.

6. Some growth-related problems may be most common or significant among organizations of a particular size while others may persist in magnitude-of-importance as long as the organization continues to grow.

7. Most growth-related problems are at least partially amenable to resolution through active and appropriate managerial intervention.

Regarding this last point, the following section outlines some of the approaches commonly used to resolve the growth-related problems that contribute to managerial complexity.

An Initial Typology of Problem Resolution Approaches

The management of complexity through the resolution of growth-related problems is an objective that may be pursued through various means. Reflecting on actual behavior in organizations, one can envision at least four approaches used to deal with managerial complexity. These approaches can be thought of as means to effect needed transitions among organizational elements or processes to states more congruent with and supportive of the organization's size. The following problem resolution approaches constitute an initial typology that may be useful in clarifying how managers deal with the phenomenon of complexity.

Diffusion of Managerial Complexity

One approach to managing complexity is to diffuse it throughout the organization. This involves, in essence, distributing the "problem" and associated organizational assignments to new individuals or subunits that are added to the organization to better enable it to handle the complicating issues that are contributing to complexity. A case in point would be the creation of a functional organization structure when a simple structure, due to increased organization size, no longer proves adequate for the purposes of effectively and efficiently coordinating the firm's operations. Another example might be establishment of special-purpose organizational subunits or task forces whose objective is to ensure the formulation and implementation of appropriate responses to specific, growth-related problems experienced by the firm. The diffusion approach to dealing with managerial complexity does not reduce the overall stock of complexity confronting the firm. Rather, it is intended to ensure that this complexity is not overwhelming to particular individuals, groups, or subunits within the organization. This is accomplished by distributing the complexity in a manner that allows it to exist without detriment to the effective and efficient overall functioning of the organization.

Reduction of Managerial Complexity

Another approach to dealing with managerial complexity is to reduce it, thereby simplifying the overall administrative task. How does one reduce the stock of managerial complexity confronting a firm? There are numerous possibilities. For example, if the activities required to accomplish particular organizational objectives can be consolidated within subunits, lower overall levels of managerial complexity may result. Such structural "modularization" approaches may reduce managerial complexity by decreasing coordination costs for the organization, by eliminating unnecessary hierarchy, and/or by simplifying the procedures through which interdependent tasks can be accomplished. Managerial complexity may also be reduced through business strategy changes. The implementation of retrenchment strategies, where the scope or level of an organization's operations are reduced, will often simplify the overall administrative task. Changes from diversification to concentration strategies may have similar effects. A third possibility for reducing the stock of managerial complexity is to engage in outsourcing of key business functions or operations. Many organizations are beginning to realize the benefits of executive search firms and alignments with temporary worker agencies as means to resolve recurring human resource problems. The employment of external marketing representatives and reliance on outside R&D services would be additional ways in which managerial complexity might be reduced.

Other means for reducing managerial uncertainty undoubtedly exist. The key element of this approach, in contrast to the diffusion approach, is the former's objective of bringing the overall growth-derived administrative challenge more in line with the firm's capabilities by simplifying the firm's operations or reallocating its traditional, internal responsibilities.

Redefinition of Managerial Complexity

Managers also deal with complexity by redefining it in ways that are better addressed through the organization's capabilities. The objective here is to consider the growth-derived problems from a number of different perspectives such that the possibility exists for finding solutions that are consistent with the organization's overall capabilities. For example, a growing firm may experience what appear to be problems in the production function in that production shortages frequently preclude the firm from being quickly responsive to or able to meet market demand. However, a more careful analysis of the "problem" may reveal that the production planning or volume difficulties can be resolved by the establishment of marketing goals which consider firm production speed and capacity levels. The administrative challenge is thus redefined from building the firm's production capacity, and dealing with the set of tasks therein implied, to something as potentially simple as having marketing and production personnel jointly represented in sales and production planning efforts. Similarly, one might redefine widespread "behavioral" problems in organizations in terms of more readily addressable reward system deficiencies.

Alternatively, and consistent with the redefinition approach to complexity management, particular organizational strengths may be used to overcome felt deficiencies in other aspects of organizational operations. For example, although this scenario is more common among larger firms, "procurement" problems are sometimes redefined by financially strong firms as low-supplier-control problems. In response, these firms may implement backward vertical integration strategies, buying their suppliers or building their own internal supply businesses. The procurement function would change with such a redefinition of the "problem," and the character of the new managerial complexity profile would be altered in ways more consistent with the organization's capabilities.

Thus, while the diffusion and reduction approaches to complexity management take the character or nature of complexity as a given, the redefinition approach asks how the experienced complexity might be reconsidered in ways that allow the organization to leverage its current capabilities in circumventing the apparent administrative problems.

Capability Building as a Response to Managerial Complexity

Finally, capability building among an organization's existing members or other system elements is a common response to managerial complexity. In this approach, the emphasis is on augmenting skills and creating new competencies within the current organizational system. The objective is to lessen the difficulty in dealing with challenges posed by the organization's growth. Some examples of capability building could involve retraining personnel or acquiring new organizational resources that complement or improve the efficiency or productive capacity of existing organizational system elements (e.g., the installation of improved communications software).

In conclusion, there are several approaches to the problem resolution process that managers choose to effect needed transitions and, in doing so, manage the complexity created through organizational growth. These approaches are not presented as mutually exclusive nor exhaustive of the ways in which managers deal with the phenomenon of complexity. Rather, their delineation is intended to demonstrate the possibility of some alternative paths through which complexity may be managed. The success of these or other approaches will determine whether an organization is able to resolve key growth-related problems, thereby transitioning to more efficient and viable operations and organizational configurations. However, the specific areas in which transitions are needed and the extent to which needed transitions are achieved will not always be clear. The following section presents one analytical framework that may facilitate the planning and evaluation of needed transitions in growing businesses.

Total Competitiveness

A research program at the University of Pittsburgh has identified a 12-factor model of total competitiveness, along with a measurement instrument for scaling each of the 12 factors, as one approach to the planning and measurement of transitions. Practicing managers were asked to identify issues they felt were important and enablers of effective competitive response in their business units. Hundreds of individual items were generated and sorted to generate 12 behavioral factors. A two-stage process resulted in the development of a behavioral instrument capable of measuring each of the 12 factors (Ahlbrandt and Slevin, 1992). Norms have been developed by collecting data from 194 business units across the country, with the following results.

❖ There are no differences in average scores between service and manufacturing business units. This means that the same norms can be used for both types of businesses.

❖ All 12 factors correlate significantly with business unit performance, measured in terms of firm financial growth over the past three years.

❖ The scale reliabilities of each of the 12 factors are high. The minimum Cronbach alpha is .86; the average is .91. Thus, the instrument appears to give robust and reliable readings on the 12 factors that are predictive of business unit success.

Total Competitiveness Defined

In today's increasingly dynamic and global business environment, firms must quickly and effectively adapt to competitive pressures. This is a difficult process and firms must be able to handle continuous change involving a variety of factors. Total competitiveness implies both profitable current operations and a continuous repositioning of key factors so that the organization is capable of being responsive to and anticipative of competitors' actions. Total Competitiveness, in terms of specific firm behavior, means scoring high on all 12 dimensions of competitiveness. The *Total Competitiveness Audit* (TCA) enables a business unit to diagnose and track its performance on all 12 competitiveness factors.

The 12 Competitiveness Factors

1. *Strategy/Direction*: Long-term goals and decisions concerning the means to achieve those goals.

2. *Human Resource Policies:* Human resource practices that support business performance, including the traditional practices of planning, staffing, appraisal, compensation, and training and development.

3. *Intra-Business Unit Communications:* Efficient and effective flow of information horizontally and vertically within the business unit; cross-functional sharing of information.

4. *Total Quality Management:* Emphasis on customer satisfaction as the ultimate performance measure; dedication to monitoring and continuously improving the quality of all operations.

5. *Product/Service Development and Improvement:* Innovative and new product/service development; involvement of all functional areas plus vendors and customers in the product/service development process.

6. *Marketing and Sales:* Responsiveness to customer needs; involvement of the marketing and sales functions in tracking and improving responses to customer requirements.

7. *Vendor Relationships:* Involvement of vendors in new product/service development and improvements.

8. *Process Improvements:* Degree to which continuous improvement is valued and achieved in all product/service production processes.

9. *Participative Management:* Empowerment of workers to make decisions through training and the sharing of information and power.

10. *Organization Structure:* The basic structure of the organization as represented by the organizational chart, including formal reporting relationships, role definition and accountability, the allocation of tasks, groupings of individuals, and structural systems for communication, coordination, and integration of activities.

11. *Business Unit Culture:* Shared norms (unwritten rules of behavior) as well as shared ideologies, values, attitudes, beliefs, and assumptions. Culture provides a social energy that guides peoples' daily behavior.

12. *International Competition:* The degree to which the business unit recognizes that it must function globally with international competitors.

TCA for Measuring Transitions

To reiterate, the Total Competitiveness Audit (TCA) provides data on 12 factors shown to correlate with firm financial performance. Importantly, this instrument has been used to successfully diagnose the status of those 12 factors in a cross-sectional sample of high-growth new ventures (Slevin and Covin, 1995). This instrument represents one approach to the diagnosis of areas where transitions are needed as well as a means to measure the degree of improvement achieved. It is possible to periodically diagnose the status of a business unit on each of the 12 factors and to monitor how these factors change as the unit effects transitions necessary for coping with the managerial complexity it faces. Anecdotal evidence suggests that as business unit size increases, substantial managerial energies must be expended to sustain these 12 factors at their desired levels (Slevin and Covin, 1995). Thus, the TCA could be a useful analytical framework for diagnosing organizational traits and measuring organizational change as we attempt to understand how firms deal with the complexities involved in high-growth management.

Implications for Future Research

Implicit in a state-of-the-art conceptual essay is a mandate to identify promising directions for future research. While the model proposed here might suggest different things for different people, two major themes emerge:

❖ *Complexity is here to stay.* Based on identifiable trends across multiple segments of the domestic and international business environments, future high-growth businesses will face even more complexity in their efforts to sustain rapid growth. Therefore, researchers must attempt to better understand the construct of complexity and provide relevant information to practitioners concerning the key variables that drive complexity as well as the ways in which complexity should be managed. Clearly, the proposed model suggests a central position for the construct of complexity in future empirical research.

❖ *Transitions are central to high growth.* Transitions and their successful management are key to business growth and success. We suggest that transitions may be meaningfully studied from a variety of perspectives and using a variety of methods. As mentioned, Ahlbrandt and Slevin's (1992) 12-factor total competitiveness model has been shown by Slevin and Covin (1995) to be a promising framework for the study of new venture growth. However, this is just one of many frameworks that may be useful in helping to define promising foci for future research efforts.

Regardless of the particular theoretical perspective or research approach adopted, some particularly promising research questions might include:

1. Which elements of the organizational system should transition with changes in firm size, and which should persist in a specific, constant state?

2. What is the proper sequencing of transitions among particular organizational system elements?

3. What are some defensible heuristics for enacting piecemeal versus quantum changes in the elements of an organizational system?

Popper (1959) suggested a criteria for theory construction that included the components of falsifiability, testability, universality, precision, and simplicity. The model presented in this chapter appears to have reasonably good marks on falsifiability, universality, and simplicity. How well it performs concerning the testability and precision criteria will be a function of the creativity and execution proficiency of future researchers as they attempt to study high-growth transitions.

Implications for Managers

The proposed model is still at an exploratory stage. While parts of the model have been the focus of empirical investigation, no empirical research has been conducted that would strongly suggest the validity of the model in its entirety. Consequently, suggestions for future managerial activity are relatively brief and broad. Nonetheless, certain key conclusions are suggested:

❖ *Complexity is here to stay for managers too.* Complexity management is not a cyclical phenomenon in which the organizational system is reset, then business as usual continues. Rather, complexity management is an ever-present managerial concern. Therefore, managers of successful, high-growth firms will likely be those who respond positively to the complexity inherent in a dynamic organizational system. Conversely, managers who fear or are ambivalent toward complexity will likely misread or otherwise mishandle signals suggesting that organizational transitions are warranted.

❖ *Clearly, transitions are inevitable.* Major and often painful transitions occur in firms of all sizes. While the high-growth example is the current case in point, transitions are inherent to the functioning of any ongoing social system. Accordingly, the ability to sense transition needs and to manage and implement the necessary changes is an essential skill in all organizational contexts. However, the mismanagement of transitions is a pervasive and root cause of many, perhaps most, organizational failures.

❖ *Thus, managers must develop new skills.* In particular, managers are challenged to develop skills that will allow them to: 1) recognize and understand the implications of complexity; 2) decide what transitions, if any, are suggested by the identified complexity; 3) manage these transitions to effect needed organizational changes; and 4) be willing and prepared to redefine or reconfigure key elements of the organizational system on an as-needed basis.

Collectively, the preceding suggests that the successful general manager of the future will be much more inclined to accept and embrace the inevitability of continuous organizational change. Correspondingly, such managers will also be more proficient at coping with complexity and transition management.

REFERENCES

Adizes, I. 1989. *Corporate Life Cycles: How and Why Corporations Grow and Die, and What To Do About It.* Englewood Cliffs, NJ: Prentice-Hall.

Ahlbrandt, R.S., and D.P. Slevin. 1992. *Total Competitiveness Audit (TCA).* Pittsburgh: University of Pittsburgh Press.

Aldrich, H.A. 1979. *Organizations and Environments*. Englewood Cliffs, NJ: Prentice-Hall.

Blau, P.M. 1970. A formal theory of differentiation in organizations. *American Sociological Review* 35:201-218.

Chandler, A. 1962. *Strategy and Structure: Chapters in the History of American Industrial Enterprise*. Cambridge, MA: MIT Press.

Churchill, N.C., and V.L. Lewis. 1983. The five stages of small business growth. *Harvard Business Review* 61(3):30-50.

Clifford, D.K., Jr. 1975. The case of the floundering founder. *Organizational Dynamics* 4(2):21-54.

Dodge, H.R., F. Fullerton, and J.E. Robbins. 1994. Stage of the organizational life cycle and competition as mediators of problem perception for small business. *Strategic Management Journal* 15:121-134.

Flamholtz, E.G. 1986. *Managing the Transition from an Entrepreneurship to a Professionally Managed Firm*. San Francisco: Jossey-Bass.

Fombrun, C.J., and S. Wally. 1989. Structuring small firms for rapid growth. *Journal of Business Venturing* 4:107-122.

Glanzer, M.S., and H.H. Clark. 1962. Accuracy of perceptual recall: an analysis of organization. *Journal of Verbal Learning and Verbal Behavior* 1:289-299.

Gregg, L.W. 1967. Internal representations of sequential concepts. In B. Kleinmuntz (ed.): *Concepts and the Structure of Memory*. New York: Wiley, 107-112.

Hambrick, D.C., and L.M. Crozier. 1985. Stumblers and stars in the management of rapid growth. *Journal of Business Venturing* 1(1):31-45.

Hanks, S.H. 1990. The organization life cycle: Integrating content and process. *Journal of Small Business Strategy* 1(1):1-12.

Hedberg, B., P. Nystrom, and W. Starbuck. 1976. Camping on seesaws: prescriptions for a self-designing organization. *Administrative Science Quarterly* 21:41-65.

Hoy, F., P.P. McDougall, and D.E. D'Souza. 1992. Strategies and environments of high-growth firms. In D.L. Sexton and J.D. Kasarda (eds.): *The State of the Art of Entrepreneurship*. Boston: PWS-Kent, 341-357.

Kazanjian, R.K. 1988. Relation of dominant problems to stages of growth in technology-based new ventures. *Academy of Management Journal* 31(2):257-279.

Klahr, D., and J.G. Wallace. 1970. The development of serial completion strategies: an information processing analysis. *British Journal of Psychology* 62:243-257.

Laughery, K.R., and L.W. Gregg. 1962. Simulation of human problem-solving behavior. *Psychometrika* 27:265-282.

Lawrence, P.R., and J.W. Lorsch. 1967. *Organization and Environment*. Homewood, IL: Irwin.

Leeuwenberg, E.L.L. 1969. Quantitative specification of information in sequential patterns. *Psychological Review* 76:216-20.

Miller, D. 1992. Environmental fit versus internal fit. *Organization Science* 3(2):159-178.

Miller, D., and P.H. Friesen. 1984a. *Organizations: A Quantum View*. Englewood Cliffs, NJ: Prentice-Hall.

Miller, D., and P.H. Friesen. 1984b. A longitudinal study of the corporate life cycle. *Management Science* 30(10):1161-1183.

Mintzberg, H. 1979. *The Structure of Organizations*. Englewood Cliffs, NJ: Prentice-Hall.

Mount, J., J.T. Zinger, and G.R. Forsyth. 1993. Organizing for development in the small business. *Long Range Planning* 26(5):11-120.

Naman, J.L., and D.P. Slevin. 1993. Entrepreneurship and the concept of fit: a model and empirical tests. *Strategic Management Journal* 14:137-153.

Popper, K.R. 1959. *The Logic of Scientific Discovery*. New York: Basic Books.

Price Waterhouse Change Integration Team. 1996. *The Paradox Principles: How High-Performance Companies Manage Chaos, Complexity, and Contradiction to Achieve Superior Results*. Chicago, IL: Irwin.

Restle, F. 1970. Theory of serial pattern learning: Structural trees. *Psychological Review* 77:481-495.

Scott, M., and R. Bruce. 1987. Five stages of growth in small business. *Long Range Planning* 20(3):45-52.

Sexton, D.L., and N.B. Bowman-Upton. 1991. *Entrepreneurship: Creativity and Growth*. New York: MacMillan.

Simon, H.A. 1962. The architecture of complexity. *Proceedings of the American Philosophical Society* 106(6):467-482.

Simon, H.A. 1979. Implementation of patterned sequences of symbols. In H.A. Simon (ed.): *Models of Thought*. New Haven, CT: Yale University Press, 292-306.

Simon, H.A., and K. Kotovsky. 1963. Human acquisition of concepts for sequential patterns. *Psychological Review* 70:334-346.

Simon, H.A., and R.K. Sumner. 1968. Pattern in music. In B. Kleinmuntz (ed.): *Formal Representation of Human Judgment*. New York: Wiley, 219-250.

Slevin, D.P., and J.G. Covin. 1995. New ventures and total competitiveness: A conceptual model, empirical results, and case study examples. In W.D. Bygrave et al. (eds.): *Frontiers of Entrepreneurship Research*. Wellesley, MA: Babson College, 574-588.

Smith, K.G., T.R. Mitchell, and C.E. Summer. 1985. Top level management priorities in different stages of the organizational life cycle. *Academy of Management Journal* 28(4):799-820.

Thompson, J.D. 1967. *Organizations in Action*. New York: McGraw-Hill.

Tushman, M.L., and E. Romanelli. 1985. Organizational evolution: A metamorphosis model of convergence and reorientation. In L.L. Cummings and B.M. Staw, B.M. (eds.): *Research in Organizational Behavior*. Greenwich, CT: JAI Press, 7:171-222.

Vitz, P.C., and R.C. Todd. 1969. A coded element model of the perceptual processing of sequential stimuli. *Psychological Review* 76:433-449.

Williams, D.S. 1972. Computer program organization induced from problem examples. In H.A. Simon and L. Siklossy (eds.): *Representation and Meaning*. Englewood Cliffs, NJ: Prentice-Hall, 143-205.

CHAPTER 6

Entrepreneurial Teams

ARNOLD C. COOPER
AND
CATHERINE M. DAILY

G ROWTH-ORIENTED NEW FIRMS ARE OFTEN BUILT around the founding team. The members of the team identify the initial venture opportunity and develop a strategy to exploit it. They are the repositories of much of the technical and management knowledge that make up the intangible assets of the firm. It is their contacts and their reputations that help the new firm gain access to resources and to attract customers, suppliers, key employees, and advisors. They provide the drive (often with enormously long hours) and the direction for the new firm. The new firm depends upon the team to such an extent that investors often indicate that they emphasize the quality of the management team more than any other single factor as they make investment decisions (Kamm et al., 1989).

This chapter is about entrepreneurial teams—how they form and break up, how they function, and how they influence new ventures. Frameworks are developed for thinking about teams, the relevant literature is reviewed, and opportunities for future research are identified.

The focus here is upon growth-oriented new firms. Lifestyle businesses or even profitable niche businesses with few prospects for growth are much less likely to be started by teams. Ventures with substantial growth prospects are more likely to be able to attract and support multiple founders. If the growth is realized, these firms are more likely to require the talents of multiple people, often with complementary skills and knowledge. This chapter also emphasizes independent new firms, rather than ventures within established corporations. Teams clearly play a role in corporate entrepreneurship, but that setting is not considered here.

Understanding entrepreneurial teams appears to have implications for both practice and research. For instance, consider the process of team formation. If certain circumstances increase the likelihood that team formation will occur, this has implications for those concerned with improving the climate for the formation of growth-
oriented firms. If teams with certain attributes are more likely to function effectively
or stay together, this has implications for lead entrepreneurs as they work to form
teams. As shall be noted, there is much about entrepreneurial teams that has not
been studied systematically, and this presents opportunities for research.

What is an Entrepreneurial Team?

The question of whether an entrepreneurial team is present may be less straightforward than it appears. Presumably it means more than simply having a sole entrepreneur with employees, even key employees. Guzzo and Dickson (1996), talking about
teams in organizations, suggest that a team is more than a group, that it involves a
sense of shared commitment. Kamm et al. (1989) suggest that it involves two or more
individuals who jointly establish a venture and who were involved in the pre-startup
activities. In a later article, the requirement was added that both would hold equity
in the firm. Watson et al. (1995) defined venture teams as two or more individuals
who jointly founded a business and were still involved in operating it jointly.
Eisenhardt and Schoonhoven (1990) defined team members to be founders if they
worked full-time in executive-level positions when the firm was founded. Roberts
(1970) felt that the key entrepreneur could be involved only part-time, if that person was the source of the key ideas and provided much of the impetus for the firm.

The variations indicate that definitions of entrepreneurial teams are not clear-cut.
One of the authors recalls interviewing a series of technical entrepreneurs about
their founding processes and asking about the founders. Responses included, "Do you
mean full-time founders or part-time founders?" and, "Do you mean only early
founders or do you include later founders?" A common occurrence was to have several key people working together to get a venture formed. Some would contribute
their efforts during evenings or weekends, while keeping full-time jobs. They would
then join the venture full-time after it had reached certain benchmarks or was able
to support them. Sometimes key people (such as an experienced marketing executive) would be enticed to join the team after the founding process was well underway. The venture would then depend greatly upon that person's reputation, contacts,
and effort, even though that person was not aboard when the early planning
occurred.

Much of the research in entrepreneurship has involved survey research. The
question of who was on an entrepreneurial team seems to have been handled in the

literature chiefly by asking the president of the venture who he or she considers to have been founders. As referred to the extant literature, this is the usual definition in mind. However, it should be recognized that one of the opportunities for research is to develop typologies of teams, recognizing varying contributions and roles within the new venture.

Why Form a Team?

Many ventures are formed by sole entrepreneurs. Certainly, this is the simplest way to proceed. Under these circumstances, it is not necessary to agree with other team members about relative contributions of time or of money or the future direction of the venture. Neither is it necessary to develop good working relationships with a partner or key members of a team. Consultation about key decisions may occur only as the entrepreneur talks to himself or herself on the drive to work. Power does not have to be shared and the business can be a vehicle for independence and for doing the kind of work one wants to do. Many entrepreneurs are so committed to their ideas and "their" business that they are not willing to bring in cofounders. Stolze (1989) noted some of the disadvantages of teams, notably that teams bring dilution of ownership, possible conflict, the challenge of being both equal and unequal, and the difficulty of reversing the decision to have a partner if things do not work out. Most entrepreneurs follow the path of not having partners. For instance, a study of 2,994 entrepreneurs who were members of the National Federation of Independent Business indicated that only 30 percent reported that they had full-time partners at the time of start-up (Cooper et al., 1990).

However, certain kinds of businesses are usually started by teams. In a review of research on high-technology startups, it was reported that the median percentage of founders with full-time partners across ten different studies was 70 percent (Cooper, 1986). In his book on building growth-oriented ventures, Timmons (1990) notes that it is very difficult to build a high-potential business without a team. Teach et al. (1986) found that over two-thirds of the 237 microcomputer software entrepreneurs they studied had two or more principals. For an *Inc.* magazine study of the 100 fastest-growing young firms in 1983, two-thirds involved two or more founders.

Vesper (1990) points out a number of reasons why some ventures are formed by teams. Multiple founders make possible a larger effort, drawing upon complementary skills and knowledge of team members. If the lead entrepreneur is willing and able to recruit other key team members, this may be an indication of that person's ability to attract and manage people, a key requirement for growth. If other key people are willing to join the team, this also serves as an initial check of the venture idea, suggesting that those in a position to assess the venture believe it has promise

(Vesper, 1990). There is also less dependence upon a single person, so that an illness or departure is less likely to cripple the venture. Finally, there is psychological support. Boyd and Gumpert (1983) identified causes of entrepreneurial stress, one of which was loneliness/isolation from persons in whom they could confide. Consistent with this, an entrepreneur in Silicon Valley some years ago, commenting upon the loneliness of the task of venture formation, said, "Sometimes you wake up in the middle of the night and wonder if you're crazy. Then it helps to recall that someone else is in it with you."

A Framework for Thinking About Teams

The framework which is proposed involves three broad categories: processes of team formation; team functioning, and influences of team makeup (Table 6.1). First, the processes of team formation is considered.

TABLE 6.1
Framework for Considering Entrepreneurial Teams

Process of Team Formation	Team Functioning	Influences of Team Makeup
• Recruiting	• Roles within team	• Team stability
• Mode of formation	• Team heterogeneity	• Firm performance
• Prior relationships	• Psychological variables	
• Relative contributions and benefits	• Consensus in decision making	
	• Relationships to strategy and structure	

Processes of Team Formation

The gestation process during which a business is formed often occurs over a considerable period of time. Reynolds and Miller (1992) found that there were a number of "entrepreneurial events," each of which might be thought of as benchmarks of progress toward venture creation. They include the principal's commitment, initial hiring, initial financing, and initial sales. He found that these events occurred in varying sequences and over extended periods, ranging from one month to 10 years.

For growth-oriented firms, one of the key activities during this period is recruiting members of the entrepreneurial team. Their efforts develop the products or services upon which the business is based; they establish the market relationships and set up the facilities. Their contacts and reputation are often critical in attracting capital and key employees.

Despite its importance, little systematic research has been done on the processes by which entrepreneurial teams are formed. Bird (1989) noted that most of the work on entrepreneurial teams has been anecdotal, sparse, and lacking in theoretical development. Many of the most fundamental questions have received little attention. How does it happen that certain people join the team at particular times and with particular commitments? To what extent do entrepreneurs try to form teams, but then give up? What factors influence whether strong teams can be formed? Most of the literature is primarily conceptual, sometimes with useful examples. These provide frameworks for thinking about team formation, possible future problems, and ways to develop effectively functioning teams (Kamm et al., 1989; Timmons, 1990; Vesper, 1990). However, there is little in the way of theory, and there has not been much presentation of data or empirical analysis.

There are many challenges in forming teams. Clearly, there must be a relationship of trust. Team members will often work long hours together, seeing more of each other than of their spouses or children. They often pool their financial resources, get second mortgages on their houses, and jointly commit what they have to the new venture. For those struggling to start a business, there is the realization that success depends not only upon one's own efforts, but also upon the contributions and effectiveness of others on the team. Trust presumably develops over time, the result of many interactions, but there has not been much investigation as to how trust develops among prospective entrepreneurial team members.

The lead entrepreneur must become aware of possible candidates to join a team and decide whether to try to recruit them. Potential team members must then decide whether to cast their lot with a new firm, even as it is being formed. Thus, there is a mutual process of judging the capabilities and commitments of others. What will they bring to the party? Teams are most effective if they reflect a balance of skills, so that the major functional activities are covered by people who have expertise in those areas (Roure and Maidique 1986). This can make the process of team formation more challenging, particularly if the lead entrepreneur has limited experience and expertise or is isolated geographically. The lead entrepreneur cannot just seek clones, people whom he or she works with all of the time, but rather people who can make contributions in areas that the lead entrepreneur may not know well. How does an engineer judge whether a potential partner in marketing is first-rate? It is also necessary to judge compatibility. Can we work together? What does this person want the business to accomplish and what is he or she willing to put in? Assessment of ethical standards is also important. Are these the kinds of people I want to cast my lot with? There has not been much research on how entrepreneurs make these assessments.

As Timmons (1990) has noted, team formation is much like marriage. After a courtship period, there is commitment, and later there may be a divorce. The relationship is certainly for "richer or poorer" and for "better or worse," although it may not be "until death do us part."

Mode of Formation

The team may be formed in different ways. One mode is to have a clearly recognized lead entrepreneur, who heads the effort from the start. That person recruits the other team members and negotiates to bring them on board.

Another mode is to have an "assembly of equals," as two or more colleagues or friends decide to pool their efforts together. Initially, they may view themselves as partners or copresidents, with equal ownership and equal say on major decisions. One might expect that teams formed in this way would be more subject to jockeying for position, and possibly less stable in the long run, but this has not been investigated.

Another dimension of team formation relates to what comes first—the venture concept or the team. Sometimes the team comes first, working together to develop the concept. Sometimes the lead entrepreneur develops the concept and then seeks team members who can help to implement the idea (Kamm et al., 1989).

Prior Relationships

How do team members get together? Do most already know each other, or are new relationships formed after the decision is made to start a company? Bird (1989) considered factors that may draw team members together: likeability, proximity, alikeness, complementarity of attributes, and mutual enjoyment. Kamm and Nurick (1993) noted that prospective team members may be attracted to others with similar beliefs and interests or who have qualities judged to be desirable. The chemistry of how people are attracted to each other appears to be important.

One pattern is for teams to be formed among people who have already worked together in a prior organization, reflecting the proximity variable in Bird's (1989) framework. It provides the setting in which they can assess each other and form relationships of trust. Research on trust in established teams found that members had more trust in their leaders if they knew that their input was considered (Korsgaard et al., 1995). Past working relationships could provide the basis for this reassurance. Eisenhardt and Schoonhoven (1990) noted that team members who have worked together have probably learned how to communicate and get along. In their study of semiconductor firms, they gathered information on the percentage of team members within each startup who had previously worked together in the same organization. As possible research opportunities are considered, one might note that the nature of these prior organizational relationships might vary. They might involve superiors and subordinates or those who did not have reporting relationships, but whose work had brought them into contact. These prior relationships may affect the time needed for the members to learn to work together as a team.

The nature of organizations in which potential entrepreneurs are located may bear upon team formation. Organizations that bring together people with different functional expertise, either through their physical location or their specific assignments, may make it more likely that cross-functional teams can be formed. Smaller firms, larger organizations organized as a series of small businesses, or organizations that utilize cross-functional teams may be settings favorable to team formation. The nature of previous relationships has not been considered in previous research, nor has there been consideration of whether particular organizational settings facilitate or hinder team formation.

Another pattern is for team members to have had prior working relationships, but not within the same organization. Thus, salespeople who call upon a company may get to know the budding entrepreneurs and may be invited to join them. People who work for dealers, for customers, for suppliers, or for professional advisors (such as consulting firms) may come into contact with those forming the team and be asked to come aboard. A team formed in this way may have greater diversity of experience, but the members may have had less opportunity to learn to work together. In terms of facilitating conditions, it seems likely that those who interact with people outside their organization are in a better position to form teams.

A particular challenge may confront lead entrepreneurs located in universities or branch manufacturing plants in small towns. Their jobs may not involve much interaction with people in other functional areas, such as marketing or finance. Off the job, there may be few opportunities to get to know potential cofounders who combine industry and technical expertise with the functional experience needed to form a balanced team. They may even lack ties with knowledgeable intermediaries who could connect them with such people. Because of their location, even if contact is made with potential cofounders in other geographic areas, those people must assess the costs and risks involved in moving to become part of the entrepreneurial team.

Teams can also be formed that draw upon family members or friends. Here it may be easier to judge compatibility because the members may be bound together by long-term relationships. However, as Bird (1989) notes, joining together to start a business poses different demands than being a spouse, a relative, or a friend. In addition, as research on family business reminds us, it may be harder to assess contributions objectively, and the personal relationships may make it difficult to manage the business professionally (Kets de Vries, 1993). A model of team performances (Slevin and Covin, 1992) suggests that a host of factors affect the team relationships and creation.

Finally, teams may be formed as a result of deliberate search. Here, the lead entrepreneur seeks to find people with the right skills and bring them aboard. No research to date has looked at how this process unfolds, including the extent to which the entrepreneur utilizes existing networks. In some cases, formal programs to train entrepreneurs and encourage entrepreneurship may serve to bring people together who share a common interest in new firm formation; team formation may subsequently occur. This raises questions about whether programs to try to bring team members together (marriage brokers of a sort) might be promising.

Relative Contributions and Benefits

As formation occurs, what do team members contribute and what do they expect to get? Some contribute the idea, the concept of a market opportunity, or a technological solution to a recognized problem. Team members also contribute their time, whether it be full-time or part-time with the assurance (or hope) of joining full-time later. Money is another contribution, including borrowing power and willingness to guarantee loans. Another contribution can be facilities or equipment already owned by one of the partners. There is also the contribution of reputation and contacts; if the person is well-respected, this can serve to bring credibility to the venture.

What do the team members get in return? Research on groups shows that people are more attracted to join groups if they feel that they will have high prestige or influence within the group (Napier and Gershenfeld, 1985). Entrepreneurial ventures offer the opportunity to fill key positions, to have a feeling of influence, and a sense that this is "their" organization. There can also be the satisfaction of building a team or pursuing a strongly felt vision. Stock ownership, whether immediate or to be vested over time, can be a major incentive. Current compensation can also be a reward, although it will usually not be very high in a startup firm. The fledgling company doesn't have many rewards to allocate, other than hope and a chance at future benefits.

What influences who gets what? Timmons (1990) has provided the most extensive discussion of the reward system and issues to be considered. When there is a clearly recognized lead entrepreneur, that will usually be reflected in all of the benefits—title, ownership, and power. Others will benefit according to what they contribute, or according to how they bargain. Outside investors may exert substantial influence, both with regard to ownership and management positions. It should be recognized that contributions occur over time, so that it is not always clear in advance the value of each partner's contributions; nor is it clear how successful the business will be. The incentives to bring people aboard may not fully reflect their future contributions. Here, flexibility is needed because some team members may not work out or some may decide to withdraw. Furthermore, future investors will look at how rewards have been allocated as one indication of the management skill of the founders. Again, no known systematic research has been done with regard to how rewards are allocated to team members, how these may be related to their initial individual goals, or how these are tied to their subsequent commitments to the firm. As a result, the following questions remain unanswered:

1. What are the processes by which teams are formed? What are the factors that influence whether efforts to assemble a team are successful?

2. What typologies describe the different patterns of team formation and different kinds of teams?

3. How does the mode of team formation affect subsequent functioning? Do teams formed by "lead entrepreneurs" tend to function more effectively (less jockeying for power)? Do they tend to be more stable (less disappointment over not being at the top)? Do those in which the ideas come first (and the team is assembled later) tend to be more successful?

4. If team members have worked together in a previous organization, are their teams more effective?

5. How do team members assess each other, particularly if they have not interacted much before? How does trust develop?

6. Are teams formed with family or friends (outside the work environment) less effective because of the difficulty of assessing capabilities?

7. How do geographic relationships affect formation? Are university-based entrepreneurs coming out of universities in nonmetropolitan areas or entrepreneurs coming out of single-function locations (such as branch manufacturing plants) less likely to form balanced teams?

8. How does the organizational structure of existing firms where potential entrepreneurs are located affect team formation? Are balanced entrepreneurial teams more likely to be formed in decentralized organizations or in those which utilize cross-functional teams?

9. What are the processes by which rewards are allocated, both initially and later? How do teams deal with the problem of unequal contributions, particularly when one has much more capital to contribute?

10. How do relative positions (equal or unequal positions of ownership or power within the organization) influence subsequent functioning?

How Do Entrepreneurial Teams Function?

As businesses are formed, the entrepreneurial teams must learn to work together. They must determine how to divide up the work and responsibilities and determine the processes by which decisions will be made. As disagreements arise, they must also determine how they will be handled.

These processes may be influenced by how the team was formed. Teams formed by a clear lead entrepreneur, particularly if that person had previously been a supervisor of others on the team, may already have well-defined relationships. Teams made up of equals, who regard everyone as having an equal say, may have more difficulty in working out their roles. If it is felt necessary to achieve consensus, this can be time-consuming and sometimes frustrating. Those who have not worked together previously, even if they have been together in social or family relationships, may also face challenges in developing working relationships.

As the new firm is formed, team members define the boundaries and distance between each other; this includes how much information, planning, and decision-making are shared (Bird 1989, 218). They also determine who will specialize in particular tasks. What Hambrick (1994) has termed "behavioral integration" (shared information exchange, collaborative behavior, and joint decision-making) may be quite high in many entrepreneurial teams. The members are self-selected and work together in a limited domain.

More is required than simply assembling dedicated people. Team building must occur, and, as Timmons (1990) notes, they must come together around a vision. The lead entrepreneur needs to create that vision and to instill passion among the members of the team. Timmons also emphasizes that such qualities as cohesion, teamwork, and commitment to the long haul are necessary attributes of the effective team. The lead entrepreneur also must take responsibility for establishing and maintaining shared values and goals among team members (Watson et al., 1995). Maintaining consistency of values and goals may help the team avoid unnecessary conflicts. Conflict may result from the pursuit of peripheral goals that utilize resources critical to the new venture. All of this suggests that lead entrepreneurs need to have strong leadership skills. Leadership styles of entrepreneurs are undoubtedly a promising topic for research, but little is known of work beyond the biographies of famous entrepreneurs.

Roles within the team may evolve. As events unfold, it may be clear that some members work harder, some make more vital contributions, and some are more assertive. As team members work closely for many weeks, strong ties may develop, arising from a sense of shared commitment. Alternatively, some may begin to get on each other's nerves. The colleague who had seemed just right begins to seem like more of a talker than a doer. Research on management teams suggests that teams which have worked together for some time will function quite differently from newly formed teams. As they work together, the team may move through different phases, with the development of trust, cohesiveness, and commitment being characteristic of effective teams (Kriegel and Brandt, 1996). Little research has been done on the ways in which these relationships evolve and how roles become defined within the newly formed firm.

All of this occurs within the context of an evolving, changing organization. The new products or services are being developed and debugged, and market relationships are being established. The first orders may be received. Efforts to raise funds, to establish facilities, and to hire key employees move forward. The firm's strategy may also be changing, sometimes even before the first sale. The entrepreneurs sometimes discover that the initial target market is less promising than they thought. They may discover that a different form of the product is more likely to generate customer interest. Fund-raising, whether successful or not, bears directly upon the development of the team. If funds become available, a larger team can be formed; part-time founders can come aboard. If funds are not available (possibly because investors are waiting to see how the venture develops), the firm may have to scale back efforts, including the size of the founding team. Teach et al. (1986) suggested that, instead of funding determining team size, it is the other way around. They reported that larger teams were able to pool more personal capital of the members and thereby provide more for the launching of their venture.

The role of the lead founder in developing the entrepreneurial team appears to be much like that of the proverbial orchestra leader (who has been likened to managers before). The lead entrepreneur directs the process as team members try to play together for the first time. But some members alternate between playing instruments they know well with those they have never played before. The lead entrepreneur keeps an eye on the audience (the market) and alters the score as they proceed if the initial audience response is not favorable. Meanwhile, negotiations are proceeding with sources of capital that will determine whether they can buy the instruments needed to finish the piece.

Team Heterogeneity

Research on top management teams suggests that a number of dimensions of team makeup may influence how entrepreneurial teams make decisions. Most of this research has examined demographic characteristics, based upon published data, and has considered these relationships within the context of established large organizations (Bantel and Jackson, 1989).

One research stream has examined the extent to which a top management team is homogeneous or heterogeneous. It has been suggested that homogeneity may result in a lack of diversity in approaches to problem-solving and "group think" (Janis, 1982). Alternatively, heterogeneity in top management team makeup has been linked to conflict (Tsui and O'Reilly, 1989). Although this might seem to be dysfunctional, Eisenhardt and Bourgeois (1988) found that successful executive teams in semiconductor start-ups combined conflict with fast decision-making. For the top management teams of 84 Fortune 500 food and oil industry firms, Murray (1989) found that heterogeneity in age, tenure, education, and occupation were related to improved performance in the oil industry (but not in the food industry). Smith et al. (1994) examined small high-technology firms and found heterogeneity of experience to be negatively related to return on investment, while heterogeneity of education showed a positive relationship. With regard to corporate innovativeness, Bantel and Jackson (1989) found a positive relationship between heterogeneity of the top management team (in functional background and educational level) and innovativeness.

However, findings relating heterogeneity to performance are not uniformly favorable. Heterogeneity can make it more difficult to interact (Hambrick, 1994) and can affect communication adversely (Zenger and Lawrence, 1989). Heterogeneity may be most beneficial in turbulent, especially discontinuous, environments and may actually be dysfunctional in stable environments (Hambrick and Mason 1984). Heterogeneity has been linked to turnover within top management teams (Wiersema and Bird, 1993), and among worker groups (O'Reilly et al., 1989). Study of work teams (not top management teams) found heterogeneity in background and expertise to be unrelated or negatively related to team effectiveness (Campion et al., 1993).

Examination of the effects of top management team heterogeneity upon communication, innovativeness, and firm performance has occurred primarily within the context of established larger firms. These organizations may have a particular need for conflict and for questioning the status quo. Although the work of Eisenhardt and Bourgeois (1988) and Eisenhardt (1989) suggest that conflict may be desirable within the entrepreneurial team, not much has been done to examine the effects of team heterogeneity within this setting.

Psychological Variables

Most of the research on top management team heterogeneity has focused upon biographical variables, possibly because of data accessibility. However, heterogeneity with regard to variables relating to psychological makeup or management style may also be important to consider. Slevin (1989, 357) asked, How important is heterogeneity within the team with regard to such variables as inclination to take risks versus being cautious, proactivity versus being reactive, and orientation toward innovation? Are balanced teams, with one member keeping another in check, more successful? Miner's research (1996) suggests a relationship between personality types and entrepreneurial success, with entrepreneurs being classified as personal achievers, real managers, empathic supersalespeople, and expert idea generators. His findings suggest that those who combine multiple types are most likely to be successful. No research has been done to date on whether particular combinations across entrepreneurial teams are likely to lead to greater effectiveness.

Consensus in Decision-Making

Some evidence suggests that consensus in decision-making is not necessarily good. Bourgeois (1985) found that consensus within the top management team with regard to goals was negatively related to firm performance. Dollinger et al. (1990) found that consensus on competitive means and consensus on strategic objectives were both negatively related to performance. They concluded that diversity is appropriate and even needed in the recruitment of top management teams in small firms. Whether this lack of consensus is equally valuable during the start-up stage is an open question. During this time there is often enormous pressure to use limited resources wisely; often there is a question of whether a firm can even get a product to the market before it runs out of cash. Lack of consensus may lead to a greater variety of approaches to problem-solving; however, it may also lead to delays while differences are worked out. Recall that teams differ in their mode of formation and in the extent to which there is the expectation of achieving consensus on major decisions. Many research possibilities exist for examining the extent to which the benefits of top management team disagreement outweigh the costs during the start-up phase:

1. How do previous relationships among team members affect roles within the team?

2. What are useful leadership styles for lead entrepreneurs? What are the contingency variables that bear upon their effectiveness?

3. How do roles within the entrepreneurial team change and what influences these changes?

4. How does heterogeneity in demographic background variables affect the functioning of entrepreneurial teams? How does heterogeneity in management style and personality types affect these teams?

5. How valuable (or dysfunctional) is consensus with regard to goals and strategic means during the start-up phase?

Relationships to Strategy and Structure

The members of the entrepreneurial team make the key decisions that shape the strategy and structure of the new firm. Their goals, their values, and their management styles will influence these decisions. The strategy adopted is likely to be built around their capabilities and what they do particularly well. These strategies are likely to be self-reinforcing, such that the initial strategy is likely to influence how the firm later evolves (Miles and Snow, 1978). As Kimberly (1979) noted, just as with a child, the initial conditions of the firm may affect its later development.

Hambrick and Mason (1984) suggest that the background characteristics of top management teams, both observable (such as age, experience, and education) and not observable (such as psychological characteristics) ones, are likely to influence strategic choices.

Little research has been done on how the characteristics of the entrepreneurial team may affect the strategy and structure of the young firm, either initially or later. The most notable work has been that by Boeker (1989), who examined initial and subsequent strategies for semiconductor firms. He found that firms which adopted an initial dominant strategy (one that placed strong emphasis upon a particular way of competing) were less likely to change than those which competed in a greater variety of ways. He also found that firms whose dominant strategies were consistent with the relative influence of particular functional groups (such as a first-mover strategy and high influence of R&D) were less likely to change. Thus, it appears that, under some conditions, initial strategies have lasting effects, and their continuance is related to the influence of particular groups within the firm. Mintzberg and Waters (1982) tracked strategy over time in an entrepreneurial firm and found that the firmly held values of the family influenced the firm for decades and that later changes often could be traced to ideas which began to develop early in the firm's history.

What attributes of the entrepreneurial team may affect firm strategy? Most likely, the primary goals of the team members, particularly the extent to which they want to emphasize growth, have a substantial influence. It also seems likely that the primary functional experience of team members are related to the business strategy adopted. The backgrounds of the founders, including their technical competencies and the markets they know well, should influence the firm's search for opportunities. The strategies of the organizations the founders left, including the extent to which they emphasized differentiation versus cost leadership, may be reflected in the way the new firm competes. Personal inclinations toward innovativeness and risk-taking may be reflected in the extent to which the firm emphasizes new products and markets.

One of the major streams of research on new firms relates to decisions about structure and administrative systems, particularly the changes that are usually necessary as a firm grows (Churchill and Lewis, 1983; Stevenson et al., 1994). Growing firms usually must move toward greater delegation, more formal reporting relationships, and greater emphasis upon policies to guide decisions. These changes mean that members of the entrepreneurial team must adapt. Their roles change and they must learn to manage in different ways than when the firm was small. Only a little research has examined how the characteristics of the founding team may influence the initial administrative systems and the ability of the founders to adjust to the changes of growth. A longitudinal study of firms in Silicon Valley found that those whose founders had come from larger organizations (more than 500 employees) were more likely to enjoy substantial growth (Cooper and Bruno, 1977). The authors speculated that one reason may be that the founders of these firms had already learned to use more formal management methods in their prior organizations and were more likely to put more formal administrative systems in place in their new firms. This, in turn, may have enabled their firms to grow with fewer problems. However, these findings have not been replicated. A study of microcomputer software start-ups found no relationship between size of previous organization and new venture size (Teach et al., 1986).

No research has yet directly examined how the backgrounds of the founding team relate to the organizational structure and administrative systems initially put in place. It may be that those founders with more formal education in management or higher levels of management experience have a better understanding of how to install and use more complex administrative processes (Hambrick and Mason, 1984). Team members with more experience in larger organizations may have developed different management styles. These background characteristics may affect the kinds of structure and systems adopted for the new firm. Some research questions in this area include:

1. How is the initial strategy of the new firm related to the functional experience of the entrepreneurial team? To what extent are the personal values of the team members reflected in what the firm chooses to emphasize?

2. How is the initial strategy of the new firm related to the competitive strategy of the organizations that the founders left?

3. How is the new firm's organization structure related to the management experience or educational training of the members of the entrepreneurial team?

4. How are the formality and complexity of the firm's administrative systems related to the background of entrepreneurial team members? Do education in management and experience in larger firms lead to greater formality and complexity?

Influences of Team Makeup
on Stability and Firm Performance

When entrepreneurial teams are first formed, there may be a feeling that the marriage can last forever. However, the reality is that many teams break up. In talking about team stability, Timmons (1990) quoted an attorney who had dealt with many high-potential ventures, saying that, within the first five years, almost every new firm had lost at least one founder. Boyd and Gumpert (1983) found, in their sample of 156 company founders, that more than two-thirds of the founders starting with partners eventually dissolved ties. Interpersonal conflict among principals was the prime reason for dissolution. A study of 250 high-technology firms reported that 48 percent of the multiple founder firms that were four or more years old had experienced the departure of at least one founder (Cooper and Bruno, 1977).

Entrepreneurial teams can break up because of conflict or because one or more members find that the business no longer constitutes a good fit with their interests or talents. Sometimes personal events, such as divorce, marriage, or midlife crisis, cause team members to become less committed to the business. Sometimes outside investors or other team members will conclude that it is time for that person to go. O'Neal (1963) specifically examined factors that could lead to conflict and "squeeze-outs" among partners. These include power lust, dissension about relative contributions, irritation with an aging founder, conflicts of interest, and unexpected changes. The impact on the firm of such break-ups can be serious. Deep hostility can develop and disagreements can sap the company. Sometimes, the very future of the company can be in jeopardy (Schellenbarger, 1991; Thurston, 1986).

Team members can also leave because the growth of the firm or changes in strategy call for different skills than they possess. Growth often requires that the team members be able to manage in the context of larger, more complex, and more formal organizations. Tashakori (1980) concluded that most entrepreneurial owner-founders were not able to make the transition to more formal, professional styles of management. Roberts (1991) referred to "founder's disease," and noted that some entrepreneurs were inadequate managers from the start and others could manage the first stages competently but not later stages. Some entrepreneurs were effective managers but differed with their outside boards about the directions their firms should take and, because of the conflict, would then leave. However, a study of 155 fast-growing firms that had been listed on the *Inc.* 100 found the founder-managed firms were just as successful as the firms headed by professional managers who had been brought in (Willard et al., 1992; see also Daily and Dalton, 1992).

Entrepreneurial team members can also choose to cash out when the firm is acquired or goes public. Some find that they are most comfortable in identifying opportunities and starting firms, rather than in managing them after they have grown. One entrepreneur described himself to one of the authors as "like a starting pitcher, who needs to be replaced in about the fifth inning."

Most of the very limited literature on stability of founding teams is "wisdom-based," and provides advice on how teams might deal with conflict or establish "escape routes" while there is still universal good feeling. Some writings address the role of the board or outside advisers in dealing with conflict. Legal arrangements can be developed that provide incentives to stay, including forms of deferred compensation, the vesting of stock ownership over time, and agreements whereby a departing owner-manager must sell stock back at cost or book value (O'Neal, 1963; Thurston, 1986).

As noted earlier, heterogeneity in the makeup of top management teams and work groups may contribute to increased turnover. Whether heterogeneity affects the stability of entrepreneurial teams has not been examined to date. Mode of formation, that is, whether there is a clear lead entrepreneur as compared with a group who see themselves as equals, may also affect team stability, but no research has been done on this. It may also be that even or uneven distribution of rewards, including stock ownership and organizational power, affects whether a team stays together.

Whether team members choose to leave a venture may also depend upon their knowledge of employment alternatives and their perception of the cost of switching. Ventures located in geographic regions where there are complexes of similar firms, such as in Silicon Valley, may suffer more defections of team members. In these areas, team members may be aware of many employment opportunities, including other venture start-ups. They may perceive that the personal costs of switching, including moving expenses and having a spouse give up a job, are low.

Entrepreneurial team members make enormous commitments and are paid primarily in hope. Firms experiencing disappointing results, those missing their benchmarks, may have more trouble in maintaining morale and in keeping their founding team members. Research on groups shows that members of "successful" groups perceived their groups to be more attractive (Napier and Gershenfeld 1985, 95). It has been said that there is no deodorant like success. Team members are likely to be more willing to stay and work out problems if it appears that the vision which originally bound them together may be realized.

Research Questions

In the discussion of processes of team formation, factors were noted that may bear upon the stability of teams. It was questioned whether teams formed by clearly recognized lead entrepreneurs would be more stable because of less jockeying for power and whether those who had previously worked together in the same organization would be more stable because they previously had been able to assess each other and would already know how to work together. Other possible research questions relating to team stability include:

1. Are teams that worked together in previous organizations more stable? Are teams formed with family or friends more stable because of long-standing ties?

2. Are teams that are more homogeneous in background variables more stable?

3. Are teams of "equals" with equal distribution of power less stable?

4. Are teams characterized by great differences in stock ownership less stable (because of perceptions of unequal rewards)?

5. Are teams that start in a geographic complex of similar firms less stable (because of perceived low costs of switching)?

6. Are firms that have deferred compensation or stock ownership vested over time characterized by more stable teams?

7. Are firms with poor financial performance characterized by less stable teams?

8. Are firms with very high growth rates characterized by less stable teams (because the growth brings with it a need for new management skills)?

Team Makeup and Firm Performance

Entrepreneurial teams are at the center of the crucial activities of new firms. Therefore, one might expect their makeup and functioning to bear upon new venture performance. However, one should also recognize that many other factors also influence performance, including the environment, the financing available, and the strategy adopted. However, these factors are not unrelated to the team, which makes decisions about what markets to enter and how to compete. The team's characteristics may also influence success in raising capital.

The individual founder or the entrepreneurial team bring human capital to the new venture. This human capital can be general, useful across a wide range of opportunities, or it can be specific, such as a particular kind of business experience (Becker, 1975). One might expect that new firm performance will be a function of the general and specific human capital available to it. In new venture formation, each member brings certain educational experience, functional experience, and industry experience, all of which can be drawn upon as the new firm struggles to survive. Each member also has contacts so that larger teams may be able to develop more extensive networks with external suppliers of information and resources. However, much may depend upon the amount of diversity in the network and the extent to which there are ties to those who can supply needed resources (Aldrich and Zimmer, 1986).

A number of studies have looked at whether a relationship exists between the presence of a founding team and new venture performance. A survey article reported that, in four out of five studies, ventures started by teams did better than those started by single founders (Cooper and Gimeno, 1992).

Performance can, of course, be measured in different ways, including survival, various measures of growth and profitability, satisfaction, and (where available) stock market performance. One study considered the effect of different human and financial capital variables on both growth and survival. It found that ventures started by teams were more likely to grow, but not more likely to survive (Cooper et al., 1994). The authors reasoned that the greater human capital of founding teams contributed to the increased likelihood of growth for their ventures. They speculated that the probability of survival did not increase for these firms because of the high rate of team breakup, which often threatened the survival of these firms.

The relationship of size of founding team to venture performance has been examined in a number of studies. A survey article reported that six out of eight studies which examined number of founders reported that larger teams performed better (Cooper and Gimeno, 1992). Eisenhardt and Schoonhoven (1990) suggested that larger teams may accelerate decision-making. They noted that larger teams also permit more specialization in decision-making and provide more people to do the enormous work of getting a firm started.

What is the optimal size for an entrepreneurial team? Roberts reported that, with his large sample of MIT-related spin-offs, the larger the team, the better the performance (Roberts, 1970; Roberts, 1991). He reported that teams with cofounders behaved differently from the start with more capital and more of an orientation toward producing hardware. Later, they developed a stronger market orientation and did more follow-on financing. Teach et al. (1986) found a positive relationship between the size of the initial venture team and the size of the new firm at the time of their survey; however, they did not determine how much of this difference was due to initial size and how much to subsequent growth.

Larger teams permit more specialization but also involve more sets of relationships among team members. As Bird (1989) notes, larger teams present possibilities of coalitions and politics. Interpersonal relationships become more complex (growing geometrically), and the team takes on the characteristics of a small group, with pressures to conform, and so on.

The empirical research might be interpreted to suggest that entrepreneurs should always strive to start in teams and that larger teams are better than smaller ones. However, Vesper (1990) cautions against assuming that teams are always better. He notes that much depends upon the nature of the venture and the nature of the lead entrepreneur. Larger scale ventures often require a team from the start; however, some kinds of firms, such as artisan ventures, do not. Entrepreneurs who have previously been highly specialized are more likely to need complementary partners, whereas those with broad experience are less likely to need them. Teams should not be formed unless each member can make complementary contributions needed by the venture.

In interpreting the previous research, one always needs to be cautious in implying causality. Ventures started with teams appear, on average, to do better. However, in order to attract team members, they must show promise, and firms with larger teams probably must show even more promise. There must be enough prospects for growth and future income to support multiple founders—clearly a test that only more promising ventures will pass. A study of initial size of firms (not whether partners were present, per se) found that larger startups (eight or more employees) were more likely to be started by teams. The founders of these firms, compared with founders of smaller startups, brought more human capital to the process, with more education, more management experience, and more industry-specific experience. They were also more committed to economic goals for their businesses, such as wealth creation (Cooper et al., 1989). Therefore, firms started by entrepreneurial teams had many other things going for them also, including the characteristics of the lead entrepreneurs. Typical research questions in this area include:

1. How does heterogeneity in general human capital (education and functional experience) and heterogeneity in specific human capital (industry experience and startup experience) relate to new firm performance? How does heterogeneity relate to satisfaction?

2. How does team size relate to the networks utilized in the founding process? How does heterogeneity in background characteristics of team members relate to the networks utilized?

3. Controlling for industry and initial capital, how does team size relate to various measures of new venture performance, including survival, growth, profitability, and satisfaction?

4. Controlling for venture performance, how does team size relate to member satisfaction? How does it relate to team stability?

Conclusions

This review reinforces the conclusion that entrepreneurial teams are at the heart of any new venture. It also makes clear that there has been relatively little empirical research examining how teams are formed, how they function, whether the teams are stable, and how they influence organizational performance.

Many different theoretical frameworks can be drawn upon in examining entrepreneurial teams. Work on small group behavior is certainly relevant. So are concepts on interpersonal attractiveness, psychological contracts, organizational roles, organizational decision-making, network theory, and human capital. Bird noted that most research on entrepreneurial teams had been anecdotal and lacking in a theoretical base; her comments were published in 1989 and still seem applicable. Few topics in entrepreneurship research are so central and yet so under-researched. There are many opportunities to look forward to in future research that will enhance understanding of entrepreneurial teams.

REFERENCES

Aldrich, H., and C. Zimmer. 1986. Entrepreneurship through social networks. In D. L. Sexton and R. W. Smilor (eds.): *The Art and Science of Entrepreneurship*. Cambridge, MA: Ballinger, 3-23.

Bantel, K., and S. Jackson. 1989. Top management and innovations in banking: Does the composition of the top team make a difference? *Strategic Management Journal* 10:107-124.

Becker, G. S. 1975. *Human Capital*. New York: Columbia University Press.

Bird, B.J. 1989. *Entrepreneurial Behavior*. Glenview, IL: Scott, Foresman.

Boeker, W. 1989. Strategic change: The effects of founding and history. *Academy of Management Journal* 32:489-515.

Boyd, D.P., and D.E. Gumpert. 1983. Coping with entrepreneurial stress. *Harvard Business Review* March-April: 46-56.

Campion, M.A., G.J. Medsker, and A.C. Higgs. 1993. Relations between work group characteristics and effectiveness: Implications for designing effective work groups. *Personnel Psychology* 46:823-850.

Churchill, N.C., and V. L. Lewis. 1983. The five stages of small business growth. *Harvard Business Review* May-June: 30-40, 48-50.

Cooper, A.C. 1986. Entrepreneurship and high technology. In D.L. Sexton and R.W. Smilor (eds.): *The Art and Science of Entrepreneurship*. Cambridge, MA: Ballinger, 153-168.

Cooper, A.C., and A. Bruno. 1977. Success among high-technology firms. *Business Horizons* 20:16-22.

Cooper, A.C., and F.J. Gimeno. 1992. Entrepreneurs, processes of founding and new firm performance. In D.L. Sexton and J.D. Kasarda (eds.): *The State of the Art of Entrepreneurship*. Boston: PWS-Kent, 301-340.

Cooper, A.C., C.Y. Woo, and W.C. Dunkelberg. 1989. Entrepreneurship and the initial size of firms. *Journal of Business Venturing* 4(5):317-332.

Cooper, A.C., W.C. Dunkelberg, C.Y. Woo, and W.J. Dennis, Jr. 1990. *New Business in America: The Firms and Their Owners*. Washington, D.C.: National Foundation of Independent Businesses.

Cooper, A.C., F.J. Gimeno, and C.Y. Woo. 1994. Initial human and financial capital as predictors of new venture performance. *Journal of Business Venturing* 9:371-395.

Daily, C.M., and D.R. Dalton. 1992. Financial performance: Founder-managed versus professionally managed firms. *Journal of Small Business Management* 30(2):25-34.

Dollinger, M.J., C.M. Daily, and C.R. Schwenk. 1990. Top management team consensus and performance in small firms. Presented at the National Academy of Management meetings, San Francisco.

Eisenhardt, K.M. 1989. Making fast strategic decisions in high velocity environments. *Academy of Management Journal* 32:543-576.

Eisenhardt, K.M., and L.J. Bourgeois. 1988. Politics of strategic decision-making: Towards a mid-range theory. *Academy of Management Journal* 31:737-770.

Eisenhardt, K.M., and C.B. Schoonhoven. 1990. Organizational growth: Linking founding team, strategy, environment, and growth among U.S. semiconductor ventures, 1978-1988. *Administrative Science Quarterly* 35:504-529.

Guzzo, R.A., and M.W. Dickson. 1996. Teams in organizations: Recent research on performance and effectiveness. In J.T. Spence, J.M. Darley, and D. . Foss (eds.): *Annual Review of Psychology*. Palo Alto, CA: Annual Reviews, 307-338.

Hambrick, D.C. 1994. Top management groups: A conceptual integration and reconsideration of the "team" label. *Research in Organizational Behavior* 16:171-213.

Hambrick, D.C., and P.A. Mason. 1984. Upper echelons: The organization as a reflection of its top managers. *Academy of Management Review* 9:193-206.

Janis, I.L. 1982. *Victims of Groupthink*. Boston: Houghton Mifflin.

Kamm, J.B., and A.J. Nurick. 1993. The stages of team venture formation: A decision-making model. *Entrepreneurship Theory and Practice* 17(2):17-28.

Kamm, J.B., J.C. Shuman, J.A. Seeger, and A.J. Nurick. 1989. Are well-balanced teams more successful? In R.H. Brockhaus et al. (eds.): *Frontiers of Entrepreneurship Research*. Wellesley, MA: Babson College, 428-429.

Kets de Vries, M.F.R. 1993. The dynamics of family-controlled firms: The good news and the bad news. *Organizational Dynamics* Winter: 59-71.

Kimberly, J. 1979. Issues in the creation of organizations: Imitation, innovation and institutionalization. *Academy of Management Journal* 22:437-457.

Korsgaard, M.A., D.M. Schweiger, and H.J. Sapienza. 1995. Building commitment, attachment, and trust in strategic decision-making teams: The role of procedural justice. *Academy of Management Journal* 38:60-84.

Kriegel, R., and D. Brandt. 1996. *Sacred Cows Make the Best Burgers*. New York: Warner.

Miles, R.E., and C.C. Snow. 1978. *Organizational Strategy, Structure and Process*. New York: McGraw-Hill.

Miner, J.B. 1996. Evidence for the existence of a set of personality types, defined by psychological tests, that predict entrepreneurial success. In W.D. Bygrave et al. (eds.): *Frontiers of Entrepreneurship Research*. Wellesley, MA: Babson College.

Mintzberg, H., and J.A. Waters. 1982. Tracking strategy in an entrepreneurial firm. *Academy of Management Journal* 25(3):465-499.

Murray, A.I. 1989. Top management group heterogeneity and firm performance. *Strategic Management Journal* 10:125-141.

Napier, R.W., and M.K. Gershenfeld. 1985. *Groups: Theory and Experience*. New York: Houghton Mifflin.

O'Neal, F.H. 1963. Minority owners can avoid squeeze-outs. *Harvard Business Review* March-April: 150-160.

O'Reilly, C.A., D.F. Caldwell, and W.P. Barnett. 1989. Work group demography, social integration, and turnover. *Administrative Science Quarterly* 34:21-37.

Reynolds, P., and B. Miller. 1992. New firm gestation: Conception, birth, and implications for research. *Journal of Business Venturing* 7:405-417.

Roberts, E.B. 1970. Influences upon performance of new technical enterprises. In A. Cooper and J. Komives (eds.): *Technical Entrepreneurship: A Symposium*. Milwaukee: Center for Venture Management, 126-149.

Roberts, E.B. 1991. *Entrepreneurs in High Technology: Lessons from MIT and Beyond*. New York: Oxford University Press.

Roure, J.B., and M.A. Maidique. 1986. Linking prefunding factors and high-technology venture success: An exploratory study. *Journal of Business Venturing* 1:295-306.

Schellenbarger, S. 1991. Cutting losses when partners face a breakup. *Wall Street Journal* May 21: B1, B2.

Slevin, D.P. 1989. *The Whole Manager*. New York: American Management Association.

Slevin, D.P., and J.G. Covin. 1992. Creating and maintaining high performance teams. In D.L. Sexton and J. Kasarda (eds.): *The State of the Art of Entrepreneurship*. Boston, MA: PWS-Kent, 358-386.

Smith, K.A., K.G. Smith, J.D. Olian, H.P. Sims, D.P. O'Bannon, and J.J. Scully. 1994. Top management team demography and process: The role of social integration and communication. *Administrative Science Quarterly* 39:412-438.

Stevenson, H.H., M.J. Roberts, and H.I. Grousheck. 1994. *New Business Ventures and the Entrepreneur*. Burr Ridge, IL: Irwin.

Stolze, W.J. 1989. *Startup: An Entrepreneur's Guide to Launching and Managing a New Venture*. Rochester, NY: Rock Beach Press.

Tashakori, M. 1980. *Management Succession: From the Owner-Founder to the Professional Manager*. New York: Praeger.

Teach, R.D., F.A. Tarpley, and R.G. Schwartz. 1986. Software venture teams. In R. Ronstadt et al. (eds.): *Frontiers of Entrepreneurship Research*. Wellesley, MA: Babson College, 546-562.

Thurston, P. 1986. When partners fall out. *Harvard Business Review* November-December: 24-34.

Timmons, J.A. 1990. *New Venture Creation*. Homewood, IL: Irwin.

Tsui, A., and C.A. O'Reilly. 1989. Beyond simple demographic effects: The importance of relational demography in superior-subordinate dyads. *Academy of Management Journal* 32:402-423.

Vesper, K.H. 1990. *New Venture Strategies*. Englewood Cliffs, NJ: Prentice Hall.

Watson, W.E., L.D. Ponthieu, and J.W. Critelli. 1995. Team interpersonal process effectiveness in venture partnerships and its connection to perceived success. *Journal of Business Venturing* 10:393-411.

Wiersema, M.F., and A. Bird. 1993. Organizational demography in Japanese firms: Group heterogeneity, individual dissimilarity, and top management team turnover. *Academy of Management Journal* 36:996-1025.

Willard, G.E., D.A. Krueger, and H.R. Freeser. 1992. In order to grow, must the founder go? A comparison of performance between founder and non-founder managed high-growth manufacturing firms. *Journal of Business Venturing* 7(3):181-194.

Zenger, T.R., and B.S. Lawrence. 1989. Organizational demography: The differential effects of age and tenure distributions on technical communication. *Academy of Management Journal* 32:353-376.

CHAPTER 7

Choice of Organizational Mode in New Business Development: Theory and Propositions

S. VENKATARAMAN

AND

IAN C. MACMILLAN

I N THIS CHAPTER ISSUES PERTINENT TO THE CHOICE of the mode of organization in creating and developing a new business—either as a de novo start-up or in an existing corporation—are discussed. Typically, entrepreneurs have what they believe to be an insight: they develop a new and functional prototype of a product that they believe is the answer to a long-standing need in the marketplace. If they can only develop, produce, and distribute this product, they believe it will be a source of much profit.

In this scenario the entrepreneur never really owns or controls most of the resources required to develop the market and establish the value-chain infrastructure. Most of these resources have to come from other individuals and institutions. Thus, the entrepreneur has to assemble, organize and execute the market development and value-chain infrastructure before he or she can realize the promised profit and prove that his or her conjecture is indeed an "insight."

A critical decision the entrepreneur faces is how to "organize" the development and execution of the new business. Stated differently, when several different alternative institutional arrangements can be used to pursue a profitable opportunity, why do entrepreneurs (either independent or corporate) choose a particular mode? What are the consequences of this choice on the distribution of risks and rewards among the different stakeholders to the new venture? This chapter seeks to understand the answers to the above questions, in particular the emphasis is on the choice of organizational mode in new business development.

We wish to thank Thomas Butler for his research assistance and literature review for this chapter.

Much emphasis has been placed on the choice of organizational mode in influencing performance in the strategy literature. The choice of mode is considered important for improving efficiencies (Coase, 1937; Williamson, 1975, 1985; Hennart, 1988; Mosakowski, 1991); reducing risk (Harrigan, 1986; Kogut, 1988; Mosakowski, 1991); improving competitive positioning (Borys and Jemison, 1989; Harrigan, 1986; Kogut, 1988; Venkatraman et al., 1994); improving complementary synergies (Borys and Jemison, 1989; Harrigan, 1986; Kogut, 1988); and finally, influencing performance (McGee et al., 1995). Though the broader literature in management has emphasized alternative organizational modes, entrepreneurship literature has virtually ignored, with very few exceptions (McGee et al., 1995; Mosakowski, 1991; Shan, 1990), the question of choice among available alternatives.

It is implicitly assumed that most (if not all) new business creation occurs within a hierarchical framework (either as a de novo start-up or as a new entity within an existing corporate body). Even if this were empirically true (for which there is no systematic, demonstrated evidence, although casual observation seems to suggest this fact), conceptually, a hierarchy is just one mode among several alternatives. Thus, it begs the theoretical question as to why this mode is the predominant one observed in practice. At a more general level, a theoretical understanding is needed for explaining why a particular mode is the optimal one in a given context. In the entrepreneurship literature, these questions have not been answered satisfactorily, and yet these fundamental questions have significant implications not only for the generation of wealth (private and social) but more importantly for the distribution of this wealth and the distribution of the risk attached to new business creation. Thus, the choice of mode may be a very fruitful area for further research within the entrepreneurship literature.

Lacking significant literature or empirical evidence in the domain of start-ups or entrepreneurship, the principal theories on organization modes in this chapter are reviewed and propositions for future empirical research are presented.

Alternative Modes

New businesses may be developed through three distinct modes:

❖ Internal development (where the value-chain and the market are largely developed using the hierarchical form of organization).

❖ Purchase of the entire value-chain necessary to exploit a profitable market opportunity (acquisition or merger mode).

❖ Some cooperative arrangements (where the value-chain and/or the market are developed through a joint-venture or a strategic alliance or a franchising/licensing arrangement between two or more parties).

Acquisitions, joint ventures, and franchising/licensing arrangements are more formal modes governed by legal requirements, while strategic alliances are more informal and more easy to create and dissolve. Table 7.1 on pp. 160–161 lays out the alternative modes in greater detail.

Theoretical Explanations

Several different theoretical approaches exist for explaining the motivations and for choice of a particular mode. Two of these approaches are efficiency-based and emphasize the governance aspects of pursuing an opportunity: transaction cost theory and agency theory. Two of the explanations emerge from the strategic management literature and focus, respectively, on competitive positioning and resource/capability base in pursuing an opportunity. A final explanation rests on sociological foundations and emphasizes imitative behavior on the part of entrepreneurs and firms in pursuing activities that are inherently complex, ambiguous, and have uncertain outcomes.

Efficiency Theories

Transaction Cost Theory

The central argument of the transaction cost theory is that the choice of a mode of organization to carry out any economic activity is a function of the transaction costs in carrying out that activity. Thus, if an entrepreneur or firm does not own or control all of the resources necessary to pursue an opportunity and must deal with other resource controllers in order to have access to all the required resources, according to the theory, the pursuit of the opportunity can be organized in any of several alternative ways. The theory posits that, other things being equal, the entrepreneur will choose that mode that minimizes transaction costs in dealing with all other resource controllers in the process of pursuing the opportunity (Williamson, 1985).

Transaction costs are costs of contracting with other resource suppliers. Thus they include writing, negotiating, monitoring, safe-guarding, and enforcing contracts and settling disputes between parties.

In the context of new business development, transaction cost theory draws attention to three critical variables that may influence the transaction costs:

❖ Level of uncertainty involved in the development of the new business.

❖ Level of information asymmetry between the focal entrepreneur or firm and the different resource suppliers.

❖ Specificity of the investments required to develop the new business opportunity.

The theory predicts that the higher the level of uncertainty, the greater the information asymmetry between resource exchangers, and the greater the specificity of investments required, the higher the likelihood of a hierarchical mode in pursuing the opportunity (Kogut, 1988; Hennart, 1988). Thus, in such instances, internal development is the preferred mode. Such a mode would minimize transaction costs. Alternatively, the lower the uncertainty, the lower the information asymmetries, and the greater the fungibility of investments required, the greater the likelihood of using more cooperative arrangements in the development of the business opportunity.

Agency Theory

Like transaction cost theory, agency theory also emphasizes the governance aspects of organizational mode. The central argument of agency theory is that the choice of mode of organization to carry out any economic activity is a function of the monitoring costs involved in the particular mode to carry out that activity (Pratt and Zeckhauser, 1985). Monitoring costs arise whenever the pursuit of a business opportunity involves a division of labor with some individuals being principals (e.g., the entrepreneur or the venture capitalist) and others acting as the agents of these principals (e.g., the employees or the entrepreneur as the agent of the venture capitalist). To the extent the interests of the principals and agents are in conflict, they influence the level of monitoring costs (Jensen and Meckling, 1976).

Virtually all business start-ups and activities involve team effort. As Alchian and Demsetz (1972, 779) describe, team production uses several types of resources and "the product is not the sum of separable outputs of each cooperating resource." New business start-ups typically bring together people and institutions in joint-production situations, where people do not have a history or repeated transactions and lack knowledge about each other's preferences and motivations. Therefore, "absent trust, resources must be invested to create forms of control other than social control" (McGrath et al., 1994, 357). Investments must also be made in monitoring and evaluating effort and performance, as well as in establishing sanctions and incentives. Often, in joint production the marginal contributions of the team members cannot be separated. Further, the efforts of the individuals involved directly to the outcomes of the joint effort are difficult to relate. To the extent such a metering problem (Alchian and Demsetz, 1972) exists, agency costs arise. In such instances those modes that aid efficient monitoring, in order to align the interests of the agent with that of the principal, is preferred. Thus, agency theory would predict that hierarchical modes would be preferred in instances where effort is unobservable and disaggregating performance on the basis of individual effort is difficult. In such cases internal development or acquisition would be preferred to cooperative arrangements because such modes allow a more direct supervision and monitoring of agent activities.

Alternatively, when either effort or performance contribution can be easily measured, more cooperative arrangements may prove to be the efficient modes.

Theories of Strategic Choice

In contrast to transaction cost and agency theories, which emphasize the efficiency aspects of the choice of mode, the next two theories emphasize the strategic aspects of the choice of mode. These two viewpoints come from the strategic management literature. The first emphasizes the competitive positioning aspects of a particular mode, while the second emphasizes the appropriability (i.e., the ease with which competitors can imitate or acquire) aspects of core competencies and capabilities in the choice of a mode.

Competitive Positioning Theory

Competitive positioning theory seeks to maximize market power. The central argument of this viewpoint is that the choice of mode is a function of the trade-off between the speed and cost of entry into a market. Those modes that optimize on this trade-off in the process of creating a new business, will be preferred to those that do not.

Unlike the transaction cost theory and the agency theory, the competitive positioning theory considers the total cost (production and transaction) in the choice of the mode (Kogut, 1988). Thus, entrepreneurs may be willing to incur higher transaction costs in the short run if a particular mode allows the entrepreneur early entry into an opportunity or if the entrepreneur can economize on other costs (such as manufacturing and distribution costs). Critical to this view is the ability to enter markets early and cheaply by exploiting certain synergies that may be available by using cooperative arrangements in the pursuit of an opportunity. Thus, an entrepreneur may consider an alliance or joint venture, even if these modes involve elaborate and costly monitoring procedures. But if the entrepreneur believes that such arrangements will result in first-mover advantage leading to absolute cost advantage or differentiation advantage with future pricing power, then he or she will be willing to sacrifice short-term transaction cost disadvantages (McGee et al., 1995).

If the uncertainties involved in the new business creation is high and the risk of loss significant, competitive positioning theory allows the early investment in the new business to be viewed within a "real options" framework. The investments made by the entrepreneur early on in the development of the venture may be considered as the price of purchasing an option to expand in the future. Once the uncertainty surrounding the new idea improves, the entrepreneur is able to make the subsequent investments—that is, exercise the option to expand—more cheaply and more quickly than those who have not yet made the investments in the opportunity.

Thus, when the uncertainties surrounding a new business development are high and the risk of loss significant, the real options framework would predict that the entrepreneur would prefer the mode that simultaneously maximizes speed of entry, preserves the right to expand if conditions prove favorable, and minimizes exit costs if conditions prove unfavorable. Thus, strategic alliances, joint ventures, and franchising/licensing may be attractive alternatives because they allow risk-sharing, quick entry, and easier dissolution if unsuccessful, relative to wholly owned activities (Kogut, 1988). Often, such modes also allow one of the parties the option of purchasing the rights to the new business at a future date (Kogut, 1988; Shan, 1990).

Appropriability Regime Theory

The appropriability regime theory (Teece, 1987) focuses attention on an entirely different dimension not considered by any of the theories discussed above, namely, the quality and durability of the insulation for the core knowledge base and capabilities of the entrepreneur or the firm. According to this viewpoint the choice of a mode is a function of the trade-off between exploiting synergies present among different resource suppliers and protecting one's own core capabilities and knowledge from leakage to these resource suppliers. When the isolating mechanisms are relatively strong, the choice of mode swings in favor of exploiting synergies with other resource suppliers. Alternatively, when the isolating mechanisms are weak, the trade-off swings in favor of protecting one's own core capabilities and knowledge at the expense of synergies.

The appropriability regime concept falls within the domain of the "resource based" view of the firm (Penrose, 1959; Wernerfelt, 1994). Under this view the central purpose of the firm is to match rare and inimitable company resources and capabilities with market opportunities to create advantages vis-à-vis competitors, which in turn will allow the entrepreneur or the firm above-normal returns. To the extent the resources and capabilities of the firm increase in value when combined with the resources and capabilities of other resource suppliers, there is a strong incentive to exploit such synergies in developing a new business. On the other hand, to the extent the value of the current capabilities and knowledge are eroded or destroyed by collaborating with other resource suppliers, through the leakage of such capabilities across the firm boundaries, the incentive to develop the new business in-house or through internal development is enhanced.

Thus, when competitive insulation is weak, more hierarchical modes are preferred, and when competitive insulation is strong, more cooperative arrangements may be preferred. Competitive insulation comes primarily from the rarity, inimitability, and isolating mechanisms surrounding the accumulated resources, capabilities, and knowledge of the firm or entrepreneur (Barney, 1991; Rumelt, 1984, 1987; and Teece, 1987).

Sociological Theory

Although there may be several different viewpoints within this domain (Oliver, 1990), this paper emphasizes one prominent theory, namely, mimetic isomorphism theory (DiMaggio and Powell, 1983).

Mimetic Isomorphism

Mimetic isomorphism places less emphasis on either efficiency or rational choice as a basis for observed regularities in the economy. Choice is influenced more by imitative behavior and the need for imitation, especially when the connection between actions and outcomes are tenuous. This imitative effect is noted when firms or entrepreneurs model their behavior after firms perceived to be similar or in their peer group (Brozen, 1951; Williamson, 1965).

Imitative behavior is assumed to economize on the costs of decision-making in a world of uncertainty and ambiguity (DiMaggio and Powell, 1983; March and Olsen, 1976). When entrepreneurs face modes with uncertain trade-offs, such as trading off transaction costs against production costs, speed against cost, and synergy against leakage of critical knowledge, imitating others becomes an attractive alternative. When one cannot clearly attribute superior performance to a particular mode, imitation presents a solution with little risk. Porter (1980) even goes to the extent of arguing that under such conditions a firm may be better off making a mimetic move, even if the move turns out to be wrong, because if the manager deviates from the prevailing industry trend and is then proved wrong, there are negative consequences for his or her career. An unwise imitative move, however, is apt to be overlooked, as long as everybody else is also pursuing it. Thus, modes take on a bandwagon pattern. In practice, we have waves of acquisitions, alliances, or new corporate ventures. In summary, mimetic isomorphism theory would predict that the choice of a mode is a function of what one's neighboring firm or reference group does or what the industry norm dictates.

Synthesis

Each of the above theories draws attention to one or two critical attributes for the choice of mode. While each theory is well-developed and consistent within its own argument, each theory often highlights one facet of choice while ignoring others. The resulting predictive power has often been limited, as evidenced by empirical studies. It is our belief that in different contexts different issues are important, and it is useful to consider these contexts in determining the optimal or most likely mode. Thus, in some instances transaction costs may be important, while in others speed of entry may be important. Ignoring the context of choice leaves out a critical variable in the entrepreneur's decision situation, which often involve trade-offs between cost, speed and insulation rather than a single dimension, such as cost or speed.

In the following section the above theories are synthesized, three critical variables in the decision situation of the entrepreneur are isolated, and a typology is developed consisting of eight contexts, for which one can identify the most likely mode in the given context. From the above theories we have chosen only three variables (which we believe are the central and significant variables) for the sake of simplicity and conceptual clarity:

❖ *Level of uncertainty surrounding the new business development.* New businesses may be categorized as high- or low-risk enterprises, depending on the level of uncertainty surrounding critical aspects of the business, such as the level of information and knowledge about customer preferences, future trends, technological standards, production processes, competitive terrain, and a host of other key factors.

❖ *Metering problem surrounding the effort and performance of key resource exchangers or principal and agents involved in the development of the business opportunity.* Recall that both transaction cost theory and agency theory depend fundamentally on the ability to detect and eliminate opportunistic behavior, and a key aspect of this ability is the ease of measuring effort and performance. Thus, activities in the business development process may be categorized on the basis of the ease with which such activities lend themselves to measurement, both for effort and for marginal product of each resource or team member. This is the metering problem (Alchian and Demsetz, 1972).

❖ *Level of insulation (or vulnerability to leakage) surrounding core technologies or capabilities of the focal entrepreneur or firm.* This construct includes tangible and intangible resources and capabilities and is measured by the quality of isolating mechanisms surrounding the core technologies, processes and routines, information, knowledge, and other critical resources.

Each variable is treated as dichotomous rather than continuous to aid conceptual clarity. Thus, Table 7.1 on pp. 160–161 lists eight distinct contexts on the basis of differences in each of the three variables and shows the particular characteristic of each context and the most likely mode for that context. As indicated previously, each of these variables has a significant impact on the choice of mode. Thus, by combining the critical variables from the significant theories and presenting them in a multidimensional framework, one is able to obtain greater insights and a more fine grained prediction about choice of modes. Although, the simplicity of the individual theories has been sacrificed, the trade-off is the greater generality in prediction and application.

Table 7.1 (pp. 160–161) offers eight propositions, consistent with eight different contexts. The proposition in the first row represents a situation in which the uncertainty of the new business development is relatively low, the metering problem is relatively high, and insulation for critical resources and capabilities is low. It is proposed that the most likely mode in this situation is a hierarchical mode. Thus, internal development or acquisition would be preferred in this context.

The existence of metering problem requires close monitoring and supervision of agents, thus suggesting a hierarchical mode. The lack of strong isolating mechanisms reduces the incentive for cooperative arrangements as critical information, knowledge, and processes are susceptible to permeate the borders of the firm and leak to the collaborator. Finally, since uncertainty is low, key players in the industry share good information and knowledge about many aspects of the business, including such trends as customer preferences, technology trends, and key success factors. Hence, competitive speed is a serious threat in this context. If the entrepreneur does not have the capacity to act with speed with the existing resources at hand, he or she is most likely to consider acquiring wholly the infrastructure required to maximize speed and internalize the acquired asset or resource. Thus, the most likely mode adopted for new business development in this context would probably be internal development or acquisition. As a corollary, it is posited that performance of entrepreneurs using other modes will be inferior to the performance of entrepreneurs using internal development or acquisition in this context.

Applying similar reasoning propositions for each of the remaining seven contexts may be developed. These propositions are listed in the first column of Table 7.1. To take another example, in the situation where uncertainty is high, metering problem is high, and insulation is weak, it is predicted that the most likely modes are acquisition or a joint venture with the option to acquire. As discussed before, since the metering problem is high and insulation is weak, a mode that simultaneously allows close monitoring and affords good protection from leakage is preferred. Since uncertainty is high, there is a need to protect downside risk and exposure. Therefore, exit costs and sharing of risks are desirable properties. Thus, if the entrepreneur has the resources to fully develop the opportunity, then internal development is the most likely choice. If the firm or entrepreneur lacks the slack resources, the entrepreneur may attempt to reduce the risk by making appropriate acquisition, or share the risk by having an equal joint venture, but with an option to acquire so that the metering

TABLE 7.1
Determinants of Alternative Modes: Propositions

Variable Proposition	Uncertainty	Metering Problem	Insulation of Core Capabilities
Prefer: Hierarchy Most likely modes: internal development or acquisition	Low Risks: Competition Goals: Maximum entry speed	High Inefficiencies Minimum transaction costs and total costs	Weak Leakage Maximum reputation, maximum protection
Prefer: Cooperative arrangement Most likely mode: Franchising/licensing	Low Risks: Competition Goals: Maximum speed	Low — Minimum total costs	Weak Leakage Maximum reputation and protection
Prefer: Hierarchy Most likely modes: Internal development/acquisition or joint venture with option to acquire	High Risks: Loss exposure, wrong standards Goals: Risk-sharing, minimum exit costs	High Inefficiencies Minimum transaction costs and total costs	Weak Leakage Maximum protection and reputation
Prefer: Hierarchy Most likely modes: Internal development/acquisition	High Risks: Loss exposure, wrong standards	Low —	Weak Leakage Maximum protection
Prefer: Hierarchy Most likely modes: Internal development or, if resource constraints, franchising/ licensing	Low Risks: Competition Goals: Maximum entry speed	High Inefficiencies Minimum transaction costs and total costs	Strong Resource constraint Maximum growth and synergies
Prefer: Cooperative arrangement Most likely modes: Strategic alliance	Low — Risks: Competition Goals: Maximum entry speed	Low — Minimum total costs	Strong Resource constraint Maximum growth and synergies

TABLE 7.1 CONTINUED
Determinants of Alternative Modes: Propositions

Variable Proposition	Uncertainty	Metering Problem	Insulation of Core Capabilities
Prefer: Cooperative arrangement	High	High	Strong
Most likely mode: Equal joint venture	Risks: Loss exposure, wrong standards Goals: risk-sharing, minimum exit costs	Inefficiencies Minimum transaction costs and total costs	Resource constraint Maximum growth and synergies
Prefer: Cooperative arrangement	High	Low	Strong
Most likely mode: Unequal joint ventures	Risks: Loss exposure, wrong standards Goals: Risk-sharing, minimum exit costs	— Minimum total costs	Resource constraint Maximum growth and synergies

problem is eventually resolved. The option to acquire or abandon the joint venture minimizes exit costs by reducing the investment in elaborate hierarchical systems even before good information is available about the opportunity. In this context we predict that the most likely modes are internal development (if slack exists), acquisition, or joint venture with option to acquire. As a corollary, we expect entrepreneurs not making such choices to have inferior performance relative to those who make the predicted choices.

In a similar vein, take the context where uncertainty is low, the metering problem is high, and insulation is strong. Here, it would be predicted that franchising/licensing, or if resource constraint does not exist, internal development are the most likely modes. Since uncertainty is low, speed of entry and development is essential, thus suggesting some form of cooperative arrangement. Since insulation is strong, there is incentive to maximize growth and synergies in order to fully exploit the market opportunity, again suggesting cooperative development. However, the metering problem eliminates close collaboration with third parties, since disputes are likely to arise about marginal contributions as well as sharing of risk and rewards. Hence, close interorganizational relationships, such as joint ventures or strategic alliances, are eliminated. In such instances, franchising and licensing offer the best of both worlds, where the institutional mechanism offers a way out of the metering problem, while at the same time maximizing growth potential. In this instance the metering problem is shifted to a third party (the franchisee) who may be more capable of solving the problem. The focal entrepreneur or firm can concentrate on market development and growth. If resources are not a constraint, internal development is also feasible in this context.

In the context where uncertainty is low, the metering problem is low, and insulation is strong, the trade-offs are between maximizing growth and maximizing speed of entry and development. Since the metering problem does not exist and since insulation is strong, the situation calls for cooperative arrangement in order to quickly and effectively exploit the market opportunity. However, joint ventures are ruled out because they require elaborate monitoring, supervising, and dispute resolution systems, which are not only inappropriate if the metering problem is low but also ineffective because speed and the ability to quickly dismantle the structure does not exist. Strategic alliance appears to be the most likely mode in this context. As a corollary, entrepreneurs or firms using other modes will have inferior performance.

As a final example, in the context where uncertainty is high, the metering problem is high, and insulation is strong, the most likely mode is an equal joint venture. As a corollary, entrepreneurs or firms using other modes will have inferior performance relative to those who adopt this mode. Since uncertainty is high, the chosen mode must allow risk-sharing and minimize exit costs. Hence, there are weak incentives for internal development and acquisition. However, since the metering problem is high, strategic alliance is also not indicated in this context. Further, given the level of uncertainty, a joint venture is more feasible than franchising/licensing arrangement. Franchisees may not have the capacity to share in the risks involved; even if they carried the risk they may charge a higher premium as compensation than a joint-venture partner would. In a joint venture both parties have knowledge of performance of the organization, and this allows both of them to share equitably in the risk and reward of the new business enterprise. On the other hand, in the franchisee system, there is information asymmetry between the franchisor and franchisee (because the franchisee does not have the performance information of the franchisor). There is no way for the franchisee to detect if the risk and reward are being shared equitably. As a result, the premium for risk is likely to be higher in this case than in a joint venture; therefore, the joint venture is likely to be a more efficient mode in this context. Given the high level of risk and metering problem, we expect an equal joint venture to be more stable and more easy to establish than an unequal joint venture.

In summary, one of the primary challenges facing a new entrepreneur is the creation and development of the functional competencies and infrastructure required to develop, manufacture, market, distribute, and service the product. The focus naturally centers upon the transactional environment of the entrepreneur. The required task for the entrepreneur is to organize each activity within the appropriate mode from myriad choices. In this chapter a framework has been offered, based on extant theories, within which to make these choices.

Conclusions

Economists have long claimed that when an innovation occurs, the innovating entrepreneur must bear all of the risks associated with the creation and early development of the business. Thus, the firm must vertically integrate (that is, choose internal development as the organization mode) from the production of raw materials to the final distribution (Smith, 1937; Stigler, 1951). This claim is made because the market is not large enough at the early stages to provide incentives for other firms or entrepreneurs to specialize in the intermediate activities in the value chain. Since division of labor is limited by the size of the market, most new business ideas are frequently implemented through the creation of a new firm (Stigler, 1951).

The preceding argument that the innovating firm must vertically integrate in all stages of the value chain would seem to hold primarily in situations of complete and radical innovation of the "creative destruction" variety. In such instances none of the existing economic or business infrastructure may be useful. To the extent some infrastructure already exists in the economy to develop the new product and new market, other modes involving more cooperative arrangements must be feasible.

Even here other scholars would argue that cooperative arrangements are difficult to accomplish for a new entrepreneur. The process of bringing into existence products and markets that currently do not exist implies that much of the information required by potential stakeholders—information such as technology, price, quantity, tastes, supplier networks, distributor networks, and strategy, among others—are not reliably available. The entrepreneur must engage in relationships with others who do not share the same "insight." The entrepreneur almost always has more information about the true qualities of the project and his or her abilities than any of the other parties. Because of this natural information asymmetry, neither buyers nor suppliers may be willing to make the necessary investments in specialized assets or formal cooperative arrangements to develop the business. Thus, there is a failure of markets.

Even if suppliers and other resource controllers were willing to overlook the uncertainty or to make the specialized investments with a due risk premium, there is the ever present danger of "opportunism" (Williamson, 1975), where the entrepreneur may not comply with contracts and agreements, for a variety of reasons. Once specialized investments are made, the entrepreneur can hold the other party "hostage" to drive more favorable bargains. Establishing cooperative relationships are difficult unless the entrepreneur is willing to make significant, irreversible, and credible commitments in the business. This drives up sunk costs and therefore downside risk.

However, organization theorists would argue that this is a highly undersocialized view of society, which does not take into account relations of trust and support networks built up over time by the entrepreneur (Granovetter, 1985). Indeed, evidence is slowly collecting to show that firms do engage in a wide variety of cooperative arrangements, including joint ventures and alliances with prior network firms and other incumbents in the industry, even in the early stages of the new firm (McGee et al., 1995; Mosakowski, 1991; Ring and Van de Ven, 1992, 1994; Shan, 1990). Such cooperative relationships based on trust and prior history of relationships do help to reduce the moral hazard problem alluded to by economists.

There is merit to both viewpoints. New firms seem to use far less of the cooperative arrangements available than do established organizations (casual observation suggests this). But it is also true that most entrepreneurs are rather well embedded in their social and economic network. They are not islands unto themselves as the more atomistic theories of economists would claim. Thus, we believe that there is a definite place for cooperative arrangements even in the life of a new firm.

For the scholarly field to understand the choice and determinants of different modes, there is no dearth of theories in this domain. The need of the hour is not more theories but high-quality empirical work in the area of mode choice in new business start-ups. The challenge facing us will be the operationalization of key theoretical constructs and obtaining good quality data.

REFERENCES

Alchian, A.A., and H. Demsetz. 1972. Production, information costs, and economic organization. *American Economic Review* 62:777-795.

Barney, J. 1991. Firm resources and sustained competitive advantage. *Journal of Management* 17(1):99-120.

Borys, B., and D.B. Jemison. 1989. Hybrid arrangements as strategic alliances: Theoretical issues in organizational combinations. *Academy of Management Review* 14(2):234-249.

Brozen, Y. 1951. Invention, innovation and imitation, *American Economic Review* 41:239-257.

Coase, R. 1937. The nature of the firm. *Journal Economica* 4:386-405.

DiMaggio, P.J., and W.W. Powell. 1983. The iron cage revisited: Instituional isomorphism and collective rationality in organizational fields. *American Sociological Review* 48:147-160.

Granovetter, M. 1985. Economic action and social structure: The problem of embeddedness. *American Journal of Sociology* 91:481-510.

Harrigan, K.R. 1986. *Managing for Joint Venture Success*. Lexington, MA: Lexington Books.

Harrigan, K.R. 1988. Joint ventures and competitive strategy. *Strategic Management Journal* 9:141-158.

Hennart, J.F. 1988. A transaction costs theory of equity joint ventures. *Strategic Management Journal* 9:361-374.

Hennart, J.F. 1991. The transaction costs theory of joint ventures: An empirical study of Japanese subsidiaries in the United States. *Management Science* 37(4):483-497.

Jensen, M., and W. Meckling. 1976. Theory of the firm: Managerial behavior, agency costs, and capital structure. *Journal of Financial Economics* 3:305-360.

Kogut, B. 1988. Joint ventures: Theoretical and empirical perspectives. *Strategic Management Journal* 9(4):319-332.

March, J.G., and J.P. Olsen. 1976. *Ambiguity and Choice in Organizations*. Bergen, Norway: Universitetsforlaget.

McGee, J.E., M.J. Dowling, and W.L. Megginson. 1995. Cooperative strategy and new venture performance: The role of business strategy and management experience. *Strategic Management Journal* 16:565-580.

McGrath, R.G., S. Venkataraman, and I.C. MacMillan. 1994. The advantage chain antecedents to rents from internal corporate ventures. *Journal of Business Venturing* 9:351-369.

Mosakowski, E. 1991. Organizational boundaries and economic performance: An empirical study of entrepreneurial computer firms. *Strategic Management Journal* 12:115-133.

Oliver, C. 1990. Determinants of interorganizational relationships: Integration and future directions. *Academy of Management Review* 15(2):241-265.

Penrose, E. 1959. *The Theory of the Growth of the Firm*. New York: John Wiley.

Porter, M.E. 1980. *Competitive Strategy*. New York: John Wiley.

Pratt. J.W., and R.J. Zeckhauser. 1985. Principals and agents: An overview. In J.W. Pratt. and R.J. Zeckhauser (eds.): *Principals and Agents: The Structure of Business*. Cambridge, MA: Harvard Business School Press, 1-35.

Ring, P.S., and A.H. Van de Ven. 1992. Structuring cooperative relationships between organizations. *Strategic Management Journal* 13(7):483-498

Ring, P.S., and A.H. Van de Ven. 1994. Development processes of cooperative interorganizational relationships. *Academy of Management Review* 19(1):90-118.

Rumelt R.P. 1984. Toward a strategic theory of the firm. In R. Lamb (ed.): *Competitive Strategic Management*. Englewood Cliffs, NJ: Prentice-Hall, 556-570.

Rumelt R.P. 1987. Theory, strategy and entrepreneurship. In D.J. Teece (ed.): *The Competitive Challenge*. New York: Ballinger, 137-158.

Shan, W. 1990. An empirical analysis of organizational strategies by entrepreneurial high technology firms. *Strategic Management Journal* 11:129-139.

Smith, A. 1937. *Wealth of Nations.* New York, Modern Library.

Stiegler, G. 1951. The division of labor is limited by the size of the market. *Journal of Political Economy* 59(3):185-193.

Teece, D.J. 1987. Profiting from technological innovation: Implications for integration, collaboration, licensing and public policy. In D.J. Teece (ed.): *The Competitive Challenge.* New York: Ballinger, 185-219.

Venkataraman, S., I.C. MacMillan, and R.G. McGrath. 1992. Progress in research on corporate venturing. In D.L. Sexton and J. Kasarada (eds.): *The State of the Art in Entrepreneurship Research.* Boston, MA: PWS Kent, 487-519.

Venkatraman, N., L. Lawrence, and J. Koh. 1994. The adoption of corporate governance mechanisms: A test of competing diffusion models. *Management Science* 40(4):496-507.

Wernerfelt, B. 1994. A resource-based view of the firm. *Strategic Management Journal* 5:171-180.

Williamson, O.E. 1965. A dynamic theory of inter-firm behavior. *Quarterly Journal of Economics* 79(4):579-607.

Williamson, O.E. 1975. *Markets and Hierarchies: Analysis and Antitrust Implications.* New York: Basic Books.

Williamson, O.E. 1985. *The Economic Institutions of Capitalism.* New York: MacMillan.

CHAPTER 8

Births and Deaths
of New Firms

BRUCE A. KIRCHHOFF

AND

ZOLTAN J. ACS

T HE ABILITY OF THE U.S. ECONOMY TO maintain full employment while providing international leadership in high-technology markets during the latter part of the 1980s was in large part due to the entrepreneurial entry and subsequent growth of new small firms (Acs and Audretsch, 1992). The role of new firm entry (and exit) is the fundamental tool for restructuring the economy.

Over the last five years, research has demonstrated that, indeed, the economy is characterized by a dynamic process of new firm entry (birth) and existing firm exit (death) which significantly alters the nature of industrial competition (Baldwin, 1995; Audretsch, 1995). This turbulence is correlated with economic growth (Reynolds and Maki, 1990) and reaffirms the theories of Schumpeter (1934) that innovations brought into the market through new firm formation by the entrepreneur play a central role in economic development. These dynamics can be expanded to incorporate not only births and deaths but also such important phenomenon as growth, decline, and survival. This has become known in the literature as post-entry performance (Mata and Audretsch, 1995). Even in former socialist societies, the evidence is rapidly expanding to demonstrate the these dynamics are a major source of growth in economic activity, realignment of competitive market shares, and increases in productivity (Johnson and Loveman, 1995). For a review of the literature, see Harrison (1994), Admiraal (1996), Acs (1996), and Butler and Greene (Chapter 12 in this book).

The popular habit among researchers is to treat the terms "births" and "deaths" as a single phrase, as if the two phenomena are indelibly linked as in human life. However, it is not unusual for newly born firms to outlive their founders and for both young and old firms to experience death. Although statistics from many data sources show that younger firms are more prone to death, statistics from multiple sources also show that younger firms are more likely to grow and make significant contributions to economic growth, both individually and collectively. In fact, the early efforts in the U.S. to identify small firm contributions to job creation (Birch, 1979; Phillips and Kirchhoff, 1988; Dunne et al., 1988) subsumed the birth and growth phenomena into the small-firm class definition, thereby obscuring the major source of small-firm job creation. However, during the last decade much progress has been made in understanding the dynamics of competition in capitalist economies and developing dynamic research methods.

Researchers in Europe have assembled multiple data sources in an effort to measure births and deaths. These have various liabilities for dynamic measurements depending on their composition. Again, however, these studies show that birth, growth, decline, and death contribute to European economies much as they do to in the United States and Canada (Storey, 1994).

The similarities in findings and differences in research methodologies are the subject of this chapter with the overall objective of demonstrating that dynamics of birth, and death are the major factors shaping capitalist economies in the world. Because of the widely differing data sources and methodologies applied by the various researchers in the world, this analysis is divided by function. In the next section previous research and review issues of data collection are discussed. In the following section the sectoral, spatial, and temporal nature of births are examined. The analysis will begin with entry because that is where the empirical research leading to recognition of dynamics in markets was first developed. Next exits are explored.

Previous Research: Births and Deaths Date Issues

In the United States, the significant research has been based upon administrative data sources that entail both measurement and sampling errors. The Dun and Bradstreet files used by Birch and the Small Business Administration files are built upon data from a credit rating service that has difficulty keeping track of ownership changes (Kirchhoff, 1994). The Bureau of the Census's Longitudinal Establishment Data File on manufacturing draws its every five-year definition of the business population from business tax forms filed with the Internal Revenue Service, which lacks the information necessary to trace ownership changes. Best efforts by multiple statisticians have not been able to trace such changes among manufacturing firms with fewer than five employees (Dunne et al., 1988). This size class undoubtedly contains the newly born firms since 90 percent of all new firms formed in 1977–78 were formed with one to four employees (Kirchhoff, 1994). Although widely used and quoted in the media, neither source is a reliable base for birth and death measurements because of ownership changes. Recent work using the Michigan State Department of Labor files, which allow tracing of ownership changes, provides useful insight into the magnitude of the error contributed by ownership changes. Birth and growth of firms contribute much more to economic growth than previously thought (Jackson, 1995).

Research on dynamics requires firm-level data (micro-data) arranged in a longitudinal format. Only by tracing individual firms from birth to death and summing their actions into appropriate categories can one measure competitive dynamics. But the only source of business statistical data in the United States was produced by government agencies, and each of these agencies is constrained by federal laws from releasing any form of data that might disclose information about individual firms. Thus, micro-data was nonexistent.

Birch created a micro-data file in the 1970s by drawing data from the Dun and Bradstreet data files and assembling it into a longitudinal file for the period 1969 through 1976. Since Dun and Bradstreet collected this data to establish credit ratings of individual firms, they had business-owner permission to transfer this data to other businesses. Thus, the data was not confidential. Birch's (1979) analysis of this file showed that 81.5 percent of the net new jobs created during this seven-year period were attributable to small firms. This finding triggered a burst of conflicting views among economists and a bevy of database development activity by the Small Business Administration (SBA). In 1980, the SBA initiated two major database development efforts. First was a major project to replicate Birch's database by assembling the biennial Dun and Bradstreet Market Identifier files into a longitudinal data base. This project began with 1976 data and created new cross-sectional files every two years until 1990, when its funding was discontinued. The file, however, became a major source of information on firm dynamics beginning with the first publication in 1982 and continuing throughout the early 1990s. The second major project started in 1980 by the SBA was cofunded with the National Science Foundation. This project was designed to develop a longitudinal micro-data file on manufacturing firms with information drawn from the Census of Manufactures. This work evolved into the Census Bureau's Longitudinal Establishment Data File that has become a second source of birth and death dynamics, with results being reported beginning in 1987 (Kirchhoff, 1994).

The earliest measurement of births and deaths of firms were done by SBA with its database. SBA matched each biennial cross-section file with the previous file. If a firm was absent from the previous file and present in the current file, SBA assumed it was the birth of a new firm. A similar algorithm was used for deaths. The results of this analysis, expressed as percent of total number of firms, is shown in the first panel of Table 8.1, p. 170, along with the net change. The Census Bureau researchers used similar definitions to analyze the Longitudinal Establishment Data file. The results of this analysis (births and deaths of manufacturing establishments only) is shown in the second panel of Table 8.1. The census results are presented with the small firms included in the births and deaths and as an annual average so that it is "crudely" comparable to the SBA results.

TABLE 8.1
Estimated Average Annual Rates of Establishment Births and Deaths from Two U.S. Data Sources

	Births			Deaths	
Year	SBDB*	LED‡		SBDB	LED
[1972-77]		10.4%			9.0%
1977-78	12.9%			9.6%	
1979-80	10.3%			10.5%	
[1977-82]		10.3%			10.0%
1981-82	7.5%			5.7%	
1983-84	11.5%			8.7%	
Mean	**10.5%**	**10.4%**		**8.6%**	**9.5%**

* The Small Business Data Base is a biennial file so births and deaths are measured every two years. The numbers reported here are the biennial rates divided by two. These rates are measured for all businesses in all industries. Adapted from: Kirchhoff and Phillips, 1991.

‡The Longitudinal Establishment Data File measures births and deaths at five year intervals. The numbers reported here are the five year rates divided by five. These rates are for manufacturing establishments only. Adapted from: Dunne, T., Roberts, M.J., Samuelson, L. 1988. Patterns of firm entry and exit in U.S. manufacturing industries. Rand Journal of Economics 19:595-615.

Availability of these two data sources led to a much better understanding of the dynamics that created Birch's original findings. In fact, the emerging research directions today do not focus on the share of net new jobs generated by small versus large firms. Gradually, researchers have shifted their focus to measuring the economic contributions of firm formation, growth, decline and death. In other words, data has become available to begin testing Schumpeter's hypothesis about capitalist economies being driven by the dynamics of entrepreneurs.

The most recent addition to micro-data files has occurred in a more local fashion. In the late 1980s, the University of Michigan's Institute for Social Research was contracted to use the Michigan Employment Security Commission's data files to construct a longitudinal micro-data file of all businesses with paid employees in Michigan. This database includes an analytical procedure that adjusts for ownership changes, since firms that change owners must report this fact to the Michigan State Department of Labor, which is recorded in their files (Brown et al., 1990). Although this database consists of only one state, it has the advantage of more accurate measures of dynamics because it adjusts for ownership changes. The reason ownership changes are identifiable is that businesses pay unemployment insurance for their employees and payments are a function of employment history. Thus, when a business changes owners, the new owners must identify each employee as working essentially in the same job but for a new owner. The Michigan State Department of Labor uses the term "successor" to define the new owner, which is the term adopted here (Brown et al., 1990).

Canada has business registration and conducts annual censuses to produce a micro-data file. This micro-data file has existed in longitudinal form since 1970. Among the most noticeable differences between the Canadian and U.S. economies is that Canada's is more heavily vested in small firms (Picot et al., 1994). However, Baldwin's (1995, 117–152) extensive comparative analysis of Canadian and U.S. manufacturing suggests that both economies are very similar in the dynamic processes of competition.

Canadian researchers have recognized the full character of dynamics among manufacturing firms in their economy for many years. The reliability of their database allows linkage of firms across ownership changes and even provides detailed analysis across four-digit Standard Industrial Classification (SIC) codes. Births are recognized as the first appearance of an establishment owned by a firm never before seen in the industry under investigation They define a "greenfield entry" as one where the firm's first appearance coincides with the appearance of the first establishment. Greenfield entry, then, represents the formation of a new firm. Deaths are analogously defined. A closedown exit occurs when a firm no longer has a plant classified in manufacturing (Baldwin and Gorecki, 1990). The average rate of entry from 1970 through 1982 is 4.9 percent, with greenfield entry as the major contributor at 4.3 percent. The average rate of exit is 6.5 percent with closedown exits accounting for 5.3 percent of this total. Note that the net changes are negative because manufacturing is a declining industry (Baldwin and Gorecki, 1990, 28).

As evident by a comparison of Table 8.2 on p. 172 with Table 8.1, the birth and death rates in Canadian manufacturing are much smaller that those reported by Kirchhoff and Phillips (1991) and Dunne et al. (1988). Either there are substantially different dynamics in Canada, or the Canadian control for ownership changes has greatly improved the reliability of the entry and exit rates by lowering them to realistic values. The strikingly lower rate cannot be ignored. Hopefully, additional research will someday resolve this dilemma.

TABLE 8.2
Annual Firm Entry and Exit Rates in the Canadian Manufacturing Sector

Year	Greenfield Entry	Acquisition Entry	Total Entry	Closedown Exit	Divestiture Exit	Total Exit
1970-71	3.4%	0.8%	4.2%	5.6%	0.2%	5.8%
1971-72	4.6%	0.4%	5.1%	4.8%	1.4%	6.2%
1972-73	4.8%	0.2%	5.0%	5.5%	0.6%	6.1%
1973-74	5.7%	0.3%	6.0%	4.3%	0.9%	5.2%
1974-75	5.9%	0.3%	6.2%	6.3%	1.1%	7.4%
1975-76	3.4%	0.2%	3.6%	5.1%	0.6%	5.7%
1976-77	1.7%	0.4%	2.1%	5.3%	0.9%	6.2%
1977-78	4.4%	0.9%	5.3%	5.0%	1.7%	6.7%
1978-79	3.4%	1.1%	4.5%	3.8%	1.6%	5.4%
1979-80	4.7%	1.1%	5.8%	4.6%	1.8%	6.4%
1980-81	2.9%	9.0%	3.8%	5.5%	1.5%	7.0%
1981-82	6.3%	1.0%	7.3%	8.3%	1.8%	10.1%
Mean	**4.3%**	**0.6%**	**4.9%**	**5.3%**	**1.2%**	**6.5%**

Adapted from: Baldwin, J.R., and Gorecki, P.K. 1990. Firm entry and exit in the Canadian manufacturing sector, working paper of the Business and Labour Market Analysis Group, Analytical Studies Branch, Statistics Canada, p. 28.

The statistics on births and deaths in manufacturing noted above have been reproduced in a book by Baldwin (1995). This book, *The Dynamics of Industrial Competition,* provides the most comprehensive analysis to date of firm dynamics, along with a lengthy statistical analysis of all aspects of birth, growth, decline, and death of Canadian firms with a primary focus on market shares, productivity, and efficiency in manufacturing. However, he does not use cohort analysis over time as a method of expressing his results and therefore does not generate statistical analyses equivalent to that produced by Kirchhoff (1994) and Jackson (1995). Yet Baldwin's work provides a strong foundation for assessing dynamics and defining competition in capitalist economies.

Existing databases do not allow reliable identification of new firms and their founders. Survey data on small businesses have consistently demonstrated greater survival (fewer deaths) and growth rates of new firms than those reported in the statistical systems of either the United States or Canada (Kirchhoff, 1994, 161–169). As noted previously, the inherent problems of using administrative data to define births and deaths are unavoidable in U.S. government statistics. One difficulty is that firms with fewer than five employees are very difficult to track even with Canada's registration system (Baldwin, 1996). Yet identification of entrepreneurs and their firms at the earliest stage of business activity and tracing them through a period of time to determine success or failure is essential to understand the entrepreneurship process. Thus, reliable statistics on births and deaths must be obtained from other sources.

Such information requires data collection from the population as a whole. Two survey efforts have been initiated in the United States, the "nascent entrepreneur" research by Reynolds, (1995) and the Wells Fargo/National Federation of Independent Business Foundation's business entries and exits survey by Dennis (1996).

A unique effort to capture longitudinal behavior of "entrepreneurs" was carried out in Wisconsin by Reynolds and White (1993). Subsequently, a second study was carried out for the United States by Reynolds (1995). In both studies, a survey of a representative sample of the population was conducted to identify "nascent entrepreneurs," that is, persons who have taken steps toward starting a new business. In both surveys, the researchers defined nascent entrepreneurs as those respondents that stated they were starting a new business and reported initiating two or more business-forming activities within the last 12 months. From these surveys, the researchers learned that 3.9 percent of the U.S. adults (Reynolds, 1995) and 4.3 percent of Wisconsin adults (Reynolds and White, 1993) are nascent entrepreneurs.

The surveys also collected a great deal of demographic information about the nascent entrepreneurs. This demographic information promises to provide considerable information beyond that currently available because such information is simply not collected by the existing government statistical groups. Historically, government data collection focuses on business functions, not on the entrepreneurs.

Nonetheless, continuing the focus on the firm formation process, Reynolds's early U.S. sample revealed that one in every 25 adults was involved with trying to start a new business in 1994. His follow-up survey six to nine months later showed that 46 percent of these individuals actually launched these businesses. Based on these results, Reynolds estimates that approximately one in every 25 adults is currently involved with trying to start a new business and between 30 and 50 percent of these individuals will actually launch these businesses within the next six to nine months (Reynolds, 1995).

Based on these estimates, one can calculate the business formation rate for a population of 280 million people as 11.2 million nascent entrepreneurs who will create between 3.4 to 5.6 million businesses. Since *Enterprise Statistics* reports 4.7 million firms in existence in 1987, this 100 percent birth rate is obviously much greater than that measured by U.S. government statistical data. Also see Phillips and Dennis in this book (Chapter 15), who reach similar conclusions.

In sum, existing data sources, both government and nongovernment, indicate a high level of firm births and deaths. However, we do not have adequate data sources to measure the universe of firm births and deaths. We can only hope that better data sources become available over time. In the meantime, existing databases have yielded many rich results.

Sectoral, Spatial, and Temporal Variations in Births

Table 8.3 shows sectorial variations in new firm births for the United States between 1978 and 1980 and is part of a much larger table of data on more than 400 industry sectors. The value of the table is that it makes a direct comparison between entry and new firm formation at the sectoral level. The first column shows the number of jobs created in entrants for low- and high-entry industries. The second column shows the wide variation in new small firm entrant's share of total firm entry, from a low of 12 percent in radio and television to a high of 100 percent in the electrotyping and stereotyping sector. The third column of the table shows net entry, defined as the number of new entrants minus the number of exits between 1978 and 1980. The final column of the table shows the ranking of the sectors according to the net entry criterion.

This table demonstrates that there is only a modest association between the measure of net entry and the measure of employment in births. It emphasizes that wide sectoral variations exist in the number of new firms entering an industry, the employment in those new firms, and the proportion of all entrants which are new firms. This suggests that different explanations are needed to understand the factors which influence the number of entrants, the number of entrants which are new firms, and the impact which those new firms have upon incumbent firms in the industry.

There is wide variation in the rates of new firm formation across countries as well as within countries. These are reflected in both international differences and differences within the same country on a regional or local basis. In the United States in 1989, the number of new firms expressed as a percentage of the working population was 0.65 percent. In the European Economic Community, it was 0.97 percent, with the highest rate of new firm formation in the United Kingdom (1.59 percent); the lowest rate of new firm formation (0.33 percent) is in the Netherlands (van der Horst, 1992). The rankings, however, do not seem to exhibit any clear economic pattern. In other words, less developed countries do not have different new firm formation rates than larger firms.

Wide variations in the rate of new firm formation are also found within the same country. Reynolds and Maki (1990) found wide variation in new firm births in the United States for different units of analysis, including states and labor market areas. For the United Kingdom, using the definition of new firm formation as being a business

TABLE 8.3
Industry Births, the Small Firm Birth Share, and Net Entry Compared between High- and Low-Birth Industries United States 1978–80

Industry	Employment in entrants	Small firm entrants' share	Net entry 1978-80	(Rank)
Radio and TV communication equipment	152,524	0.1220	90	(47)
Miscellaneous plastic products	149,065	0.4672	687	(4)
Motor vehicle parts and accessories	120,334	0.1260	235	(17)
Electronic computing equipment	118,833	0.1964	224	(21)
Electronic components	92,107	0.3312	284	(12)
Machinery, except electrical	77,612	0.7501	1,904	(2)
Primary lead	210	0.1154	-3	(311)
Chewing and smoking tobacco	142	0.3067	-5	(234)
Millinery	112	0.8803	-24	(404)
Space propulsion units and parts	100	0.5856	-4	(317)
Chewing gum	90	1.0000	0	(277)
Electrotyping and stereotyping	16	1.0000	-12	(370)

Source: Acs, Z.J., and D.B. Audretsch. 1989. The social and economic consequences of entrepreneurship. In D.L. Sexton and J. Kasarda (eds.): *The State of the Art of Entrepreneurship*. Boston: PWS-Kent, 47-67.

newly registered for value-added tax, Keeble et al. (1993) found wide variation in the country. The new firm formation rates in the total economy between 1980 and 1990 varied widely in the United Kingdom. The rates of formation were virtually three times higher in some areas than in others. A strong clustering of high rates of new firm formation occurred in London and in the bordering counties of southeast England.

A wide spatial variation is found in the former West Germany. Fritsch (1992), using social insurance statistics, shows that the birth rate of new firms in 1986 varied markedly, but a spacial pattern seems to occur, with higher rates in the areas around the northern, western, and southern borders. Relatively lower rates were found in the east.

In the United Kingdom, data on company incorporations are available for more than 70 years, even though limited companies constituted less than 20 percent of businesses there in 1990. Immediately after World War II an increase in company registrations occurred; however, it fell back by 1948. From then on, it rose until 1964, when it fell again for a four-year period. In 1968 it began to rise again, peaking in 1973, then falling sharply in 1974, but rising in virtually all subsequent years.

The Theory of New Firm Births

The traditional view can be found in the literature of industrial organization. The prime focus of the industrial economist's attention is upon the pricing and output decisions of firms already in an industry, rather than upon new firms entering that industry. Economists identify at least five types of entry, only one of which involves starting a new firm. Why do firms enter an industry? A level of profits in excess of long-run equilibrium induces entry into the industry. The new firm provides an equilibrating function in the market, in that the level of prices and profits are restored to the long run competitive level. This is the traditional model of entry where entry in any industry is a function of the difference between expected post-entry level of profits minus the lung-run level of profit expected in the industry.

Little consensus has emerged in the literature on the importance of long-run profits on entry. The level of profits has been found to have only a weak positive impact on entry decisions. Geroski and Schwalback (1991) found a positive link between profits and entry in five out of six studies.

If our interest is in explaining the formation of new firms, as opposed to entrants, then as Acs and Audretsch (1992) have pointed out, there is little reason to assume that small firm entry is an exact replica of large firm entry.

A crude distinction can be made between the work of industrial economists and labor economists. While the industrial economist studies the exogenous firm, the labor economist examines new firm formation as a decision exercised by the individual (entrepreneur) in the context of the labor market. Thus, for the labor economist the focus shifts from an exogenous firm to individuals.

The labor market economists interested in new firm formation derive intellectual inspiration from the work of Knight (1921). Jovanovic (1982) and Holmes and Schmitz (1995), among others, have all reinterpreted Knights's theory of the decision confronting each economic agent to become either an employee in an incumbent enterprise or an entrepreneur, that is, start a new firm, in terms of a model of income choice. The income choice model states that the probability of an agent starting a new firm is a function of the expected profits accruing from such a new firm, minus the wage that the agent would earn if he or she chose to be employed by an incumbent firm.

The model of income choice has been used as a framework for estimating those individual characteristics shaping the choice between starting a new firm and working (Evans and Leighton, 1990; Dolton and Makepeace, 1990; Blanchflower and Oswald, 1990; Blanchflower and Meyer, 1991). These characteristics relate to the personality of the individual, human capital, and ethnic origin of individuals and are summarized in four studies in Table 8.4.

TABLE 8.4
Factors Influencing Self-Employment

Factors	Evans and Leighton (1990) (US)	Dolton and Makepeace (1990) (UK)	Blanchflower and Oswald (1990) (UK)	Blanchflower and Meyer (1991) (Australia)
Married	+	*	o	*
Divorced	+	o	o	o
Education	+	*	*	+
Children	*	*	*	o
Unemployed	+	*	+	o
Previous wage	-	*	*	o
Experience	*	o	o	+
Age	*	+	*	*
Ethic	*	*	*	*
Sex	*	+	*	*
Social class	o	*	o	o
School type	o	+	o	o
Region/urban	*	o	*	+
Inheritance/liquidity	+	o	+	o
Personality	o	o	+	o
Manager	o	o	*	*
Family in business	o	o	*	o

Key
+ Variable is statistically positively significant in the study.
- Variable is statistically negatively significant in the study.
* Variable included in the equation, but not shown to be significant.
o Variable not included in the equation.

Several conclusions can be drawn from this table. The first is that although all four studies are addressing a broadly similar issue, there must be some risk of omitted variable bias since none appear to include all variables. Only four variables appear in all of the studies: ethnic, sex, age, and education, and only three variables appear with a significant coefficient. The studies do not provide strong support for the impact of family and cultural influences on the self-employment decision. Also, family circumstances, with the exception of the Evans and Leighton (1990) study in the United States, appear to exert only a modest influence.

Spatial Variation in New Firm Formation

As already discussed, wide-ranging variation in the spacial rate in new firm formation occurs. The factors used to explain this spatial variation in new firm birth rates are closely related to and, in some instances, derived from the industrial and labor market economist's approaches (Reynolds and Maki, 1990; Reynolds and Storey, 1993).

As Table 8.5 shows, eight basic types of factors are identified: 1 relates to population, 2 to unemployment, 3 to wealth, 4 to qualifications and occupations, 5 to the characteristics of the enterprises in the area, 6 to housing, 7 to the local government, and 8 to policy. The precise variables chosen to measure these factors do vary somewhat. The table examines these hypotheses for five countries: Sweden, France, United Kingdom, Germany, and United States. For each country there are two measures. The first examines the birth rates of new firms over a period of time, dividing that by the active population, or employed population, in the area. The second measure is the number of births of new firms normalized by the existing stock of businesses, called "the stock measure."

The overall findings from the cross-national studies is that there are differences in the extent to which particular variables explain national differences. The overall results suggest that prior population growth in an area is a significant and consistent positive inducement to new firm formation rates. Such was the case in three out of the five countries studied. In other words, formation rates are higher in urban areas than in rural areas. Unemployment and changes in the unemployment rate appear to have a broadly positive impact upon new firm formation, except in Sweden where changes in unemployment have a negative impact and in the United Kingdom where there is no impact. It is also clear that geographical areas having a high proportion of their employment in small firms are more likely to have higher rates of new firm formation. The impact of other variables is more mixed, with none of the public policy variables having any identifiable impact.

The role of public policy in new firm start-ups has been examined by Danson (1995), who looked at the role of Scottish Enterprise in its role as facilitator of new

TABLE 8.5
Factors Influencing Spatial Variations in New Firm Formation

Factor Variables	France		Germany		Sweden		UK		US	
	Pop	Stk	Pop	Stk	Pop	Stk	Pop	Stk	Pop	Stk
1. Population 25-44 yrs.	-	*	*	*	o	o	o	o	*	*
In-migration/growth	+	+	*	+	+	+	+	+	+	+
Density/urban	+	+	*	*	+	(+)	+	+	*	*
2. Unemployment level	+	+	*	+	+	*	*	*	+	+
Change in unemployment	*	*	+	+	-	-	*	*	*	*
3. Wealth	*	*	o	o	o	o	*	*	o	o
GDP growth	o	o	*	*	*	+	(+)	+	+	+
4. Qualifications	*	-	o	o	*	*	*	*	-	-
% managers	*	+	*	(+)	o	o	+	*	+	+
5. Firm size	+	+	+	+	+	(-)	+	-	+	*
Specialization index	+	*	*	*	o	o	o	o	*	+
6. Owner-occupied housing	-	-	*	*	*	-	*	*	*	*
House prices	o	o	o	o	o	o	+	+	+	+
Land prices	o	o	*	*	o	o	o	o	o	o
Secondary housing	+	*	o	o	o	o	o	o	o	o
7. Socialist voters	*	*	o	o	*	*	-	+	o	o
Local govt. expenditure	o	o	*	*	o	o	*	*	-	-
8. Policy	o	o	o	o	*	*	*	*	o	o
n	96	96	74	74	80	80	64	64	382	382
R2	[0.84]	[0.87]	0.80	0.69	0.45	0.60	0.80	0.77	0.59	0.53

Notes: Pop = births/active population.
Stk = births/stocks of firms.

Key
+ Variable is significant at 5% level, positively associated.
- Variable is significant at 5% level, negatively associated.
( ) Variable significant only at 10% level.
* Variable is not significant.
o Variable is not included.
[ ] Indicates unadjusted R2.

Adapted from Reynolds, P.D., and D.J. Storey. 1993. Local and regional characteristics affecting small business formation: A cross-national comparison. Paris: OECD.

firm formation. The study looks at many subtle and complex issues that face entrepreneurs in starting and nurturing businesses. They conclude that gender and culture are often overlooked issues.

Temporal Variation in Rates of New Firm Formation

This section provides a brief overview of five studies, two for the United States, two for the United Kingdom, and one multicountry study. Two of the studies are concerned primarily with unemployment (Johnson et al., 1988; Robson and Shah, 1989), one with innovation (Audretsch and Acs, 1994), and the last two with macroeconomic variation (Highfield and Smiley, 1987; Acs and Evans, 1994).

The first major factor affecting new firm formation over time is the unemployment rate. Unemployment affects agents in two different but related ways. First, unemployment reduces the average alternative opportunity cost of entering self-employment. One would therefore expect to see a positive correlation between entry into self-employment and whether a particular individual is unemployed. Evans and Leighton (1990) have shown that individuals who have experienced a spell of unemployment are roughly twice as likely as individuals who are working to become self-employed. They are also less likely to survive.

Second, unemployment may be associated with a depressed economy in which the revenues that entrants into self-employment might expect are depressed. One would therefore expect to see a negative correlation between business formation rates and economy-wide or region-wide unemployment rates. Several studies for the United Kingdom, summarized by Storey (1991), find that the rate of new business formation is lowest in regions with the highest unemployment rate.

The second major group of factors influencing firm formation rates is profitability. Arguably, new firm formation will be higher when income from self-employment is higher or when stock prices are higher, on the grounds that this will attract individuals to start businesses. The third group refers to interest rates, so when real interest rates are high, access to capital is usually restricted and new firm formation rates will be lower. The fourth major group that effects new firm formation is the structure of the economy. The shift from manufacturing to services would have a positive impact on new firm formation.

The overall level of economic activity is the fourth major factor that might effect firm formation. Technology measures to what extent new firms can enter industries that are science-based, and the small firm innovation rate measures the extent of new firm entry in those industries where small firms have the innovative advantage.

Table 8.6, shows the results of five studies using time series data. All of the studies have used unemployment. Four studies show that increases in the unemployment rate

TABLE 8.6
Time Series Studies of New Firm Formation

Concept	Variable Used	Johnson (1988) (UK)	Robson/Shaw (1989) (UK)	Highfield/Smiley (1987) (US)	Audretsch/Acs (1994) (US)
Labor market	Unemployment	+	+	+	+
Profitability	Self-employment income	o	+	o	o
Interest rate	Real interest rate	o	-	-	-
Cyclical indicator	GDP	+	o	o	+
Technology	Basic science	o	o	o	-
Small firm innovation rate		o	o	o	+

Key
\+ Variable is positively significant.
\- Variable is negatively significant.
o Not applicable.

is associated with increases in the rate of new firm formation. However, Acs and Evans (1994) find that for a sample of 24 countries over two decades that the correct sign is negative when other variables are controlled for. The results for GDP are also mixed. While GDP growth has a positive effect in the United Kingdom, for the Office for Economic Cooperation and Development (OECD) as a whole, GDP growth has a negative effect on the self-employment rate. The results show that firms are pulled by higher level of income and self-employment income. The findings with interest rates are broadly consistent with theorizing. That is, when real interest rates are low, new firm formation will be higher. Basic science does not promote the start of new firms; however, the small firm innovation rate, which measures the extent of knowledge outside of the firm, does promote the start-up of new firms. These results are consistent for both the United States and the United Kingdom. The female labor force participation rate has a negative impact on new firm births, and structural change (the shift from manufacturing to services) also promotes new firm births.

Perhaps the key conclusion from this section on entry is the huge importance of new firms to the economy. The statistical evidence cited herein suggests that between 5 and 15 percent of the stock of firms could be new in the economy in any given year. The second key result is that the new firm formation rate varies from sector to sector, from region to region, from country to country, and from time to time.

The Death of Small Firms

One fundamental characteristic of small firms is that births and deaths are highly correlated. Between 1980 and 1986, according to the Small Business Administration database, 2,513,000 new establishments started in the United States. This represents a gross entry rate of 56 percent. During the same time 2,027,000 establishments exited from the whole economy. This represents a gross exit rate of 45 percent, a net birth rate of 10.8 percent, or 1.8 percent a year. However, for manufacturing Dunne et al. (1989) show that small manufacturing plants had an exit rate that was twice as high as large plants.

Before analyzing the numbers, it would help to take a more careful look at the definitions of exit. Business bankruptcy data are provided by the Statistical Analysis and Reports Division of the Administrative Office of the U.S. Courts. These data are reported under federal bankruptcy regulations when businesses file bankruptcy petitions. A business bankruptcy is a legal recognition that a company is insolvent. Business bankruptcy data are more likely to include self-employed persons and new, very small firms than are business failures.

Business failures are collected and published by the Dun and Bradstreet Corporation (D&B). These data represent businesses that are no longer in D&B's list of active business during their latest survey due to failure or the filing of a bankruptcy petition. A business failure is defined as an enterprise that ceases operation with a loss to one or more creditors. It should be kept in mind that about 75 percent of dissolutions in the Dun and Bradstreet file are voluntary.

Data on business terminations are collected from State Employment Security Agencies and submitted quarterly to the U.S. Department of Labor, Employment, and Training Administration. If a firm has employees, it is required to withhold quarterly federal income tax for each employee, and pay quarterly unemployment insurance premiums under the FICA laws. Therefore, when a firm terminates operations (that is, ceases to employ people), the respective State Employment Security Agency has a record since no more tax payments are received.

How many firms go out of business each year? Figure 8.1 shows the number of business bankruptcies between 1984 and 1994, and Figure 8.2 shows the number of business failures. Both measures exhibit similar patterns, although the magnitudes are slightly different. The business termination rate is much larger, with 803,127 terminations in 1994. Each date on exit measures a different aspect of the firm. There is no unambiguous measure of firm exit.

FIGURE 8.1
Number of Business Bankruptcies 1984–1994

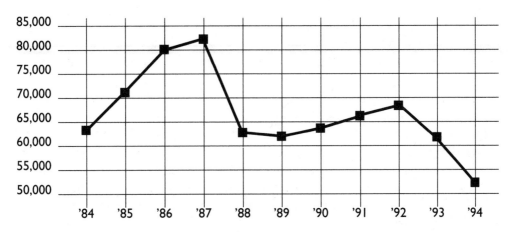

Source: Office of U.S. Courts.

FIGURE 8.2
Business Failures for the U.S. 1985–1995

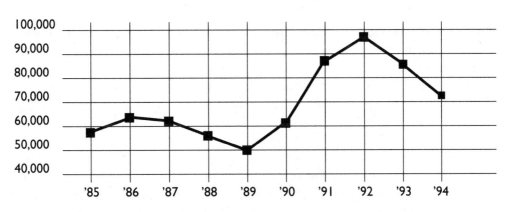

Source: Dun and Bradstreet Corp., Business Failure Record.

Some Theoretical Issues

The developments of exit have proven less powerful than those of entry, growth, or survival. The economists basic assumption is that in the long run, firms which are losing money will exit the industry. In the short run, firms that earn a quasi rent will also survive. A more sophisticated model has been worked out by Reid (1991, 1993) and Baden-Fuller (1989). The decision whether or not to close the firm may depend on the relative net costs of continuance versus immediate closure. The model can be expressed as:

$$\Pi < rC - c'$$

where Π is present value of anticipated profit in the coming period, C is residual value of the plant if scrapped now, r is rate of interest, and c' is the present value of anticipated capital gains in scrap value from deferring the closure. The model shows that the continue-versus-liquidate decision depends upon the relationship between the owners of the business, the bank, and other creditors. It also depends on the legal framework establishing creditor priority. Although the model is useful in explaining why existing plants or firms will go out of business, it is not very useful in explaining why the failure rate of new firms is so high.

Jovanovic (1982) assumes that both the individuals themselves and financial institutions such as banks are ignorant, before that individual starts a business, of whether or not the business will be successful. It is only by being an entrepreneur that the individual is able to obtain information on success, and the same applies to the bank. As a result, both banks and entrepreneurs modify their behavior over time, which it has been termed "the learning model." The value of Jovanovic's model is that it provides some explanation why young firms have lower rates of survival than older firms.

There are three variables that seem to be related to survival: firm size, firm age, and firm growth. The firm growth rate decreases with firm size and firm age. Therefore, holding the firm size constant, increased age is associated with lower failure rates. Firm survival is positively related to firm size and firm age.

Survival and growth of new entrants has been examined by Audretsch (1991). Looking at a sample of 11,314 manufacturing firms from 1976 to 1986, he found that the average entry firm size in 1976 was about eight employees. The mean initial size of the firms still in existence in 1982 was higher. That is, for those firms surviving six years, the start-up mix was slightly larger. The mean size of firms existing throughout the period seems to be greater than those not surviving. For example, in 1978 the group of firms surviving throughout the entire sample period exhibited a mean size of 12.01 employees, which is considerably greater then the mean size of 10.70 employees for all firms still in existence as of 1978. Not only does the initial start-up size of surviving firms tend to be larger, but the growth rates tend to be higher. These results confirm earlier findings by Phillips and Kirchhoff (1989).

Other issues that economists have not paid much attention to when looking at death is the issue of harvesting the business or succession in a family business.

Research Agenda: What Next?

Births and deaths are just two measures of the dynamics of a capitalist economy. How firms enter, survive, grow, decline, and exit provides the key to understanding the dynamics of economic development. Over the past decade a great deal of progress has been make in developing better data sets and in understanding the role of entrepreneurship as it is represented in the statistics of firm births and deaths. Future research should focus on even better understanding how firm births and deaths affect economic development. This calls for closer collaboration between entrepreneurship researchers, economists, and sociologists.

In the first state-of-the-art conference at Baylor University in 1980, an entire section was devoted to "Entrepreneurship and Progress"—entrepreneurship in economic development, entrepreneurship in the less-developed world, the theory of entrepreneurship in economic growth, the role of the entrepreneur in innovation, elaboration on entrepreneurs and innovation, and the environment for entrepreneurship. Many references were made to the work by economists that is very relevant to current research. What is especially important is to measure the contribution that entrepreneurship makes to economic growth, productivity, and technological change. The work in this area by Baldwin (1995), Kirchhoff (1994), and Audretsch (1995) were instrumental in moving the field in the right direction.

REFERENCES

Acs, Z.J. (ed.). 1996. *Small Firms and Economic Growth*. Cheltenham, U.K.: Edward Elgar Publishers.

Acs, Z.J., and D. Evans. 1994. The determinants of variations in self-employment rates across countries and over time. CIBER Working Paper 51, University of Maryland at College Park.

Acs, Z.J., and D. B. Audretsch. 1992. The social and economic consequences of entrepreneurship. In D.L. Sexton and J. Kasarda (eds.): *The State of the Art of Entrepreneurship*. Boston: PWS-Kent, 45-67.

Admiraal, P.H. (ed.) 1996. *Small Business in the Modern Economy*. Oxford: Basic Blackwell.

Audretsch, D. 1991. New firm survival and the technological regime. *Review of Economics and Statistics* 68:520-526.

Audretsch, D.B. 1995. *Innovation and Industry Evolution.* Cambridge, MA: MIT Press.

Audretsch, D.B., and Z.J. Acs. 1994. New-firm startups, technology, and macroeconomic fluctuations. *Small Business Economics* 6:439-449.

Baden-Fuller, C.W.F. 1989. Exit from declining industries in the case of steel castings. *Economic Journal* 99:949-961.

Baldwin, J.R., and P.K. Gorecki. 1990. Firm entry and exit in the Canadian manufacturing sector, a working paper of the Business and Labour Market Analysis Group, Analytical Studies Branch, Statistics Canada.

Baldwin, J.R. 1995. *The Dynamics of Industrial Competition.* Cambridge, UK: University Press.

Baldwin, J.R. 1996. Telephone conversations between Bruce Kirchhoff and John Baldwin on April 30 and May 1, 1996.

Birch, D. 1979. The job generation process. Unpublished report, prepared by the Massachusetts Institute of Technology Program on Neighborhood and Regional Change for the Economic Development Administration, Department of Commerce, Washington, DC.

Blanchflower, D.G., and A.J. Oswald. 1990. Self-employment in the enterprise culture. In R. Jowell, S. Witherspoon, and L. Brook (eds.): *British Social Attitudes: The Seventh Report.* Aldershot, UK: Gower Publishing.

Blanchflower, D.G., and B.D. Meyer. 1991. Longitudinal analysis of young entrepreneurs in Australia and the United States. *Small Business Economics* 6:1-19.

Brown, C., J. Connor, S. Heeringa, and J. Jackson. 1990. Studying (small) business with the Michigan Employment Security Commission Longitudinal Database. *Small Business Economics* 2(4):261-278.

Danson, M. (ed.). 1995. Special issue on new firm formation and regional economic development. *Small Business Economics* 7(2):81-172.

Dennis, W.J., Jr. 1996. *Wells Fargo/NFIB Foundation Series on Business Entries and Exits.* Washington, DC: NFIB Education Foundation.

Dolton, P.J., and G.H. Makepeace. 1990. Self-employment amongst graduates. *Bulletin of Economic Research* 42(1):35-53.

Dunne, T., M.J. Roberts, and L. Samuelson. 1988. Patterns of firm entry and exit in U.S. manufacturing industries. *Rand Journal of Economics* 19:595-615.

Dunne, T., M.J. Roberts, and L. Samuelson. 1989. The growth and failure of U.S. manufacturing plants. *Quarterly Journal of Economics* 104:671-698.

Evans, D.S., and L.S. Leighton. 1990. Small business formation by unemployed and employed workers. *Small Business Economics* 2(4):319-330.

Fritsch, M. 1992. Regional differences in new firm formation: Evidence from West Germany. *Regional Studies* 26(3):96-101.

Geroski, P.A., and J. Schwalbach. 1991. *Entry and Market Contestability: An International Comparison.* Cambridge, MA: Basil Blackwell.

Hall, G. 1992. Reasons for insolvency amongst small firms—A review and fresh evidence. *Small Business Economics* 4(3):237-50.

Hall, G., and B. Young. 1991. Factors associated with insolvency amongst small firms. *International Small Business Journal* 9(2):54-63.

Harrison, B. 1994. *Lean and Mean*. Boston: Basic Books.

Highfield, R., and R. Smiley. 1987. New business starts and economic activity: An empirical investigation. *International Journal of Industrial Organization* 5(1):51-66.

Holmes, T.J., and J.A. Schmitz. 1995. On the turnover of business firms and business managers. *Journal of Political Economy* 103(5):72-94.

Jackson, J.E. 1995. Firm size and the dynamics in a market economy. Working paper, University of Michigan.

Johnson, S., and G. Loveman. 1995. *Starting Over in Eastern Europe*. Cambridge, MA: Harvard Business School Press.

Johnson, S., R. Lindley, and C. Boulakis. 1988. An exploratory time series analysis of self-employment in Great Britain. Project Report, DE Programme, Institute for Employment Research, University of Warwick.

Jovanovic, B. 1982. Selection and the evolution of industry. *Econometrica* 50:649-70.

Keeble, D., S. Walker, and M. Robson. 1993. *New Firm Formation and Small Business Growth: Spatial and Temporal Variations and Determinants in the United Kingdom*. U.K. Department of Employment, Research Series No. 15, September, London.

Kirchhoff, B.A. 1994. *Entrepreneurship and Dynamic Capitalism*. Westport, CT: Praeger.

Kirchhoff, B.A., and B.D. Phillips. 1989. Innovation and growth among new firms in the U.S. economy. In R. Brockhaus et al. (eds.): *Frontiers of Entrepreneurship Research*. Wellesley, MA: Babson College.

Kirchhoff, B.A., and B.D. Phillips. 1991. Are small firms still creating the new jobs? In N. Churchill et al. (eds.): *Frontiers of Entrepreneurship Research*. Wellesley, MA: Babson College.

Knight, F.H. 1921. *Risk, Uncertainty and Profit*. New York: Houghton Mifflin.

Mata, J., and D.B. Audretsch. 1995. The post-entry performance of firms. *International Journal of Industrial Organization* 13(4):413-614.

Phillips, B.D., and B.A. Kirchhoff. 1989. Formation, growth and survival; small firm dynamics in the U.S. Economy. *Small Business Economics* 1(1):65-74.

Phillips, B.D., and B.A. Kirchhoff. 1988. The effect of firm formation and growth on job creation in the United States. *Journal of Business Venturing* 3(4):261-272.

Picot, G., J. Baldwin, and R. Dupuy. 1994. Have small firms created a disproportionate share of new jobs in Canada? A reassessment of the facts. Working paper of the Business and Labour Market Analysis Group, Analytical Studies Branch, Statistics Canada.

Reid, G.C. 1991. Staying in business. *International Journal of Industrial Organization* 9:545-556.

Reid, G.C. 1993. *Small Business Enterprise: An Economic Analysis.* London: Routledge.

Reynolds, P.D., and D.J. Storey. 1993. Local and regional characteristics affecting small business formation: A cross-national comparison. Paris: OECD.

Reynolds, P.D., and W.R. Maki. 1990. *Business Volatility and Economic Growth.* Final project report to the U.S. Small Business Administration, Contract No. SBA 3067-OA-88.

Reynolds, P.D. 1995. The national study of U.S. business start-ups: Background and progress report. Presented at the Conference on Dynamics of Employment and Industry Evolution, University of Mannheim, Germany, January 1995.

Reynolds, P.D., and S. White. 1993. Wisconsin's Entrepreneurial Climate Study. Milwaukee, WI: Marquette University Center for the Study of Entrepreneurship. A report prepared for the Wisconsin Housing and Economic Development Authority.

Robson, M., and A. Shah. 1989. A Capital Theoretic Approach to Self Employment in the U.K. Department of Economics, University of Newcastle upon Tyme (mimeo).

Schumpeter, J.A. 1934. *The Theory of Economic Development.* Cambridge, MA: Harvard University Press.

Storey, D.J. 1994. *Understanding the Small Business Sector.* London: Routledge.

Storey, D.J. 1991. The birth of new firms—does unemployment matter?—a review of the evidence. *Small Business Economics* 3:167-78.

Van der Horst, R. 1992. The volatility of the small business sector in the Netherlands. Presented at the International Conference on Small Business, OECD, Montreal, Canada, May 24-27.

Entrepreneurship Education

Entrepreneurship Education

T HE FIELD OF ENTREPRENEURSHIP EDUCATION has grown from the early 1980s to the present time. The magnitude and rate of growth in academics can and has been measured by the number of endowed positions, the number of courses and/or programs developed, the number of students in the courses, and the number of universities that now recognize entrepreneurship as a viable vocational choice for graduates.

Entrepreneurship education research can be characterized by four different effectiveness areas: research content, pedagogy, effectiveness programs, and learning styles. In addition, education can also be classified on the basis of age and/or the experience of students. In this section the emphasis is on the education of primary and secondary students as well as university students and practicing entrepreneurs.

In the past the majority of research activities have been directed toward course content and have addressed issues such as what should be taught to entrepreneurship students at the university level to prepare them to either initiate their own venture, work in an emerging venture, or to be employed in a company that provides goods and services to emerging firms. Initially, the course content focused on starting a business. However, as distinctions were drawn between small business and entrepreneurship content shifted from starting to growing the business.

As content evolved, changes in pedagogy were also required, and entrepreneurship courses became more interdisciplinary and more in line with the activities of real-world entrepreneurs. With this shift case studies and business plans became the norm along with guest visits from specialists addressing such issues as legal aspects, taxation, intellectual property, business valuation, and contracts.

The popularity of the early courses resulted in students requesting more information, which led to the development of a series of courses and in some cases a major or minor in entrepreneurship. In 1980, the first three majors in entrepreneurship were established at Babson, Baylor, and the University of Southern California. The development of multiple courses and majors also signaled the acceptance and support of faculty administrators.

The question, Have we really made a difference? begs for research on the effectiveness of courses or programs. A considerable amount of research has been directed to the activities of students since leaving the classrooms. Issues such as the number of businesses started, the growth of these businesses, and their economic contributions have been studied. They all address entrepreneurship students but, for the most part, lack comparison to a control group.

Education research in general has been directed toward primary, secondary, and university students. Only limited efforts have been directed toward the special needs of the entrepreneurship student or practicing entrepreneur. In Chapter 9, the state of the art of entrepreneurship education for primary and secondary students is discussed by Kourilsky and Carlson, and a number of programs are described. Then the learning styles of both university students and entrepreneurs are examined by Young in Chapter 10 in an effort to increase the effectiveness of entrepreneurship education.

Entrepreneurship Education for Youth: A Curricular Perspective

MARILYN L. KOURILSKY

AND

SHEILA R. CARLSON

THIS CHAPTER ANALYZES THE CURRENT STATUS of entrepreneurship curricula at elementary school through high school levels and provides recommendations for state-of-the-art development and dissemination of curricula. The chapter begins with a discussion of high school students' current knowledge of and attitudes toward entrepreneurship and entrepreneurship education. Next, elementary school through high school entrepreneurship curricula that have been widely disseminated are reviewed. Finally, seven habits are proposed for enhancing the state of the art in entrepreneurship education.

Youth's Knowledge of and Attitudes Toward Entrepreneurship and Entrepreneurship Education

In 1994, a Gallup Poll was conducted to gather reliable national data about the "market demand" for entrepreneurship education. The survey sampled high school students' beliefs about the degree of entrepreneurship education received throughout their schooling, their knowledge of basic entrepreneurship concepts, and their attitudes toward becoming an entrepreneur. The poll results are now being utilized to inform researchers, curriculum developers, disseminators, policymakers, and other stakeholders of key "market opportunities" for entrepreneurship education (Gallup, 1994). Some of the salient findings of this poll revealed that almost nine out of ten high school students (86 percent) rate their knowledge of entrepreneurship as "very poor to fair." This self-assessment proved to be accurate. Their average entrepreneurship knowledge score was only 44 percent. Further, approximately four out of five high school students believe that more entrepreneurship should be taught in the schools. About 70 percent of the students surveyed want to start a business, and 68 percent indicate that, if they become successful entrepreneurs, they have an obligation to give something back to their communities beyond providing jobs.

The Gallup Poll clearly revealed that there is a *demand* for entrepreneurship education among high school students. Although 84 percent indicated a desire to learn more about entrepreneurship, 85 percent also reported they were taught "a little about" or "practically nothing about" business and entrepreneurship throughout their years of schooling. Seventy-three percent of our high school students stated they want to "be my own boss," but believed they lack the requisite knowledge to pursue such a course.

A surprising and provocative result of the survey was the finding that 69 percent of the students want to start a business of their own. Among African-American youths the percentage was even higher (80 percent). The challenge is to meet the existing demand for entrepreneurship education. Subsequent focus groups have revealed that high school students no longer trust large corporations or government for their economic survival. The deluge of personal experiences with downsizings and layoffs have led them to the conclusion that the most realistic way to ensure economic security and wealth creation is through self-employment—to *make* a job, not *take* a job.

What is currently being done to meet this high demand for entrepreneurship education both within and outside-of-school environments (e.g., in youth organizations)? The answer is, Not enough! There are existing programs. However, a number of important curricular issues—such as pilot testing, evaluation, and proven replicability—have been given only nominal attention at best by many of these programs. In the next sections of this chapter, entrepreneurship education will be defined. Then the programs that address this area will be discussed. Although it is strongly believed that a need for concrete effectiveness data through rigorous program evaluations exists, lack of such data did not exclude programs from the scope of this chapter's review, provided they met the criteria stated above.

Current Status of Entrepreneurship Curricula

A true entrepreneurship education program must successfully educate students in the following core areas of entrepreneurship:

❖ Identification or recognition of a market opportunity and the generation of a business idea (service or product) to address the opportunity.

❖ Marshaling and commitment of resources in the face of risk to pursue the opportunity.

❖ Creation of an operating business organization to implement the opportunity-motivated business idea (Kourilsky, 1995; Sahlman and Stevenson, 1992).

Many programs that purport to be entrepreneurship education programs are in reality business management or economic education programs. Although some of the latter are effective (e.g., Junior Achievement and the Rural Entrepreneurship through Action Learning [REAL] high school curricula), they at present *"miss the heart of the entrepreneurship process"* because *"key personal entrepreneurship experiences are either missing entirely or are fatally compromised by group dilution and by intervention of the teacher and the school"* (Kourilsky, 1995). Business management—oriented programs, in particular, tend to familiarize students with skillsets useful in day-to-day business operations, as opposed to providing students with personal learning experiences related to opportunity recognition, marshaling of resources in the face of risk, and venture initiation. Thus, these business management programs may or may not advance entrepreneurial behavior.

The small number of programs that do meet some or all of the previously stated criteria for core entrepreneurship education can be characterized as being at one of four stages of curricular development:

❖ *Pilot*: curriculum is implemented in carefully monitored settings and evaluated for effectiveness

❖ *Enhancement*: curriculum is revised and refined in response to pilot assessments.

❖ *Custom transfer*: curriculum is tested for its ability to successfully transfer to different markets.

❖ *Mass transfer*: educators and youth group leaders throughout the country are trained in the delivery of the curriculum, and there is large-scale dissemination of the research-based curriculum.

The goals of currently available entrepreneurship curricula may also vary. Some of these programs are *entrepreneurship awareness* curricula and have as their goal to introduce students to entrepreneurship as a career alternative and to the role of the entrepreneur in the economy. Other programs are *entrepreneurship readiness* curricula that provide basic knowledge of the concepts and first-level skills of entrepreneurship, so that students are "ready" to start a business. Finally, there exists several *entrepreneurship application* curricula with goals, for example, of having students apply their entrepreneurship knowledge, skills, and behaviors through actual entrepreneurship experiences—frequently in the context of the students starting their own businesses.

The entrepreneurship education programs considered in this chapter will be described below in terms of 1) target audience, 2) goals and salient characteristics, 3) appropriateness for different age levels and environments, and 4) the extent of empirical verification of the program's effectiveness. An attempt has been made to include all programs that even approximate the stated definition of core entrepreneurship education. Also included are several curricula that have been disseminated before successful completion of piloting and evaluation when the initial results indicate potential for long-term success.

Elementary School Curricula

YESS!/Mini-Society

YESS!/Mini-Society (Youth Empowerment and Self-Sufficiency) is a curricular enhancement embedded in the Mini-Society Framework (Kourilsky, 1974). The program is a self-organizing, interdisciplinary, experienced-based entrepreneurship readiness program targeted primarily for children between the ages of eight and twelve.

A primary goal of the program is to enhance youth empowerment and self-sufficiency. To accomplish this goal, the program provides a framework within which participants develop an understanding of and gain personal experience with the principles and practices of entrepreneurship. Students create societies, establish their own economies, and even develop unique currencies for their societies. They then independently develop products, services, and businesses to address opportunities they identify in their classroom marketplaces. After their various firsthand entrepreneurship experiences, students are helped by their teachers (through formal debriefings) to explore the concepts underlying what they have done. The program is easily integrated with other subject areas taught during the day. The program is customarily conducted for approximately one hour per day, three days a week, for a minimum of 10 weeks.

Although this program was originally targeted as an in-school instructional system for third through sixth grade students, it has been successfully implemented at different age levels in a variety of in-school environments, in both public and private schools, and out-of-school settings, such as after-school girls' and boys' clubs. The program has also been implemented successfully in some school districts as separate required courses in entrepreneurship for sixth and seventh grade middle school programs.

Persuasive evidence indicates that typical students who participate in the program enhance their ability to apply the principles and practices of personal entrepreneurship, practice entrepreneurial and economic decision-making, and recognize entrepreneurship as a viable option for their personal career choices. The program also enhances students' attitudes toward school and learning and increases their locus of control (perception of their own influence on what happens in their lives). These positive empirical research findings for the program reflect the results of numerous research studies conducted since the pilot-testing of the original framework in 1974 and published in refereed journals (Carlson, 1994; Cassuto, 1980; Graff, 1982; Hopkins, 1989; Koon, 1995; Kourilsky, 1974, 1976, 1979, 1980, 1981; Kourilsky and Ballard-Campbell, 1984a, 1984b; Kourilsky and Campbell, 1981; Kourilsky and Graff, 1986; Kourilsky and Hirshleifer, 1976; Kourilsky and Murray, 1981; Kourilsky and Ortiz, 1985; Ortiz, 1982).

Entrepreneur Invention Society

The Entrepreneur Invention Society is a YESS!/Mini-Society curricular enhancement targeted for upper elementary students in grades four through six; typically they have previously participated in the YESS!/Mini-Society program. The Entrepreneur Invention Society is an experience-based entrepreneurship readiness program targeted for within-school audiences and for participants in out-of-school settings, such as girls' and boys' clubs, who are at the concrete operational stage of cognitive development. Program participants have been children at high, medium, and low scholastic levels and from dissimilar ethnic and socioeconomic backgrounds.

The program is an experience-based interdisciplinary curriculum designed to foster and integrate the process of invention and the knowledge, skills, and attitudes of entrepreneurship. It accomplishes these goals by teaching aspiring young inventors to recognize opportunities, conceive and develop inventions associated with the identified opportunities, analyze target markets, develop marketing strategies, formulate business plans, and finally, create viable businesses for their innovations. Other important goals of this entrepreneurship education initiative are the enhancement of participants' self-esteem, locus of control, and creativity.

The program was originally pilot-tested in five states with several hundred children. The curriculum was modified and enhanced based on evaluation results. A standardized teacher training model has been developed, and the program is at the initial stage of mass transfer. Comprehensive training workshops are being conducted for educators across the country.

The program has been subjected to quantitative and qualitative research evaluations. Pretest/posttest comparisons drawn from this experimental research reveal that this program has a significant effect on students' entrepreneurial thinking, entrepreneurial application skills (including pricing and marketing), occupational aspirations, and originality. Regression analysis further revealed that the success of the program's participants is independent of gender, giftedness, scholastic achievement, and parental occupation. These results demonstrate that students' conceptual and practical knowledge of the fundamentals of entrepreneurship, as well as their attitudes toward entrepreneurship, are enhanced by their participation in the program.

Middle and Secondary School Curricula

An Income of Her Own

An Income of Her Own, developed in 1992 by Joline Godfrey, offers several entrepreneurship awareness programs targeted for teenage women between the ages of 13 to 18 who are from diverse ethnic groups, socioeconomic backgrounds, and scholastic achievement levels. The program has been implemented within schools, in after-school girls' clubs, and in other community agencies and summer resident camps.

The mission of the program is to provide young women with both opportunities to explore entrepreneurship and economic literacy to help prepare them for independence and economic well-being. Toward this end, it attempts to cultivate the notion among adolescent women that entrepreneurship is a viable career choice—and seeks to provide them with the principles and practices they will need in order to achieve successful business ventures if they choose to pursue such a course.

Among the entrepreneurship awareness experiences offered by the program are several flexible components, including one-day out-of-school or within-school awareness conferences, a nationally advertised business plan competition, and a summer resident camp. A brief description of each of the components follows.

The 13- to 18-year-old target audience age appears most appropriate for the current program. Adolescent men could also profit from the program's awareness conferences, business plan competitions, and summer resident business camps. Also, it has been determined from verbal feedback following informal pilot tests that the awareness conferences are also appropriate as community events or as within-school events.

New modules are continually being added to the curriculum, and the different components are in various stages of development. The formats of the one-day awareness seminars and the business plan competition have been standardized, piloted, and enhanced based on informal evaluation. These programs are in the mass transfer phase.

The program appears to have replication potential. Since its inception in 1992, approximately 10,000 young women have reportedly been exposed to the awareness component at locations including Boston, Los Angeles, San Francisco, San Jose, Washington, DC, and the Cherokee Nation in Oklahoma.

The national business plan competition sponsored by the program is advertised in national teenage women's magazines, through awareness conferences, and at summer business camps. The purpose of the competition is to invite young women to consider personal entrepreneurship. Entrants are not required to have any previous business background in order to apply to this loose-format competition.

Although several comprehensive evaluative research studies by outside agencies are in progress, the only empirical evidence of effectiveness currently available are anecdotal reports from previous participants. These reports are generally quite positive and suggest that the program is effective in stimulating interest in entrepreneurship and enhancing the self-esteem of the young women who participate.

Program for Acquiring Competence in Entrepreneurship

The Program for Acquiring Competence in Entrepreneurship (PACE) is an in-school readiness program that was originally developed in 1976 by the International Development Laboratory. The curriculum was revised and updated by the Center on Education and Training for Employment at Ohio State University, who developed the third PACE edition in 1994. The curriculum is available for three separate levels of instruction:

❖ Level 1 is primarily targeted for high school students as a single-semester course in entrepreneurship or as supplementary entrepreneurship materials to be infused in other courses.

❖ Level 2 is provided as a full major or as elective courses primarily for community college students.

❖ Level 3 is targeted for adult education students interested in start-up ventures.

The central goal of the program is to impart basic entrepreneurship skills necessary for success in initiating and building business ventures. Separate student goals for each PACE level are as follows:

❖ Level 1 introduces students to basic entrepreneurship concepts and skills and develops awareness of entrepreneurship as a viable career option.

❖ Level 2 promotes students' comprehension and application of entrepreneurship concepts and skills and develops recognition of personal venture opportunities.

❖ Level 3 applies advanced entrepreneurship concepts and skills to the planning and preparing for actual implementation of a personal business venture.

Evidence gathered over the past 20 years concerning the effectiveness of the curriculum has been informal. Anecdotal accounts of student success at each of the levels have been reported by various instructors who have implemented the curriculum and administered its test instruments. Although some anecdotal reports have noted students initiating business ventures after program participation, estimates of the number of actual start-ups were not available.

EntrePrep

EntrePrep is a year-long out-of-school entrepreneurship readiness/internship program for motivated college-bound students who have completed the eleventh grade. The program is initiated between targeted students' junior and senior years of high school. The experience-based program was developed by Marilyn Kourilsky in 1995. The program was designed as a proactive entrepreneurship education intervention for students who are high-potential "boomerang" candidates. Boomerang individuals have successful academic track records and often multiple college degrees, who upon discovering their services are undervalued in the corporate marketplace, "boomerang" back to their parents' homes as they try to sort out what to do next.

The rationale for targeting high school students who have completed their junior year is twofold. First, these adolescents are at the "society-reformer" stage and tend to engage in idealistic-logical thought (Piaget, 1967; Wadsworth, 1989). Such young people are, in general, eager to become involved in projects like internships, where the voluntary contribution of their knowledge and expertise assists and is valued by others. Second, entering high school seniors typically experience "senioritis"—a sudden and often spectacular loss of motivation to learn anything, do anything academic, or think about anything in their lives other than the fact that high school is almost over. The curriculum presents entrepreneurship as a career alternative and attempts to promote the focusing of thought processes and the conscious consideration of personal life goals in these young people.

A primary goal of the curriculum is to develop in participants a background of entrepreneurship knowledge, skills, experiences, and attitudes that will enable them to identify opportunities and initiate successful business ventures should they ever become "boomerang" displaced (or career-displaced in general). The program also actively supports the pursuit of college education including $1,000 fellowships for participants who successfully complete the program.

Evaluations of the implementations reveal that the curriculum significantly impacts both cognitive and affective outcomes. Pretest/posttest comparisons reveal significant gains in entrepreneurship awareness, entrepreneurship concept acquisition, and ability to apply the principles and practices of successful application of entrepreneurship concepts and skills. Also significant gains in positive attitudes toward entrepreneurship, including the desire to pursue personal entrepreneurship were noted. A posttest of the Gallup entrepreneurship questions was administered to participants who had completed only the orientation and summer institute but not the internship phase of the program. EntrePrep students scored 77 percent compared with the national average of 44 percent among high school students.

National Foundation for Teaching Entrepreneurship

The National Foundation for Teaching Entrepreneurship (NFTE) was developed by Steve Mariotti in 1987. Early target audiences for the readiness/introductory application entrepreneurship program were various at-risk youth populations, including individuals in detention and handicapped or disadvantaged youngsters in grades kindergarten through high school and up to the age of 24 years. The current stated target audience for this experiential program is lower-income students in grades 8 through 12 from primarily urban areas. The NFTE program is implemented in out-of-school settings such as summer business camps, as after-school programs at local youth service agencies, and through in-school offerings as a semester or full-year entrepreneurship course.

The basic mission of the program is to introduce at-risk and inner-city youth to the world of business by teaching the basics of entrepreneurship and how to start and maintain a small business. This mission is carried out through several programs, similar in framework, that are custom-fitted for different environments. A core introductory application program is offered for one-semester within-school courses, two-week summer business camps, and for after-school youth organization programs. A fundamentals program is available for implementation settings with limited time frames, such as short-term after-school programs or one-week summer business camps. Students who participate in a fundamentals program experience many of the same activities as students in the core program. However, since the text materials and experiences are so abbreviated, this program is considered to be an entrepreneurship awareness experience rather than an introductory readiness program.

Students in either program are introduced to the fundamentals of entrepreneurship through teacher-directed lessons, field trips, and traditionally organized write-in workbooks. The central theme around which the principal components are organized is "buy low, sell high."

The curriculum appears to have been written for an audience assumed to be at the stage of formal operations. However, a substantial body of research suggests that a noticeable fraction of the target audience is unlikely to have reached the formal operations stage (Elkind, 1962; Kohlberg and Meyer, 1972; Kuhn et al., 1977; Schwebel, 1975; Wadsworth, 1989). Thus, since there is a strong possibility that many of the students in the target audience are still at the stage of concrete operations, they will be hard-pressed to fully comprehend and apply the entrepreneurship concepts presented without the assistance of a curriculum whose construction is appropriate to their stage of cognitive development.

Although the program is currently being disseminated nationwide, the curriculum has been subjected to only limited informal pilot-testing procedures. Program developers indicate that the program has been revised several times since its inception in 1988. Some modifications to the latest version of the curriculum were based upon recommendations from an external preevaluative study conducted by Hahn (1994) at Brandeis University.

A multisite pretest/posttest comparison group study of the program is currently being implemented in response to preevaluation findings that characterized previous evaluation efforts as unorganized—and recommended a more structured and comprehensive evaluation study. The evidence that exists at present concerning its effectiveness is chiefly anecdotal. Program participants often give positive reports about the impact on their self-esteem and their desire to pursue entrepreneurship. Reports from alumni indicate some of them have started businesses.

The Hahn preevaluation study cited previously did sample partial responses of a selected participant group to a program-developed entrepreneurship concept acquisition pre- and post-test. Although the results indicated some level of increase in posttest scores for 42 percent of the students who participated in the program, and some level of decrease in posttest scores for 12 percent of the same students, neither the increases nor the decreases in entrepreneurship acquisition were found to be statistically significant.

Educational Designs that Generate Excellence

Educational Designs that Generate Excellence (EDGE), developed in 1993 by former NFTE associate Scott Shickler, provides a set of entrepreneurship awareness, readiness, and introductory application programs. EDGE targets at-risk and mainstream youth between the ages of 12 and 19 with programs designed for in-school settings at junior and senior high schools and for other settings, such as after-school or summer camp programs offered by youth and community outreach organizations.

The primary goal of the program is to use entrepreneurship as a catalyst to prepare young people for economic success—as valued employees or as business owners. Other goals are to strengthen self-esteem, foster a sense of purpose, and encourage the continuation of participants' education. The various programs are structured similarly to those offered by NFTE.

The curricular focus of the program is similar to the NFTE programs and centers around students forming individual retail flea market and trade fair-style businesses. A wholesale purchasing club made available through EDGE corporate offices plays an important role in the small businesses individual students open as participants. As with the NFTE program, risk is minimized as participants are given a set amount of capital to invest in the purchase of wholesale items from the club, which they will subsequently sell at higher retail prices. Start-up funds are not repaid, and any profits earned are retained by individual students.

Anecdotal reports suggest that the curriculum can be implemented to some degree in the seventh through twelfth grade. The core text is targeted at a ninth-grade readability level. No evidence based on systematic research and evaluation is available with respect to the effectiveness of the program. Anecdotal reports and informal results of pretests and posttests (developed by the author of EDGE) suggest that students may be learning some entrepreneurship concepts and developing entrepreneurial attitudes.

New Youth Entrepreneur

The New Youth Entrepreneur (Kourilsky et al., 1995) is an experience-based entrepreneurship readiness program targeted for use with middle school students in the eighth grade and high school students in the ninth and tenth grades, as both an in-school and an after-school program. It is based on a program initially developed by the Education, Training and Enterprise Center (EDTEC) in 1985 (Bocage and Waters, 1985). The curriculum is generally designed for youngsters at an average scholastic level.

The primary goals of the program are to impart basic entrepreneurship knowledge, skills, and attitudes which enable students to initiate ventures of their own. The affective dimension of the curriculum seeks to build positive attitudes toward entrepreneurship in general and toward the personal practice of entrepreneurship—and to enhance student self-esteem.

The role of the teacher in the curriculum is that of a facilitator who guides participants through firsthand, real-world entrepreneurship experiences that enable them to construct their own knowledge, make decisions, and bear the consequences of their decisions. The program is typically implemented through service organizations in out-of-school settings. It has also been implemented for entrepreneurship clubs and as a one-semester course for within-classroom settings. The first three modules have been incorporated in school-to-work programs as part of their entrepreneurship awareness component. Outside-of-school implementation periods vary with local requirements.

The New Youth Entrepreneur was originally targeted as an in-school or after-school program for eighth through tenth grade students. However, the program has been successfully implemented at the seventh, eleventh, and twelfth grades as well and utilized in a variety of out-of-school settings by organizations such as the Peace Corps, Cities Within Schools, Department of Housing and Urban Development (HUD), and Future Farmers of America (FFA).

The New Youth Entrepreneur is at the dissemination stage and is being implemented nationwide though the use of a small cadre of certified trainers. After the 1995 development effort was completed, each module of the New Youth

Entrepreneur curriculum was pilot-tested—and subsequently enhanced based on the pilot results—before program dissemination was initiated. The program was also pilot-tested for its ability to successfully transfer to a variety of markets, and the development of standardized teacher training procedures are in progress. The 12 modules of the curriculum have been translated into Spanish, and piloting of the Spanish version in bilingual environments is in process.

Evaluative studies have established that the program is effective in multiple environments, including middle school and within or outside of high school. Persuasive research evidence from several experimental studies across multiple sites affirms the impact on both cognitive and affective learning. The program appears to be especially effective for at-risk students, as suggested by their average posttest score of 81 percent on the Gallup entrepreneurship questions (compared with the national average of 44 percent).

A number of the programs cited above have been evaluated by their developers or have had program evaluations that have not been published in refereed journals. For copies of these evaluations and more detailed information on the programs, please contact the authors at the Center for Entrepreneurial Leadership Inc., 4900 Oak Street, Kansas City, MO 64112.

The remaining section of this chapter provides recommendations for enhancing the effectiveness of entrepreneurship education and discusses techniques and approaches to develop entrepreneurship education programs in grades K–12.

Seven Habits of Effective Entrepreneurship Curriculum Development

The state of the art of K–12 entrepreneurship education may best be described as "to be determined." Although seven out of every 10 high school students want to start their own business and four out of five want more entrepreneurship education provided, the preceding examination of the field reveals that it is inconclusive whether and to what extent this striking market demand is being satisfied.

It appears that there is a "mixed bag" of nationally disseminated curricula currently available to prospective implementers. Some of the curricula have been "rigorously tested"; others have been "rigorously marketed" with only anecdotal evidence offered by the developers that the programs are indeed accomplishing their goals. This observation is not meant to imply that the latter programs are necessarily not achieving their goals; it simply suggests that rhetoric, as opposed to quantitative or qualitative research evidence, is being offered as the prime indicator of success.

Students today want to *make* a job rather than *take* a job. Entrepreneurship educators and developers can do much to ensure students are receiving the benefits of quality programs. The following recommendations are offered in an effort to accelerate the state of the art in entrepreneurship education by creating a larger pool of exemplary entrepreneurship education programs with maximum potential for research-validated effectiveness in diverse settings.

Habit 1

An entrepreneurship curriculum should be about entrepreneurship. There is a strong (and growing) demand for entrepreneurship education. Given the shortage of programs available to meet the demand, it is not surprising that off-target programs—in areas such as economic education, business management, leadership development, and cooperative learning—are being seized upon and relabeled as plausible substitutes. Such programs are generally well-intentioned, often add value to the student learning process, and provide content that can be related to entrepreneurship. Economics can help students understand the relationship between entrepreneurship and a market economy; business management skills are important to the success of a business already operating; leadership development and cooperative learning can enhance the effectiveness of the entrepreneurial development team (Kourilsky, 1995; Slaughter, 1996). However, such programs do not focus on the key themes of entrepreneurship. For example, "buy wholesale, sell retail" may be a useful rubric for understanding the gross margins of certain classes of retail businesses, but it is not a sufficiently robust theme for providing students with a solid grasp of the concepts and skills of entrepreneurship. As we discussed earlier, a true entrepreneurship education program must focus on and successfully educate students in the core areas of entrepreneurship: the identification or recognition of a market opportunity, the generation of a business idea to address the opportunity; the marshaling of resources in the face of risk to pursue the opportunity; and the creation of an operating business venture to implement the business idea (Kourilsky, 1995; Sahlman and Stevenson, 1992).

Habit 2

An entrepreneurship curriculum should be experiential or experience-based. Those individuals who are attracted to entrepreneurship typically are *doers* who span a broad range of intellectual abilities; they are active rather than passive. They can tolerate ambiguity and tend to engage in nonlinear as opposed to linear thinking. They learn *especially well* in environments that promote experiential learning. Evidence has shown that their learning is even more enhanced when the instruction is *experience-based*, i.e., when the concepts which arise during the experiences are isolated, reviewed, and reinforced through formal debriefings (Kourilsky, 1979, 1983). In many of the curricula reviewed, the only experiential learning that occurred was in the context of field trips—or possibly at the culmination of the program if a student decided, for example, to start a business. The instructional approaches throughout the curricula often were didactic and directive, interleaved with fill-in-the-workbook-type activities. The authors recommend that prospective curricular innovators weave and integrate experiential learning opportunities *throughout* their curricula—rather than as uncertain by-products of culminating activities. All chapters or sections of their curricula should provide opportunity for active as opposed to passive learning in order to accommodate the learning styles and maximize entrepreneurship concept acquisition and understanding for those students who have the potential entrepreneur's typical learning profile. Otherwise, curricula developers may find that in practice their curricula are perceived as "traditional textbook" in approach—an approach that has been shown to "lose and bore" many of the nontraditional learners that entrepreneurship educators are most interested in targeting.

Habit 3

An entrepreneurship curriculum should be based on principles of learning theory. Key learning principles such as task analysis, generative learning, and developmental readiness should be applied throughout a curriculum to maximize learning and retention (Hunter, 1974; Kourilsky and Quaranta, 1987).

Almost all the curricula examined included specification of instructional goals and objectives. However, several did not reflect a careful instructional task analysis for meeting their goals and objectives. *Task analysis* includes two functions that are very important to the successful design of a curriculum:

1. Breaking down of complex concepts and learning tasks into collections of simpler learning components and steps.
2. Careful sequencing of those components and steps to optimize the instructional cohesiveness and effectiveness of the curriculum in general.

In an arithmetic curriculum, an individual who will be learning to multiply first needs to have learned how to add. Similarly, in a well-sequenced entrepreneurship curriculum, students should not be asked to develop business plans before they understand business plan learning components such as target markets, income statements, and balance sheets; nor should they be asked to perform present value analysis before the skills and concepts it requires—such as calculation of interest and return on capital—have been verified. When performing curricular task analysis, the developer must first take into account the baseline or entry level knowledge of the learners. The developer then must design and order the sequence of learning components and steps so that it starts at the learners' baseline and proceeds all the way to the curriculum's objectives with an intellectual flow that corresponds to students' natural learning processes.

Several of the curricula reviewed also were not sensitive to the generative learning needs of the entrepreneurship student. The concept of *generative learning*—synthesized from contemporary brain research—clarifies that the brain is not a passive consumer of information. During the learning process, it actively tries to construct meaningful relationships between unfamiliar concepts and familiar knowledge and experiences that may be relevant (Wittrock, 1974). As students construct connections between previous experience (the familiar) and new conceptual knowledge (the unfamiliar), they generate a meaning consistent with their perceptions or interpretations. Thus, when curriculum writers construct explanations and examples, they must be aware of and draw upon the previous knowledge and experiences of their target student audience. Only then will the curriculum be able to tap into the generative learning capabilities of the students and enable them to link the unfamiliar, the new concepts and knowledge of entrepreneurship, to the familiar cognitive terrain of their previously acquired knowledge, understandings, observations, and interactions. The authors further recommend that curriculum writers use the enhancement stage of the curricular process to refine their explanations and examples after ascertaining whether and to what extent learners could make meaningful connections between them and their own knowledge and experiences. A final caution to developers is that a curriculum should not be targeted for too many audiences because learners in different age groups and from different backgrounds usually cannot relate generatively to the same examples and explanations.

Finally, the authors observed that some of the curricula were written without adequately considering the developmental readiness of the learner. A curriculum must be appropriate to the *developmental stage* of its target audience. Jean Piaget's theory of cognitive development describes the intellectual stages individuals traverse as they construct and acquire knowledge during their physical development years (Piaget, 1952). For example, in the stage of *concrete operations*, individuals are able to solve problems systematically that involve real, observable objects and/or concrete events that have occurred in their own experiences. It is not until the stage of *formal operations* however, that they have the readiness to reason logically and abstractly, test hypotheses, and deal with "made-up" or hypothetical problems. Applying this example, developers of curricula targeting students primarily at the concrete operations stage would have to be careful not to employ instructional methods (e.g., graphs, abstract word problems, and theoretical what-if scenarios) that require the student to be functioning intellectually at the stage of formal operations.

It is clear from the above discussion that developers who aspire to the creation of effective entrepreneurship curricula should ensure that all aspects of the curricula reflect and are consistent with research-informed learning theory and principles.

Habit 4

An entrepreneurship curriculum should evolve through all four stages of development (pilot, enhancement, custom transfer, and mass transfer). Skipping any of these stages will generally compromise the ultimate quality and effectiveness of a curriculum. For example, if a curriculum does not go through a pilot stage during which formative evaluation is conducted, it is very difficult to ascertain what the student is learning, what parts of the curriculum are accomplishing their objectives, and what parts of the curriculum need refining. It is not unusual for programs to skip the pilot stage and proceed immediately to dissemination. When such programs subsequently find that they are not accomplishing the objectives of their curricula, their final evaluations often have a natural bias toward the assumption that the problem lies with the instructors and/or with the students. The dissemination investment already in place makes it very painful to consider objectively the very real possibility that there might be inherent deficiencies in the curricula themselves. As another example, if an aspiring curriculum innovator decides to skip the curricular stage of custom transfer, it is quite possible to conclude that the curriculum appears effective in general when in fact its effectiveness may have been largely a consequence of the particular characteristics of the environment in which it was piloted or of the particular talents or charisma of the instructor who was implementing the pilot. Thus, it is important—in addition to piloting—to implement and evaluate a curriculum at multiple sites with diverse environments and types of instructors. This step helps the developer to ascertain which indications of effectiveness can be attributed to the strengths of the curriculum itself rather than to the unique characteristics of the pilot instructors or environment. It also provides additional opportunities to enhance the curriculum for more reliable impact across different student populations, instructors, and learning environments.

Once a curriculum has been demonstrated to be reliably replicable and capable of achieving its alleged outcomes across varying environments, it may then be a candidate for further dissemination and even for mass transfer—especially if it also can be demonstrated that the curriculum is affordable and cost-effective.

Habit 5

Certified instructor training (and training of trainers) programs should be initiated for a curriculum intended for mass transfer. Once a program has progressed through the first two stages of curricular development—pilot testing and curriculum enhancement—the introduction of formalized instructor training should be given priority attention for those programs targeted for widespread dissemination. This is an important step for developers whose goals include effective control of the *quality* of implementation during the custom and mass transfer stages. Curriculum innovators will want to be sure that the implementers identified for the first stage of dissemination (custom transfer) are thoroughly knowledgeable and proficient with respect to the program's rationale, salient characteristics and components, subject matter content, and methodology and sequencing. Currently, the programs reviewed that already include an instructor certification component (with one exception) rely on simple attendance at a training workshop as the criterion for awarding certification; certification does not require confirmation of postworkshop performance by attendees based on substantive measures. If quality control is a serious objective, then using workshop attendance as the sole criterion for certification is, in general, a recipe for meaningless or, at best, misleading certification. Attendance of a certification candidate by itself provides almost no reliable information about the degree to which the candidate absorbed the workshop content and is capable of implementing what was absorbed. Will such a candidate be on-target and effective during implementation? Thus, the authors maintain that requirements for instructor training certification must include postworkshop candidate performance (or postworkshop performance of the candidate's students) with respect to clearly defined, research-informed criteria that can be systematically and consistently measured.

Similarly, curriculum innovators will want to be sure that a certified pool of trainers of trainers is in place for the widespread dissemination stage (mass transfer) of the program. This step can be a major challenge even for sophisticated and experienced dissemination experts. Of course, the most natural candidates for trainers of trainers are instructors who are already effective in implementing the program directly for youngsters in their own classrooms (or in their own outside-of-school groups). However, curriculum developers should be aware that careful screening is usually needed to identify the surprisingly few out of this group (perhaps two out of 10, if you are fortunate) who also possess the instructional aptitude to train their *peers* how to implement the same program without major dilution of program objectives and overall quality. This major challenge notwithstanding, the successful development and maintenance of a cadre of effective, performance-certified trainers of trainers is a critical hurdle developers must clear in order to engage in program mass transfer dissemination without sacrificing program quality and ultimately, program longevity.

Habit 6

Curricular goals should be compatible with the organization and constraints of target implementation sites. Within-school settings typically limit student application experiences to class business projects with very limited (if any) personal creative freedom to identify opportunities and with virtually no personal student risk with respect to marshaling or investing resources, or they allow student groups to manage an existing predefined and usually failure-proof operation like the student store or a school fair. Since these experiences are really cooperative-learning-oriented projects in business management rather than true entrepreneurship applications, curricular goals for in-school programs are best focused on entrepreneurship awareness and readiness through experience-based methodologies. Environments sponsored by outside-of-school organizations or after-school clubs are much more flexible arenas for curricula whose goals include moving students from entrepreneurship readiness into true entrepreneurship application experiences. Curricular innovators who foster organizational alliances that link appropriate in-school and after-school curricula increase the likelihood that young people will experience the natural progression of moving from awareness of entrepreneurship, to readiness for entrepreneurship, and finally to the successful application of entrepreneurship principles and practices by creating ventures of their own.

Habit 7

An entrepreneurship curriculum should undergo systematic evaluation and enhancement on an ongoing basis. If the ultimate goal of the curricular initiator is to secure multiple long-run adoptions nationally, it is imperative that the curriculum routinely undergo ongoing cycles of systematic curricular evaluation and enhancement. The evaluations should utilize multiple measures (either norm-referenced or criterion-referenced) and multiple sample populations to study both anticipated and unanticipated outcomes of the curriculum. Such evaluations can provide substantive evidence of the curriculum's effectiveness in areas of success—and guidance for curricular enhancement in areas requiring improvement.

The evaluation process in general should be *student-centered*. It should focus on the outcomes related to student learning and on the implications for enhancing that learning. *When appropriate,* multisite quantitative experimental design studies (e.g., pretest/posttest treatment and control groups with adequate sample sizes) should be conducted. Care should be taken that tests utilized in such studies are valid and reliable instruments. Developers of entrepreneurship education programs should also consider formalized qualitative evaluations of their programs, such as studies based on in-depth focused interviews of certified trainers and practitioners.

The trend unfortunately appears to be to disseminate a curriculum before demonstrating its success, and then to conduct extensive teacher training to promote replication of the untested programs. Perhaps some developers elect to rush their innovations to the market because they hope to achieve quick entry into the field while the window of opportunity they perceive is still open. In other cases, it may be that the authors of unevaluated curricula lack the funding (or do not wish to use their funding) to conduct systematic research and development.

The authors believe that both of these approaches reflect curricular strategies which are nonentrepreneurial in the long run. Ultimately, the consumers of unevaluated curricula will assert their sovereignty. When the instructional costs for such curricula are no longer subsidized (i.e., when the educational delivery agents themselves must bear the financial costs of buying the materials and implementing the programs), they may indeed ask the following questions:

❖ What are the proven benefits to the students of a program under consideration?

❖ What is the cost per student of implementing the program?

❖ Are the benefits of the program worth the costs?

Eventually, when prospective program implementers must spend their own money, they will want to see hard data that confirms that the program really works—that it actually accomplishes its alleged results—and that the results merit the required financial investment. Thus, the final habit for curriculum developers recommended by the authors is to pursue with top priority an ongoing program of tightly designed quantitative and qualitative evaluation studies.

REFERENCES

Bocage, A., and G. Waters. 1985. *New Entrepreneurs*. Camden, NJ: Education, Training, and Enterprise Center.

Carlson, S.R. 1994. Entrepreneurship Education for the Multiple Cognitive-Developmental Levels of Third Graders: Differential Impacts of Three Experience-Based Programs. Unpublished doctoral dissertation, University of California, Los Angeles.

Cassuto, A.E. 1980. The effectiveness of the elementary school mini-society program. *Journal of Economic Education* 11(2):59-61.

Elkind, D. 1962. Quantity conceptions in junior college students. *Journal of Social Psychology* 57:459-65.

Gallup Organization and National Center for Research in Economic Education. 1994. *Entrepreneurship and Small Business in the United States: A Survey Report on the Views of the General Public, High School Students, and Small Business Owners and Managers*. Kansas City, MO: Center for Entrepreneurial Leadership.

Graff, E.E. 1982. Economic Reasoning and Decision-Making of Third and Fourth Graders. Unpublished doctoral dissertation, University of California, Los Angeles.

Hahn, A. 1994. *Themes and Findings from the NFTE Pre-Evaluation Project: Toward Clear Standards and Standard Operating Procedures*. New York: National Foundation for Teaching Entrepreneurship.

Hopkins, M.C. 1989. Using Mini-Society to Teach the Florida Minimum Objectives in Economics. Unpublished masters thesis, University of West Florida.

Hunter, M.H. 1974. *Enhancing Teaching*. New York: Macmillan.

Kohlberg, L. and R. Meyer. 1972. Development as the aim of education. *Harvard Educational Review* 42(4):449-496.

Koon, S. 1995. The Relationship of Implementation of an Entrepreneurial Development Innovation to Student Outcomes. Unpublished doctoral dissertation, University of Missouri, Kansas City.

Kourilsky, M.L. 1974. *Beyond Simulation: The Mini-Society Approach to Instruction in Economics and Other Social Sciences*. Los Angeles: Educational Resource Associates.

Kourilsky, M.L. 1976. Perceived versus actual risk-taking in Mini-Societies. *Social Studies* 67(5):191-197.

Kourilsky, M.L. 1979. Optimal intervention: An empirical investigation of the role of the teacher in experience-based instruction. *Journal of Experimental Education* 47(4):339-345.

Kourilsky, M.L. 1980. Predictors of entrepreneurship in a simulated economy. *Journal of Creative Behavior* 14(3):175-198.

Kourilsky, M.L. 1981. Economic socialization of children: Attitude toward the distribution of rewards. *Journal of Social Psychology* 115:45-57.

Kourilsky, M.L. 1983. *Mini-Society: Experiencing Real-World Economics in the Elementary School Classroom*. Menlo Park, CA: Addison-Wesley.

Kourilsky, M.L. 1990. Entrepreneurial thinking and behavior: What role the classroom? In C.A. Kent (ed.): *Entrepreneurship Education: Current Developments, Future Directions*. New York: Quorum Books.

Kourilsky, M.L. 1995. Entrepreneurship education: Opportunity in search of curriculum. *Business Education Forum* 50(10):11-15.

Kourilsky, M.L., C. Allen, A. Bocage, and G. Waters. 1995. *The New Youth Entrepreneur*. Camden, NJ: Education, Training and Enterprise Center.

Kourilsky, M.L., and M. Ballard-Campbell. 1984a. Sex differences in a simulated classroom economy. *Sex Roles: A Journal of Research* 10(1-2):53-66.

Kourilsky, M.L., and M. Ballard-Campbell. 1984b. Mini-society: An individualized social studies program for children of low, middle, and high ability. *Social Studies* 75(5):224-228.

Kourilsky, M.L., and M. Campbell. 1981. The influence of instructional intervention on entrepreneurial attitudes of elementary school children. In D.L. Sexton and P.M. Van Auken (eds.): *Entrepreneurship Education*. Waco, TX: Baylor University Press.

Kourilsky, M.L., and E.E. Graff. 1986. Children's use of cost-benefit analysis: Developmental or non-existent. In S. Hodkinson and D. Whitehead (eds.): *Economic Education: Research and Development Issues*. Essex, UK: Longman Group.

Kourilsky, M.L., and J. Hirshleifer. 1976. Mini-Society vs. token economy: An experimental comparison of the effects on learning and autonomy of socially emergent and imposed behavior modification. *Journal of Educational Research* 69(10):376-381.

Kourilsky, M.L., and E. Keislar. 1983. The effect of the success-oriented teacher on pupil's perceived personal control and attitude toward learning. *Contemporary Educational Psychology* 8(2):158-167.

Kourilsky, M.L., and T. Murray. 1981. The use of economic reasoning to increase satisfaction with family decision-making. *Journal of Consumer Research* 8:183-188.

Kourilsky, M.L., and E.G. Ortiz. 1985. The Mini-Society and mathematical reasoning: An exploratory study. *Social Studies Review* 13:37-48.

Kourilsky, M.L., and M. Quaranta. 1987. *Effective Teaching: Principles and Practice*. Chicago: Scott, Foresman.

Kuhn, D., N. Langer, L. Kohlberg, and N. Hann. 1977. The development of formal operations in logical and moral judgment. *Genetics Psychology Monograph* 95:115.

National Business Education Association. 1995. Entrepreneurship education standards. In *National Standards for Business Education*. Reston, VA: National Business Education Association.

Ortiz, E.G. 1982. Mathematical Reasoning and Economic Cognition of Third and Fourth Grade Students: A Case Study of the Mini-Society Instructional System. Unpublished doctoral dissertation, University of California, Los Angeles.

Piaget, J. 1952. *The Origins of Intelligence in Children*. New York: W. W. Norton.

Piaget, J. 1967. *Six Psychological Studies*. New York: Vintage.

Sahlman, W.A., and H.H. Stevenson. 1992. *The Entrepreneurial Venture: Readings*. Cambridge, MA: Harvard Business School Publications.

Schwebel, M. 1975. Formal operations in first year college students. *Journal of Psychology* 91(1):133-141.

Slaughter, M.P. 1996. Seven keys to shaping the entrepreneurial organization. In R. Smilor and D.L. Sexton (eds.): *Leadership and Entrepreneurship*. Westport, CT: Quorum Books, 99-110.

Wadsworth, B.J. 1989. *Piaget's Theory of Cognitive and Affective Development*. White Plains, NY: Longman.

Wittrock, M.C. 1974. Learning as a generative process. *Educational Psychologist* 11:87-95.

CHAPTER 10

Entrepreneurship Education and Learning for University Students and Practicing Entrepreneurs

JOHN E. YOUNG

URRENTLY, THE ADJECTIVE "ENTREPRENEURIAL" is used in a host of varying contexts and embodies a wide variety of meanings and implications. For instance, entrepreneurial knowledge is on occasion referred to as the concepts, skills, and mentality associated with operating major corporations with greater flexibility, innovation, and responsiveness (Kao, 1991a). Entrepreneurial knowledge has also been associated with the formulation of comprehensive economic development plans to encourage the growth of new businesses within targeted geographic areas. For example, state governments have examined the value of such concepts, applied to the development of new and existing businesses within targeted industries or areas within the state (Eisinger, 1990). As a result of these applications, today there are researchers as well as administrators investigating and utilizing entrepreneurship concepts in government (Wortman, 1986). However, in this chapter and in the academic field of entrepreneurship, entrepreneurial knowledge is restricted to the concepts, skills, and mentality individual business owners employ in the process of starting and operating their growth-oriented businesses.

The utility of well-founded entrepreneurial knowledge lies in its value for increasing the effectiveness of new ventures as well as small- and medium-sized businesses. For instance, valid *concepts* that could enhance the effectiveness of new ventures and small firm operations would include a conceptual knowledge of the functional areas of traditional management education. However, such concepts would also include a knowledge of business creation (e.g., Gartner, 1989) and a knowledge of how to act

The author wishes to thank Sean Murray for invaluable assistance during the preparation of this chapter.

entrepreneurially (Bailey, 1986), taking quick advantage of opportunities as they occur (Peters, 1987) while avoiding or managing vulnerabilities and threats (Mackenzie, 1991). A knowledge of well-grounded *skills and behaviors* would include a knowledge of oral presentation skills, interpersonal skills, or the ability to construct a business plan. Some examples of valid *mentalities* would include an understanding of how to promote creative thinking (Lipper, 1987), develop and create a vision (Bird and Jelinek, 1988), embrace change as a catalyst for learning (Stumpf et al., 1991), and utilize opportunistic thinking (Timmons et al., 1995).

The purpose of this chapter is to present an overview and a perspective based on research pertaining to the quest for entrepreneurial knowledge and to consider the learning processes used by university students as well as practicing entrepreneurs. Specific questions include:

❖ What drives the desire of each for entrepreneurial knowledge?

❖ What are the characteristic learning similarities and differences of each?

❖ What are their knowledge acquisition processes?

❖ What are some approaches for assessing the outcomes of their entrepreneurship education and learning?

The Desire for Entrepreneurial Knowledge

In order to examine the quest for knowledge and the learning processes used by university students and practicing entrepreneurs, some initial clarification of the use of terms is in order. In this chapter, *entrepreneurship education* is considered the structured, formal conveyance of entrepreneurial knowledge. *Entrepreneurial knowledge* refers to the concepts, skills, and mentality individual business owners use during the course of starting and developing their growth-oriented businesses. *Entrepreneurial learning* refers to the active and cognitive processes individuals employ as they acquire, retain, and use entrepreneurial knowledge. The present assessment of the quest for entrepreneurial knowledge begins with an examination of the motives for acquiring such knowledge.

University Students

University students are motivated to study entrepreneurship for a variety of reasons. Based upon an analysis of all of the graduates of one program, observations of the author and others (e.g., Kuratko and Naffziger, 1993–94), several motives of university students for taking entrepreneurship courses and enrolling in such programs are apparent. For example, perhaps the most compelling reason for studying entrepreneurship at the university level is the desire to start one's own business and be one's own boss (Monroy and Reichert, 1993–94). Some students plan to start their own businesses immediately after completing their formal university training; others operate their own companies while enrolled in university courses; and still others take the courses or enroll in such programs with the intent of eventually starting their own enterprises. While the majority of students enrolled in such programs may ultimately intend to start their own businesses, this is not the only reason for enrolling in formal university courses and programs.

University students also enroll in entrepreneurship courses to acquire knowledge that will be helpful in promoting their careers in larger organizations. Specifically, knowledge pertaining to starting and operating growing companies can be useful for boosting one's career in either large corporations, nonprofit organizations, or government agencies that have significant numbers of small- and medium-sized business clients. Similarly, large corporations and nonprofit organizations seeking to act more entrepreneurially also hire entrepreneurial studies majors, particularly at the graduate level. Government agencies with entrepreneurs or small firm clients would also find entrepreneurial knowledge beneficial. Thus, while the knowledge acquired in university programs relates to new ventures and the operation of growth-oriented enterprises, this knowledge and perspective can be considered useful by the hiring officials of large corporations and organizations (see Kuratko and Naffziger, 1993–94).

Entrepreneurial knowledge can also represent a personal competitive advantage for students seeking to establish a basis for careers as independent professionals. For example, careers as independent lawyers, public accountants, consultants, physicians, dentists, and others could all benefit from this knowledge, since such professionals are, in effect, independent business owners.

Many students desire to acquire such knowledge because they, in fact, would prefer to work for growing small- and medium-sized businesses as employees. Entrepreneurial studies curricula sensitize students regarding how to

❖ Work with minimal resources.

❖ Wear many hats among several functional areas within a company

❖ Appreciate and develop venues for customer responsiveness.

❖ Develop an overall company-wide perspective for strategy development and problem-solving as opposed to a narrow functional perspective.

Some university students enroll in entrepreneurship courses as their own personal insurance against corporate restructuring and layoffs, which may occur later in their careers. This perspective of instilling an entrepreneurial spirit (Tan et al., 1995) within university students as insurance against corporate restructuring and economic downturns has been embraced by the upper levels of university administrations in at least three countries: Mexico, Singapore, and Sweden. Currently, no universities in the United States have embraced entrepreneurship courses as curricular policy, as a form of social insurance.

Finally, some students enroll in entrepreneurship courses as a result of their own intellectual curiosity with no conscious intention of actually employing the knowledge. These students aim to broaden their understanding of business and seek answers to questions such as, What is the significance of the emerging trend of entrepreneurship? What does it mean to be an entrepreneur? How do entrepreneurs function under conditions of ambiguity, adversity, and personal or professional risk? (Stumpf et al., 1991, 692). Practicing entrepreneurs, on the other hand, have very different motives for desiring to acquire entrepreneurial knowledge.

Practicing Entrepreneurs

Practicing entrepreneurs are moved to acquire entrepreneurial knowledge for substantially different reasons and motives from those of university students. Practicing entrepreneurs are motivated to acquire such knowledge in order to solve the novel problems they face in their enterprises. Novel problems are those which the entrepreneur has not faced previously. Novelty results from several sources, including changes in the external or internal environments of a business, or from modifications in the entrepreneur's goals. Novelty also results when new ideas are generated and expressed, when new ideas are combined with existing ideas and techniques, or when existing ideas and techniques are combined in a new way. These novel problems, which motivate learning, are in contrast to routine or recurring problems, which typically do not inspire a strong need to learn. Ideally, entrepreneurs should develop, or have their associates develop, rules and standard operating procedures (SOPs) for handling routine problems that are typically well-specified and have clearly delineated goals (Greeno and Simon, 1988).

Entrepreneurs are motivated to engage in learning processes as a response to both internally and externally generated novel problems. Internally generated problems are those that evolve as a result of the activities taking place within the operating domain of the entrepreneur's business. In contrast, externally generated problems are those that emerge independently or outside the domain of the operations or activities of the business or new venture. Generally speaking, the entrepreneur's desire to acquire entrepreneurial knowledge is reactive in nature to either internally or externally generated novel problems. Proactively motivated entrepreneurial learning processes are somewhat difficult to identify because problem-solving activities taken in response to problems, as well as those taken in response to opportunities, are both triggered as responses to situations that develop within the entrepreneur's internal or external environments.

In addition to classifying problems that stimulate entrepreneurial learning as either internally or externally generated, problems facing entrepreneurs can also be classified as either simple or complex learning efforts. Simple learning efforts are those problems which the entrepreneur is capable of understanding and solving alone, that is, without the assistance of others within the business. In contrast, complex learning projects are those in which the entrepreneur requires the cooperation of others within the business in order to be understood or solved. Designations of simple versus complex would also, of course, be a function of the entrepreneur's:

❖ Current skills and knowledge base.

❖ Problem-solving style.

❖ Available resources for solving the problem.

❖ The organization's culture.

❖ Various "political" factors.

❖ The stage of growth and development of the firm.

Following this reasoning and using terminology first introduced by Swinth (1971), we see that the complex/novel problem represents the entrepreneur's most challenging learning situation. Table 10.1 on p. 220 presents actual examples (Young and Sexton, 1996b) of internally and externally generated problems that could stimulate motivation to engage in learning responses by practicing entrepreneurs.

University and Practitioner Entrepreneurial Learning

Both university students and practicing entrepreneurs learn processively. They engage in active and cognitive processes in order to acquire the entrepreneurial knowledge they desire. The active processes are the actions and means employed to acquire such knowledge, while the cognitive processes refer to the storage and retrieval of such knowledge from long-term memory. These procedures become integrated, forming an active, developing, and constantly renewing way of learning for the individual.

The similarities between student and practitioner learning are numerous. For instance, both come to their learning environments with previously acquired knowledge, attitudes, and predispositions. Both learn through the enhancement of their long-term memories by accumulating new information regarding new business start-ups or the growth of their businesses. Both are compelled to modify their existing organized knowledge structures or cognitive schemata (Rumelhart, 1980) pertaining

TABLE 10.1
Internally and Externally Generated Problems
and Learning Responses of Practicing Entrepreneurs

	Internally Generated		**Externally Generated**	
Simple	Stimulus	Repeated employee turnover.	Stimulus	Competitor introduces new product.
	Response	CEO develops first set of formal hiring guidelines.	Response	CEO investigates and locates new competitive products in response.
	Stimulus	Need for timely, accurate, financial statements.	Stimulus	Company experiences adverse relations with industry association and suppliers.
	Response	CEO acquires and learns new financial software.	Response	CEO establishes external relations with mentors to "learn the ropes" in terms of effective industry relationships.
Complex	Stimulus	Continuous operating questions from employees.	Stimulus	Repeated violation of federal operating regulations.
	Response	CEO coordinates and directs the development of the company's first operating manual.	Response	CEO leads and directs company's first comprehensive operating manual.
	Stimulus	Key employee quits.	Stimulus	Company acquires its first government contract.
	Response	CEO and management team develop new operating procedures.	Response	CEO leads and directs the establishment of new offices and operating procedures in order to comply with contract.

to venture initiation or the growth of their companies. But, despite the many similarities between university and practitioner entrepreneurial learning, there are several differences as well.

While a vast amount of research has been conducted regarding university entrepreneurship education and programs (Block and Stumpf, 1992), not as much attention has been given to elaborating the differences between university and practitioner entrepreneurial learning. Four differences between these two groups clearly emerge. For example, the research of Knowles (1980, 1984) indicates that the self-concept of younger, college-age students tends to be more dependent, while the self-concept of older practicing entrepreneurs is more self-directing and independent. Also, practicing adult entrepreneurs have an accumulated reservoir of work and life experiences they use as learning resources. Additionally, they possess a greater state of readiness for learning, including entrepreneurial learning. Finally, entrepreneurs are typically more concerned with the immediate application of their knowledge. Therefore, they tend to be more problem-centered in their learning efforts (Knowles, 1980). Young and Sexton (1996a) captured these differences between practicing adult and younger, students of entrepreneurship in summary form in Table 10.2. With

TABLE 10.2
Differences between Practicing Adult Entrepreneurs and Pre-Adult Students of Entrepreneurship

Variable	Practicing Adult Entrepreneur	Pre-Adult
Self-Concept	A mature self-concept, entrepreneur knows who he or she is, with clear personal goals and aspirations.	Still searching for self-identity, developing self-concept and belief structures.
Experience	Brings to learning situation an accumulated reservoir of business and life experiences which become an increasing resource for learning.	Has limited entrepreneurial, business, and life experiences. Requires learning situations that approximate real-world entrepreneurial experiences.
Readiness	Has a readiness to learn directly related to his or her role and responsibilities as a lead entrepreneur.	Has no direct entrepreneurial responsibilities associated with the outcome and effectiveness of the learning project.
Application	Is more problem-centered, concerned with the immediate application of knowledge.	Is more subject-centered, concerned with the long-term development and application of knowledge.

these differences in mind, the unique challenges and processes of university versus practitioner entrepreneurial learning will be considered in greater detail.

University-Based Education and Learning

University-Based Education and Pedagogy

University-based entrepreneurship curricula represent formally structured methods for conveying entrepreneurial knowledge. The fundamental purpose of formally constructed entrepreneurship education, including university-based curricula, is to prepare enrolled participants in thought and action to create and successfully administer growing, profitable enterprises, and in so doing, enhance the welfare of society (Hood and Young, 1993a, 116). Formally constructed entrepreneurship education, in this case university-based instruction, is concerned with the conveyance of entrepreneurial knowledge and developing the focused awareness that precludes flawed thinking, as it relates to opportunity recognition and the creation of new ventures, as well as the pursuit of such opportunities through the subsequent profitable growth of businesses (Hood and Young, 1993a, 116).

Frequently, university students enrolled in entrepreneurship courses lack the knowledge of business basics (Gartner and Vesper, 1994); typically, they lack actual experience in entrepreneurship. Therefore, the challenge for university entrepreneurship education curricula is to devise learning situations resulting in familiarization with business and entrepreneurship basics and replication of authentic entrepreneurship environments. Effective entrepreneurship curricula will ensure ecological validity (Murphy, 1986) during the processes of instruction, and require students to encounter materials and situations that match, as much as possible, the daily experiences they would face in their subsequent entrepreneurial careers (Hood and Young, 1994; Gartner and Vesper, 1994).

Research on entrepreneurship education has long advocated that the most effective approaches for conveying entrepreneurial knowledge are those which require students to engage in active learning processes. The volume of research in this area suggesting active, hands-on pedagogies for university learning is now comprehensive and includes a long list of researchers. For instance, Zeithaml and Rice (1987) indicated that students should learn by actually working with small businesses experiencing difficulties. Also, Haines (1988) discouraged traditional lecture settings, and recommended instead clinical, learn-by-doing situations. McMullan and Long (1987) stressed hands-on experience and real-world projects. Sexton and Bowman-Upton (1984, 1987) were significant contributors to the early research on pedagogical techniques, advocating that students work with existing entrepreneurs and encountering ambiguity and risks in unstructured situations. Stumpf et al. (1991)

suggested behavioral simulation for teaching the concepts and skills for entrepreneurship, and Gibb (1993) emphasizes the learn-by-doing processes experienced as in an actual small business.

Effective active, or experiential pedagogical, techniques are characterized by traits of concreteness, involvement, dissonance, and reflection (Hutchings and Wutzdorff, 1988). These same traits were related to entrepreneurship pedagogies by Hood and Young (1994). Problem-based learning is a specific form of active learning in which learning results within the process of resolving a problem. In this approach, the problem is encountered first in the learning process in contrast to formats in which the problem is presented to students after they have been provided with facts or principles that students can apply later (Barrows and Tomblyn, 1980). Hence, students experience true learning, through the process of discovery, as they search for and find solutions to the problems they face. Hood and Young (1994) listed 45 specific pedagogical techniques, suggested by successful entrepreneurs, which could be adapted to an active, problem-based, university-based curriculum.

In addition to class-affiliated pedagogical techniques, extracurricular learning activities such as student clubs, student-run businesses, student venture trade shows (see Vesper, 1993), and entrepreneurship-related economic development projects (e.g., Miners and Young, 1995) should be encouraged. This research builds from the premise that effective pedagogies for transferring entrepreneurial knowledge within university settings should be action-based. It further suggests that a problem-based format provides a more effective approach to action-based pedagogies.

University-Based Entrepreneurial Learning

University instructors that adopt active learning approaches typically believe that genuine learning, a more or less permanent enhancement of long-term memory, cannot occur without activity on the part of the students. These instructors employ active methodologies in these programs, taking the position that passive absorption or rote memorization cannot be called true learning (Alder, 1988). Rather, true learning, the process of discovery that results in expanded knowledge, includes far more than a surface orientation, which characterizes the mere memorization of facts. Instead, true learning comprises a deep orientation, which focuses on understanding, comprehension, and critical thinking (Pintrich, 1988).

For university students, true learning encompasses learning both the requisite concepts and procedures for successful entrepreneurship (Hood and Young, 1994). Conceptual knowledge entails the reformulation of their existing structures of entrepreneurial knowledge. Procedural knowledge entails the learning of new skills and habits (Squire et al., 1993) for successful entrepreneurship. For example, students would not only conceptually learn and understand the principles of marketing, as they relate to new ventures or businesses, but they also would practice sales procurement activities or assist businesses in designing and implementing such sales procurement activities. The design activities might well include developing steps for prospecting or closing company sales. Finally, as part of the mentoring process, those students who own their own businesses should be instructed in the techniques and methodologies of self-directed entrepreneurial learning through their own independent learning projects whenever possible and appropriate.

Practitioner Learning and Education

Practicing entrepreneurs also learn processively. They learn in real time, during the process of actually solving, or attempting to solve, the real problems they face. For example, Reuber and Fischer (1993) confirm in a study of Canadian biotechnology and telecommunications firms in which entrepreneurs believe that actual problem-solving experience, in their current firms, provides the foundation of their most meaningful learning.

Practitioner Entrepreneurial Learning

Practicing entrepreneurs engage in self-directed entrepreneurial learning when they take the initiative alone, or with the help of others, for planning, conducting, and evaluating their own learning activities (Young and Sexton, 1996a). Most of the learning activities engaged in by practicing entrepreneurs are in the self-directed mode. In this mode of learning, the entrepreneur takes the primary responsibility for the acquisition of knowledge that takes place in numerous settings, including the office, in the field, at home, or in formal classrooms. However, to say that entrepreneurs learn on their own is not to say that they learn alone. The entrepreneur's self-directed learning frequently entails collaboration and cooperation with others, (e.g., Gibb, 1993). For example, elements of the entrepreneur's personal and extended networks, such as suppliers, trade associations, associates within and outside the business, even competitors and customers, can assist in the learning process (Dubini and Aldrich, 1991; Johannisson, 1991). Additionally, information resources such as libraries, electronic media, and university-related assistance programs (Silva-Castan, 1994) can be engaged in helping the entrepreneur to learn. Since entrepreneurs typically are the top ranking officers within their own companies, they lack associates of equal rank within the business. As a result, many entrepreneurs experience a sense of psychological isolation (Boyd and Gumpert, 1983) during the processes of self-directed learning.

Earlier, it was suggested that entrepreneurs are motivated to learn as a result of the externally or internally generated problems they face. Entrepreneurs engage in self-directed learning, as opposed to seeking formal education and training or sub-contracting the problem-solving to others, for several reasons. Prominent among the reasons are:

1. Perceived immediate need for required knowledge.

2. Lack of availability of the precise class or workshop that meets their needs.

3. Lack of time to engage in a formal learning program.

4. The desire to structure the learning effort as they like.

5. The desire to keep the learning styles they use flexible.

6. The desire to take advantage of their own learning styles.

When entrepreneurs engage in highly deliberate efforts to gain knowledge and skill, or to change in some other way on behalf of their business, the efforts can be referred to as learning projects. This classic definition of learning projects, which is now applied to entrepreneurship, was first introduced by Tough (1978) and was previously related to entrepreneurs by Guglielmino and Klatt (1993).

Two proposed patterns for self-directed entrepreneurial learning are linear and non-linear. Applying a framework suggested earlier by Knowles (1975), Young and Sexton (1996a) report that the linear approach suggests that entrepreneurs systematically:

❖ Diagnose their learning needs.

❖ Formulate their learning goals.

❖ Identify human and material resources for learning.

❖ Choose and implement appropriate learning strategies.

❖ Evaluate learning outcomes.

However, such a neatly segmented, linear approach is probably rarely demonstrated by entrepreneurs in the course of their self-directed learning efforts. Instead, a nonlinear methodology is more likely. The nonlinear approach suggests that the entrepreneur may attempt multiple learning paths, dictated by necessity, evolving interests, cognitive barriers that may exist due to prior knowledge and experience within the business, and even the entrepreneur's own degree of optimism (e.g., Woo et al., 1992). The nonlinear approach emphasizes hands-on experience, practice, and trial-and-error as entrepreneurs move on to new levels of learning and understanding (Berger, 1990). During these learning processes, entrepreneurs naturally enhance their long-term memories for successful problem-solving by trying various and divergent paths for solving their problems.

Entrepreneurs learn in several areas as they work toward the solutions of novel problems. Gatewood et al. (1995) suggest that individuals who succeed at going into business are eager learners and become proficient at using new knowledge for adapting to new and changing circumstances.

During the course of operating a growing business, the entrepreneur's major areas of learning include marketing, financing, as well as designing and developing management systems and structures. For instance, Sargent and Young (1991) described a dynamic view of learning that takes place during the entrepreneur's continual search for financing. Similarly, Slovin and Young (1992) described how, in order to learn new methods and modes of financing as their businesses grow, entrepreneurs out of necessity are required to break out of their habitual financing problem-solving domains. Habitual problem-solving domains were defined as the recurring collection of ideas and actions that can be activated by an entrepreneur at any given time (Yu, 1980). The entrepreneur's habitual domains are bounded by his or her current knowledge regarding how to proceed in search of information for problem-solving (Woo et al., 1992). The implication is that, as the entrepreneur starts and grows a business, the habitual domains in the major areas of learning must continually expand as the business itself evolves through succeeding plateaus.

Finally, Young and Sexton (1995) explain that learning for practicing entrepreneurs is cumulative in nature and when entrepreneurs initiate new growth processes, their domain knowledge is frequently spotty. They noted that as entrepreneurs become dissatisfied with the current state of their knowledge in a given domain, they engage in mental experimentation. In turn, the mental models (Norman, 1983) they have formulated of their environments, problems, current operations, or plans are modified accordingly. Thus, entrepreneurial success is significantly determined by the degree of congruence between the entrepreneur's cognitive schema and mental models and the actual operating environments (Guth et al., 1991). In addition to the self-directed, cognitive, and procedural aspects of practitioner entrepreneurial learning, entrepreneurs also engage in structured, formal entrepreneurship education.

Practitioner Entrepreneurial Education

Most successful entrepreneurs engage in self-directed learning over time. Occasionally, however, they also engage in formal, structured entrepreneurship education or training. It is useful to think of the entrepreneur's engagement in formal education or training as a resource acquisition process.

The challenge of determining when a practicing entrepreneur should engage in formal, structured entrepreneurship education is becoming increasingly important in today's rapidly changing and information-rich environment. Given such an environment, the questions arise for the entrepreneur whether and at what point to 1) engage formal education and 2) to select the appropriate venues for such education.

The decision to engage in formal education involves a realistic self-assessment of the entrepreneur's level of knowledge and skills, as well as a similar assessment of others on the venture team or within the business. Generally, entrepreneurs perform tasks within their perceived realm of responsibility, for which they believe they have the capabilities. These perceived capabilities include: an interest in performing the task, adequate conceptual knowledge and skills, and adequate resources—including equipment and time—for performing the task. Other activities within the perceived realm of responsibility are either delegated, subcontracted, or not performed. The perspective taken here is that the entrepreneur will engage in formal, structured education when a net benefit is perceived for doing so.

The determination of a net advantage or benefit for engaging in structured entrepreneurship education will vary for every situation and within every process. The decision to engage in education can be influenced by several considerations or variables, including:

❖ Is the need for the knowledge urgent?

❖ Does the entrepreneur have any previous experience or exposure relevant to the needed conceptual knowledge or skills?

❖ Is there a desire for a short-term fix or for a more durable application of the knowledge and solution to the problem?

❖ Should the entrepreneur delegate the responsibility for acquiring the knowledge, or should the knowledge be acquired personally?

❖ Are there opportunity costs involved in acquiring the knowledge?

❖ Is a source of formal education that meets the entrepreneur's needs readily available?

❖ Is the source of formal instruction amenable to the entrepreneur's learning styles?

Several of these variables contrast with the reasons entrepreneurs use for engaging in self-directed learning. Generally speaking, entrepreneurs will undertake formal education when they perceive that the knowledge they will receive will be useful in solving the novel problems they face. A mapping function, a concept similar to a decision tree network, can be developed for 1) considering variables affecting the entrepreneur's decision to engage in formal education, and 2) predicting what specific personal entrepreneurship education strategies will be enacted (see Khandekar and Young, 1980; Tan et al., 1994).

Currently, much of the education for potential and practicing entrepreneurs appears aimed at specific niche populations or markets, a fact reflecting the nature of the funding for many of these education initiatives. For instance, structured, formal education programs for low-income potential entrepreneurs (e.g., Balkin, 1989; Hood and Young, 1993b) and entrepreneurs living in economically depressed areas (Birley and Westhead, 1992) are frequently developed. However, education and training for owners of ongoing or existing businesses appears to be less prevalent than training for new ventures (Gibb, 1983). Nevertheless, such programs have been conducted, and linkages between entrepreneurship education and improved managerial skills have been discovered (Barnes and Jones, 1995). For example, successful programs for existing businesses have been conducted for women and minority entrepreneurs with positive impact reported on the operating effectiveness of the businesses (Price and Monroe, 1992). Effective education programs would teach entrepreneurs how to approach self-directed learning, thereby teaching them how to learn (Johannisson, 1991).

Entrepreneurship Education and Learning Outcomes

University-Based Programs

Monroy and Reichert (1993–94) explained that traditional outcome assessment measures, such as objective and subjective instruments used in traditional management education, may not tap into reliable indices of entrepreneurship education at the university level. Earlier, McMullan and Long (1987) suggested that the goals and outcome measures of university entrepreneurship programs should be measured in terms of their socioeconomic impact. They went on to suggest outcome indicators such as number of companies created, number of jobs created, and other measures. Before that, McMullan et al. (1986) assessed the socioeconomic impact of an actual entrepreneurship outreach program based at a Canadian university, which utilized M.B.A. students, who, in the process of pursuing their degrees, assisted local businesses.

It was Hoy (1993–94) who suggested that in order to assess the outcomes of university-based programs, the stakeholders of such programs must first be determined. After identifying the programs' stakeholders, Hoy indicated that long-term and short-term objectives for such programs can be formulated. He further suggested that after identifying program stakeholders, a program's mission, goals, and outcome measures can be established.

Hood and Young (1995) depict a general process model for entrepreneurship education which closely fits Hoy's recommendation. The model calls for four basic steps. As the first step, they recommend that an entrepreneurship program should be anchored in a clearly defined strategic philosophy, which validates the basis of a clear program mission. The mission should fit the overall mission of the host organization or college. Hood and Young (1995) suggest that, in serving the various stakeholders, the mission should determine strategic and tactical plans, operating plans, guidelines, projects, and procedures. They call this first step in their model, "the development of a conceptual framework and mission."

The second step in their model contends that a comprehensive entrepreneurship program should reach a consensus regarding the design and development of teaching content without infringing on the academic freedom of any instructional faculty. This step involves developing content materials and reaching agreement with respect to what should be taught. The third step is called "the application of teaching methodologies for true learning." It concerns the selection of methodologies to be used for true learning of entrepreneurship concepts, procedures, and mentalities. Finally, the fourth step in this process model is called "monitoring, evaluation, and measuring methods." These processes and techniques evaluate outcomes and should, of course, be linked with and fit the program's overall philosophical foundation and strategic mission, reflecting in turn the philosophy and mission of the host organization. Each of the four elements in the general model evolves, and each mutually affects and interacts with every other element as the program designers and implementors themselves continually learn to adapt to their changing environments (Hood and Young, 1995). The general model for entrepreneurship education applied to university-based programs is depicted in Figure 10.1.

FIGURE 10.1
A General Model for Entrepreneurship Education

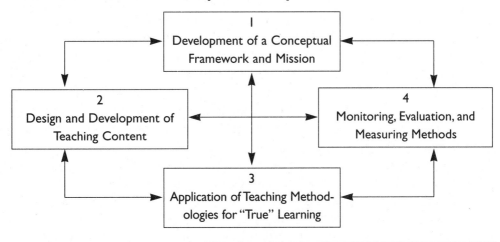

Practicing Entrepreneurs

As stated earlier, when entrepreneurs engage in self-directed learning, they diagnose their own learning needs, formulate their own learning goals, choose their own learning strategies (which may include formal, structured learning if such resources are available), and evaluate their own learning outcomes. From this understanding, it follows that the effectiveness of measuring the outcomes of self-directed learning would entail a straightforward, honest comparison of the entrepreneur's initial learning goals with the outcomes that evolve from a particular learning project. Entrepreneurs more experienced and knowledgeable regarding the self-directed approach could in fact develop their own individual learning plans (Young and Sexton, 1996a). These plans could be linked to the anticipated development of their ventures or businesses but should be flexible enough to allow them to take advantage of unforeseen opportunities and problems (Clifford, 1976).

Of course, when entrepreneurs engage in formal, structured education, traditional instruments such as surveys, interviews, and questionnaires can be administered both during the education process and to course graduates. Structured and unstructured instruments could be used for such assessments, and statistics pertaining to the entrepreneur's new venture or business could be analyzed before and after exposure to these structured educational efforts. The literature on various philosophies and methodologies for such program evaluation is extensive (e.g., Mohr, 1995; Patton, 1990). Finally, using frameworks pertaining to entrepreneurial learning, modifications in schemata, mental models, and frames of reference could also be assessed; similarly the progress of the learner, from novice to expert, can be tracked and analyzed.

Future Research Directions

This chapter commenced by considering three important concepts. Specifically, entrepreneurial knowledge was defined, then distinctions were made between the notions of entrepreneurial learning—the acquisition and retention of entrepreneurial knowledge in long-term memory, and entrepreneurship education—the structured, formal conveyance of entrepreneurial knowledge. Based on these three fundamental ideas, the current status of research for entrepreneurship education and learning for university students and practicing entrepreneurs was examined. Now the current status and future directions of research for these topic areas are summarized.

Present approaches to the consideration of entrepreneurship education and entrepreneurial learning suggest that they may be emerging as two distinct but strongly related subfields in entrepreneurship. While the learning and education approaches to entrepreneurial knowledge are distinct, in reality, neither can be adequately considered without reflection upon and consideration of the other. The status of previous and current research, as well as directions for future investigation of entrepreneurial learning for university student and practicing entrepreneurs, is depicted in Table 10.3.

Entrepreneurial Learning

Table 10.3 indicates that previous and current research on entrepreneurial learning in university-based programs have considered the active learning processes university students undertake in order to acquire knowledge. The vast amount of this research advocates active, participatory learning. The research also considers the

TABLE 10.3
The State of Entrepreneurial Learning and Education Research

University-Based	Practicing Entrepreneurs
Previous and Current Research	**Previous and Current Research**
Active processes	Active processes
Active learning through experiential approaches	Information search
Problem-based and other experiential approaches	Previous experience and search
Contrasts between memorization and "true learning"	Self-directed search
Focus on concepts, skills, and mentality development	Cognitive processes
Extra-curricular learning venues	Learning styles
	Cognitive schemata
Future Directions	**Future Directions**
Cognitive development	Active processes
Schematic development	Self-directed search
Mental models	Search behavior
Long-term memory enhancement	
	Cognitive processes
	Novice versus experts
	Schematic development
	Mental models
	Enhancement of long-term memory
	Learning failures

development of the conceptual base, skills, and mentalities most appropriate for successful entrepreneurship. However, no research has been conducted regarding the cognitive processes students use to acquire entrepreneurial knowledge.

Future studies examining learning for university students should include consideration of the cognitive processes that enhance students' long-term knowledge bases. Cognitive development of schemata, mental models of students, and approaches for encouraging evolution of entrepreneurial knowledge in long-term memory provide examples of topics that should be addressed.

Meanwhile, research regarding the learning processes of practicing entrepreneurs has just begun. Previous research can be divided into the examination of the entrepreneur's active and cognitive learning processes. Topics for future research regarding the learning processes of entrepreneurs are numerous, and this area of investigation should develop rapidly. For instance, both the areas of active and cognitive processes require a great deal of additional research. Activities involved in the self-directed search of entrepreneurs have only recently begun to be addressed, and general issues related to the entrepreneur's search behavior require further investigation. The consideration of the cognitive processes of entrepreneurs has also just begun. Areas such as the cognitive processes of novice versus expert entrepreneurs, schematic development of successful versus unsuccessful practitioners, development of mental models, and general enhancement of long-term memory over time are all issues requiring further research. Analysis of learning failures from the perspective of cognition represents another potentially intriguing area of study. Finally, the study of entrepreneurial learning for both university students, as well as practitioners, should be more closely linked with considerations of formal, structured, entrepreneurship education. Table 10.4 reflects previous and current research and future research directions for entrepreneurship education.

Entrepreneurship Education

The topic of entrepreneurship education has received considerably more attention than the area of entrepreneurial learning. Within the area of entrepreneurship education, university-based education has been researched most extensively. Specifically, issues pertaining to the subject matter of entrepreneurship—can it be taught, what to teach; how to teach and evaluate outcomes—have received the most attention. A great deal of research has also been conducted regarding program development—the evolution of university programs and their evaluation (e.g., Ronstadt, 1990; Vesper, 1993).

A great deal of research is still needed in this extensively examined area of entrepreneurship education. Additional research is required in the area of instructional delivery; for instance, research regarding the further development and evaluation of

TABLE 10.4
The State of Entrepreneurship Education Research

University-Based	Practicing Entrepreneurs
Previous and Current Research	**Previous and Current Research**
Subject Matter	Program Evaluations for Potential and
Can it be taught?	Existing Entrepreneurs
What to teach?	Niche markets such as low-income
	individuals, economically depressed
Instructional Delivery	areas, women, minorities, etc.
How to teach (perspective, pedagogies,	
and technologies)	Evaluation of Pedagogical Approaches
Evaluation of education outcomes	Simulation, etc.
Program Development	
Evolution of programs	
Analysis and evaluation of programs	
Future Directions	**Future Directions**
Instruction and Delivery	Program Evaluations for Growth-Oriented
Pedagogies and teaching technologies	and Technology Entrepreneurs
Evaluation of teaching processes and	
refinement of evaluation of outcomes	General Models of Instruction
Faculty Development and Evaluation	Pedagogical Methods and Techniques

pedagogies and teaching technologies is needed. Research pertaining to the evaluation of teaching processes and further research refining the assessments of teaching outcomes are required. Finally, while some discussion of the development of entrepreneurship faculty has occurred, there is much need for research in this area.

Research regarding formal education for practicing entrepreneurs has focused primarily on niche markets. The evaluation of programs for low-income, economically depressed areas, and other specialty topics has been undertaken. Also, the evaluation of some specific pedagogical approaches has occurred. Future directions for research on formal, structured education programs should include niches for growth-oriented entrepreneurs and technology entrepreneurs, areas which seem to have been neglected. General models for education for entrepreneurs need to be developed, and greater emphasis on the development and evaluation of specific pedagogical methods and techniques, suitable for use for practicing entrepreneurs should be encouraged.

In today's rapidly changing environment, perspectives on entrepreneurial knowledge, entrepreneurial learning, and education are likewise constantly changing. Future prospects for research on these topics, as they relate to university students and practicing entrepreneurs, are limited only by the imagination of the investigators. Clearly, such research will be continually needed if entrepreneurs are to remain competitive and significant contributors to their respective national economies.

REFERENCES

Adler, M.J. 1988. Teaching, learning, and their counterfeits. In M.J. Adler (ed.): *Reforming Education: The Opening of the American Mind*. New York: Macmillan, 167-175.

Bailey, J.E. 1986. Learning styles of successful entrepreneurs. In R. Ronstadt (ed.): *Frontiers of Entrepreneurship Research*. Wellesley, MA: Babson College, 199-210.

Balkin, S. 1989. *Self-Employment for Low-Income People*. New York: Praeger.

Barnes, L., and S. Jones. 1995. Small business training programs in Victoria: A survey of course content and effectiveness. *Journal of Enterprising Culture* 3(1):1-57.

Barrows, H., and R. Tomblyn. 1980. *Problem-based Learning*. New: Springer.

Berger, N. 1990. A Qualitative Study of the Process of Self-Directed Learning. Doctoral dissertation, Division of Educational Studies, Virginia Commonwealth University, Richmond, VA.

Bird, B., and M. Jelinek. 1988. The operation of entrepreneurial intention. *Entrepreneurship Theory and Practice* 13(2):21-29.

Birley, S., and P. Westhead. 1992. A comparison of new firms in "assisted" and "non-assisted" areas in Great Britain. *Entrepreneurship and Regional Development* 4(4):299-338.

Block, Z., and S.A. Stumpf. 1992. Entrepreneurship education research: Experience and challenge. In D.L. Sexton and J.D. Kasarda (eds.): *The State of the Art of Entrepreneurship*. Boston: PWS-Kent, 17-42.

Boyd, D., and D. Gumpert. 1983. The loneliness of the entrepreneurs. In J.A. Hornaday et al. (eds.): *Frontiers of Entrepreneurship Research*. Wellesley, MA: Babson College, 180-191.

Clifford, D.K. 1976. The case of the floundering founder. *McKinsey Quarterly* (Winter):30-45.

Dubini, P., and H. Aldrich. 1991. Personal and extended networks are central to the entrepreneurial process. *Journal of Business Venturing* 6(5):305-313.

Eisinger, P. 1988. *The Rise of the Entrepreneurial State*. Madison, WI: University of Wisconsin Press.

Eisinger, P. 1990. Do the American states do industrial policy? *British Journal of Political Science* 20:509-535.

Entrepreneurial Studies Alumni Directory. 1996. Robert O. Anderson Schools of Management, University of New Mexico, Albuquerque, NM.

Gartner, W.B. 1989. Who is an entrepreneur? is the wrong question. *Entrepreneurship Theory and Practice* 13(4):47-68.

Gartner, W.B., and K.H. Vesper. 1994. Experiments in entrepreneurship education: Success and failures. *Journal of Business Venturing* 9(3):179-187.

Gatewood, E.J., K.G. Shaver, and W.B. Gartner. 1995. A longitudinal study of cognitive factors influencing start-up behaviors and success of venture creation. *Journal of Business Venturing* 10(5):371-391.

Gibb, A.A. 1983. Small business challenge to management education. *Journal of European Industrial Training* 7(5):3-8, 38-39.

Gibb, A.A. 1993. The enterprise culture and education. *International Small Business Journal* 11(3):11-34.

Greeno, J.G., and H.A. Simon. 1988. Problem solving and reasoning. In R.C. Atkinson et. al. (eds.): *Stevens' Handbook of Experimental Psychology.* New York: John Wiley and Sons, 589-672.

Guglielmino, P.J., and L.A. Klatt. 1993. Entrepreneurs as self-directed learners. In J.S. Devlin and M.M. Trevino (eds.): *Proceedings 38th World Conference ICSB,* Las Vegas, Nevada, June 20-23, pp. 206-216.

Guth, W.D., A. Kumaraswamy, and M. McErlean. 1991. Cognition, enactment and learning in the entrepreneurial process. In N. Churchill et al. (eds.): *Frontiers in Entrepreneurship Research.* Wellesley, MA: Babson College, 242-253.

Haines, G.H., Jr. 1988. The ombudsman: Teaching entrepreneurship. *Interfaces* 18(5):23-30.

Hood, J.N., and J.E. Young. 1993a. Entrepreneurship's requisite areas of development: A survey of top executives in successful entrepreneurial firms. *Journal of Business Venturing* 8(3):115-135.

Hood, J.N., and J.E. Young. 1993b. Entrepreneurship as a route out of poverty and low-income status: Realities, barriers, and hope. In J.S. Devlin and M.M. Trevino (eds.): *Proceedings 38th World Conference ICSB,* Las Vegas, Nevada, June 20-23, pp. 193-201.

Hood, J.N., and J.E. Young. 1994. Methods for conveying entrepreneurial knowledge: Perceptions of top executives from successful entrepreneurial firms. *Journal of Enterprising Culture* 1:297-320.

Hood, J.N., and J.E. Young. 1995. Entrepreneurship education and economic development: Bridging the gap. *Entrepreneurship, Innovation, and Change* 4(2):133-147.

Hoy, F. 1993–94. Evaluating short-term vs. long-term learning outcomes. In F. Hoy et al. (eds.): *The Art and Science of Entrepreneurship Education,* 2 vols. Berea, OH, pp. 215-220.

Hoy, F., T.G. Monroy, and J. Reichert (eds.). 1993–94. *The Art and Science of Entrepreneurship Education,* 2 vols. Berea, OH.

Hutchings, P., and A. Wutzdorff. 1988. Experiential learning across the curriculum: Assumptions and principles. In P. Hutchings and A. Wutzdorff (eds.): *New Directions for Teaching and Learning* 35:5-19.

Johannisson, B. 1991. University training for entrepreneurship: Swedish approaches. *Entrepreneurship and Regional Development* 3(1):67-82.

Kao, J.J. 1991a. *The Entrepreneurial Organization*. Englewood Cliffs, NJ: Prentice Hall.

Kao, J.J. 1991b. *Managing Creativity*. Englewood Cliffs, NJ: Prentice Hall.

Khandekar, R., and J.E. Young. 1980. Selecting a legal form: A strategic decision. *Journal of Small Business Management* 23:47-55.

Knowles, M.S. 1975. *Self-Directed Learning*. New York: Association Press.

Knowles, M.S. 1980. *Modern Practice of Adult Education: From Pedagogy to Androgy*, 2nd ed. New York: Cambridge Books.

Knowles, M.S. 1984. *The Adult Learner: A Neglected Species*, 3rd ed. Houston: Gulf Publishing.

Kuratko, D.F., and D.W. Naffziger. 1993–94. The integral role of experience in quality entrepreneurship education. In F. Hoy et al. (eds.): *The Art and Science of Entrepreneurship Education*, 2 vols. Berea, OH, pp. 337-344.

Lipper, A., III. 1987. If constructively creative divergent equals entrepreneur ... how can we help create more of them? *Journal of Creative Behavior* 21:214-218.

Mackenzie, K.D. 1991. *The Organizational Hologram: The Effective Management of Organizational Change*. Boston: Kluwer.

McMullan, W.E., and W.A. Long. 1987. Entrepreneurship education in the nineties. *Journal of Business Venturing* 3:1-10.

McMullan, W.E., W.A. Long, and J.B. Graham. 1986. Assessing economic value added by university-based outreach programs. *Journal of Business Venturing* 1:225-240.

Miners, I., and J.E. Young. 1995. University-based entrepreneurship programmes as vehicles for state-level economic development: A case study. *The Journal of Entrepreneurship* 4(2):185-214.

Mohr, L. B. 1995. *Impact Analysis for Program Evaluation*. Thousand Oaks: CA.: Sage Publications.

Monroy, T., and J. Reichert 1993–94. Learning outcomes assessment: Serendipitous findings. In F. Hoy et al. (eds.): *The Art and Science of Entrepreneurship Education*, 2 vols. Berea, OH, pp. 185-200.

Murphy, D.A. 1986. Designing systems that train learning ability: From theory to practice. *Review of Educational Research* 56(1):1-30.

Norman, D.A. 1983. Some observations on mental models. In D. Genter and A.L. Stevens (eds.): *Mental Models*. Hillsdale, NJ: Erlbaum.

Patton, M.Q. 1990. *Qualitative Evaluation and Research Methods*. Thousand Oaks, CA: Sage.

Peters, T. 1987. *Thriving on Chaos*. New York: Harper and Row.

Pintrich, R.R. 1988. Student learning and college teaching. In R.E. Young and K.E. Eble (eds.): *New Directions for Teaching and Learning* pp. 71-86.

Price, C., and S. Monroe. 1992. Educational training for women and minority entrepreneurs positively impacts venture growth and development. In N.C. Churchill et al. (eds.): *Frontiers of Entrepreneurship Research*. Wellesley, MA: Babson College, pp. 216-230.

Reuber, A.R., and E.M. Fischer. 1993. The learning experiences of entrepreneurs. In N.C. Churchill et al. (eds.): *Frontiers of Entrepreneurship Research*. Wellesley, MA: Babson College, pp. 234-242.

Ronstadt, R. 1990. Emerging structures in entrepreneurship education: Curricular designs and strategies. *Entrepreneurship Theory and Practice* 14(3):55-70.

Rumelhart, D. 1980. Schemata: The building blocks of cognition. In R. Spiro et al. (eds.): *Theoretical Issues in Reading Comprehension*. Hissdale, NJ: Erlbaum, 33-58.

Sargent, M., and J.E. Young. 1991. The entrepreneurial search for capital: A behavioural science perspective. *Entrepreneurship and Regional Development* 3:237-252.

Sexton, D.L., and N.B. Bowman. 1984. Entrepreneurship education: Suggestions for increasing effectiveness. *Journal of Small Business Management* 22(2):18-25.

Sexton, D.L., and N.B. Bowman. 1987. Evaluation of an innovative approach to teaching entrepreneurship. *Journal of Small Business Management* 25(1):35-43.

Silva-Castan, J.R. 1994. The relationship between institutions of higher education and small business in the United States. *Journal of Enterprising Culture* 2(3):771-798.

Slovin, M.B., and J.E. Young. 1992. The entrepreneurial search for capital: An investment in financial relationships. *Entrepreneurship, Innovation, and Change* 1(2):177-193.

Squire, L.R., B. Knowlton, and G. Musen. 1993. The structure and organization of memory. *Annual Review of Psychology* 3:453-495.

Stumpf, S.S., R.L.M. Dunbar, and T.P. Mullen. 1991. Simulation in entrepreneurship education: Oxymoron or untapped opportunity? In N. Churchill et al. (eds.): *Frontiers in Entrepreneurship Research*. Wellesley, MA: Babson College, pp. 681-695.

Swinth, R.L. 1971. Organizational joint problem-solving. *Management Science* 18:320-335.

Tan, T.M., W.L. Tan, and J.E. Young. 1994. A conceptualization of the entrepreneurial infrastructure: The case of Singapore. In R. Zutshi et al. (eds.): *Proceedings of the 5th ENDEC World Conference on Entrepreneurship*, July 7-9, Singapore.

Tan, W.L., L.K. Tan, W.H. Tan, and S.C. Wong. 1995. Entrepreneurial spirit among tertiary students in Singapore. *Journal of Enterprising Culture* 3(2):211-227.

Timmons, J., D. Muzyka, H. Stevenson, and W. Bygrave. 1987. Opportunity recognition: The core of Entrepreneurship. In N. Churchill et al. (eds.): *Frontiers of Entrepreneurship Research*. Wellesley, MA: Babson College, 109-123.

Tough, A. 1978. Major learning efforts: Recent research directions. *Adult Education* 28(4):250-263.

Vesper, K.H. 1993. *Entrepreneurship Education 1993*. Los Angeles: Entrepreneurial Studies Center, UCLA.

Woo, C., T. Folta, and A. Cooper. 1992. Entrepreneurial search: Alternative theories of behavior. In N.C. Churchill et al. (eds.): *Frontiers of Entrepreneurship Research*. Wellesley, MA: Babson College, 681-695.

Wortman, M.S. 1986. A unified framework, research topologies, and research prospectus for the interface between entrepreneurship and small business. In D.L. Sexton and R.W. Smilor (eds.): *The Art and Science of Entrepreneurship*. Cambridge, MA: Ballinger, 273-331.

Young, J.E., and D.L. Sexton. 1995. Explicit learning: When entrepreneurs know what they know. In R. Zutshi et al. (eds.): *Proceedings 6th ENDEC World Conference on Entrepreneurship*, December 7–9, Shanghai, China, pp. 64-70.

Young, J.E., and D.L. Sexton. 1996a. The nature of entrepreneurial learning. Working paper, Kansas City, MO: Center for Entrepreneurial Leadership, E.M. Kauffman Foundation.

Young, J.E., and D.L. Sexton. 1996b. Assessing the entrepreneurial learning process. Working paper, Kansas City, MO: Center for Entrepreneurial Leadership, E.M. Kauffman Foundation.

Yu, P.L. 1980. Behavior bases and habitual domains of human decision/behavior—concepts and applications. In G. Fandel and T. Gal (eds.): *Multiple Criteria Decision Making: Theory and Applications*. New York: Springer-Verlag.

Zeithaml, C.P., and G.H. Rice, Jr. 1987. Entrepreneurship/small business education in American universities. *Journal of Small Business Management* 25(1):44-50.

Broader Dimensions of Entrepreneurship

Broader Dimensions of Entrepreneurship

I N THE EARLY 1980S A DISTINCTION BEGAN to emerge that separated the areas of small business and entrepreneurship. The distinction was growth, and entrepreneurs were defined as persons who sought opportunity and the resources necessary to pursue that opportunity. The desire and opportunity or the will and skill to grow separated entrepreneurial (growth-oriented) firms from the no resources, no opportunity pursuance attitude of most of the small businesses and large corporate organizations.

With the definition of growth via opportunity recognition and resource gathering, entrepreneurship researchers began to examine a number of other areas beyond those of business start-up and ownership. In this section Upton and Heck discuss the family business dimension of entrepreneurship and conclude that research in this specialty area, although much like entrepreneurship in the mid-1980s, is following the same path. They argue that with the exception of family issues, the problems faced by family businesses are no different from mainstream entrepreneurship.

Butler and Greene examine another dimension in their discussion of ethnic entrepreneurship. In this area, historical accounts of African-American entrepreneurs date back to the turn of the century. By tracing entrepreneurship as a generational phenomenon, they identify clear paths of demarcation and change in this group of ethnic entrepreneurship.

McDougall and Oviatt review and provide an update on the changes in the state of the art in entrepreneurship research in the international area since the 1990 conference. They conclude that changes in technology production quality have contributed to significant and worldwide competition. These new aspects of global competition have brought about a new wave of entrepreneurial ventures and overcome the barriers of distant communication through technological advancement.

Hisrich and Young introduce a new dimension in entrepreneurship with their discussion of entrepreneurial activities in the not-for-profit sector. Drawing upon past research, they conclude that innovation is a dimension present among both the for-profit and not-for-profit sectors and that opportunity recognition and pursuance are common in both areas.

CHAPTER 11

The Family Business Dimension of Entrepreneurship

NANCY B. UPTON

AND

RAMONA K. Z. HECK

INTEREST IN THE FIELD OF FAMILY BUSINESS is slowly growing. By the mid-1980s Lansberg et al. (1988) noted that scholarly writings about entrepreneurship outnumbered family business 15 to 1. A computer search of the ABI/INFORM computerized citation search yielded an approximate ratio of 2 to 1 for works between 1985 and 1996; however, research works are still in developmental stages. Reviews of the literature revealed an orientation toward "anecdotes, folklore, war-stories and 'expert opinion'" (Desman, 1992; Desman and Brush, 1991, 61). This mirrors early entrepreneurship research (Paulin et al., 1982). Conceptual frameworks are often lacking; a broad, comprehensive family-business theoretical framework is yet to be developed, and rigorous analytical techniques are only emerging (Wortman, 1994). Research is narrow in scope focusing primarily on transitional events, few studies are comparative, and little has been replicated. This chapter provides an overview of the definitional issues and the consequences of overly broad definitions, explores the relationship between entrepreneurship and family business, and reviews the research literature. Finally, suggestions for further research will be delineated.

Defining Family Business

There is a need for a succinct definition of family business and for convergence within certain areas of interest to entrepreneurship researchers. Wortman (1995) contends that more than 20 definitions are in use and that each researcher develops one to suit his or her needs; Handler (1989b) notes a lack of definitional consensus. Most definitions seem to revolve around family ownership, family involvement, family control, and/or the intention to transfer the family firm. For example, Donnelley (1964, 94) suggests that a family firm is one which has been closely identified with at least two generations of a family and which has had an influence on company policy and on family interests. Barnes and Hershon (1976) and Schwartz and Barnes (1991, 270) define a family firm to be one in which controlling ownership is held by an individual or by members of a single family and the company is managed by a family member. Ward (1987) defines a family firm by its transfer to a subsequent generation. Daily and Thompson (1994) assert that this multigenerational dimension may distinguish family business from entrepreneurship.

Definitions are important for replication purposes and for purposes of determining the characteristics of the population (Handler, 1989b; Riordan and Riordan, 1993). Three commonly held assumptions are that family firms are:

❖ The most prevalent organizational form and contribute significantly to GNP and wages.

❖ Small, but include one-third of the Fortune 500.

❖ Prone to short lives with only one-third surviving to the second generation.

One assumption that seems to be made by family business writers is that all sole proprietorships are family firms (Kirchhoff and Kirchhoff, 1987, 25). Somewhere between 75 and 90 percent of all firms in the United States are often counted as family-owned and operated (Barnes and Hershon, 1976; Holland, 1981), even though these figures are based on Small Business Administration reports that do not support such criteria. These quoted figures are the number of small businesses, not family firms. All sole proprietorships are not family businesses.

Hershon (1975) suggested that half of the GNP is produced by family firms and that they employ half of the workforce. He, too, cites statistics from the Small Business Administration that claim that small businesses provide 51 percent of the jobs and 43 percent of the GNP. Again, how many of these small businesses are family firms? He also wrote that there were 1 million corporations and that 980,000 are privately owned family firms. They may be closely-held, but are they family firms? It may depend on the definition. Dreux (1990) suggests that one could conservatively estimate that there are 1.7 million business entities that are family-owned and controlled, excluding sole proprietorships.

A number of authors also indicate that one-third of the Fortune 500 are family-owned and controlled. In 1955 Fortune magazine printed that 175 of the largest U.S. corporations had close relatives or in-laws holding management jobs in the same firm. Donnelley (1964) writes that 20 percent of the Fortune 500 show evidence of "significant family management and/or proprietary interest." Sheehan (1967) in a later *Fortune* article wrote that in about 150 of the *Fortune* 500, controlling ownership rested in the hands of an individual or the members of a single family. Burch (1972) studied 450 large companies and determined that 42 percent of the largest publicly held corporations are controlled by one person or family. No one has replicated the earlier *Fortune* work, and the number of firms on the 500 list that are truly family owned, controlled, and/or managed is unknown.

Beckhard and Dyer (1983a, 1983b) stated, but do not document, that only 30 percent of family firms survive the transition to the second generation. Most failure statistics quoted today cite Ward's (1987) study of 200 Illinois manufacturers. Using the *Illinois Manufacturing Guide,* he tried to track these firms from the years 1924 through 1984. The firms he chose had to have at least 20 employees and to have been in operation for at least five years. If a firm "disappeared" in subsequent issues of the guide, he tried to determine why, although for some he could not determine the actual cause for the disappearance. The reader is not told how the initial 200 were deemed to actually be family firms or if they were just founder-managed. In addition, his strategy of tracking firms by last names to determine family or nonfamily ownership leaves open the possibility of firms transferred to family members with different last names. Ward is not clear on how he determined if, in 1924, the companies had the *intention* of transferring to the next generation. Ward, himself notes several limitations to the study, including convenience sampling.

Is Family Business Entrepreneurship?

There is some debate as to whether family business is entrepreneurship (Hoy and Verser, 1994). A quick survey of entrepreneurship and small business texts reveals chapters on family business. Both the Babson Research Conference and the Entrepreneurship Division of the Academy of Management have accepted papers on family business. In 1994 an entire issue of *Entrepreneurship Theory and Practice* was devoted to family firm research.

Litz (1995) provides various definitions of entrepreneurship and states that the core issue of entrepreneurship is "organizational initiative," and that is different from family business. Hoy et al. (1992, 341) argue that entrepreneurship is not restricted to a single act but is instead, "a label we attach to a multidisciplinary field," one in which they state encompasses family business. Hart and Stevenson (1994) argue that the development of a family business originates with an entrepreneur and is a natural extension of entrepreneurship. Poza (1989) provides an excellent example of entrepreneurship as "organizational initiative" in the family firm. Gundry and Welsch (1994) believe that entrepreneurship has grown and matured to the point where separate dimensions (such as family business) are becoming specialties.

Many authors have suggested that role models are an important determinant of entrepreneurial behavior (e.g., Brockhaus and Horowitz, 1986; Cooper, 1986; Holland, 1983; Shapero and Sokol, 1982; Timmons, 1986). Social learning theory has linked parental role modeling and a preference for an entrepreneurial career (Scherer et al., 1989). Scott and Twomey (1988) also found a link between parental role model and a preference for entrepreneurship. Matthews and Moser (1995) in a longitudinal study of business school graduates found that those, especially males, reporting a family firm had more interest in small business ownership.

Family firms seem to outperform nonfamily firms on a number of dimensions (Kirchhoff and Kirchoff, 1987; Kleiman et al., 1995). This finding seems to hold for family firms internationally (Donckels and Frolich, 1991; Dunn, 1995; Stoy Hayward, 1992). Financially this high performance is attributed to a unified economic vision and a hypothesized lower agency cost. Family firms are thought to be more concerned for the long-run, measuring results over decades, not quarters (Porter, 1992). One aspect of the financial picture is the sweat equity, internal funding, and sacrifices families will make for their firms (Donnelley, 1964; Harris et al., 1994; Rosenblatt et al., 1985).

Family contributions to productivity have been explored by Kirchhoff and Kirchhoff (1987). Family firms are thought to have a greater commitment to quality (Davis and Stern, 1980; Lyman, 1991), a higher emphasis on maintaining the value of the company's name (Davis and Stern, 1980), and a higher level of concern and caring for needs of the employees and communities (Astrachan, 1988; Covin, 1994; Davis and Stern, 1980; Harris et al., 1994).

Survey of Family Business Research Literature

Systems Perspective

Family business research is heavily influenced by a systems approach. The social science application of systems theory as applied to organizations was offered in writings by Churchman (1957, 1979) and Miller and Rice (1967, 1970). In the family business literature, family firms are seen as the interaction of two systems (Davis and Tagiuri, 1981) or as a system in its entirety (Cox, 1996; Whiteside and Herz-Brown, 1991).

Derived from clinical observations and empirical work, family systems theory has suggested typologies for describing families (Constantine, 1986; Cox, 1982; Imig, 1996; Kantor and Lehr, 1975; Olson, 1986; Owen et al., 1992). One scheme describes four major family systems types: closed, random, open, and synchronous (Constantine, 1986; Kantor and Lehr, 1975). The family systems types vary depending on how family members interact on a number of dimensions, including seeking power, affection, substance, and meaning via their use of space, time, matter, and energy. In a closed family, family members maintain their often traditional intrafamily relationships and roles more intensively than other nonfamily relationships and roles. Family "intensity" in the firm has been linked to a higher performance goals and strategic planning (Gundry and Welsch, 1994). Though difficult to observe or study as distinct from the closed family type, the synchronous family type denotes those families in unanimous agreement on most family matters, including values, goals, and behaviors. It has been argued that goal and value congruence may be a competitive advantage of family firms (Hart and Stevenson, 1994). The random family type is at the other end of the continuum from the closed family. Individuals dominate over the family dimension with likely as many relationships and roles outside the family as within. The open family type is a mixture of the closed and random type. Such a family type includes family members who attempt to work together as a unit to achieve harmony between the individuals in the family.

The family system goes through sequential stages throughout the time frame of a family generation and over time between generations. This family life course encompasses the notions of life trajectories, transitions, and the timing of retirement (Moen, 1996). Nelton (1986) has pointed out the difficulty that a family generation is often 25 years compared to the average business life cycle of less than 20 years.

Transitioning the Family Firm

Since the research by Christensen in 1953, the majority of research in the family business area has focused on succession issues. There is within the literature an assumption that family succession should occur and that failure is not continuing ownership and management to the next generation. However, Malone (1989) found that 26 percent of business owners felt family continuity was undesirable, particularly so for founders. Bowman-Upton and Dugat (1987) in a survey of 178 firms who defined themselves as family businesses found that none of them founded the business with the intent of providing their children a job and only 40 percent were concerned with family succession. In a random national survey of family firms, it was discovered that the majority wish to transfer ownership and control to their children (MassMutual, 1995).

While owners may wish to transfer control to their children, successor selection is obviously difficult. Dean (1992) found that less than 20 percent of 236 African-American family firms had selected a successor. Internationally, studies indicate that 47.8 percent of Korean and 46 percent of Japanese entrepreneurs have chosen a successor, which in the majority of instances, is a family member (Ouh, 1995). An Australian study indicates that up to 60 percent of family firms plan to appoint a family member as the next CEO (Moores and Mula, 1993). For those who wish to transfer ownership and management control to the next generation, there are a plethora of prescriptive works encouraging planning relative to succession, estates, financials, and strategic moves (e.g., Danco, 1982; Jaffe, 1990; Ward, 1987).

Although many authors argue that a written succession plan may be critical to business continuity (Beckhard and Dyer, 1983a; Handler, 1990), there is an overall lack of succession planning in family firms (Bowman-Upton and Dugat, 1987; Dean, 1992; MassMutual, 1995; Ward, 1987). Surveys indicate that succession planning occurs in less than 25 percent (MassMutual, 1995) to 40 percent (Mandelbaum, 1994). Of the firms, Astrachan and Kolenko (1994) in a random national sample of family firms, found that while 42 percent had a written business plan, only 21 percent had a written succession plan.

Significant questions remain as to what constitutes adequate planning (Fiegener et al., 1994). Some evidence suggests that smaller businesses do not do the planning necessary to continue to the next generation (Ambrose, 1983; Bowman-Upton and Dugat, 1987). Malone (1989) found a significant positive correlation between strategic planning and continuity planning. Astrachan and Kolenko (1994) also found a positive relationship between strategic planning and long-term survival and success.

Resistance to succession planning is common (Handler and Kram, 1988; Lansberg, 1988; Rosenblatt et al., 1985). Factors that influence resistance are multilevel and include individual, organizational, familial and environmental (Lansberg, 1988; Malone, 1989). Lansberg (1988) coined the term "succession conspiracy" to explain why all the stakeholders (e.g., family, advisors, and nonfamily managers) conspire in the resistance.

The Role of the Founder

Barnes and Hershon (1976, 105) suggest that the problem of succession is often the most acute in family firms, where the original entrepreneur hangs on as he watches others try to help manage or take over his business, while his heirs feel overshadowed and frustrated. According to Davis and Stern (1980, 223), the involvement of the entrepreneur can seriously constrain the firm's ability to grow. However, the founder resists letting go (Ambrose, 1983; Bowman-Upton, 1989; Schein, 1985; Sonnenfeld and Spence, 1989).

A number of reasons are posited for why the founder resists letting go. One line of reasoning asserts that the resistance can be traced to psychological issues. Levinson (1971) traces the resistance to the meaning of the business for the founder: mistress, baby, and extension of ego. Davis and Tagiuri (1989, 73) found that the father is often emotionally attached to his company as to a child, and this relationship competes with his attachment to his son. A number of authors propose that letting go is tied up with death: signing one's own death warrant (Barnes and Hershon, 1976), preparing for death (Beckard and Dyer, 1983a, 61), or retirement equated with euthanasia (Sidwell, 1989, 391). Other authors suggest that the business fulfills deep-seated psychological needs such as the need to control (Handler, 1994) and dominate and that letting go means giving up power (Berenbeim, 1984; Danco, 1980; Davis, 1982; Dyer, 1986; Lansberg, 1988). Peay and Dyer (1989) found entrepreneurs with a high need for personal power were much less likely to plan for succession than those with a high need for social power. Malone (1989) found that succession planning is positively influenced by an internal locus of control.

Two major barriers to exit have been suggested based on the work of Sonnenfeld (1988, 358). These are heroic stature (position of power that top leaders hold) and heroic mission (or the leader's sense that he has a unique ability to fulfill the responsibilities of his job). The typology of exit styles these authors have developed is based on the entrepreneur's mastery of heroic stature and heroic mission. Four styles of letting go have been identified: monarch, general, ambassador, and governor. While examining family firms, Sonnenfeld and Spence (1989) found that monarchs are in command of smaller firms, retain close control over strategic decisions, are most troubled by both barriers to exit, and are usually forced out after a long tenure. Generals are also forced out but plot their return. Ambassadors lead larger firms, recognize when it is time to leave, and do so gracefully. They tend to maintain contact with the business in an advisory capacity. Governors rule for a specified, limited time frame in the largest companies. Sonnenfeld and Spence found that family firm owners are more likely to be monarchs or generals. When comparing the family-firm CEOs to nonfamily CEOs, they discovered that family-firm founders saw no reason to ever let go, while nonfamily CEOs looked forward to retirement.

The Successor's Role

Throughout the literature are suggestions that successors are either a disaster (Blotnick, 1984) or the source of growth and regeneration (Poza, 1989). Boswell (1972) found that 53 percent of older firms were in a state of decline, and the majority of them were run by an inheritor-successor. Blotnick's (1984) study of the financial performance of 837 profitable family firms before and after the succession event revealed that less than 20 percent of the heirs had been able to maintain a growth rate sufficient to keep pace with inflation. Actually, a few studies have examined the experiences of the successor generation (Barach et al., 1988; Birley, 1986; Blotnick, 1984; Goldberg and Wooldridge, 1993; Patrick, 1986; Seymour, 1993; Stavrou, 1996; Upton, 1990) or how successors are developed as leaders (Fiegener et al., 1994). A few studies have also focused on multiple successors (Friedman, 1991; Swogger, 1991) or the effects of choosing among them (Barnes, 1988). Barnes describes "incongruent hierarchies" that exist when an individual in the lower family hierarchy attains a higher level in the business system.

Most research has revealed that sons are usually groomed (Blotnick, 1984; Finney and Wambsganss, 1990; Montagno et al., 1991). Davis and Tagiuri (1981) found the typical type of family pair is father and son. Early research on family firms suggests that issues specific to father-son relationships cloud rational business decision-making necessary for successful transitions (Alcorn, 1982; Danco, 1982; Levinson, 1971). At times, the working relationship may be characterized as tense due to the son's conflict with his father around issues of power, authority, and competition (Davis, 1982; Rosenblatt et al., 1985), or the son's internal conflict between parental approval and autonomy (Patrick, 1986). Davis and Tagiuri (1989) investigated the quality of the father-son work relationship as a function of their respective stages of life. They found that the quality of the work relationship improves as the father moves into his fifties (50-59) and the son gets beyond his twenties (23 to 32) and dramatically worsens when the father is in his sixties (60 to 69) and the son is between 34 to 40.

The literature on women in family business is extremely sparse. Bowman-Upton and Sexton (1987) found women in stereotypical positions (e.g., secretary or bookkeeper) in family firms and only considered as successors when no male was available. Dumas (1988, 1989) describes daughters as invisible successors. In surveying seminar participants, Salganicoff (1990) confirmed those findings when she discovered that less than 22 percent prepared for a career in the family firm and only 27 percent felt they were expected to enter the business. Iannerelli (1992) explored career experiences and found that daughters while growing up spend less time in the family business, develop fewer skills, and are encouraged less than their brothers.

Particular advantages for women in family firms include: flexibility, access to traditionally male-dominated industries, and job security. Salganicoff (1990) contends that some of the characteristics by which women define themselves contribute greatly to the success and survival of the business. One of the major responsibilities of women in the family firm is to maintain kinship ties and to pass to the next generation family traditions and family history (Lyman, 1988).

Process of Succession

Most authors agree that succession is a process, not an event. Further, it may be argued that various stages exist and possess characteristic problems (McGivern, 1989) or opportunities (Handler, 1994). Further, various aspects of the process have positive and negative influences (Barach and Granitsky, 1995; Barach et al., 1988; Dumas et al., 1995; Goldberg and Wooldrige, 1993; Handler, 1992; Lansberg and Astrachan, 1994; Seymour, 1993).

A number of stage models have been developed to capture the succession experience (Churchill and Hatten, 1987; McGivern, 1989). Longenecker and Schoen (1978) describe the first two stages as early attempts to promote the successor's interest and knowledge of the firm, which may lead to a career choice. Iannarelli (1992) and Dumas et al. (1995) note the importance of early presocialization. The Longenecker and Schoen model notes the entry of the potential successor into the business somewhere between the "introductory" and "functional" stage. Harvey and Evans (1994) convey the concept of a strategic window of opportunity to have the successor enter the firm and use the skills and expertise he or she has acquired elsewhere. Dumas et al. (1995) discuss three events related to the decision to join a family firm:

❖ Changes in educational pursuits.

❖ Difficulty in establishing a profession.

❖ Changes in the family firm.

A number of factors influence the offspring's decision to enter the firm (Birley, 1986). Stavrou (1996) found the intention to enter the family business significantly related to individual needs, goals, skills, and abilities. She described the decision not to enter the business as related to family membership, family dynamics, values, relationships, needs, and desires.

Two common entry strategies are advocated: low-level entry (via summer jobs and low-level employment) or delayed entry (gaining work experience outside the family firm first). Barach et al. (1988) found that low-level entry was more common. The sample suggested the potential entrant learn from the ground up and slowly earn credibility rather than enter ready to "rock the boat." In a study of family-owned firms in Kansas, Finney and Wambsganss (1990) found that founders learn to operate a business by working for others but successors learn to run the family firm by working in it. Forty-two percent felt the successor should work through the ranks of the organization, and 43 percent wanted the successor to work as their assistant. Only 14 percent felt outside experience was necessary.

The quality of the succession experience was studied by Handler (1992) and a model developed. She found that from the successor's perspective if career, psychosocial needs (i.e., development of personal identity in context of family business), and lifestage fulfillment needs are met and if the individual has the potential to exert personal influence, then the experience will be positive. Handler (1992) found four relational influences that she considers central to the experience: degree of mutual respect (see also Stempler, 1988) and intergenerational understanding, sibling accommodation, commitment to family firm succession (see also Lansberg and Astrachan, 1994), and the extent of tension due the lack of separation of family and business issues (see also Astrachan and Kolenko, 1994; Malone, 1989; Upton, 1990). All but the latter are hypothesized to positively affect the succession experience.

Seymour (1993) developed a model of family influences on leadership succession and tested the effect of intergenerational relationships on leadership continuity. He found a significant positive relationship in the quality of the work relationship between the owner/manager and successor. The quality of their work relationship significantly enhanced the prediction of successor training. These findings support earlier research concerning the quality of the leader-successor relationship in succession (Lansberg and Astrachan, 1994; Patrick, 1986; Ward, 1987). Goldberg and Wooldridge (1993) see the successor characteristics of self-confidence and managerial autonomy as critical determinants. Their findings suggest that the successor must take control of the process, especially in the later stages described in the Longenecker and Schoen model.

In a comparative analysis of successor development in 236 family and 121 nonfamily firms, Fiegener et al. (1994) report significant differences in successor development approaches with the family firms taking what they termed a riskier approach. Family firms rate formal education and on-the-job training as less important than nonfamily firms and formalize the successor process to a lesser extent. On the other hand, family firms are more involved in mentoring and rely more heavily on network-building experiences as a means of developing successors.

Professionalizing the Family Firm

There is a pervasiveness in much of the literature that family participation in the business is negative. Munson (1963) suggests that in an industry where family management is a virtue, the overall quality of management will not be high. Early writings considered professionalizing to mean bringing outsiders into the firm to provide objectivity and rationality to an emotional milieu. It seemed as if professional management and family management were mutually exclusive (Levinson, 1971). The family was seen as not able to run the business in the best interest of the business because of a conflict of interest between the person and the firm (Christiansen, 1953). Donnelley (1964) wrote of families who abuse the family firm by using the business to serve personal needs, possessing poor profit discipline, and having excessive nepotism.

Much of the literature also paints an unfavorable picture of family influence on organizational decision-making, with the family being described as irrational (e.g., Dyer, 1994; Hollander and Elman, 1988; Kahn and Henderson, 1992; Upton and Seaman, 1991). However, both Kahn and Henderson and Upton and Seaman found decision-making driven by a desire to satisfy the needs of both the family and business.

Welsch's (1993) comparative analysis of German family and nonfamily firms found no significant differences in the way they approach the tasks of human resource management and management succession. Further he found that older family firms are as professional as nonfamily firms. However, Kleinsorge (1994) in a comparative analysis of nursing homes, found family-owned ones to be less efficient on a number of economic factors.

Retaining Professional Managers

Dyer (1989) writes that the primary reasons professional managers are retained are:

❖ Lack of management talent in the family.

❖ To change the norms and values of the business operations.

❖ To prepare for leadership succession acting as an interim leader.

However, the values, views, and assumptions of professional managers are usually in direct conflict with the founder, and this may lead to problems in their relationship and decline in profitability. Dyer suggests three alternatives for integrating professional management into the family firm:

❖ Professionalize members of the owning family.

❖ Professionalize nonfamily employees currently working in the business.

❖ Bring in outside professional management talent.

When choosing the latter, developing the relationship between the manager and the family is very important. Dyer (1986) suggests using role clarification meetings, team-building sessions. To professionalize the current family and nonfamily managers would require the development of sound human resource management (Lansberg, 1983). Astrachan and Kolenko (1994) reported the results of the large-scale MassMutual/Gallup survey and found that family businesses engage in several human resource practices that influence organizational survival.

Board of Directors

A common piece of advice for family firms is to have an active board with outside directors (Danco and Jonovic, 1981; Stern, 1986). The advantages of outside board members include an objective point of view (Sidwell, 1989), holding family management accountable, setting executive salaries, and asking challenging questions (Danco and Jonovic, 1981; Ford, 1989; Schwartz and Barnes, 1991; Ward and Handy, 1988). Despite the proposed advantages, Nash (1988) suggests that less than 10 percent of all closely held firms have a board with outside directors beyond the company attorney. This finding holds for firms internationally (Gallo, 1995). Resistance to placing outsiders on the board is due to concern for privacy and loss of control (Heidrick, 1988), director liability (Schipani and Siedel, 1988), and family member opposition (Schwartz and Barnes, 1991).

Barach (1984) finds that outsiders are freer of family and/or hierarchical pressures, and yet Dyer (1986) relates that outside directors' decision-making may be influenced by family dynamics (e.g., the Lee Iacocca–Henry Ford II dispute and the board's reaction). Alderfer (1988) agrees and notes that subgroup dynamics can affect board operations, effectiveness, and board-family relations. Jonovic (1989) suggests that outside board members may be too diplomatic and not give timely, objective advice. Schwartz and Barnes (1991) found outsiders provided the least help in the areas of day-to-day operations or issues of family conflict. Ford (1989) discovered that outside directors are of less value because of their lack of knowledge about the firm and its environment and lack of availability to the firm. Schwartz and Barnes (1991) noted the debate and point out that outsiders should not include close friends, advisors, or retired executives because they are not unbiased or objective. After surveying 262 CEOs on board-related matters, they found that larger and older firms have a higher percentage of outside boards; however, very large and very small ones do not. When asking CEOs to rate the value of their board, there were significant differences between all-family and outside boards, with all-family boards getting the lowest score. Highest scores went to boards with five or more outsiders. Ward and Handy (1988) found that two outsiders are the critical demarcation for adding value to the board.

Strategy and Growth Issues

Family firms are likely to struggle with growth issues (Peiser and Wooten, 1983) and are unlikely to use formal strategic planning (Brown, 1995; Rue and Ibrahim, 1996; Silverzweig and D'Agostino, 1995; Ward, 1987). However, Rue and Ibrahim (1996) found family firms engage in more planning than previously thought, with over half of their sample reporting written long-range plans and 97 percent reporting some specific plans related to growth.

Daily and Dollinger (1992) found that family firms pursued strategies that differed from those of their professionally managed counterparts. Specifically, family owned and operated firms pursued more active growth-oriented strategies. In a later study Daily and Thompson (1994) compared strategic postures based on ownership structure. They found no significant differences in strategic posture based on ownership structure between founder-managed firms, family firms, and professionally managed firms. In addition, no effect on firm growth occurred by either ownership structure or strategic posture.

There are conflicting findings concerning growth in the family firm (Harris et al., 1994). Alcorn (1982) wrote that accommodating growth in the family-firm is a large obstacle. In a study of goals of successful family firm owners, Tagiuri and Davis (1992) found growth goals were not highly ranked. Malone and Jenster (1992) note that one of the critical differences between owner-managed and family-managed firms is growth. Past research has shown that inherited firms have lower growth rates than start-ups or buyouts (Dunkelburg and Cooper, 1982) and that founder firms grow more rapidly than those run by a successor (Begley and Boyd, 1986). Daily and Dollinger (1992) found that the majority of family firms adopted the defender strategy in which growth is not actively sought but achieved through operating efficiencies and incremental process improvements. There is some support that this may be indicative of family firms across the globe (Gallo, 1995; Ouh, 1995).

Benedict (1979) found successful family firms use a great deal of uncompensated or under-compensated family labor. The companies that practiced this had fewer business failures and were more likely to experience long-term growth. A number of authors have found growth to be restricted due to limited financial resources, reluctance to share ownership and a desire to grow via internally generated funds (Barry, 1975; Berenbeim, 1984; Friedman and Friedman, 1994; Miller and Rice, 1967). Internal financing of growth seems to be prevalent internationally (Ouh, 1995).

Other factors that seem to influence growth in the family firm are lower market share and less participation in global markets (Gallo, 1995), an overconcentration in industries which are less capital intensive and have lower barriers to entry (Ward, 1988b), lack of skilled management (Miller and Rice, 1967), goal conflict between active and nonactive family members (Hoy and Verser, 1994), and an inflexible organization (Barry, 1975).

A final aspect of growth is the role the successor plays in regenerating the family firm. Poza (1988) describes the process as the revitalization activity prior to succession: pursuing strategies to grow the family firm and supporting entrepreneurial activity in the next generation. He develops a model for growth in the family firm that includes setting the stage for interpreneurship and continued growth through changes in strategy, organizational change and development, financial restructuring, and family behavior. According to Poza, barriers to growth in the family firm include:

❖ Absence of a growth vision.

❖ Distance from customers, employees, operations, and the competition.

❖ Nervousness about time and money.

❖ Large overheads.

❖ Obsession with data and logic.

❖ Inappropriate boundaries between management, owners, and successor.

When assessing strategies for growth, Poza notes that while diversification and specialization are options, family firms can capitalize on the diverse talents of off-spring through a process he calls "entrepreneurial approximations," that is, sponsoring new ventures within the family constellation. Upton et al. (1995) found most successful firms started by undergraduates were spin-offs from the family firm.

The idea that subsequent generations rejuvenate the family firm (Barnes and Hershon, 1976; Ward, 1987, 1988a, 1988b) is prevalent in the literature. Barnes and Hershon describe the successor generation as eager and likely to go beyond traditional practices. Sonnenfeld and Spence (1989) found that greater increases in income and earnings per share were correlated with a smoother departure and succession.

Research Modeling

Miller and Rice (1967) first described the family business as an example of two inter-connected subsystems. Davis and Stern (1980) described a central triangle in family firms consisting of "family organizational behavior, structure and behavior of the task system, and legitimizing structure." Others have tried to model the family firm with two interlocking circles, that is, the concept of the family firm as a joint, interacting, or overlapping system. The two-circle models, or dual systems, usually portray a family system and a business system, with the family firm consisting of the overlap between these two basic systems (Dyer and Handler, 1994; Lansberg, 1983; McCollom, 1988). Both systems, family and business, have been characterized by distinct and often incongruent needs, role requirements, rules, values, and cultures. While McCollom adhered to the two-system view, the idea of the family system as the key integration mechanism of the family firm was acknowledged. Although it has been noted that these systems influence each other, most writers have examined ways in which the family system impinges upon, and possibly jeopardizes, the business system (Bowman-Upton et al., 1991). Further, a view of the family firm as a total system has yet to be fully developed.

Other researchers have represented the family firm by using a three-circle model in varying degrees of interlocking: the family, owners, and managers involved in the family firm. Davis and Tagiuri (1981) used such a model to denote the unique bivalent attributes of the family firm. Lansberg (1988) used these three interlocking circles to identify major players in succession and their underlying motivations. Hoy and Verser (1994) have offered further details and delineation of concepts within these three arenas. Churchill and Hatten (1987) linked the three-circle model to the human life cycle experienced by various family members involved in the family business. Their resulting four-stage model of the family firm raised suggestions for variables to study in each stage: owner-managed business; training and development of the new generation, partnership between the generations; and transfer of power.

Still other researchers strongly suggest that the family firm be viewed as a single entity or system (Hollander and Elman, 1988). Whiteside and Herz-Brown (1991) argue strongly against the dual-system view of the family business because such a view leads to biases, such as stereotyping of subsystem functioning, inconsistent and inadequate analysis of interpersonal dynamics, exaggerated notions of subsystem boundaries, and underanalysis of whole system characteristics. Cox (1996) emphasizes the importance of recognizing that the family system is the basis of the functioning of the family firm and also treats the family business as a system in its entirety.

The Continuing Need for Research

The family business field of study is emerging and would be greatly enhanced by increasing the amount and quality of applied research (Task Force, 1995). Such applied research is impaired by the lack of a well-established national statistical series and high-quality, comprehensive data sources. None currently exist in the United States sufficient to study simultaneously both the business and the family. Data regularly published by the Small Business Administration do not distinguish between family and nonfamily firms.

A dearth of good research on family businesses merits attention (NE-167R Technical Committee, 1993). First, research about transitioning could address:

❖ How succession differs for family dyads other than the father and son as well as for the female founders/owners.

❖ Mentoring processes and experiences of older generations.

❖ Venture capital used to fund transitions and harvesting practices.

Second, if family firms have a longer planning horizon, what is the effect of congruency or incongruency of family and firm goals? Are there specific strategies that are more "family-friendly" such as entrepreneurial team building?

Third, the growth rates of family firms, problems of strategic regeneration in the family firm, and nature of the strategies used to grow have not been addressed. The difficulties of limited funding, informal venture capital, and the use of venture creation need to be explored.

Fourth, there is the need to develop an integrative family business approach or model. Good exploratory investigation could then proceed.

Finally, the study of the family behind the business is essential in understanding not only the business but learning more about the environments within which entrepreneurs live and flourish, especially relative to ethnicity, firm size, and the firm's life course.

REFERENCES

Alcorn, P.B. 1982. *Success and Survival in the Family-Owned Business.* New York: McGraw-Hill.

Alderfer, C.P. 1988. Understanding and consulting to family business boards. *Family Business Review* 1(3):249-261.

Ambrose, D. 1983. Transfer of family-owned business. *Journal of Small Business Management* 21(1):49-56.

Astrachan, J.H. 1988. Family firm and community culture. *Family Business Review* 1(2):165-190.

Astrachan, J.H., and T.A. Kolenko. 1994. A neglected factor explaining family business success: Human resource practices. *Family Business Review* 7(3):251-262.

Barach, J.A. 1984. Is there a cure for the paralyzed family board? *Sloan Management Review* (Fall):3-12.

Barach, J.A., and J.B. Ganitsky. 1995. Successful succession in family business. *Family Business Review* 8(2):131-155.

Barach, J.A., J. Gantisky, J.A. Carson, and B.A. Doochin. 1988. Entry of the next generation: Strategic challenges for family business. *Journal of Small Business Management* 26(2):49-56.

Barnes, L.B. 1988. Incongruent hierarchies: Daughters and younger sons as company CEOs. *Family Business Review* 1(1): 9-21.

Barnes, L.B., and S.A. Hershon. 1976. Transferring power in the family business. *Harvard Business Review* 54(4):105-116.

Barry, B. 1975. The development of organization structure in the family firm. *Journal of General Management* 3(1):42-60.

Beckhard, R., and W.G. Dyer, Jr. 1983a. Managing change in the family firm—Issues and strategies. *Sloan Management Review* 16(2):59-65.

Beckhard, R., and W.G. Dyer, Jr. 1983b. Managing continuity in the family-owned business. *Organizational Dynamics* 12(1): 5-12.

Begley, T.M., and D.P. Boyd. 1986. Executive and corporate correlates of financial performance in smaller firms. *Journal of Small Business Management* 24(2):8-15.

Benedict, B. 1979. Family firms and firm families: A comparison on Indian, Chinese, and Creole firms in Seychelles. In S.M. Greenfeld et al. (eds.): *Entrepreneurs in Cultural Context.* Albuquerque, NM: University of New Mexico Press.

Berenbeim, R. 1984. *From Owner to Professional Management: Problems in Transition* (Report no. 851). New York: Conference Board.

Birley, S. 1986. Succession in the family firm: The inheritor's view. *Journal of Small Business Management* 24:36-43.

Blotnick, S. 1984. The case of the reluctant heirs. *Forbes* 134:180.

Boswell, J. 1972. *The Rise and Decline of Small Firms*. London: Allen and Unwin.

Bowman-Upton, N. 1989. Transition planning and business succession for women entrepreneurs. In O. Hagen et al. (eds.): *Women-Owned Businesses* . New York: Praeger, 151-182.

Bowman-Upton, N., and S. Dugat. 1987. Family business succession: Issues for the founding entrepreneur. *Proceedings of the United States Association for Small Business and Entrepreneurship*, Milwaukee, WI, 11-14.

Bowman-Upton, N., S.L. Seaman, and P. Dyer. 1991. A preliminary analysis of family system types in family business. In *Proceedings of the US Association for Small Business and Entrepreneurship*. San Diego, CA, 150-156.

Bowman-Upton, N., and D.L. Sexton. 1987. Family business succession: The female perspective. *Proceedings of the International Council on Small Business*. 68-73.

Brockhaus, R.H., and P.S. Horwitz. 1986. The psychology of the entrepreneur. In D.L. Sexton and R.W. Smilor (eds.): *The Art and Science of Entrepreneurship*. Cambridge, MA: Ballinger Publishing, 68-73.

Brown, R. 1995. *Family Business: Rethinking Strategic Planning*. Paper presented to the 40th Annual International Council on Small Business, Sydney, Australia, June 18–21.

Burch, Jr., P.H. 1972. *The Managerial Revolution Reassessed*. Lexington, MA: Lexington.

Christiansen, C.R. 1953. *Management Succession in Small and Growing Enterprises*. Cambridge, MA: Harvard University Press.

Churchill, N.C., and K.J. Hatten. 1987. Non-market based transfers of wealth and power: A research framework for family businesses. *American Journal of Small Business* 12(2):53-66.

Churchman, C.W. 1957. *The Systems Approach*. New York: Dell.

Churchman, C.W. 1979. *The Systems Approach and Its Enemies*. New York: Basic Books.

Constantine, L.L. 1986. *Family Paradigms: The Practice of Theory in Family Therapy*. New York: Guilford.

Cooper, A. 1986. Entrepreneurship and high technology. In D.L. Sexton and R.W. Smilor (eds.): *The Art and Science of Entrepreneurship*. Cambridge, MA: Ballinger, 153-168.

Covin, T.J. 1994. Profiling preference for employment in family-owned firms. *Family Business Review* 7(3):287-296.

Cox, E. S. 1982. Family Structure and External Openness: A Two-Dimensional Model. Unpublished doctoral dissertation, University of Southern California, Los Angeles.

Cox, E.S. 1996. The family firm as a foundation of our free society: Strengths and opportunities. *Proceedings of the Cornell University Conference of the Entrepreneurial Family*, New York City, March 18–20.

Daily, C.M., and M.J. Dollinger. 1992. An empirical examination of ownership structure in family and professionally managed firms. *Family Business Review* 5(2):117-136.

Daily, C.M., and S.S. Thompson. 1994. Ownership structure, strategic posture, and firm growth: An empirical examination. *Family Business Review* 7(3):237-250.

Danco, L.A. 1980. *Inside the Family Business*. Cleveland, OH: University Press.

Danco, L.A. 1982. *Beyond Survival: A Business Owner's Guide for Success*. Cleveland, OH: University Press.

Danco, L.A., and D. Jonovic. 1981. *Outside directors in the family-owned business*. Cleveland: University Press.

Davis, J.H. 1982. The Influence of Life Stage on Father-Son Work Relationships in Family Companies. Unpublished doctoral dissertation, Business Administration, Harvard University.

Davis, J.H., and R. Tagiuri. 1981. The Incidence of Work Relationships Between Relatives in the Family Business. Unpublished paper, Harvard Business School.

Davis, J.H., and R. Tagiuri. 1989. The influence of life stage on father-son work relationships in family companies. *Family Business Review* 2(1): 47-74.

Davis, P., and D. Stern. 1980. Adaptation, survival, and growth of the family business: An integrated systems perspective. *Human Relations* 34 (4):207-224.

Dean, S.M. 1992. Characteristics of African-American family-owned businesses in Los Angeles. *Family Business Review* 5(4):373-395.

Desman, R. 1992. Family business: The state of the notion 1991. *Proceedings of Annual Conference of Family Firm Institute (FFI)*. Brookline, MA: FFI, 295-305.

Desman, R., and C. Brush. 1991. Family business: The state of the notion. *Proceedings of Annual Conference of the FFI*. Brookline, MA: FFI, 59-63.

Donckels, R., and E. Frolich. 1991. Are family businesses really different? European experiences from STRATOS. *Family Business Review* 4(2):149-160.

Donnelley, R. G. 1964. The family business. *Harvard Business Review* 42(4):93-105.

Dreux, D.R., IV. 1990. Financing family business: Alternatives to selling out or going public. *Family Business Review* 3(3):225-244.

Dumas, C. 1988. Daughters in Family-Owned Businesses. An Applied Systems Perspective. Unpublished doctoral dissertation. The Fielding Institute, Santa Barbara, CA.

Dumas, C. 1989. Understanding of father-daughter and father-son dyads in family-owned businesses. *Family Business Review* 2(1):31-46.

Dumas, C., J.P. Dupuis, F. Richer, and L. St-Cyr. 1995. Factors that influence the next generation's decision to take over the family firm. *Family Business Review* 8(2):99-120.

Dunkelburg, W.C., and A.C. Cooper. 1982. Patterns of small business growth. *Academy of Management Proceedings*, 409-413.

Dunn, B. 1995. Success themes in Scottish family enterprises: Philosophies and practices through generations. *Family Business Review* 8(1):17-28.

Dyer, W.G., Jr. 1986. *Cultural change in family firms: Anticipating and managing business and family transitions*. San Francisco: Jossey-Bass.

Dyer, W.G., Jr. 1989. Integrating professional management into a family-owned business. *Family Business Review* 2(3):221-235.

Dyer, W.G., Jr. 1994. Potential contributions of organizational behavior to the study of family-owned businesses. *Family Business Review* 7(2):109-132.

Dyer, W.G., Jr., and W. Handler. 1994. Entrepreneurship and family business: Exploring the connections. *Entrepreneurship: Theory and Practice* 19 (1):71-83.

Fiegener, M.K., B.M. Brown, R.A. Prince, and K.M. File. 1994. A comparison of successor development in family and nonfamily businesses. *Family Business Review* 7(4):313-329.

Finney, B.J., and J.R. Wambsganss. 1990. Family-owned firms in Kansas: Results of a survey. *Kansas Business Review* 14(1):22-31.

Ford, R.H. 1989. Establishing and managing boards of directors: The other view. *Family Business Review* 2(2):142-146.

Friedman, S. 1991. Sibling relationships ad intergenerational succession in family firms. *Family Business Review* 4(1):3-20.

Friedman, M., and S. Friedman. 1994. *How to Run a Family Business*. Cincinnati: Better Way.

Gallo, M. 1995. The role of family business and its distinctive characteristic behavior in industrial activity. *Family Business Review* 8(2):83-98.

Goldberg, S.D., and B. Wooldridge. 1993. Self-confidence and managerial autonomy: Successor characteristics critical to succession in family firms. *Family Business Review* 6(1):55-73.

Gundry, L.K., and H.P. Welsch. 1994. Differences in familial influence among women-owned businesses. *Family Business Review* 7(3):273-286.

Handler, W.C. 1989a. Managing the Family Firm Succession Process: The Next-Generation Family Member's Experience. Unpublished doctoral dissertation, School of Management, Boston University.

Handler, W.C. 1989b. Methodological issues and considerations in studying family businesses. *Family Business Review* 5(3):257-276.

Handler W.C. 1990. Succession in family firms: A mutual role adjustment between entrepreneurs and next-generation family member. *Entrepreneurship Theory and Practice* 15(1):37-51.

Handler, W.C. 1992. The succession experience of the next generation. *Family Business Review* 5(3):283-307.

Handler, W.C. 1994. Succession in family business: A review of the research. *Family Business Review* 7(2):133-158.

Handler, W.C., and K.E. Kram. 1988. Succession in family firms: The problem of resistance. *Family Business Review* 1(4):361-379.

Harris, D., J.I. Martinez, and J.L. Ward. 1994. Is strategy different for the family-owned business? *Family Business Review* 7(2):159-174.

Hart, M.M., and H.H. Stevenson. 1994. Entrepreneurs and the Next Generation: Management Advantages and Challenges in a Family Business. Paper presented at the Babson Entrepreneurship Research Conference, Houston, TX.

Harvey, M., and R.E. Evans. 1994. The impact of timing and mode of entry on successor development and successful succession. *Family Business Review* 7(3):221-236.

Heidrick, G.W. 1988. Selecting outside directors. *Family Business Review* 1(3):271-277.

Hershon, S.A. 1975. The Problem of Management Succession in Family Businesses. Unpublished doctoral dissertation, Business Administration, Harvard University.

Holland, J.L. 1983. Making vocational choices: A theory of careers. In S.H. Osipow (ed.): *Theories of Career Development*. Englewood Cliffs, NJ: Prentice Hall.

Holland, P.J. 1981. Strategic Management in Family Business: An Exploratory Study of the Development and Strategic Effects of the Family-Business Relationship. Unpublished doctoral dissertation, University of Georgia.

Hollander, B.S., and N.S. Elman. 1988. Family-owned businesses: An emerging field. *Family Business Review* 1(2):145-164.

Hoy, F., P.P. McDougall, and D.E. Dsouza. 1992. Strategies and environments of high-growth firms. In D.L. Sexton and J.D. Kasarda (eds.): *The State of the Art of Entrepreneurship*. Boston: PWS-Kent, 341-357.

Hoy, F., and T.G. Verser. 1994. Emerging business, emerging field: Entrepreneurship and the family firm. *Entrepreneurship Theory and Practice* 19(1):9-24.

Iannerelli, C.L. 1992. The Socialization of Leaders in Family Business: An Exploratory Study of Gender. Unpublished doctoral dissertation, University of Pittsburgh.

Imig, D. 1996. Systems and paradigms: A conceptual approach to the study of succession and family business. *Proceedings of the Cornell University Conference of the Entrepreneurial Family*, New York City, May 18–20.

Jaffe, D.T. 1990. *Working with the Ones You Love*. Berkeley, CA: Conari Press.

Jonovic, D.J. 1989. Outsider review in a wider context: An alternative to the classic board. *Family Business Review* 2(2):125-140.

Kahn, J.A., and D.A. Henderson. 1992. Location preferences of family firms: Strategic decision-making or "Home Sweet Home." *Family Business Review* 5(3):271-282.

Kantor, D., and W. Lehr. 1975. *Inside the Family: Toward a Theory of Family Process*. New York: Harper Colophon.

Kirchhoff, B.A., and J.J. Kirchhoff. 1987. Family contributions to productivity and profitability in small businesses. *Journal of Small Business Management* 25(4):25-31.

Kleiman, B., J.W. Petty, and J. Martin. 1995. Family controlled firms: An assessment of performance. *Family Business Annual* 1:1-10.

Kleinsorge, I.K. 1989. *Comparing Nursing Homes on the Basis of Ownership: A Survey of Oregon Administrator's Perceptions*. Working paper, Oregon State University, College of Business, Corvallis.

Kleinsorge, I.K. 1994. Financial and efficiency differences in family-owned and non-family-owned nursing homes: An Oregon study. *Family Business Review* 7(1):73-86.

Lansberg, I.S. 1983. Managing human resources in family firms: The problem of institutional overlap. *Organizational Dynamics* (Summer):30-46.

Lansberg, I.S. 1988. The succession conspiracy. *Family Business Review* 1(2):119-143.

Lansberg, I.S., and J.H. Astrachan. 1994. Influence of family relationships on succession planning and training: The importance of mediating factors. *Family Business Review* 7(1):39-59.

Lansberg, I.S., E. Perrow, and S. Rogolsky. 1988. Family business as an emerging field. *Family Business Review* 1(1):1-8.

Levinson, H. 1971. Conflicts that plague the family business. *Harvard Business Review* 49(2):90-98.

Litz, R.A. 1995. The family business: Toward definitional clarity. *Family Business Review* 8(2):71-82.

Longenecker, J., and J. Schoen. 1978. Management succession in family business. *Journal of Small Business Management* 16(3):1-6.

Lyman, A. 1988. Life in the family circle. *Family Business Review* 1(4):383-398.

Lyman, A. 1991. Customer service: Does family ownership make a difference? *Family Business Review* 4(3):303-324.

Malone, S.C. 1989. Selected correlates of business continuity planning in the family business. *Family Business Review* 2(4):341-353.

Malone, S.C., and P.V. Jenster. (1992). The problem of the plateaued owner-manager. *Family Business Review* 5(1):25-41.

Mandelbaum, L. 1994. Small business succession: The educational potential. *Family Business Review* 7(4):369-375.

MassMutual. 1995. *Family Business: 1995 Research Findings*. Springfield, MA: MassMutual.

Matthews, C.H., and S.B. Moser. 1995. The impact of family background and gender on interest in small firm ownership: A longitudinal study. In *Proceedings of the ICSB 40th World Conference*. Sydney, Australia: Institute of Industrial Economics, 245-262.

McCollom, M. E. 1988. Integration in the family firm: When the family system replaces controls and culture. *Family Business Review* 1(4):399-417.

McGivern, C. 1989. The dynamics of management succession: A model of chief executive succession in the small family firm. *Family Business Review* 2(4):401-411.

Miller, E.J., and A.K. Rice. 1967. *Systems of Organization*. London: Tavistock.

Miller, E.J., and A.K. Rice. 1970. *Systems of Organization: The Control of Task and Sentient Boundaries*. New York: Barnes and Noble.

Moen, P. 1996. A life course approach to the entrepreneurial family. *Proceedings of The Cornell University Conference of The Entrepreneurial Family*, New York City, March 18–20.

Montagno, R.V., D.F. Kuratko, and J.S. Hornsby. 1991. *Family Business Succession: A Study of Cultural Diversity*. Paper presented during the Sixth Annual National Conference, USAS-BE, San Diego, CA, October 7–9.

Moores, K., and J. Mula. 1993. *Managing and Controlling Family Owned Businesses: A Life Cycle Perspective of Australian Firms*. Gold Coast, Australia: Bond University.

Munson, F.C. 1963. *Labor Relations in the Lithographic Industry*. Cambridge, MA: Harvard University Press.

Nash, J.M. 1988. Boards of privately held companies: Their responsibilities and structure. *Family Business Review* 1(3):263-269.

NE-167R Technical Committee. 1993. Family business: Interaction of work and family spheres. Unpublished research grant proposal, Cornell University, Department of Consumer Economics and Housing.

Nelton, S. 1986. *In Love and in Business: How Entrepreneurial Couples Are Changing the Rules of Business and Marriage*. New York: Wiley.

Olson, D.H. 1986. Circumplex model VII: Studies and FACES III Validation. *Family Process* 25:337-351.

Ouh, Y. 1995. Cultural basis of skills for success in small and medium enterprises: The Korean Cases. In *Proceedings of the ICSB 40th World Conference*, Sydney, Australia. 77-97.

Owen, A.J., B.R. Rowe, and J.E. Gritzmacher. 1992. Building family functioning scales into the study of at-home income generation. *Journal of Family and Economic Issues* 13:299-313.

Patrick, A. 1986. Family Business: Offspring's Perceptions of Work Satisfaction and Their Working Relationship with Their Father. Unpublished doctoral dissertation, The Fielding Institute, Santa Barbara, CA.

Paulin, W.L., R.E. Coffey, and M.E. Spaulding. 1982. Entrepreneurship research: Methods and directions. In C.A. Kent, D.L. Sexton, and K.H. Vesper (eds.): *Encyclopedia of Entrepreneurship*. Englewood Cliffs, NJ: Prentice Hall, 352-373.

Peay, T.R., and W.G. Dyer, Jr. 1989. Power orientations of entrepreneurs and succession planning. *Journal of Small Business Management* 27(1):47-52.

Peiser, R.B., and L.M. Wooten. 1983. Life-cycle changes in small family businesses. *Business Horizons* (May-June):58-65.

Porter, M.E. 1992. Capital disadvantage: America's failing capital investment system. *Harvard Business Review* 70:65-82.

Poza, E.J. 1988. Managerial practices that support interpreneurship and continued growth. *Family Business Review* 1(4):339-359.

Poza, E.J. 1989. *Smart Growth: Critical Choices for Business Continuity and Prosperity*. San Francisco: Jossey-Bass.

Riordan, D.A., and M.P. Riordan. 1993. Field theory: An alternative to systems theories in understanding the small family business. *Journal of Small Business Management* 31(2):66-78.

Rosenblatt, P.C., L. deMik, R.M. Anderson, and P.A. Johnson. 1985. *The Family in Business.* San Francisco: Jossey Bass.

Rue, L.W., and N.A. Ibrahim. 1996. The status of planning in smaller family-owned business. *Family Business Review* 9(1):29-43.

Salganicoff, M. 1990. Women in family business: Challenges and opportunities. *Family Business Review* 3(2):125-137.

Schein, E.H. 1985. *Organizational Culture and Leadership: A Dynamic View.* San Francisco: Jossey-Bass.

Scherer, R.F., J.S. Adams, S.S. Carley, and F.A. Wiebe. 1989. Role model performance: Effects on development of entrepreneurial career preference. *Entrepreneurship Theory and Practice* 15:53-71.

Schipani, C.A., and G.J. Siedel. 1988. Legal liability: The board of directors. *Family Business Review* 1(3):279-285.

Schwartz, M.A., and L.B. Barnes. 1991. Outside boards and family business: Another look. *Family Business Review* 4(3):269-285.

Scott, M., and D. Twomey. 1988. The long-term supply of entrepreneurs: Student's career aspirations in relation to entrepreneurship. *Journal of Small Business Management* 26: 5-13.

Seymour, K.C. 1993. Intergenerational relationships in the family firm: The effect on leadership succession. *Family Business Review* 6(3):263-281.

Shapero, A., and L. Sokol. 1982. The social dimensions of entrepreneurship. In C.A. Kent et al. (eds.): *Encyclopedia of Entrepreneurship.* Englewood Cliffs, NJ: Prentice Hall, 72-88.

Sheehan, R. 1967. Proprietors in the world of big business. *Fortune* (June 15): 179.

Sidwell, P. 1989. An interview with Leon Danco. *Family Business Review* 2(4):381-400.

Silverzweig, S., and N. D'Agostino, Jr. 1995. A promising workshop model. *Family Business Review* 8(3):221-238.

Small Business Administration. 1978. *Facts about Small Business and the U.S. Small Business Administration.* Washington, DC: Government Printing Office.

Small Business Administration. 1994. *The State of Small Business: A Report to the President.* Washington, DC: Government Printing Office.

Sonnenfeld, J.A. 1988. *The Hero's Farewell: What Happens When Chief Executives Retire.* New York: Oxford University Press.

Sonnenfeld, J.A., and P.L. Spence. 1989. The parting patriarch of a family firm. *Family Business Review* 2(4):355-375.

Stavrou, E. 1996. Intergenerational Transitions in Family Enterprise: Factors Influencing Offspring Intentions to Seek Employment in the Family Business. Unpublished doctoral dissertation, Business and Public Management, George Washington University.

Stempler, G. 1988. The Study of Succession in Family Owned Businesses. Unpublished doctoral dissertation, George Washington University.

Stern, M.H. 1986. *Inside the Family-Held Business*. New York: Harcourt Brace Jovanovich.

Stoy Hayward. 1992. *The Stoy Hayward/BBC Family Business Index*. London: Stoy Hayward.

Swogger, G., Jr. 1991. Assessing the successor generation in family businesses. *Family Business Review* 4(4):397-411.

Tagiuri, R., and J.A. Davis. 1992. On the goals of successful family companies. *Family Business Review* 5(1):43-62.

Task Force of the International Family Business Program Association. 1995. Family business as a field of study. *Family Business Annual* (Sec. II, pp. 1-8). Nashville, TN.

Timmons, J. A. 1986. Growing up big: Entrepreneurship and the creation of high-potential ventures. In D.L. Sexton and R.W. Smilor (eds.): *The Art and Science of Entrepreneurship*. Englewood Cliffs, NJ: Prentice Hall, 223-240.

Upton, N.B. 1990. Children in the family business: The successors perspective. *Proceedings of 4th Annual FFI*. Brookline, MA: Family Firm Institute, 72-76

Upton, N.B., and S.L. Seaman. 1991. Rational decision-making in the family firm. Working Paper Series 221991, Waco, TX: Baylor University.

Upton, N., D.L. Sexton, and C. Moore. 1995. *Have We Made a Difference? An Examination of Career Activity of Entrepreneurship Majors since 1981*. Paper presented to the Babson Entrepreneurship Research Conference, London, England, April 9–12.

Ward, J.L. 1987. *Keeping the Family Business Healthy*. San Francisco: Jossey-Bass.

Ward, J.L. 1988a. The active board with outside directors and the family firm. *Family Business Review* 1:223-229.

Ward, J.L. 1988b. The special role of strategic planning for family businesses. *Family Business Review* 1(2):105-117.

Ward, J.L., and J.L. Handy. 1988. A survey of board practices. *Family Business Review* 1(3):289-308.

Welsch, J.H.M. 1993. The impact of family ownership and involvement on the process of management succession. *Family Business Review* 6(1):31-54.

Whiteside, M., and F. Herz-Brown. 1991. Drawbacks of a dual system approach to family firms: Can we expand our thinking? *Family Business Review* 4 (4):383-395.

Wortman, M.S., Jr. 1994. Theoretical foundations for family-owned business: A conceptual and research-based paradigm. *Family Business Review* 7(1):3-27.

Wortman, M.S., Jr. 1995. Critical issues in family business: An international perspective of practice and research. In *Proceedings of the ICSB 40th World Conference*, Sydney, Australia: Institute of Industrial Economics, 53-76.

CHAPTER 12

Ethnic Entrepreneurship: The Continuous Rebirth of American Enterprise

JOHN S. BUTLER
AND
PATRICIA G. GREENE

T HE PURPOSE OF THIS CHAPTER IS TO EXAMINE the literature that looks at the process by which ethnic and racial groups develop, manage, and maintain business enterprise. Ethnic entrepreneurship is the formation of enterprises by an individual who uses some type of support, instrumental and/or expressive, from the ethnic community of which the entrepreneur is a member (Bonacich and Modell, 1980; Portes and Sensenbrenner, 1993; Light, 1980; Waldinger et al., 1990). This literature has a distinguished history that dates back to the late 1800s. Although all of this literature will not be reviewed, consideration will be given to the history of entrepreneurship and ethnicity, with an emphasis on the context in which the literature developed. This is necessary because, in addition to studies of ethnic entrepreneurship through the years, a strong theoretical framework emerged as studies started to unfold around the turn of the century. Next, an extension of this theoretical framework as applied to African-American entrepreneurs will be considered. The chapter concludes with a review of the treatment of ethnic entrepreneurship in the business literature and suggestions for future research.

Discussion of Previous Research

The Emergence of a Theoretical Framework

The early impetus for the study of entrepreneurship and ethnicity lay in the attempt by scholars to understand how immigrants, or new members of host societies, develop a sense of economic stability. In the late 1800s Georg Simmel (1950) referred to what we today call ethnic entrepreneurs as strangers or traders. Simmel, as well as Bonacich and Modell (1980), noted that throughout history economists consistently reported the stranger as the trader, and vice versa.

The stranger concept evolved in scholarship during a time when communities were evolving from traditional to modern societies. In traditional societies, trade and the people who brought it, were not welcomed (Hamilton, 1978; Bonacich and Modell, 1980). Strangers were seen as being only in the pursuit of money, considered a negative characteristic in such societies (Bonacich and Modell, 1980; Sjoberg, 1960). It was a time when subsistence agriculture and home crafts were in decline. New traders represented the city, cosmopolitan values, customs that were strange, and a different kind of life.

Because no one else wanted to engage in trade, distinctive ethnic minorities began to occupy the position. Bonacich and Modell (1980) sum up the relationship as one in which distinctive ethnic minorities assumed the role of traders, partly because no one else in the society would do so. Since trading was considered dirty work, outsiders with identifiable cultural differences were allowed to fulfill the need for money-lenders and other middlemen. If the outsiders became assimilated to the host society, they too began to despise the middleman role and were less willing to continue in that role. However, as traders and outsiders they were disdained by members of the host society, complicating and postponing the process of assimilation. A state of equilibrium resulted, equating the trader as outsider (Bonacich and Modell, 1980).

These early ideas are the building blocks for present theoretical frameworks for the study of ethnic entrepreneurship. The major idea is that entrepreneurship is socially embedded, and not strictly economic or the function of the psychological make-up of individuals.

The contemporary study of ethnic entrepreneurship, and the importance of social embeddedness, can be traced to the works of Max Weber (1930) and Joseph Schumpeter (1934). Weber argued that the very foundation of competitive capitalism, innovation, sacrifice, and hard work, grew out of religious philosophy and could not be separated from capitalism when one seeks clues for the emergence of business activity. Weber's argument was that capitalism in Europe received a critical stimulus from Protestant thinkers such as Calvin and Luther, a boost which allowed the continent to break away from guild traditionalism. Weber (1978) introduced notions of the boundedness of and the maintenance of enforceable trust within social networks (Spener 1995). Schumpeter (1934) argued that the entrepreneur was at the very center of all business activity and that business activity was tied to social values and relationships. Like Weber, he argued that the source for understanding entrepreneurial behavior lay in the social structure of societies and the value structures that they produce.

Weber, building on Simmel's concept of the stranger, was one of the first to formalize the relationship between business activity, immigration, minority status, societal exclusion, and entrepreneurship. He brought together all of the strangers and traders that Simmel noted in his work, recognizing that members of minority groups, restricted from participation in the state due to discrimination, focus their energies on economic activities. Weber noted these recognizable patterns of economic behaviors driven by discrimination in groups such as Poles in both Russia and Eastern Prussia, Huguenots in France during the reign of Louis XIV, Nonconformists and Quakers in England, and the Jewish people throughout most of history. Weber's insights provided an early theoretical guiding light, which is still present today, for the general understanding of entrepreneur behavior.

One stimulus for the development of Weber's insights was his interest in understanding why Catholics, a minority group in Germany, had not developed a strong entrepreneurial culture. The obverse of that question was why Protestants were more likely to be engaged in entrepreneurial behavior. Weber concluded that the religious tenets of Catholics, with the emphasis on being one with the church and working toward the rewards of the afterworld, served to decrease the entrepreneurial spirit. On the other hand, as noted above, Protestant thinkers provided a philosophical platform that stressed the importance of earthly rewards (Weber, 1930). Thus the earliest explanation for entrepreneurial behavior revolved around the importance of religion and the social experiences of a group.

Sombart (1982) challenged Weber's notion that Protestantism was the fundamental source of the entrepreneurial spirit. Building on Weber's statement that entrepreneurship had been a characteristic of excluded groups in societies, he concentrated on the experience of European Jews and brought them into the forefront of the relation between ethnicity and entrepreneurship. Sombart connected the shifting of economic life from southern Europe to the northwest with the migration of segments of the Jewish population. He described the contribution of the Jews as influencing modern capitalism, both as to its outward form and its inward spirit.

During the early stages of the development of the literature on ethnicity and entrepreneurship, scholars documented the existence of this entrepreneurial type in all countries around the globe. The Chinese in Singapore (Fallers, 1967), the Coptic Christians in Egypt (Hamilton, 1978), Jews in the United States (Rinder, 1958), the Ibo in Nigeria (Waterbury, 1972), Greeks in Egypt (Becker, 1940), and Arabs in China (Hamilton, 1978).

The historical scholarship, which is grounded in the stranger-as-trader metaphor, manifests itself today in frameworks designed to understand the ethnic entrepreneurship experience. Two major theories involve ethnic enclaves and middlemen. It is important to point out that many studies of ethnic entrepreneurship do not explicitly utilize these theories, but they nevertheless influence a significant amount of the literature.

Enclave theory examines "self-segregated" communities of ethnic immigrants, communities that have as their major concern the creation of business enterprise and the development of a labor market within the broader market of the host country (Nee and Nee, 1986; Portes and Bach, 1985; Wilson and Portes, 1980). The enclave economy is thus composed of both an economic and cultural component. The ethnic enclave can be seen as a segmented sector of the larger economy, a partially autonomous enclave economic structure constituting a very distinct labor market (Zhou, 1992). Scholars who utilize enclave theory stress the positive cultural identity of the group, and how members rely on resources within the ethnic community in order to develop, manage, and maintain business enterprise. Such a community helps immigrants to successfully adjust to an advanced capitalist society and avoid the bottom of the socioeconomic structure of societies (Zhou, 1992).

Middleman theory is similar to enclave theory in its specification of the importance of business enterprise. Instead of enterprises being located in one geographic area within a city, members of the ethnic group establish enterprises all over the city and are intertwined with the overall business economy. As the term suggests, studies in this theoretical tradition concentrate on ethnic groups who concentrate in the middle of the structure of capitalism: those who act as middlemen in the movement of goods and services. They are found as labor contractors, rent collectors, moneylenders, and brokers. Thus, playing the middleman position means that they negotiate products between producer and consumer, owner and renter, elite and masses, and employer and employee (Zenner, 1991; Bonacich and Modell, 1980). Because of the importance of immigration to historical as well as the contemporary studies of ethnic entrepreneurship, both enclave and middleman frameworks begin their analysis with theories of immigration.

The Importance of Immigration

The study of the movement of ethnic groups around the globe is central to much of the research on ethnic entrepreneurship. Push-pull theories of migration, which have guided this research, are concerned with economic, social, and political factors that force people to leave their native land and seek opportunities in more fertile land (Piore, 1975; Portes and Bach, 1985). Negative political forces push those with the entrepreneurial spirit to the shores of America and other free-world markets. Commenting on the growth of Cuban entrepreneurs in Florida 20 years after the Cuban Revolution, Gilder (1984) characterized the Cubans as the latest immigrant arrivals to contribute to America's entrepreneurial growth. Gilder attributed the continuing revival and rebirth of the United States to its immigrant flow.

As groups move around the globe, research termed "migration networks and immigrant entrepreneurship" has developed to explain the phenomenon (Light et al., 1993). This research examines how migration networks link migrants, former migrants, and nonmigrants who share a common origin and destination in a bond of friendship and shared community origin (Light, 1972; Portes and Bach, 1985). The research also seeks to measure the solidarity and independence of those who chose to migrate, which might influence new entrepreneurial or job opportunities (Sell, 1983; De Jong and Fawcett, 1981, De Jong and Gardner, 1981). This literature argues that migration networks promote the independence of migratory flows for two basic reasons: they lead to an autonomous social structure that supports immigration, and they permit the reduction of social, economic, and emotional costs associated with immigration (Light et al., 1993; Hugo, 1981; Findley, 1977).

It has been argued that once fully underway, networks generate economic growth which promotes their continued survival. Although they might ultimately collapse and disintegrate, they often outlive the economic conditions that created them. This is because of the capacity of immigrant entrepreneurs to create the very economic opportunities that migration networks require for continued survival (Light et al., 1993).

The importance of networks for immigrant stability has been examined around the globe. These include case studies and analysis for Paris and Berlin (Morokvasic, 1993), Canada and Israel (Razin, 1993), Russia and Israel (Lerner, 1994), France (Simon, 1993), and Britain (Bhachu, 1993). In the United States these studies include but are not limited to Asian Indians in Southern California (Leonard and Tibrewal, 1993), Chinese in New York (Wong, 1988; Zhou, 1995), Koreans in Los Angeles (Min, 1988), Armenians in Los Angeles (Der-Martirosian et al., 1993), and Cubans in Florida (Portes and Bach, 1985).

Muller (1993) argued that the connections that skilled immigrants bring with them improve the technological standing of America, increase the standard of living for the middle class, and facilitate the resurgence of inner cities. From an international perspective, Kotkin (1992) argues that the success in the new global economy is determined by the connections which immigrant entrepreneurs carry with them around the world. This research on immigration is in stark contrast to the research that views the process as being detrimental to the economic success of America. It points to the fact that the entrepreneurial process which immigrants bring with them must be considered in the overall historical debate focusing on immigration in advanced countries around the globe.

Ethnic Entrepreneurs and Capital Formation

The foundation of all business is financial capital. One of the most interesting areas of research is how immigrant ethnic groups develop and maintain a capital base. Rotating credit systems and various kinds of community fund development have stood at the center of research in this area (Light, 1972; Geertz, 1962; Tenenbaum, 1993). These funds have been referred to as "contribution clubs," "slates," "mutual lending societies," "pooling clubs," "thrift groups," and "friendly societies" (Geertz, 1962, 242).

Rotating credit systems vary as much by operation as they do by name. The basic procedure usually involves the creation of more capital than an individual can accumulate. Members of the defined group are asked to contribute to an organized fund. Various rules exist for the distribution of the funds upon accumulation of an amount determined as sufficient. In some cases a lottery is held to see which person will benefit from the fund. In other cases, sealed bids are submitted to see who will benefit from the capital (Light, 1972). Repayment terms, including whether or not interest is paid, depend on the cultural norms.

The ethnic enterprise research has documented the use of such arrangements by immigrants to the United States in general (Russell, 1984; Woodrum, 1981). Specific studies have reported variations of the system for West Indians and Haitians in New York City (Bonnett, 1981), Chinese in New York City (Wong, 1979), and Japanese Americans (Woodrum, 1981). For ethnic groups that have been in America for generations, more formalized means of capital formation have been developed. Certain groups have developed their own banking institutions, including people of African descent (Butler, 1991), Cuban Americans (Portes and Bach, 1985), and the Chinese in New York (Zhou, 1992).

Research has also found that although there are nontraditional kinds of ways to raise capital, the great majority of ethnic entrepreneurs also use personal savings and money from family members (Min, 1988). In many cases members of ethnic groups come to the United States with enough financial capital to open and maintain an enterprise (Kotkin and Kishimoto, 1988). As an immigrant ethnic group develops economic stability within a country, the use of traditional banking becomes more of a reality. With established credit ratings, capital formation becomes a function of business performance rather than ethnic ties (Greene and Butler, 1996).

Ethnic Entrepreneurs and Nonfinancial Resources

It could be argued that the documentation of nonfinancial resources by immigrant entrepreneurs forms the core of this research area. The management, maintenance and success of ethnic enterprises depend upon the resources and strategies employed by business owners. As noted by Waldinger et al. (1990), strategies are related to the intersection of opportunity structures and group characteristics as ethnic entrepreneurs adjust to the resources available to them and build on the characteristics of their group.

Labor from the ethnic community constitutes a chief element of the success of enterprises. Joseph A. Pierce (1947/1996) points out the importance of black labor for African-American entrepreneurs from the beginning to the middle of the 20th century. Bonacich and Modell (1980) document the importance of an ethnic labor force in their studies of Japanese in California at the turn of the century. Not only did the Japanese Americans build a strong business community by utilizing immigrant labor, they also created conflict with white labor because the latter felt that the price of labor was being decreased significantly. For years the Japanese-American workers were prohibited from joining white labor unions. When white labor finally asked the immigrant Japanese to join the unions, the Japanese Americans rejected the invitation for fear of discrimination in an open labor market. Instead, they worked in their ethnic community.

The dynamics of the ethnic labor force—how it is utilized for the success of enterprises and how it can create divisions of class within a class—has been documented for the Chinese in New York (Kwong, 1987). Waldinger (1985) has shown how Dominican entrepreneurs in New York recruited labor from a common city in the Dominican Republic. Chinatown in New York City has relied upon an ethnic force (Zhou, 1992), as have Cubans in Miami (Portes and Bach, 1985; Portes and Manning, 1986), Asians in the Russian Far East (Patsiorkovsky et al., 1995), and immigrant entrepreneurs in general (Bailey and Waldinger, 1991).

The literature also reflects potential negative aspects of sometimes working within an ethnic labor market. There is a spirited debate over the advantages and disadvantages of ethnic labor markets. On one hand, the manner in which ethnic labor is sometimes used is considered exploitative. The alternative view is that there is little basis for such a claim and, indeed, that a charge of exploitation is meritless without a consideration of alternative labor conditions and opportunities. Training and skills for the ethnic workplace are, for the most part, realized on the job (Aldrich and Waldinger, 1990). Research continues to show that family members play a crucial role in ethnic enterprises; most often this labor is unpaid.

Ethnic community resources may serve many purposes. Greene and Butler (1996) described a Pakistani community incubator that brought community resources under one managerial umbrella. Contrasting the ethnic community incubator with research on traditional incubators, they showed how resources were geared not only toward the creation of business enterprise but also toward the teaching of language skills, health care for the elderly, youth and sports, teaching religious education, and the creation of enterprises.

Ethnic Enclave Research

Research on ethnic enterprise reached a new level of sophistication with the development of enclave theory. In addition to carrying out research on ethnic groups, these theorists argued that some ethnic groups developed business communities which provide immigrants with equal, if not better, opportunities than can be found in the larger host society. In addition, the theory strikes at the very essence of the relationship between assimilation and being successful in America. It contradicts the classical assimilation view that segregation retards the economic stability of minority group members.

Central to understanding the enclave perspective is dual economy theory, which suggests two structural idea types: A center economy with a high degree of corporate and bureaucratic organization, great diversification, technologically progressive means of production and distribution, and national and international accounts, along with a peripheral economy composed of firms that are small, dominated by one individual, use outdated techniques of production, and operate in small restricted markets. The center economy is structured to reduce or eliminate competitive forces, while the peripheral economy is somewhat powerless against, and subject to, forces of competition (Averitt, 1968). In order to understand the dynamics of labor participation in America, one must understand that workers will participate in the economy in either the center or peripheral economy. When workers are placed, one is concerned with the issue of dual labor markets (Kalleberg and Sorensen, 1979).

Essentially, the labor market is divided into good jobs and bad jobs, or the primary sector and the secondary sector, which produce different outcomes for workers, including pay, benefits, career opportunities, different rates of turnover or commitment, different types of discipline, and different returns to education. Positive things for workers are found in the primary sector. Overall, immigrant and minorities are more likely to be found in the secondary sector (Butler, 1991; Butler and Herring, 1991).

Research has pointed out that the terms "ethnic economy" and "ethnic enclave economy" must be distinguished from each other. The idea of an ethnic enclave economy emerges out of the labor segment literature, whereas the concept of ethnic economy comes out of the literature dealing with middleman minorities. The differences are important because the latter does not address location of enterprises (Light et al., 1994).

An examination of the enclave economy thesis (Wilson and Portes, 1980; Portes and Bach, 1985) not only revealed that Cubans in Miami developed ethnic enterprises, but the authors also advanced the enclave economy hypothesis that immigrants in an enclave labor market received earning-returns to human capital commensurate with earning-returns of immigrants in the primary labor market. The Cuban refugees in Miami were able to replicate the labor market of the host society, complete with both primary and secondary sectors. The enclave economy analysis has also been used to increase our understanding of Chinese economic behaviors in New York City (Zhou, 1992). However, the dynamics of enclave analysis has generated a major debate over conceptualization, analysis, and findings (Sanders and Nee, 1987). This debate has served to bring the importance of ethnic entrepreneurship for economic stability to the forefront of immigrant entrepreneurship in America.

Race and Gender: Beyond Immigrant Entrepreneurship

Related to, but distinguished from, the tradition of immigrant entrepreneurship is the research on people of African descent and women around the globe. Although there is overlap between this research and citations above, studies on race and gender have entered the literature as a distinct subject. Obviously, the issue of immigration, for native American blacks and women, is taken out of the theoretical equation.

Research has argued that African Americans followed many of the patterns of ethnic entrepreneurship from the 1700s to the present, with the most activity developing after the Civil War and lasting up until the middle 1950s (Butler 1991). Indeed, the documentation of this activity started before the turn of the 20th century, about the same time that Weber was conceptualizing his ideas (Weber, 1930). The historical research of DuBois (1898), Minton (1913), and Pierce (1947/1996) has served as the basis for the discussion of enclave theory and middleman theory within the African-American tradition (Butler, 1991).

This reconstruction of African-Americans in business reveal that in 1910 they were more likely than any other ethnic group in America to be self-employed (Levenstein, 1995). It has been shown that this is the group that was responsible for building early African-American communities, constructing over 200 private schools throughout the South, and starting the tradition of college matriculation among African Americans (Butler, 1991). However, the middleman explanation as applied to this population can best be described as truncated. This is the only minority group in the United States that operated in contemporary times under legal constraints regarding business practices, including such things as location and clientele. The limitation of entrepreneurial opportunities that resulted from the de jure constraints caused a large segment of the African-American population to lose the tradition of entrepreneurship. The outcome can be classified as an "economic detour" and begins to help us understand the differences observed between the entrepreneurial behaviors of members of certain ethnic groups and African Americans (Butler, 1991).

Present research on African American enterprise concentrates on those in the inner city (Horton and Lundy-Allen, forthcoming; Horton, 1992) and those that are located outside of the inner city (Boston, 1994; Sonfield, 1993; Graves, 1988). The inner-city research concentrates on rebuilding American communities and the many problems associated with that task. African-American entrepreneurship outside of the inner city concentrates on the population getting back on mainstreet, doing business enterprise anywhere in the city. One branch of this literature traces the number of African-American enterprises (Boyd, 1991a; Horton and De Jong, 1991) and analyzes the business environment and characteristics of the business owner (Boyd, 1991b).

An important but neglected area in the study of entrepreneurship is the role of women. Very little explicit attention is paid to ethnic women in the literature; it is usually restricted to references to women as unpaid family workers often working long and hard in the background. Westwood and Bhachu (1988) offer a collection of analytical approaches to the role of women in British ethnic economies, emphasizing the articulation between race and class relations, cultures, and gender. Phizacklea (1988) describes the ethnic business literature as mostly "gender blind," and he attributes much of the success of ethic entrepreneurs to using resources unavailable to native business owners. One of the most important of these resources is low and unpaid family workers, most of whom are women.

Research by scholars such as Peter Berger (1988) also point to the fact that women do play important roles in the development and "success" of ethnic entrepreneurs. This line of research stresses the importance of the family structure and women's role in that structure vis-à-vis business enterprise (Mariz, 1988; Martin, 1990).

The theme of a lack of gender specificity in research on ethnic economies drives Dallalfar's recent work on Iranian women entrepreneurs (1994). However, opposed to the exploitative situations described by Phizacklea and Westwood and Bhachu, Dallalfar describes entrepreneurship as a path to empowerment for the women in this study. Dallalfar's study is additionally unique in that it recognizes ethnic women involved in entrepreneurial activities without the direct participation of a spouse or father. In the sample described, Iranian women are benefiting from the ethnic resources of the community, including the creation of capital, provision of labor, and networks providing instrumental types of assistance. The women are seen as providing a benefit to the community through the creation of employment opportunities for other ethnic women who may lack the necessary skills or education to compete in the primary labor market.

Other examples of female ethnic entrepreneurs can be found that cause one to question the limited knowledge held of these women. A recent investigative report by *The New York Times* described a garment industry sweatshop owned by a Chinese woman. Maggie Zheng, described as "a fashionable woman in her early 30's," who assumed ownership of the business when her brother, the former owner, fled town owing the workers backpay of approximately $80,000 (Lii, 1995). An interview of a Pakistani woman business owner in a southwestern city revealed a polished, experienced, professional enjoying a lucrative return from her business participation (Greene, 1993).

Our understanding of women's entrepreneurial behaviors in the ethnic economy remains polarized. Most theoretical treatments of ethnic entrepreneurship either do not include women as part of the discussion or aggregate them as an exploited ethnic labor resource. However, research and trade publications are beginning to offer an alternative view, one in which women are active participants in entrepreneurial activities, with and without the participation of a spouse.

Ethnic Entrepreneurship in the Business Literature

Discussion of the entrepreneurial behaviors of groups defined by ethnicity or race have appeared sporadically in the business literature over the past few decades. The theoretical basis for these studies often drew on the early sociological frameworks. Glade (1967) briefly reviewed early works on cultural influences on economic decision-making and proposed the use of situational analysis to better understand ethnic entrepreneurs, positing that ethnic groups traditionally engaged in trading occupations acquire a differential advantage in developing entrepreneurial activities. Leibenstein (1968) proposed theoretical categories to explain the responsiveness of entrepreneurs to various motivations and explicitly used the concept of outsiders to describe a group drawn to entrepreneurship. The group was seen to face reduced opportunity costs of entrepreneurship due to restrictions from certain economic opportunities.

More recently, Reynolds (1991) includes the study of ethnicity and entrepreneurship in his exegesis on the contribution of sociology to the study of entrepreneurship. Reynolds describes the dominant theme underlying minority entrepreneurship as blocked economic opportunities in the majority society. The challenge placed is to understand the differential behaviors and contexts of various ethnic groups.

In order to understand behaviors within contexts, we must first be familiar with the characteristics of the group under study. Most of the business literature dealing with minority entrepreneurship approaches the topic from a descriptive perspective. These works vary in their conceptualization of minority groups, unit of analysis, and theoretical disciplines. Drawing from an economic perspective, Kirchhoff et al. (1982) and Borjas (1986) each present an overview of rates and trends of minority entrepreneurship. Kirchhoff et al. use the 1972 and 1977 Survey of Minority-Owned Business Enterprises database to show varying ownership rates between minority groups. While acknowledging regional differences, these authors found the lowest participation rates for Blacks, the second highest, but fastest growing for Hispanics, and the highest rate of ownership participation for Asians (i.e., Japanese, Chinese, and Filipino). Borjas, using U.S. Census data from 1970 and 1980, examines the propensities for immigrant and native born groups to be self-employed, finding that the likelihood of being self-employed is 11.7 percent for native-born, versus 16.5 percent for immigrants. Borjas explicitly draws from ethnic enclave theory, concluding that the enclave effect does indeed increase the likelihood of being self-employed.

In one of the earliest comparisons between Black and white business owners, Hornaday and Aboud (1971) searched for racial differences in characteristics of their respondents. The authors found that white owners had been in business longer, were less likely to be separated or divorced, more likely to have graduated from college, and more likely to have based their business on a "special idea." Hornaday and Aboud also explored for racial differences in an assortment of psychological measures but the only significant difference found was in a measure of benevolence. A later study of the personal values of Black and white small business owners found similar value orientations for both groups (Watson and Simpson, 1987).

The demographics of business owners defined by their race and/or ethnicity has been another approach to the field. Gomolka (1977) used data from 220 members of a minority business organization to describe characteristics of minority business owners and their businesses. The minority organization, and thus the sample frame, included members who reported themselves as Black, American Indian, Asian, Eskimo, Aleut, Puerto Rican, Chicano, or as from Central or South America. Gomolka compared his sample with an earlier study of white businessmen in the manufacturing industry and found the minority sample to be younger and better educated but from similar family backgrounds as the white businessmen.

DeCarlo and Lyons (1979) did bring gender into the equation through a comparison of minority and nonminority female entrepreneurs. These authors used many of the same measures as Hornaday and Aboud (1971) to analyze personal characteristics. The sample was drawn from a selection of business directories, including those of women-owned and minority-owned firms. The racial/ethnic composition of the sample was Black, Hispanic, American Indian, white, or other. In comparing the minority entrepreneur to the white entrepreneur, the typical minority female was found to be married, older, started her business when older (although it was not her first business), and less likely to be a college graduate. The comparison of personality scales did produce significant differences in six of the nine measures.

Van Fleet and Van Fleet (1985) place their study in the inner city to examine the question of the viability of business for both Black- and white-owned businesses. The urban environment of the 63 businesses targeted for study was predominately Black and largely poor. However, race was found to have less of a relationship with business success than did the assets of the firm.

Hisrich and Brush (1986) used a government listing of minority business to obtain responses from 217 minority business owners. The research questions included not only basic demographic data, but explored the issues of business problems as well. The sample composition included Black, Hispanic, Asian, and American Indian business owners. The typical minority business owner was concluded to be the eldest child of a blue-collar family, held a college degree and had related industry experience, was married and had children, and was primarily motivated by achievement, opportunity, and job satisfaction. The two problems mentioned most often by the respondents were obtaining lines of credit and a lack of business training.

Using data from the late 1960s and early 1970s, Auster (1988) examined Black and white business owners in three urban areas in order to describe characteristics of both the owners and the business. Black business owners were found to have fewer years of both education and business experience. Black businesses were found to be smaller and less profitable. Auster did not, however, find significant differences between the survival rates of Black- and white-owned businesses. (Survival rates after six years at the same site were .47 and .50, respectively.) Auster posits that one explanation for the lack of a significant difference in survival rates is that the Black business owners lacked alternative employment options, a reoccurrence of the decreased opportunity cost explanation previously offered by Leibenstein (1968). She concludes with the suggested public policy implications that increased funding and business training to Black business owners have the potential for improving the profitability of their businesses, and ultimately the underlying problems of the urban neighborhoods.

Policy implications have been an underlying theme of much of the work of Bates in his long-term analysis of black economic development and banking relationships (Bates and Bradford, 1979; Bates, 1993). Bates (1985) suggests that the shape of minority entrepreneurship is a result of limited access to financial capital, education, and training and society's perceptions of appropriate roles for minorities. Using a data set created from matching files in the Dun and Bradstreet Financial Profiles with records of minority business listings (Bates and Furino, 1985), Bates finds a positive relationship between human and financial capital and business profitability. In addition, Bates documents the entry of better educated minority business owners into industrial sectors considered nontraditional minority enterprises, such as skill-intensive services, manufacturing, and heavy construction. This reflects a movement away from the traditional sectors of personal services and retail.

Value orientations of small business owners were the focus of analysis for Enz et al. (1990). These authors used data from 153 minority business owners listed in the National Minority Business Directory and a control group of 99 business owners from a state industrial directory. The ethnic/racial composition of the sample was described as mostly Black and Hispanic, with smaller numbers of Asians and American Indians. The respondents were tested on the importance of six organizational value dimensions and the perceived similarity of those values with their customers. Significant differences were found between the minority and nonminority owners on every dimension and differences between the similarity of owner possessed values and perceived customer values were found on all but one dimension. The authors found no significant between-group differences for the minority owners.

Feldman et al. (1991) make an important contribution to the study of minority entrepreneurship in two ways. First, by turning their attention to the process of business formation and, second, by including between group comparisons within the minority sample. These authors obtained 172 responses from a survey mailed to members of a local minority business development center. The sample was approximately half Hispanic, with the remainder of the respondents being Black (20.3 percent), Asian (10.5 percent), and American Indians (10.5). When compared to a study of members of the National Federation of Independent Business Owners (NFIB) (Cooper and Dunkelberg, 1986), the authors found the minority sample to be more likely to have an immigrant parent and more likely to have a college education. Between group comparisons showed Asians to be far more likely to have an immigrant parent than Blacks, 77.8 percent and 2.9 percent, respectively. In addition, the American-Indian business owners were more likely to come from "foreign stock" than the Black business owners. Asian business owners (84 percent) were much more likely to have a college education than American Indians (33 percent), Hispanics (51 percent), and Blacks (54 percent). Approximately 37 percent of the NFIB sample had a college degree. The minority businesses were found to be in construction, service, and professional businesses, while the NFIB sample reported greater participation in retail and "other."

Feldman et al. use Cooper and Dunkelberg's four typical paths to ownership:

❖ Start-up
❖ Purchase
❖ Inheritance
❖ Promotion

Minority business owners of each race and ethnicity were found to be much more likely to enter business ownership through their own start-up activities. This finding is attributed to a recent emergence of minority entrepreneurship.

Theory in the field of ethnic entrepreneurship includes discussion of capital resources available to members of certain ethnic communities. Chotigeat et al. (1991) provide an exceptionally detailed explanation of rotating saving and credit societies (RSCS), including participation procedures and motivation of participants. The authors conclude that the RSCS are the preferred method of financing among some groups of Asian immigrants and that the RSCS will continue to play an important role in the founding of immigrant businesses.

Social performance is another area examined for minority differences. Thompson and Hood (1993) used a sample drawn from a private business directory, resulting in data from 32 minority and 137 nonminority owners. The racial/ethnic composition of the sample is assumed to be largely Hispanic because of the location of the study. Minority-owned firms were found to contribute more dollars to charitable organizations, particularly religious organizations, than nonminority owned firms.

Conclusions

The theoretical study of ethnic entrepreneurship is based on an extensive body of works, primarily within the field of sociology. This literature is grounded by the importance of a community dimension inherent in the business creation process. Studies across groups, eras, and locations consistently find significant contributions of community resources to the entrepreneurial activities of group members. Both middleman minority theory and ethnic enclave theory help us better understand the phenomena of ethnic entrepreneurship.

The study of African-American entrepreneurs is grounded in a variation of ethnic entrepreneurship theories, referred to as an economic detour. Black business owners largely do not benefit from community resources, and their business practices and outcomes differ accordingly. Black business owners have been the subject of much public policy debate regarding business assistance programs as a path to economic development.

The study of minority entrepreneurship raises many issues about potential generalizations. A theoretical understanding that includes the context and situation of the economic behaviors of a group defined by race, ethnicity, or religion provides for a better interpretation and utilization of research findings. Studies that combine groups which differ dramatically by access to group resources and entrepreneurial strategies result in findings more difficult to interpret and provide results of limited use to both academics and practitioners.

The study of ethnic or minority entrepreneurship needs to draw from a broader sense of methodology, one that emphasizes the theoretical grounding not only of the research question but of the appropriate population and sample selection as well. Studies that recognize group differences will result in findings which help us learn from and about the entrepreneurial activities of these groups.

Areas for Future Research

One of the keys to understanding entrepreneurial activities in general is the process by which ethnic entrepreneurs develop and maintain an enterprise. In a real sense, the fundamental elements of the entrepreneurial process come from understanding the population. The theoretical ideas, and data that support them, have been around for generations. The integration of interdisciplinary boundaries provides a framework in which to organize research questions related to both characteristics of the owner and business, as well as the business process. This framework can be organized along four dimensions:

❖ The community

❖ The individuals within the community

❖ The business

❖ The process of business creation

One intriguing research agenda deals with entrepreneurial differences within particular ethnic communities. This line of research needs to help us better understand community boundaries and norms. An initial approach would deal with the recognition of group definition, or what unites the community, be it ethnicity, race, or religion. Indeed, a historical approach to the migratory patterns and traditional economic behaviors of the group would help provide the context for the group's contemporary economic activities. While longitudinal studies are often called for as necessary to understand a phenomena, in this area it is particularly essential in order to understand generational trends toward and away from business ownership.

A more micro-oriented level of analysis is also necessary to better understand ethnic entrepreneurship. One question that needs to be addressed is why different economic outcomes of businesses are observed and reported within the ethnic community if the businesses are founded through similar processes and with some similarity of resource input? What is it that the individual brings to the equation? In addition, the gender of the entrepreneur is of particular interest in linking the individual business owner to the context of the community. Cultural norms contribute greatly to understanding the economic activities of individual female ethnic entrepreneurs.

Ethnic businesses have been stereotyped as small service activities and retail shops that survive largely by the use of exploitative family labor relationships. From the business perspective, much remains to be learned about the actual enterprises. Information is starting to surface that broadens the portrait of ethnic enterprise by industrial sector, size, scope, and profitability. A framework that provides a means of comparing these businesses across dimensions of community and individual owner-ship would be a significant contribution to the field.

As research in mainstream entrepreneurship shifts from trait research to process, so must we consider the process of business creation for ethnic entrepreneurs, rec-ognizing potential differences in that creation process by the two previously men-tioned dimensions, the community context and the individual entrepreneur. The types of questions that need to be explored include the effect of an ethnic enclave on the business creation process, how resources are identified, acquired, and deployed within various ethnic groups, and what type of strategies provide the most leverage for ethnic-based resources.

Attention to and extension of each of these questions, along with integration across the suggested research dimensions, across disciplines, and with mainstream entrepreneurship research will begin to move us away from stereotypes of ethnic entrepreneurs, their business creation processes, and the resultant businesses to a better understanding of this phenomena.

REFERENCES

Aldrich, H.E., and R. Waldinger. 1990. Ethnicity and entrepreneurship. *Annual Review of Sociology* 16:111-135.

Auster, E.R. 1988. Owner and organizational characteristics of black-and white-owned busi-nesses. *American Journal of Economics and Sociology* 47(3):331-344.

Averitt, R.T. 1968. *The Dual Economy: The Dynamics of America Industry Structure*. New York: Norton.

Bailey, T., and R. Waldinger. 1991. Primary, secondary, and ethnic labor markets: A training system approach. *American Sociological Review* 56:432-445.

Bates, T. 1993. *Banking on Black Business*. Washington, DC: Joint Center for Political and Economic Studies.

Bates, T. 1985. Entrepreneur human capital endowments and minority business viability. *Journal of Human Resources* 20(4):540-554.

Bates, T., and W. Bradford. 1979. *Financing Black Economic Development*. NY: Academic Press.

Bates, T., and A. Furino. 1985. A new nationwide data base for minority business. *Journal of Small Business Management*: 23(2):41-52.

Becker, H. 1940. Constructive typology in the social sciences. In H.E. Barnes, H. Becker, and F. Barnett Becker (eds.): *Contemporary Social Theory*. New York: Appleton-Century-Crofts.

Berger, P.L. 1988. An East-Asian development model? In P.L. Berger and M.H.H. Hsiao (eds.): *In Search of an East Asian Development Model*. New Brunswick, NJ: Transaction Publishers.

Bhachu, P. 1993. Twice and direct migrant Sikhs: Caste, class, and identity in pre- and post-1984 Britain. In G. De Jong and R. Gardner (eds.): *Immigrant and Entrepreneurship: Culture, Capital, and Ethnic Networks.* New Brunswick, NJ: Transaction Publishers.

Graves, E.G. 1988. Brady Keys does franchising right. *Black Enterprise.* 19(2).

Bonacich, E., and J. Modell. 1980. *The Economic Basis of Ethnic Solidarity: Small Business in the Japanese American Community.* Berkeley: University of California Press.

Bonnett, A. 1981. *Institutional Adaptation of West Indian Immigrants to America.* Washington, DC: University Press of America.

Borjas, G.J. 1986. The self-employment experience of immigrants. *Journal of Human Resources* 21:485-506.

Boston, T.D. 1994. Black entrepreneurship and economic development: A case study of Atlanta. Paper presented at the meetings of the Association for the Study of Afro-American Life and History. Department of Economics, Georgia Tech University, Atlanta, GA.

Boyd, R.L. 1991a. Black entrepreneurship in 52 metropolitan areas. *Sociology and Social Research* 75:409-429.

Boyd, R.L. 1991b. A contextual analysis of Black self-employment in large metropolitan areas, 1970–1980. *Social Forces* 70:409-429.

Butler, J.S. 1991. *Entrepreneurship and Self-Help among Black Americans: A Reconsideration of Race and Economics.* Albany: State University of New York Press.

Butler, J.S., and C. Herring. 1991. Ethnicity and entrepreneurship. *Sociological Perspectives* 34:79-94.

Chotigeat, T., P.W. Balsmeier, and T.O. Stanley. 1991. Fueling Asian immigrants' entrepreneurship: A source of capital. *Journal of Small Business Management* 29(3):50-61.

Cooper, A.C., and W. Dunkelberg. 1986. Entrepreneurship and paths to business ownership. *Strategic Management Journal* 7:53-68.

Dallalfar, A. 1994. Iranian women as immigrant entrepreneurs. *Gender and Society* 8(4):541-561.

De Jong, G.F., and J.T. Fawcett. 1981. Motivations for migration: An assessment and a value-expectancy research model. In G.F. De Jong and R.W. Gardner, (eds.): *Migration Decision-Making.* New York: Academic Press.

De Jong, G., and R.W. Gardner (eds.). 1981. *Migration Decision-Making.* New York: Academic Press.

DeCarlo, J.F., and P.R. Lyons. 1979. A comparison of selected personal characteristics of minority and non-minority female entrepreneurs. *Journal of Small Business Management* 17:22-229.

Der-Martirosian, C., G. Sabagh, and M. Bozorgmehr. 1993. In G. DeJong and R.W. Gardner (eds.): *Immigrant and Entrepreneurship: Culture, Capital, and Ethnic Networks.* New Brunswick, NJ: Transaction Publishers.

Du Bois, W.E.B. 1898. *The Negro in Business*. Atlanta: Atlanta University Press.

Enz, C.A., M.J. Dollinger, and C.M. Daily. 1990. The value orientations of minority and non-minority small business owners. *Entrepreneurship Theory and Practice* 15(1):23-35.

Fallers, L.A. 1967. *Immigrants and Associations*. The Hague: Mouton.

Feldman, H.D., C.S. Koberg, and T.J. Dean. 1991. Minority small business owners and their paths to ownership. *Journal of Small Business Management* 29(4):12-27.

Findley, S.E. 1977. *Planning for Internal Migration*. Washington, DC: Department of Commerce, Bureau of the Census, International Statistical Programs Center.

Geertz, C. 1962. The rotating credit association: A 'middle rung' in development. *Economic Development and Cultural Change* 10(April):241-263.

Gilder, G. 1984. *The Spirit of Enterprise*. New York: Simon and Schuster.

Glade, W.P. 1967. Approaches to a theory of entrepreneurial formation. *Explorations in Entrepreneurial History* 4(3):245-259.

Gomolka, E. 1977. Characteristics of minority entrepreneurs and small business enterprises. *American Journal of Small Business* 2(1):12-21.

Greene, P.G. 1993. Women in entrepreneurship: A case study of the role of the spouse in the ethnic business community. Working Paper, University of Texas at Austin.

Greene, P.G., and J.S. Butler. 1996. The ethnic community as a natural business incubator. *Journal of Business Research* 36(1):51-59.

Hamilton, G. 1978. Pariah capitalism: A paradox of power and dependence. *Ethnic Groups* 2:1-15.

Hisrich, R.D., and C. Brush. 1986. Characteristics of the minority entrepreneur. *Journal of Small Business Management* 24:1-8.

Hornaday, J.A., and J. Aboud. 1971. The characteristics of successful entrepreneurs. *Personnel Psychology* 24:141-153.

Horton, H.D. 1992. A sociological approach to black community development: Presentation of the Black organizational autonomy model. *Journal of the Community Development Society* 23:1-9.

Horton, H., and G.F. De Jong. 1991. Black entrepreneurs: A sociodemographic analysis. *Research in Race and Ethnic Relations* 6:105-120.

Horton, H.D., and B. Lundy-Allen. Forthcoming. *Rebuilding Black Communities: Black Community Development in Contemporary America*. Ames, IA: Iowa State University Press.

Hugo, G.J. 1981. Village-community ties, village norms and ethnic and social networks: A review of evidence from the Third World. In G.F. De Jong and R.W. Gardner (eds.): *Migration Decision-Making*. New York: Pergamon.

Kalleberg, A., and A. Sorensen. 1979. The sociology of labor markets. *Annual Review of Sociology* 5:351-379.

Kirchhoff, B.A., R.L. Stevens, and N.I. Hurwitz. 1982. Factors underlying increases in minority entrepreneurship: 1972–1977. In K.H. Vesper (ed.): *Frontiers of Entrepreneurship Research*. Wellesley MA: Babson College Center for Entrepreneurial Studies.

Kotkin, J. 1988. *The Third Century*. New York: Crown.

Kotkin, J. 1992. *Tribes: How Race, Religion and Identity Determine Success in the New Global Economy*. New York: Random House.

Kwong, P. 1987. *The New Chinatown*. New York: Hill and Wang.

Leibenstein, H. 1968. Entrepreneurship and development. *American Economic Review* 58(2):72-83.

Leonard, K.B., and C.S. Tibrewal. 1993. In G. DeJong and R.W. Gardner (eds.): *Immigrant and Entrepreneurship: Culture, Capital, and Ethnic Networks*. New Brunswick, NJ: Transaction Publishers.

Lerner, M. 1994. Immigrant entrepreneurial enclaves: The case of Russian immigrants in Israel. Paper presented at the Babson Entrepreneurship Conference, Wellesley, MA, June 9-11.

Levenstein, M. 1995. African American entrepreneurship: The view from the 1910 census. *Business and Economic History* 24(1):106-121.

Light, I. H. 1972. *Ethnic Enterprise in America: Business Welfare Among Chinese, Japanese and Blacks*. Berkeley: University of California Press.

Light, I. 1980. Asian enterprise in America: Chinese, Japanese, and Koreans in small business. In S. Cummings (ed.): *Self-Help in Urban America: Patterns of Minority Economic Development*. Port Washington, NY: Kennikat Press.

Light, I., P. Bhachu, and S. Karageorigis. 1993. Migration networks and immigrant entrepreneurship. In G. DeJong and R.W. Gardner (eds.): *Immigrant and Entrepreneurship: Culture, Capital, and Ethnic Networks*. New Brunswick, NJ: Transaction Publishers.

Light, I., G. Sabagh, M. Bozorgmehr, and C. Der-Martirosian. 1994. Beyond the ethnic enclave economy. *Social Problems* 41(1):65-80.

Lii, J. 1995. Week in sweatshop reveals grim conspiracy of the poor. *New York Times*, Sunday, March 12.

Mariz, C. 1988. The religious factor in economic development among the urban poor in Brazil. Unpublished doctoral dissertation, Boston University.

Martin, D. 1990. *Tongues of Fire*. Oxford: Blackwell.

Min, P.G. 1988. *Ethnic Business Enterprise: Korean Small Business in Atlanta*. New York: Center for Migration Studies.

Minton, H.M. 1913. Early History of Negroes in Business in Philadelphia. Read before the American Historical Society, March 1913.

Morokvasic, M. 1993. Immigrants in garment production in Paris and in Berlin. In G. DeJong and R.W. Gardner (eds.): *Immigrants and Entrepreneurship: Culture, Capital, and Ethnic Networks*. New Brunswick, NJ: Transaction Publishers.

Muller, T. 1993. *Immigrants and the American City*. New York: New York University Press.

Nee, V., and B. Nee. 1986. *Longtime Califom': A Study of American China Town*. Stanford, CA: Stanford University Press.

Patsiorkovsky, V., S. Fugita, and D.J. O'Brien. 1995. Asians in small business in the Russian Far East: A historical overview and comparison with Asians on the American West Coast. *International Migration Review* 29(2):566-573.

Phizacklea, A. 1988. Entrepreneurship, ethnicity, and gender. In S. Westwood and P. Bhachu (eds.): *Enterprising Women*. New York: Routledge.

Pierce, J.A. [1947] 1996. *Negro Business and Business Education*. New York: Plenum.

Piore, M. J. 1975. Notes from a theory of labor market stratification. In R.C. Edwards, M. Reich and D.M. Gordon (eds.): *Labor Market Segmentation*. Lexington, MA: D.C. Health.

Portes, A., and R.L. Bach. 1985. *Latin Journey: Cuban and Mexican Immigrants in the United States*. Berkeley: University of California Press.

Portes, A., and R.D. Manning. 1986. The immigrant enclave: Theory and empirical examples. In S. Olzak and J. Nagel (eds.): *Competitive Ethnic Relations*. Orlando, FL: Academic Press.

Portes, A., and J. Sensenbrenner. 1993. Embeddedness and immigration: Notes on the social determinants of economic action. *American Journal of Sociology* 98:1320-1350.

Razin, E. 1993. Immigrant entrepreneurs in Israel, Canada, and California. In G. DeJong and R.W. Gardner (eds.): *Immigrants and Entrepreneurship: Culture, Capital, and Ethnic Networks*. New Brunswick, NJ: Transaction Publishers.

Reynolds, P.D. 1991. Sociology and entrepreneurship: Concepts and contributions. *Entrepreneurship Theory and Practice* 16:47-70.

Rinder, N.B. 1958. Stranger in the land: Social relations in the status gap. *Social Problems* 6:253-260.

Russell, R. 1984. The role of culture and ethnicity in the degeneration of democratic firms. *Economy, Industry, Democracy* 5:73-69.

Sanders, J.M., and V. Nee. 1987. Limits of ethnic solidarity in the enclave economy. *American Sociological Review* 52:745-767.

Schumpeter, J.A. 1934. *The Theory of Economic Development: An Inquiry into Profits, Capital, Credit, Interest and the Business Cycle*. New York: McGraw-Hill.

Sell, R. 1983. Analyzing migration decisions: The first step—whose decision? *Demography* 20:299-311.

Simmel, G. 1950. The stranger. In K Wolf (ed.): *The Sociology of Georg Simmel*. Glencoe, IL: Free Press.

Simon, G. 1993. Immigrant entrepreneurs in France. In G. DeJong and R.W. Gardner (eds.): *Immigrants and Entrepreneurship: Culture, Capital, and Ethnic Networks*. New Brunswick, NJ: Transaction Publishers.

Sjoberg, G. 1960. *The Pre-Industrial City: Past and Present*. Glencoe, IL: Free Press.

Sombart, W. 1982. *The Jews and Modern Capitalism*. New Brunswick, NJ: Transaction Publishers.

Sonfield, M.C. 1993. Progress and success in the development of Black-owned franchise units. *Review of Black Political Economy* 22(2):73-88.

Spener, R. 1995. Entrepreneurship and Small-Scale Enterprise in the Texas Border Region: A Sociocultural Perspective. Dissertation, Department of Sociology, The University of Texas at Austin.

Tenenbaum, S. 1993. *A Credit to Their Community*. Detroit, MI: Wayne State University Press.

Thompson, J.K., and J.N. Hood. 1993. The practice of corporate social performance in Minority- versus nonminority-owned small businesses. *Journal of Business Ethics* 12:197-206.

Van Fleet, E.W., and D.D. Van Fleet. 1985. Entrepreneurship and black capitalism. *American Journal of Small Business* 10:31-40.

Waldinger, R. 1985. Immigration and industrial change: A case study of the New York apparel industry. In M. Tienda and G. Borjas (eds.): *Hispanic Workers in the United States Economy*. New York: Academic Press.

Waldinger, R., H. Aldrich, R. Ward, et al. 1990. *Ethnic Entrepreneurs*. Newbury Park, CA: Sage Publications.

Waterbury, J. 1972. *North for the Trade: The Life and Times of a Berber Merchant*. Berkeley: University of California Press.

Watson, J.G., and L.R. Simpson. 1987. A comparative study of owner-manager personal values in Black and White small businesses. *Academy of Management Journal* 21(2):313-319.

Weber, M. 1930. *The Protestant Ethic and the Spirit of Capitalism*. New York: Charles Scribner and Sons.

Weber, M. 1978. *Economy and Society: An Outline of Interpretive Sociology*. Berkeley: University of California Press.

Westwood, S., and P. Bhachu. 1988. *Enterprising Women*. New York: Routledge.

Wilson, K.L., and A. Portes. 1980. Immigrant enclaves: An analysis of the labor market experiences of Cubans in Miami. *American Journal of Sociology* 86:295-319.

Wong, C. 1979. *A Chinese American Community: Ethnicity and Strategies*. Singapore: Chopman Enterprises.

Wong, B. 1988. *Patronage, Brokerage, Entrepreneurship and the Chinese Community of New York*. New York: AMS Press.

Woodrum, E. 1985. Religion and economics among Japanese Americans: A Weberian study. *Social Forces* 64:191-204.

Woodrum, E. 1981. An assessment of Japanese American assimilation, pluralism, and subordination. *American Journal of Sociology* 87:157-169.

Zenner, W. 1991. *Minorities in the Middle: A Cross-Cultural Analysis*. Albany: State University of New York Press.

Zhou, M. 1992. *Chinatown: The Socioeconomic Potential of an Urban Enclave*. Philadelphia: Temple University Press.

Zhou, M. 1995. Low-wage employment and social mobility: The experience of immigrant Chinese women in New York City. *National Journal of Sociology* 9(1):1-30.

CHAPTER 13

International Entrepreneurship Literature in the 1990s and Directions for Future Research

PATRICIA P. MCDOUGALL

AND

BENJAMIN M. OVIATT

THE TOPICS OF ENTREPRENEURSHIP AND INTERNATIONAL business have perhaps been the two most explosive fields of study within U.S. business schools within the last decade. International entrepreneurship, as the juxtaposition of the two words implies, is at the intersection of these two growing areas of interest.

Until recently, international business scholars focused on large, mature corporations. Today, many large multinational firms are changing shape, creating all manner of networks and alliances, downsizing, and spinning off divisions. New ventures are also becoming international from inception. Recognizing this evolution in a celebration of 25 years of international business research in the *Journal of International Business Studies*, Wright and Ricks (1994) highlighted international entrepreneurship as one of three important newly emerging research thrusts. While entrepreneurship researchers have long addressed a limited number of international issues, such as exporting and cross-cultural comparisons, the primary focus of entrepreneurship research has been domestic. However, today's use of low-cost, rapid, worldwide, communication technology and transportation, decreasing government protectionist policies, and the lack of geographically protected market niches has made it possible, if not necessary, for many of today's entrepreneurial firms to view their operating domains as international.

The Georgia Tech Center for International Business Education and Research and the Georgia State University Institute of International Business provided support for this research. We wish to thank Crystal Godsey for her comments and her assistance in the library search.

FIGURE 13.1

The Domain of Academic Literature on Organizations

		Geographic Scope	
		Domestic	**International**
Entrepreneurial		I	II
Large, Established		III	IV

Adapted from McDougall, P.P., Oviatt, B.M., and Brush, C. (1991). A symposium on global start-up: Entrepreneurial firms that are born international. Presentation at the annual Academy of Management meeting, August 11–14, Miami.

Figure 13.1 depicts our sense of the domain of scholarly literature on business organizations. There has been a substantial body of research in quadrants I, III, and IV. Research in quadrant I has been the preserve of entrepreneurship scholars, and quadrant IV has been preserve of international business scholars. Multiple functional areas have focused on quadrant III. Quadrant II, a more sparsely studied area, is the subject of this paper. It represents international entrepreneurship, an important, emerging arena of study.

In the last edition of *The State of the Art of Entrepreneurship,* papers appeared on international joint ventures (Hisrich, 1992) and entrepreneurship education in Europe (Brockhaus, 1992). In addition, several other contributors in the book highlighted concerns about their topics that went beyond those of a North American audience. Now there are signs that the international aspect of entrepreneurship is emerging as a distinct arena of academic inquiry and entrepreneurial interest. Thus, the focus is not on one or two topics; instead, it is cast broadly to describe and classify many international issues being considered when entrepreneurship researchers conduct their work.

The purpose of this chapter is to identify, categorize, and analyze the research on international entrepreneurship. In keeping with the theme of this book, the most recent five years of research are examined. By limiting the review to a narrow time span, the research can be examined in more depth, reflect the state of the art, and provide more thoughtful advice about future directions for research in international entrepreneurship.

The chapter begins by providing a definition of international entrepreneurship, and the process we used in conducting the literature review. Seven areas are identified into which the research can be categorized, and the research is then discussed within each of these categories. Finally, future research directions are presented to guide the field into the next millennium.

Definition of International Entrepreneurship

This is not the first attempt at a definition of international entrepreneurship. McDougall's (1989) study comparing domestic and international new ventures provided a narrow definition of the term that effectively excluded all established firms. At a 1992 workshop, a special task force within the Entrepreneurship Division of the Academy of Management specifically addressed the issue of a definition of international entrepreneurship. The task force had previously sent a questionnaire on international entrepreneurship activities to its membership. Both the questionnaire and the consensus of workshop participants reflected that narrowing the definition of international entrepreneurship was not the right thing to do, at least at that time. The task force concluded that international entrepreneurship needs a broad domain and that it should be encouraged rather than striving for a definition that can be put in boldface in a textbook (Giamartino et al., 1993).

It is generally accepted that international business concerns firm-level business activity that crosses national borders and is focused on the relationship between businesses and the international or foreign environment in which they operate (Wright and Ricks, 1994). This focus includes both firms that have business activities that cross national borders and comparisons of domestic business activity in more than one country. There is less agreement about the meaning of entrepreneurship. However, in the broadest sense, it concerns the proactive assumption of financial, psychological, and social risk in an effort to create value and growth with the expectation that residual rewards or costs will accrue to the persons making that effort (see Hisrich and Peters, 1995). Thus, entrepreneurship may take place in established organizations or new ventures and in nonprofit or for-profit organizations. In this chapter international entrepreneurship is defined as *new and innovative activities that have the goal of value creation and growth in business organizations across national borders*. Thus, international entrepreneurship concerns value creation and growth activities that span national borders, and cross-border comparisons of domestic business activities. Cross-border comparisons of entrepreneurs would be included, as the entrepreneur is central to the organization.

This definition highlights interest in businesses and excludes international entrepreneurial activity within nonprofit and government organizations because the generally accepted definition of international business excludes them. Research on nonprofit or governmental efforts to foster international entrepreneurial business activity is included as the outcome of these efforts was central to the definition. Corporate entrepreneurship and joint-venture formation by large corporations has been excluded from this review. Although a joint venture represents a new venture, and as such is central to the domain of entrepreneurship, only that research in which an entrepreneurial firm was one of the joint venture partners is included. Also, franchising has recently received increased attention within the field of entrepreneurship. If the franchiser was an entrepreneurial franchiser, or if the focus of the study was on the franchisee, the article was included. If the focus was on a large established franchiser, the study was considered to be corporate entrepreneurship and excluded.

Notably, this definition differs from the definition that many U.S. entrepreneurship scholars hold, in that research in a setting outside of the United States with no cross-border or cross-cultural business activity comparison was excluded. For example, a study of an Italian entrepreneur who focused exclusively on his or her domestic market and in which the author made no cross-border comparison would not be included. This type of research offers important insights and has been instrumental in broadening the domain of U.S. researchers. But as academia globalizes and adopts a more geocentric viewpoint, this type of research should be regarded as domestic entrepreneurship.

Literature Search Methodology

Guidance for the identification of target publications came indirectly from leading academics in the fields of entrepreneurship and international business. *The Journal of Business Venturing* published the results of a survey of leading entrepreneurship scholars rating journals as a potential outlet for publication (MacMillan, 1993). Twenty journals were identified as "appropriate" to "outstanding" as an outlet for publication. Journals ranked as "not appropriate as an outlet for publication" were excluded from the search. In addition, a listing of the most frequently cited journals in *Journal of International Business Studies* recently appeared (Chandy, 1994), and the top 15 listed journals were chosen as a guide to the best international journals. Not surprising, there were seven duplications on the two lists.

The Journal of International Marketing was added to the survey, as this journal began in 1993 and would not have been included in either listing. Also included are articles from Babson College's *Frontiers of Entrepreneurship Research* because many foreign entrepreneurship scholars traditionally attend this conference. Also, the conference has encouraged the presentation of ongoing research projects, and therefore, emerging areas of interest within the field are prevalent in these books. However, if an article from *Frontiers* also appeared later in a journal (e.g., Manigart, 1994), only the journal article was included, as this represented the most current version of the research. We apologize for studies inadvertently left out and for our focus on English language and North American journals.

Framing the International Entrepreneurship Research of the 1990s

As interest in international entrepreneurship has developed, two articles (Brockhaus, 1991; Carsrud, 1991) have appeared that attempted to describe academic entrepreneurship issues around the world. One article (Giamartino et al., 1993) has attempted to draw boundaries around the area. In a previous section, an attempt was made to refine that definition, and in this section the work is categorized within international entrepreneurship into seven topics. In the chapter appendix, beginning on p. 309, international entrepreneurship studies are summarized and placed into the context of these seven major topics—Cooperative Alliances, Economic Development Initiatives, Entrepreneur Characteristics and Motivations, Exporting and Other Market Entry Modes, New Ventures and IPOs, Transitioning Economies, and Venture Financing. These are the topics of greatest research activity within international entrepreneurship. To a large extent, the topics mirror the research on domestic entrepreneurship, with two notable exceptions being Exporting and Other Market Entry Modes and Transitioning Economies. In numerous instances articles overlapped two or more topic areas. Each article was categorized by its central thrust or into the category for which the results appeared to make the largest contribution. This judgment especially affected articles relating to economic initiatives. For example, there were several articles we classified as Exporting and Other Market Entry Modes in which government initiatives to foster export activities were also key to the article. Thus, the number of articles listed within each topic may not correctly reflect the actual level of research interest. The following seven sections summarize insights from the studies on each topic.

Cooperative Alliances

As cooperative alliances have been embraced by the business community, they have received increasing interest from researchers. Numerous recent studies on the topic have appeared in domestic entrepreneurship research (e.g., Larson, 1992). Only a relatively small number of studies were located that focused on the involvement of entrepreneurial firms in international cooperative alliances (Coviello and Munro, 1992; Hara and Kanai, 1994; Howard, 1990; Shan, 1990; Tallman and Shenkar, 1990). As previously noted, all newly formed international joint ventures are clearly entrepreneurial organizations and within the domain of international entrepreneurship but are included in this review only if one or more of the parent firms is an entrepreneurial firm. The research that was deleted offers important insights, but the sheer volume of this research is beyond the scope of this broad review.

Although small in number, these five studies span the globe with samples representing activity in New Zealand, Japan, United States, Germany, and Korea. There are in-depth, longitudinal case studies, as well as large-size samples using secondary data.

A strong theoretical base (e.g., transaction cost models and internalization theory) guides research in this topic. However, the authors of two of the studies note the difficulty of applying to today's small firms some of the well-accepted models and theories that were developed to explain the activities of large firms.

Cooperative Alliances, perhaps more than any of the other six topics identified, reflects the basic restructuring of business in the industrialized world as firms adapt to compete in the global economy. As the author of one of these studies notes, the large, vertically integrated corporation of yesteryear, driven by standardized mass markets and rigid mass-production technologies, has decentralized in response to the increased demand for more specialized products, nonstop technological innovation, and cheaper and more flexible computer-based production technologies (Howard, 1990). Cooperative alliances lie at the heart of both international business and entrepreneurship, and one would expect continued emphasis from researchers in both fields.

Economic Development Initiatives

The four studies presented under this topic greatly under-represent the research actually occurring in this area. In numerous studies, a focus on economic development initiatives is a substantive aspect but not the central focus. For instance, several of the exporting studies included sections addressing governmental exporting assistance policies. Also, in several instances it was somewhat of an arbitrary decision to classify studies as Economic Development Initiatives or Transitioning Economies, and the latter was chosen in order to highlight the emergence of the latter topic.

Not surprisingly, these studies do not coalesce into a standard recipe for economic initiatives. Assistance with financing and logistic-related problems are highlighted as critical needs. One study recommends a minimalist approach, advocating that the best thing governments in poorer nations can do is to simply remove some of the hurdles (e.g., price controls and trade regulations) facing entrepreneurs. Three of the five studies do, however, repudiate targeted projects and suggest more general nurturing policies and programs. The remaining study focuses specifically on technology and outlines guidelines for developing an infrastructure for technological entrepreneurship.

Entrepreneur Characteristics and Motivations

Just as research on entrepreneur traits and characteristics has been a major component of research in the field of entrepreneurship, there is a major body of this work within the narrower field of international entrepreneurship. All nine studies under this topic have large-size samples, the smallest being 163 and the largest being 2,423 respondents, and all use cross-sectional questionnaires. This topic, more than any of the others that were classified, represents research efforts in multiple countries. For example, several of these studies are drawn from the Society of Associated Researchers of International Entrepreneurship (SARIE) database. This international research effort represents data from 2,278 venture initiators and 1,733 nonventure initiators in 15 countries.

Five of the studies found important cultural differences between entrepreneurs. However, two of the studies, both from the SARIE database, concluded that entrepreneurs share a distinctive pattern of fundamental beliefs, and these beliefs transcend cultures. A consistent explanation for these seemingly contradictory results is not apparent.

Across studies, it is generally assumed that the label—"entrepreneur"—identifies similar economic, social, and individual roles in every culture. This assumption may not be valid, and certain contingent relationships, involving cultural and economic variables, have been ignored. For example, entrepreneurs may arise out of economic necessity, or they may create new ventures to reach their individual potential in an environment that nurtures such efforts. Also, certain comparisons between entrepreneurs and nonentrepreneurs may be valid in some countries but not in others due to vast differences in their roles.

Exporting and Other Market Entry Modes

These 13 studies constitute the most active topic of research in the arena of international entrepreneurship. Mailed questionnaires represented the prominent source of data. Regrettably, there were no longitudinal studies. While nearly all of the studies utilized samples from within a single country, two of the studies made cross-cultural comparisons. The statistical analyses employed by these researchers represented some of the most sophisticated methods examined.

The methodology of one study in particular, a literature review of 26 empirical studies on the export activity of firms within their home country, merits attention. Many of these 26 studies had been published only in Italian and, as such, were not accessible to many researchers. Researchers from other countries should consider similar efforts to increase the dissemination of knowledge.

Size is examined in five of the studies, with mixed results. Three studies found that size acted as a constraint on exporting or influenced the choice of entry mode. Two studies found no effect, leading one author to reject the widely held proposition that size is positively related to export intensity.

The group of studies on exporting is the most mature of those considered here. However, the group of studies reported since 1990 seems to be suffering from diminishing marginal returns to research efforts. A number of literature reviews have been published periodically over the years (e.g., Aaby and Slater, 1989; Bilkey, 1978) and familiar concepts seem to have been reconsidered by the studies done during the 1990s. The problem is that beyond having a group of top managers and owners that are dedicated to exporting, the conditions that lead to exporting success are highly dependent on the measure of success, the local environment, and organizational conditions. Thus, little can be said beyond, "It all depends." Even this most developed group of studies lacks a strong theoretical base. At the end of most of the studies there are few calls for vital additional work beyond calls for more efforts to predict success. However, because exporting seems to depend so much on local conditions in a world of heterogeneous environments, the likelihood that additional efforts will yield valuable results is discouraging. Yet the strong rationale presented by Czinkota (1994), that today's marketplace is so well-suited for small firms to successfully export, leads to the conclusion that with some theoretical redirection this may continue to be a critical area for research.

New Ventures and IPOs

This group of studies is focused on the firm level, including firms from the United States, Europe, Asia (primarily Japan), and even West Africa. Data sources and methods of analysis are quite varied, ranging from explanations and interpretations of personal experiences to mailed surveys, longitudinal case studies based on multiple data sources, and regression equations for the analysis of secondary data.

The 12 studies of new ventures included in this group are wide-ranging. Demand growth, an abundance of small firms, and an urban population were shown to have a strong positive effect on the number of firm births in the United States, Japan, and Western Europe. In the resource-starved countries of West Africa, the legitimization provided by social connections and the entrepreneur's willingness to support family, friends, and the larger community were judged vital in the successful formation of a new business.

A series of six studies considered aspects of international new ventures, or firms that are international from inception. Evidence was provided that this type of venture is increasing throughout much of the world because many new ventures require resources from multiple countries, because markets and competition span national borders, and because entrepreneurs recognize that their firms need to have internationally adapted internal processes from inception. Case studies described how international new ventures formed, how they communicated, and because traditional international business theory does not adequately explain the existence of international new ventures, new theoretical frameworks were explored that combined entrepreneurship and international business concepts.

The studies in this group showed that new venture success is dependent on a variety of entrepreneurs, strategy, and industry influences in all countries. Interestingly, *successful* U.S. and Japanese new ventures have significant similarities. However, among ventures that were successful enough to issue initial public offerings (IPOs), Japanese ventures were larger, more often led by the founder even though they were older, and more focused on new products, research, and capital investment than were U.S. ventures. The latter were more interested in exploiting their existing market and buying other companies, usually leaving R&D spending at pre-IPO levels.

This group of studies shows some evidence of theoretical development and the use of more thoughtful sample selection and sophisticated analysis methods. However, it is still clear that researchers need to make a better connection with the community of practicing entrepreneurs to determine the vital questions that remain to be answered about international new ventures and the important differences between new ventures in various countries.

Transitioning Economies

Many prominent North American entrepreneurship researchers have been involved in recent entrepreneurship initiatives in Central and Eastern Europe; however, as noted earlier, much of their writing is about entrepreneurship *within* a specific country and as such should be considered domestic entrepreneurship. However, five studies were identified within this area for which there is cross-border activity or a comparative focus.

The most striking characteristic of these studies is that only one had an actual sample of firms. The others were a single case study or, more typically, company examples drawn from the experiences of the researchers and previously published reports and data. This may be reflective of the lack of quality secondary data and the greater difficulty of surveying firms in these economies.

The authorship of the case study on a Czechoslovakian international new venture is noteworthy as it represents a fruitful approach to international entrepreneurship research. An American professor and a Czechoslovakian professor teamed with the founder of the venture to write the case study, allowing the venture to be examined through three very different lenses.

Researchers of firms in transitioning economies paint an exciting, challenging, and at times dismaying picture, with numerous successful entrepreneurial examples. Calls for Western assistance and foreign direct investment appear in three of the studies. This area clearly represents a fruitful area of study for the field's pioneers.

Venture Financing

This group of 10 publications compares U.S., European, and Asian venture capital firms, informal investors, and other sources of venture financing. Eight of these studies focus on Europe, the other two focus on Asia, and four of them make comparison with U.S. venture capital firms. Five of the studies employ cross-sectional data derived from questionnaires, two use a variety of secondary data sources and are longitudinal. One cross-sectional study uses both primary and secondary sources, one study does not describe the source of data, and one article is derived from the author's personal experience and knowledge. In summary, these studies focus mainly on developed countries where the means of financing new ventures tends to be mature, and the empirical methods vary in sophistication.

According to these studies, investors in the United States, Europe, and Asia appear to have similar criteria for choosing ventures to support. That is, they all are most concerned that the ventures be run by a highly regarded entrepreneur or team of entrepreneurs. While that often means that entrepreneurs have a track record of business success, positive network (including family) relationships are also important for obtaining the support of venture capitalists, especially in Asia. The articles also highlight national differences among venture financiers. U.S. investors emphasize technology investments, are willing to take greater risks, and appear to be more involved in the management of the ventures they invest in. The U.S. venture capital industry is also older and advantaged because of strong secondary markets for financial securities. European financiers appear to be more conservative and seem to earn lower returns usually. Some of that result may be due to Europe's more sluggish economy. Venture capital firms in Europe that specialized in particular types of investments tended to have higher risks and better returns. National differences within the European samples were also apparent. Asian (particularly Japanese) investors, are less interested in financial returns than in learning about new technologies.

At the last state-of-the-art conference, Timmons and Sapienza (1992) described the great expansion and general characteristics of venture capital throughout the world. In general, the comparative studies we have found since then appear to be initial efforts at providing a more fine-grained description of venture financing in various countries. However, the effort lacks a theory to guide it. Moreover, these studies seem to be motivated by a general curiosity about venture financing conditions in various countries rather than by any vital questions that have been posed by either academics or practitioners.

What Have We Learned, and Where Should We Go?

International entrepreneurship is not an academic discipline. It is an arena in which many disciplines apply and extend their theories in an attempt to discover and explain facts about entrepreneurship across national borders. It is expected that such efforts will result in an understanding of the successful promotion, formation and management of 1) business ventures in various countries and 2) business ventures whose activities span national borders. Our review of seven groups of 62 publications that have appeared from 1990 to 1995 indicates that researchers have only recently begun to enter the international entrepreneurship arena. Much remains to be done.

The results of the survey suggested the seven groups of research questions on international entrepreneurship that appear below. Undoubtedly, other people can add to the list, and the important questions will certainly change over time. It is believed the best source of future questions will be the international entrepreneurs themselves and the best source of answers will be theoretically driven, methodologically varied, and rigorous empiricism.

1. Do the social, individual, and economic conditions and processes that encourage the formation of new ventures differ among regions of the world, nations, and subnational cultures? If so, what are those differences?

2. What should governments and private voluntary organizations do to encourage the development of entrepreneurship in economically underdeveloped nations and economies in transition? What should governments and private voluntary organizations do to promote the internationalization of small and new domestic ventures?

3. Do the environmental conditions, venture activities, and entrepreneur characteristics that distinguish successful from unsuccessful entrepreneurial firms differ among regions of the world, nations, or subnational cultures? If so, what are those differences?

4. Are the number of international new ventures (new ventures that are international from inception) expanding? In what countries or locations? Why? What distinguishes them from domestic new ventures? How can they simultaneously manage the risks of newness, small size, and international activity? What determines the survival and long-term prosperity of an international new venture?

5. How do cross-border cooperative alliances involving entrepreneurial firms begin? What are their most important functions for such firms? What are the criteria for success, and how do those criteria differ among regions, nations, and subnational cultures? Once established, how do cross-border cooperative alliances evolve over time? What is the relationship between small or new ventures and large established multinational enterprises in cross-border alliances?

6. What theoretical framework might help organize and clarify the seemingly disparate mass of empirical results we have available about exporting by small and new ventures?

7. How do venture capital firms and informal investors in entrepreneurial firms differ across regions, nations, and subnational cultures?

In answering these research questions, scholars in international entrepreneurship should recognize the benefits and opportunities for multidisciplinary collaboration. However, the literature indicates that those opportunities remain largely untapped. Finance, marketing, management, sociology, and economics scholars continue their segregated work even when evidence comparing entrepreneurship across nations makes it clear complex forces influence how entrepreneurial activity begins and evolves. In the future, research funding and universities must support multidisciplinary teams of researchers; academic meetings must include scholars with a variety of backgrounds, and journals must publish papers from more than one discipline.

An emphasis on collaboration between academic disciplines will yield several benefits. First, most researchers recognize that explanations of complex phenomena, such as the successful internationalization of a small new venture, require the use of contingency theories. A multidisciplinary team of researchers is more likely to discover the most powerful contingencies, rather than the contingencies favored by the assumptions of a particular discipline. Second, bringing more approaches to bear on a question will likely lead to the use of more sophisticated theory. Sophisticated multilevel theories will help identify the complex processes that intervene between broad economic conditions and entrepreneurially motivated individuals to produce viable new ventures in various nations. Third, too many of the articles reviewed were devoid of theory, hypotheses, or even research questions. Multidisciplinary work will require that different and sometimes conflicting assumptions and theories be made explicit, and that is likely to produce more rigorous work.

It is hoped that future researchers will devote more effort to making their work rigorous. The review revealed too many published articles in which research questions were not stated, definitions were unclear, measures and samples were not adequately explained, scant attention was paid to validity and reliability, and very speculative statements were not distinguished from empirical results. Being a newly emerging arena of inquiry may necessitate research on what in more mature arenas would appear to be simple questions. Such questions still deserve rigorous research methods, else a flawed foundation is established for future work. Assuring appropriate research methods is a responsibility of both researchers and the journal reviewers who consider their work.

Many of the articles reviewed compared samples from various countries, and some, but not enough, of that work attempted to choose the national sites in systematic ways that matched their research questions. Unfortunately, some locations in the world, such as South America, seemed underrepresented. Collaboration between researchers located in various countries and cultures is the best way to ensure a variety of nations and cultures are included.

It is believed that rigorous international entrepreneurship research can be conducted by a single individual and by small local teams. The survey indicates that thoughtful research by such people is ongoing. However, the most influential research in international entrepreneurship is likely to be a significant collaborative challenge. Almost by definition, it requires the work of scholars in multiple countries and the expertise of scholars in multiple disciplines. Those facts suggest that such research will be expensive, time-consuming, and contentious. Thus, sponsors will be needed to provide funding; a diverse cadre of researchers in varied locations who are willing to devote years of effort must be recruited, and distinguished academic entrepreneurs will be needed to lead that effort.

REFERENCES

Aaby, N., and S.F. Slater. 1989. Management influences on export performance: A review of the empirical literature. *International Marketing Review* 6:7-26.

Abetti, P.A., F.M. O'Such, and S. Porowski. 1992. Planning and building the infrastructure for technological entrepreneurship—part II: Field studies in Poland. In N.C. Churchill et al. (eds.): *Frontiers of Entrepreneurship Research*. Babson Park, MA: Babson College, 469-480.

Abetti, P.A., and P.A. Wheeler. 1990. Planning and building the infrastructure for technological entrepreneurship: Field studies in the U.S.A., France and Mexico. In N.C. Churchill et al. (eds.): *Frontiers of Entrepreneurship Research*. Babson Park, MA: Babson College, 422-436.

Agarwal, S., and S.N. Ramaswami. 1992. Choice of foreign market entry mode: Impact of ownership, location and internalization factors. *Journal of International Business Studies* 23:1-27.

Baum, J.R., J.D. Olian, M. Erez, E.R. Schnell, K.G. Smith, H.P. Sims, J.S. Scully, and K.A. Smith. 1993. Nationality and work role interactions: A cultural contrast of Israeli and U.S. entrepreneurs' versus managers' needs. *Journal of Business Venturing* 8:499-512.

Beamish, P.W., R. Craig, and K. McLellan. 1993. The performance characteristics of Canadian versus U.K. exporters in small and medium sized firms. *Management International Review* 33:121-137.

Bilkey, W.J. 1978. An attempted integration of the literature on the export behaviour of firms. *Journal of International Business Studies* 9:33-46.

Bonaccorsi, A. 1992. On the relationship between firm size and export intensity. *Journal of International Business Studies* 23:605-635.

Bonaccorsi, A. 1993. What do we know about exporting by small Italian manufacturing firms? *Journal of International Marketing* 1:49-75.

Brockhaus, R.H., Sr. 1991. Entrepreneurship education and research outside North America. *Entrepreneurship Theory and Practice* 15:77-84.

Brockhaus, R.H., Sr. 1992. Entrepreneurship education and research in Europe. In D.L. Sexton and J.D. Kasarda (eds.): *The State of the Art of Entrepreneurship*. Boston: PWS-Kent, 560-578.

Carsrud, A.L. 1991. Entrepreneurship and enterprise formation: A brief perspective on the infrastructure in Europe. *Entrepreneurship Theory and Practice* 15:69-75.

Chandy, P.R. 1994. The impact of journals and authors on international business research: A citational analysis of *JIBS* articles. *Journal of International Business Studies* 25:715-728.

Choy, C.L. 1990. Sources of business financing and financing practices: A comparison among U.S. and Asian countries. *Journal of Business Venturing* 5:271-275.

Coviello, N., and H. Munro. 1992. Internationalizing the entrepreneurial technology-intensive firm: Growth through linkage development. In N. C. Churchill et al. (eds.): *Frontiers of Entrepreneurship Research*. Babson Park, MA: Babson College, 430-440.

Czinkota, M.R. 1994. A national export assistance policy for new and growing businesses. *Journal of International Marketing* 2:91-101.

Dichtl, E., H. Koeglmayr, and S. Mueller. 1990. International orientation as a precondition for export success. *Journal of International Business Studies* 21:23-40.

Diomande, M. 1990. Business creation with minimal resources: Some lessons from the African experience. *Journal of Business Venturing* 5:191-200.

Dyson, E. 1991. Micro capitalism: Eastern Europe's computer future. *Harvard Business Review* 69:26-37.

Erramilli, M.K., and D.E. D'Souza. 1993. Venturing into foreign markets: The case of the small service firm. *Entrepreneurship Theory and Practice* 17: 29-41.

Giamartino, G.A., P.P. McDougall, and B.J. Bird. 1993. International entrepreneurship: The state of the field. *Entrepreneurship Theory and Practice* 18:37-42.

Hara, G., and T. Kanai. 1994. Entrepreneurial networks across oceans to promote international strategic alliances for small businesses. *Journal of Business Venturing* 9:489-507.

Harper, M. 1991. Enterprise development in poorer nations. *Entrepreneurship Theory and Practice* 15:7-11.

Harrison, R.T., and C.M. Mason. 1991. Informal venture capital in the U.K. and the U.S.A. A comparison of investor characteristics, investment preferences and decision-making. In N.C. Churchill et. al. (eds.): *Frontiers of Entrepreneurship Research*. Babson Park, MA: Babson College, 469-481.

Hisrich, R.D. 1992. Joint ventures: Research base and use in international markets. In D.L. Sexton and J.D. Kasarda (eds.): *The State of the Art of Entrepreneurship*. Boston: PWS-Kent, 520-559.

Hisrich, R.D., and M.P. Peters. 1995. *Entrepreneurship: Starting, Developing, and Managing a New Enterprise*. Chicago: Irwin.

Holzmüller, H.H., and H. Kasper. 1991. On a theory of export performance: Personal and organizational determinants of export trade activities observed in small and medium-sized firms. *Management International Review* 31:45-70.

Hoy, F., M. Pivoda, and S. Machrle. 1992. A virus theory of organizational transformation. In N.C. Churchill, et al. (eds.): *Frontiers of Entrepreneurship Research*. Babson Park, MA: Babson College, 481-494.

Howard, R. 1990. Can small business help countries compete? *Harvard Business Review* 68:88-103.

Hurry, D., A. Miller, and E.H. Bowman. 1992. Calls on high-technology: Japanese exploration of venture capital investments in the United States. *Strategic Management Journal* 13:85-101.

Jaffe, E.D., and H. Pasternak. 1994. An attitudinal model to determine the export intention of non-exporting, small manufacturers. *International Marketing Review* 11:17-32.

Keeley, R.H., J.B. Roure, M. Goto, and K. Yoshimura. 1990. An international comparison of new ventures. In N.C. Churchill et al. (eds.): *Frontiers of Entrepreneurship Research*. Babson Park, MA: Babson College, 472-486.

Kolvereid, L. 1992. Growth aspirations among Norwegian entrepreneurs. *Journal of Business Venturing* 7:209-222.

Kotabe, M., and M.R. Czinkota. 1992. State government promotion of manufacturing exports: A gap analysis. *Journal of International Business Studies* 4:637-658.

Landström, H. 1993. Informal risk capital in Sweden and some international comparison. In N.C. Churchill et al. (eds.): *Frontiers of Entrepreneurship Research*. Babson Park, MA: Babson College, 496-510.

Larson, A. 1992. Network dyads in entrepreneurial settings: A study of the governance of exchange relationship. *Administrative Science Quarterly* 37:76-104.

Lerner, M., and Y. Hendeler. 1993. New entrepreneurs and entrepreneurial aspirations among immigrants from the former USSR in Israel. In N.C. Churchill et al. (eds.): *Frontiers of Entrepreneurship Research*. Babson Park, MA: Babson College, 562-575.

Levie, J. 1993. Can governments nurture young growing firms? Quantitative evidence from a three-nation study. In N.C. Churchill et al. (eds.): *Frontiers of Entrepreneurship Research*. Babson Park, MA: 198-211.

Levie, J. 1994. Can governments nurture young growing firms? Qualitative evidence from a three-nation study. In W.D. Bygrave et al. (eds.): *Frontiers of Entrepreneurship Research.* Babson Park, MA: Babson College, 514-527.

Lim, J., T.W. Sharkey, and K.I. Kim. 1991. An empirical test of an export adoption model. *Management International Review* 31:51-62.

Lyles, M.A., N.M. Carter, and I.S. Baird. 1994. Partnering in establishing new ventures: The experience in Hungary. In W.D. Bygrave et al. (eds.): *Frontiers of Entrepreneurship Research.* Babson Park, MA: Babson College, 430-444.

MacMillan, I.C. 1993. The emerging forum for entrepreneurship scholars. *Journal of Business Venturing* 8:377-381.

Manigart, S. 1994. The founding rate of venture capital firms in three European countries (1970 to 1990). *Journal of Business Venturing* 9:525-541.

Manigart, S., P. Joos, and D.D. Vos. 1992. The performance of publicly traded European venture capital companies. In N.C. Churchill et al. (eds.): *Frontiers of Entrepreneurship Research.* Babson Park, MA: Babson College, 331-344.

Matsuda, S., P. Vanderwerf, and P. Scarbrough. 1994. A comparison of Japanese and U.S. firms completing initial public offerings. *Journal of Business Venturing* 9:205-222.

McDougall, P.P. 1989. International versus domestic entrepreneurship: New venture strategic behavior and industry structure. *Journal of Business Venturing* 4:387-400.

McDougall, P.P., B.M. Oviatt, and C. Brush. 1991. A symposium on global start-ups: Entrepreneurial firms that are born international. Presentation at the annual Academy of Management meeting, August 11–14, Miami.

McDougall, P.P., S. Shane, and B.M. Oviatt. 1994. Explaining the formation of international new ventures: The limits of theories from international business research. *Journal of Business Venturing* 9:469-487.

McGrath, R.G., and I.C. MacMillan. 1992. More like each other than anyone else? A cross-cultural study of entrepreneurial perceptions. *Journal of Business Venturing* 7: 419-429.

McGrath, R.G., I.C. MacMillan, and S. Scheinberg. 1992. Elitists, risk-takers, and rugged individualists? An exploratory analysis of cultural differences between entrepreneurs and nonentrepreneurs. *Journal of Business Venturing* 7:115-135.

Muzyka, D., S. Birley, B. Leleux, G. Rossell, and F. Bendixen. 1993. Financial structure and decisions of venture capital firms: A Pan-European study. In N.C. Churchill et al. (eds.): *Frontiers of Entrepreneurship Research.* Babson Park, MA: Babson College, 538-552.

Muzyka, D., W. Bygrave, B. Leleux, and M. Hay. 1993. Entrepreneurs' perceptions about realizing enterprise value: A Pan-European perspective. In N.C. Churchill et al. (eds.): *Frontiers of Entrepreneurship Research 1993.* Babson Park, MA: Babson College, 270-285.

Muzyka, D.F., and M.G. Hay. 1994. European management buy-out funds: Opportunity selection criteria. In W.D. Bygrave et al. (eds.): *Frontiers of Entrepreneurship Research.* Babson Park, MA: Babson College, 346-360.

Muzka, D.F., M.K. de Vries, and M. Ullmann. 1991. Cross-cultural aspects of entrepreneurship: A European view. In N.C. Churchill et al. (eds.): *Frontiers of Entrepreneurship Research*. Babson Park, MA: Babson College, 545-561.

Ohe, T., S. Honjo, M. Oliva, and I.C. MacMillan. 1991. Entrepreneurs in Japan and Silicon Valley: A study of perceived differences. *Journal of Business Venturing* 6:135-144.

Oviatt, B.M., and P.P. McDougall. 1994. Toward a theory of international new ventures. *Journal of International Business Studies* 25:45-64.

Oviatt, B.M., P.P. McDougall, M. Simon, and R.C. Shrader. 1991. A new venture without geographic limits: Case history of a global start-up. In N.C. Churchill et al. (eds.): *Frontiers of Entrepreneurship Research. 1991,* Babson Park, MA: Babson College, 64-78.

Oviatt, B.M., P.P. McDougall, M. Simon, and R.C. Shrader. 1993. Heartware International Corporation: A medical equipment company "Born International," parts A, B, and C. *Entrepreneurship Theory and Practice* 18:111-128.

Ramaseshan, B., and M.S. Patton. 1994. Factors influencing international channel choice of small business exporters. *International Marketing Review* 11:19-34.

Ray, D.M. 1991. International opportunity identification in small Canadian exporting firms. In N.C. Churchill et al. (eds.): *Frontiers of Entrepreneurship Research*. Babson Park, MA: Babson College, 159-173.

Reynolds, P.D., D.J. Storey, and P. Westhead. 1994. Regional characteristics affecting entrepreneurship: A cross-national comparison. In W.D. Bygrave et al. (eds.): *Frontiers of Entrepreneurship Research*. Babson Park, MA: Babson College, 550-564.

Roure, J.B., R. Keeley, and T. Keller. 1992. Venture capital strategies in Europe and the U.S. Adapting to the 1990's. In N.C. Churchill et al. (eds.): *Frontiers of Entrepreneurship Research*. Babson Park, MA: Babson College, 345-359.

Seringhaus, F.H.R. 1993. Comparative marketing behaviour of Canadian and Austrian high-tech exporters. *Management International Review* 33:247-269.

Shan, W. 1990. An empirical analysis of organizational strategies by entrepreneurial high-technology firms. *Strategic Management Journal* 11:129-139.

Shane, S., L. Kolvereid, and P. Westhead. 1991. An exploratory examination of the reasons leading to new firm formation across country and gender. *Journal of Business Venturing* 6:431-446.

Tallman, S.B., and O. Shenkar. 1990. International cooperative venture strategies: Outward investment and small firms from NICs. *Management Internationa Review* 4:299-315.

Timmons, J.A., and H.J. Sapienza. 1992. Venture capital: The decade ahead. In D.L. Sexton and J.D. Kasarda (eds.): *The State of the Art of Entrepreneurship*. Boston: PWS Kent, 402-437.

Tyebjee, T. 1990. The internationalization of high tech ventures. In N. C. Churchill et al. (eds.): *Frontiers of Entrepreneurship Research*. Babson Park, MA: Babson College, 452-467.

VanderWerf, P.A. 1991. Tests of performance correlates in the high-speed circuit industry. In N.C. Churchill et al. (eds.): *Frontiers of Entrepreneurship Research*. Babson Park, MA: Babson College, 638-651.

Vesper, J.F., K.H. Vesper, and B. Cho. 1994. International communication in a start-up. In W.D. Bygrave et al. (eds.): *Frontiers of Entrepreneurship Research*. Babson Park, MA: Babson College, 565-577.

Walters, P.G.P., and S. Samiee. 1990. A model for assessing performance in small U.S. exporting firms. *Entrepreneurship Theory and Practice* 14:33-50.

Welfens, P.J.J. 1992. Foreign investment in the East European transition. *Management International Review* 32:199-218.

Wright R.W., and D.A. Ricks. 1994. Trends in international business research: Twenty-five years later. *Journal of International Business Studies*. 25:687-701.

Yang, E.A., R.G. McGrath, I.C. MacMillan, and W. Tsai. 1991. Three faces of entrepreneurship: An exploration of values of entrepreneurs from mainland China, Taiwan and the United States. In N.C. Churchill et al. (eds.): *Frontiers of Entrepreneurship Research*. Babson Park, MA: Babson College, 562-576.

Appendix Table 13.1
International Entrepreneurship Literature 1990–1995

Authors, Year	Key Issues	Sample	Research Method	Data Analysis	Dependent Variable
Brockhaus, 1991	Entrepreneurship programs outside U.S., Canada, & Western Europe	N/A	Highlights Japan, Southeast Asia, Egypt, South Africa, Kenya, & India	N/A	N/A
	Principal Findings & Recommendations: A rich diversity of entrepreneurship programs are described. Some entrepreneurship courses are appearing in college & university curriculums, but major source of training, education, & research is government or quasi-governmental agencies.				
Carsrud, 1991	Academic entrepreneurship in Europe	N/A	Perspectives of an American working in Europe	N/A	N/A
	Principal Findings & Recommendations: Pivotal differences between Europe & North America result from European active & central government orientation toward small/medium enterprise development, combined with traditional government ownership of critical industries. European emphasis on regional economic development. N.A. emphasis on individual entrepreneur, venture, or capital market. European organizations for entrepreneurship, and small business are growing at a rapid rate.				
Giamartino, McDougall, & Bird, 1993	Internationalization of the field of entrepreneurship	147 members of Academy of Management Entrepreneurship Division	Mailed questionnaire, pre-conference workshop discussion	Descriptive statistics	N/A
	Principal Findings & Recommendations: Members held a broad definition of international entrepreneurship. Few schools offer course work in international entrepreneurship, and there are few plans to do so. Most identified barriers in international research were funding & time constraints.				
Cooperative Alliances					
Coviello & Munro, 1992	Role of linkages in technology venture internationalization	4 New Zealand case studies	Interviews, longitudinal	N/A	N/A
	Principal Findings & Recommendations: Smaller technology-intensive entrepreneurial firms do not follow stages of internationalization more common to larger firms. Linkage partners tended to play a dominant role in ventures' internationalization processes, e.g., providing international marketing support.				
Hara & Kanai, 1994	Technology strategic alliances	1 small Japanese & 3 small U.S. companies comprising an alliance	Case study, interviews with entrepreneurs in the companies	N/A	N/A
	Principal Findings & Recommendations: Suggests that for small independent firms, creation of alliances across national boundaries is a social event that relies upon the building and nurturing of a series of entrepreneurial networks. Key to success is "networker of networks," a key person or company whose role is to create a global network of local networks. Social events, such as international symposia, exchange programs, or conventions are important mechanisms for identifying potential partners.				

Authors, Year	Key Issues	Sample	Research Method	Data Analysis	Dependent Variable
Howard, 1990	Small business networks & public entrepreneurship	N/A	Cites company & country examples, reports	N/A	N/A
Principal Findings & Recommendations: Argues importance of networks for small businesses, citing examples from Germany, Japan, and Silicon Valley. New rules for small business competition: forge close relationships with customers, suppliers, and partners, maintain a creative tension between competition and cooperation, and focus on continual innovation. Presents examples of some initiatives ("public entrepreneurship") that are helping small manufacturing companies compete.					
Shan, 1990	Technology cooperative relationships	278 new biotechnology U.S. firms	Secondary data from Paine Webber's Biotechnology Industry, FactBook, cross-sectional	Logistic regression	Inter-firm cooperative arrangement
Principal Findings & Recommendations: Firms are more likely to seek cooperative arrangements in commercializing their products in foreign countries.					
Tallman & Shenkar, 1990	Cooperative ventures for firms from NICs	340 small/medium-sized Korean firms seeking overseas cooperative ventures	Secondary data (strategic proposals from firms), cross-sectional	Cross tabulations, chi-square tests	None
Principal Findings & Recommendations: Current models of international firm and of cooperative ventures shown to have limited application to small NIC firms. Small NIC firms have strategic concerns different from those of the large MNCs typically studied.					

Economic Development Initiatives

Authors, Year	Key Issues	Sample	Research Method	Data Analysis	Dependent Variable
Abetti & Wheeler, 1990	Technology-based regional economic development	Case histories from France & Mexico, survey data on >600 U.S. technology ventures	Experiences in U.S., Republic of Ireland, France, & Mexico, uses case studies & survey data to illustrate points	N/A	N/A
Principal Findings & Recommendations: Presents guidelines for developing, operating, & marketing an infrastructure for technological entrepreneurship.					
Harper, 1991	Enterprise development in poorer nations	N/A	Draws on past experiences of working in poorer nations	N/A	N/A
Principal Findings & Recommendations: Most initiatives by foreign agencies designed to encourage enterprise in poorer nations cause more problems than benefits. Argues for a minimalist approach, i.e., reducing the amount of government and foreign involvement. Accessible credit at reasonable interest rates is one of the most effective programs.					

Authors, Year	Key Issues	Sample	Research Method	Data Analysis	Dependent Variable
Kotabe & Czinkota, 1992	Assistance needs of export firms	162 U.S. exporting manufacturers	Mailed questionnaire, interviews with state export assistance providers, cross-sectional	Descriptive statistics, ANOVA, factor analysis	Requirements & benefits of exporting, export related problems
Principal Findings & Recommendations: Benefits of exporting mainly increased competitiveness both at home and in foreign countries rather than profitability, except in experienced exporters where profits also seen. Even experienced exporters need assistance. Assistance most desired with logistic-related problems followed closely by legal and foreign market intelligence assistance. More export assistance desired by early stage exporters than is being provided.					
Levie, 1993	New venture government support	185 young growing manufacturing firms from Denmark, Ireland, & Scotland	Secondary data from several commercial databases, cross-sectional	Descriptive statistics	Type of government support
Principal Findings & Recommendations: Focused government subsidies are negatively associated with early firm growth.					
Levie, 1994	Government nurturing policies toward young firms	6 cases from Denmark, Ireland, & Scotland	1 longitudinal & 5 retrospective cases, comparison to census data	Pattern-matching	N/A
Principal Findings & Recommendations: Governmental selective nurturing policies (i.e., "picking winners") has specific unintended negative effects on early growth. Proposed that general nurturing (i.e., skills and information flow enhancement) does promote early growth as intended.					
Entrepreneur Characteristics & Motivations					
Baum, Olian, Erez, Schnell, Smith, Sims, Scully, & Smith, 1993	Comparative characteristics of entrepreneurs & managers	370 Israeli & U.S. entrepreneurs & managers	Survey, cross-sectional	ANOVA	Need for achievement
Principal Findings & Recommendations: Entrepreneurs showed significantly higher needs for autonomy and affiliation and no difference with managers on needs for achievement and dominance. Israelis manifested higher needs for affiliation, autonomy, and dominance. U.S. sample showed higher need for achievement. Interaction between country and role affects needs for affiliation and dominance. Suggests cultural differences are important.					
Kolvereid, 1992	Growth aspirations of Norwegian entrepreneurs, international tangential to study	250 Norwegian new venture entrepreneurs, comparisons to British & New Zealand entrepreneurs —SARIE database	Mailed questionnaire, cross-sectional	Factor analysis, cross tabulations, Chi-square	Revenue growth aspirations, employment growth aspirations
Principal Findings & Recommendations: Firms with revenue and employment growth aspirations are significantly further from their customers and have a higher percentage of sales exported than firms with no growth aspirations. In comparing sample with data on British & New Zealand entrepreneurs notes the higher reluctance to grow of Norwegian entrepreneurs.					

Authors, Year	Key Issues	Sample	Research Method	Data Analysis	Dependent Variable
Lerner & Hendeles, 1993	Distinctions between salaried & self-employed immigrants	1530 Russian immigrants in Israel	Personal interviews conducted in home, cross-sectional	T-tests; multiple regression	Distinctions between salaried & self-employed immigrants & between those aspiring to a salary
	Principal Findings & Recommendations: Self-employment rate low compared to the general Israeli population. Aspiration to be an entrepreneur higher than actual rate. Business and managerial experience prior to immigration the primary predictor of differences between those who want to be entrepreneurs and those who want salaried position.				
McGrath & MacMillan, 1992	Entrepreneur perceptions about themselves	770 entrepreneurs from 9 countries	Questionnaires, cross-sectional	Stepwise discriminant analysis, significance tests	Region: Anglo, Chinese, Nordic
	Principal Findings & Recommendations: Suggests there is a basic set of beliefs entrepreneurs hold about themselves and about others in their society that, from the perspective of the entrepreneur, differentiate the two. This set of beliefs transcends cultures and these perceived differences may be linked to entrepreneurial activity.				
McGrath, MacMillan, & Scheinberg, 1992	Cultural differences in beliefs & values of entrepreneurs & non-entrepreneurs	1,217 entrepreneurs & 1,206 non-entrepreneurs in 8 countries	Part of multinational study, questionnaire, cross-sectional	Stepwise discriminant analysis	Entrepreneur/non-entrepreneur
	Principal Findings & Recommendations: Entrepreneurs found to have a characteristic value orientation aligned along Hofstede's dimensions—high power-distance, high individualism, low uncertainty avoidance, and high masculinity. Results suggest entrepreneurs share a distinctive pattern of fundamental beliefs, no matter what their base culture.				
Muzyka, Vries, & Ullmann, 1991	Cross-cultural motivations of entrepreneurs	163 entrepreneurs in 6 European countries	Questionnaires administered in personal interviews, cross-sectional	Histograms, significance testing	N/A
	Principal Findings & Recommendations: Motivations and influences for becoming entrepreneur vary from country to country. Entrepreneurial management practice does not vary significantly. European Community initiatives for fostering entrepreneurial activity need to be sensitive to individual country drivers.				
Ohe, Honjo, Oliva, & MacMillan, 1991	Differences in U.S. & Japanese entrepreneurs	184 Silicon Valley & 125 Japanese entrepreneurs	Mailed survey, cross-sectional	Descriptive statistics	N/A
	Principal Findings & Recommendations: U.S. high-tech and Japanese entrepreneurs both require a certain minimum perceived personal and corporate difference to become entrepreneurs. Because of the weak entrepreneurial environment in Japan, Japanese entrepreneurs require a strong perceived personal difference than U.S. entrepreneurs. They also differ in background (occupation of father, education).				

Authors, Year	Key Issues	Sample	Research Method	Data Analysis	Dependent Variable
Shane, Kolvereid, & Westhead, 1991	Entrepreneur motivations for starting ventures	597 venture initiators in Great Britain, Norway, & New Zealand	From SARIE database, cross-sectional	Factor analysis, significance tests	N/A
	Principal Findings & Recommendations: Only the desire for job freedom motivated venture initiators across gender and national boundaries. All other reasons were determined by an interaction of gender and nationality. Points out that results are disheartening for those who quest for a universal explanation of why venture initiators start businesses.				
Yang, McGrath, MacMillan, & Tsai, 1991	Cross-cultural values of entrepreneurs	531 entrepreneurs from China, Taiwan, & U.S.	Questionnaire, cross-sectional	Discriminant analysis	Country
	Principal Findings & Recommendations: Taiwan & China share many values and exhibit similar entrepreneurial behavioral patterns, but U.S. different. Argues that culture important to consider in future studies of entrepreneurial motivations and behavior and highlights need to utilize international samples for defining a universally applicable paradigm for entrepreneurship.				

Exporting and Other Market Entry

Authors, Year	Key Issues	Sample	Research Method	Data Analysis	Dependent Variable
Agarwal & Ramaswami, 1992	Foreign market entry modes	97 U.S. leasing firms	Mailed questionnaire, cross-sectional	Factor analysis, cross-tabulation logistic regression	Choice of entry mode—no involvement, exporting, licensing, JV, & sole venture
	Principal Findings & Recommendations: Size acts as constraint on firms entering international markets. Smaller firms with limited multinational experience have higher propensity for no entry or entry through a JV mode in high potential markets. Results indicate the smaller, less multinationally experienced firms need to complement their resource needs in order to service a potentially attractive foreign market.				
Beamish, Craig, & McLellan, 1993	Export performance	106 U.K. & 91 Canadian small/medium sized exporters	Mailed questionnaire, cross-sectional	Pearson correlations	Export performance: export intensity & export profitability
	Principal Findings & Recommendations: U.K. export performance related to use of direct sales distribution, wide product offerings, long-term distributor relations and broad geographic market focus. Canadian export performance related to superior product characteristics and diversification of market focus.				
Bonaccorsi, 1992	Influence of size on exporting	Mediocredito Centrale survey on Italian manufacturing firms	Secondary data from large banking institution, cross-sectional	ANOVA, nonparametric Kruskall-Wallis test	Firm size
	Principal Findings & Recommendations: Export intensity is not positively related to firm size. Presents arguments for rejecting the widely accepted proposition that organization size is positively related to export intensity.				

Authors, Year	Key Issues	Sample	Research Method	Data Analysis	Dependent Variable
Bonaccorsi, 1993	Literature review of Italian firm exporting	N/A	Reviews 26 empirical studies on export activity of small Italian firms (many of these studies are published only in Italian)	N/A	N/A
Principal Findings & Recommendations: Small Italian exporters succeed despite their lack of control of marketing mix variables and absence of formalized international marketing programs. Product quality, product innovation, flexibility, and adaptation to individual customers are key success factors. Many prefer to limit international commitment to exporting, mainly through agents and representatives. Informational sources are mainly personal sources. Government export support policies do not play a great role in their success.					
Czinkota, 1994	Government export assistance policy	N/A	Article based on speech delivered by author to National Economic Council	N/A	N/A
Principal Findings & Recommendations: Rational small firms successfully exporting into today's market—customization of operations crucial for niche marketing, clear lines of accountability make easier to handle exceptions, flexible decision-making framework, short response time, and most to gain from experience curve effects. Identifies dimensions that should guide export assistance efforts—clarity of purpose, tightness of focus, coordination of approaches, emphasis on strengths, targeting of crucial factors, and boldness of vision.					
Dichtl, Koeglmayr, & Mueller, 1990	Export inclination	104 German small/medium-sized firms	Mail questionnaire & personal interview, cross-sectional	Histograms, regression, cluster analysis, comparisons to samples from Finland, Japan, South Africa, & South Korea	Export sales
Principal Findings & Recommendations: Develops measurement procedure for distinguishing between managers who are not foreign market-oriented and will be less likely to participate in export activities in export activities from foreign market-oriented colleagues.					
Erramilli & D'Souza, 1993	Foreign market entry choice	141 U.S. service firms engaged in international operations	Mailed questionnaire, cross-sectional	Correlation & regression	Cultural distance between home & host country, FDI
Principal Findings & Recommendations: In higher level capital intensity industries, small firms are less likely than large service firms to enter culturally distant markets and to choose FDI modes of entry. For lower capital intensity there is no difference between small and large firms.					
Holzmuller & Kasper, 1991	Export performance	103 Austrian small/medium-sized firms	Questionnaire administered via personal interview, cross-sectional	Regression analysis, factor analysis, causal modeling	Export ratio
Principal Findings & Recommendations: Export performance primarily determined by organization characteristics and dimensions of organization culture, and only secondarily by individual psychostructural value-oriented and objective features of decision-makers' characteristics. Company size (range of 50 to 1,000 employees) had little effect.					

Authors, Year	Key Issues	Sample	Research Method	Data Analysis	Dependent Variable
Jaffe & Pasternak, 1994	Intention to export	85 nonexporters & 48 previous exporters from northern Mexico	Questionnaire administered using notebook computer, cross-sectional	Confirmatory factor analysis, regression	Intention to export
	Principal Findings & Recommendations: Managerial perception of organizational readiness is a predictor of intention to export. Perception of firm differential advantage and risk of doing business abroad did not influence export intention.				
Lim, Sharkey, & Kim, 1991	Test of export adoption model	438 small U.S. manufacturing firms	Mail questionnaire, cross-sectional	LISREL	N/A
	Principal Findings & Recommendations: Empirical support for export adoption model. The four-stage export decision process proceeds from awareness to interest to adoption.				
Ramaseshan & Patton, 1994	Antecedents of channel choices of small business exporters	62 exporters of water filtration & purification equipment	Mailed questionnaire, cross-sectional	Stepwise logistic regression	Type of channel
	Principal Findings & Recommendations: Small firms with higher exports (% total sales volume) and stronger international family heritage tend to use independent channels (outside sales agents, distributors in home country). Small firms with high service requirement products tend to use integrated channels (company sales force, middlemen in a foreign country). The traditional "rules of thumb" in channel selection are not followed by sample.				
Seringhaus, 1993	Comparative exporting marketing behavior	74 Canadian & 49 Austrian small/medium-sized exporters	Self-administered questionnaires, cross-sectional	Discriminant analysis	Country
	Principal Findings & Recommendations: High-tech exporters in Canada and Austria differ in their outward orientation, cultural skills, perceived importance of information sources and market research practices.				
Walters & Samiee, 1990	Export performance	146 U.S. firms drawn from *American Export Register*	Mailed questionnaire, cross-sectional	Factor analysis, multiple regression	Export performance: after tax profit margins, growth in export sales, & export proportion of sales
	Principal Findings & Recommendations: Variables correlated with small firm export success vary according to measure of export performance. In comparison to large firms, small firms exported to fewer countries and were less likely to have specialized exporting unit and to conduct export planning and data collection.				

New Ventures & IPOs

Authors, Year	Key Issues	Sample	Research Method	Data Analysis	Dependent Variable
Diomande, 1990	Starting a business in a resource-starved environment	N/A	Examples/anecdotes related to African ventures, makes comparisons to starting a venture in developed country	N/A	N/A
	Principal Findings & Recommendations: Describes venture start-up process in West Africa and argues that it is not always appropriate to try to export venture formation techniques from developed countries.				
Keeley, Roure, Goto, & Yoshimura, 1990	New venture performance criteria	127 venture-capital backed firms from 4 European countries, Japan, & U.S.	Business plans & financial histories, longitudinal	Descriptive statistics, regression	Internal rate of return
	Principal Findings & Recommendations: Research supports the general view that performance is related to the founders' characteristics, industry, & strategy; however, specific influences vary between countries.				
Matsuda, Vanderwerf, & Scarbrough, 1994	Comparative study of firm characteristics	24 U.S. & 79 Japanese newly public firms	Mailed questionnaires, cross-sectional	Chi-square tests, Kolmogorov-Smirnov test	N/A
	Principal Findings & Recommendations: Japanese firms were older, larger, and more often led by original founders. The post-IPO investment strategies of Japanese firms focused on new product development, increase in R&D spending, and investment in capital plant. U.S. firms left R&D spending at pre-IPO level and reported interest in exploiting existing markets and buying other companies.				
McDougall, Shane, & Oviatt, 1994	International new ventures	24 international new ventures from 10 countries	Case studies, longitudinal	N/A	N/A
	Principal Findings & Recommendations: Formation process of international new ventures is not explained by existing theory from the field of international business, specifically—monopolistic advantage theory, product cycle theory, stage theory of internationalization, oligopolistic reaction theory, nor internalization theory.				
Oviatt & McDougall, 1994	Theory of international new ventures (INV)	N/A	Draws on theory & case examples to present a framework for formation of INVs	N/A	N/A
	Principal Findings & Recommendations: Four necessary and sufficient elements are needed for existence of sustainable international new ventures—organizational formation through internalization of some transactions, strong reliance on alternative governance structures to access resources, establishment of foreign location advantages, and control over unique resources.				
Oviatt, McDougall, Simon, & Shrader, 1991	Formation of international new ventures (global start-ups)	6 international new ventures	Interviews with 6 INVs & 1 venture capitalist, company documents, case study of 1 venture	Descriptive statistics	N/A
	Principal Findings & Recommendations: Six forces drive the creation of global start-ups: best resources may not be in your own back yard, financing may be easier, economies of scale drive entrepreneurs to seek global markets, rapid world-wide communications mean competitors react quickly, success may depend on establishing world-wide standard, and domestic inertia is difficult to overcome. Stage theories of internationalization are challenged.				

Authors, Year	Key Issues	Sample	Research Method	Data Analysis	Dependent Variable
Oviatt, McDougall, Simon, & Shrader, 1994	International new venture formation	1 U.S.-based international new venture	Case analysis	N/A	N/A
Principal Findings & Recommendations: Case of INV presented in three parts. Venture headquartered in the U.S., production was in Holland, product's first public exhibition in Canada, and early sales in Brazil & Spain. Venture eventually failed.					
Ray, 1991	New venture international opportunity identification	86 Canadian exporting firms from BOSS database	Mailed questionnaire, cross-sectional	Descriptive statistics	None
Principal Findings & Recommendations: Industry experience, previous business experience and international travel are the most important factors in international opportunity identification.					
Reynolds, Storey, & Westhead, 1994	Processes affecting new firm births	New firm birth rate data in France, Germany, Ireland, Italy, Japan, Sweden, UK, & US	Multiple sources of secondary data, longitudinal	Regression	Firm birth rates
Principal Findings & Recommendations: Three processes—growth in demand, a population of business organizations dominated by small firms, and a dense, urbanized context—were found to have an impact on birth rates in most countries. Other processes—related to unemployment, personal wealth, liberal political climate, or government actions—had weak or mixed effects.					
Tyebjee, 1990	Internationalization of new high technology ventures	105 U.S. high tech start-ups	Mailed questionnaire using Corptech directory	Descriptive statistics, regression	International involvement (% revenues derived from sales made directly or indirectly into foreign markets)
Principal Findings & Recommendations: Argues traditional export-based measures of international involvement are too myopic in today's global business world and presents a modified measure. Factors which lead a firm into international involvement are different from those which make that involvement successful. Management's activities and adaptation of the product are strongest factors affecting success.					
VanderWerf, 1991	Cross-cultural new venture performance	12 U.S. & Japanese ventures	Interview & questionnaire, longitudinal, total population examined	T-tests, Fisher-Exact tests, cluster analysis	Average sales by year since first sale compared to average of population
Principal Findings & Recommendations: Except for being startups, the higher-performance U.S. ventures more closely resembled Japanese ventures than they did other U.S. ventures. Higher-performance U.S. ventures were those with less management experience outside industry, independent organizations, and employed aggressive strategies.					

Authors, Year	Key Issues	Sample	Research Method	Data Analysis	Dependent Variable
Vesper, Vesper, & Cho, 1994	Communication issues in an international start-up	1 Canadian international new venture	Case study, interviews & examination of written correspondence, longitudinal	Frequency counts & content analysis of written correspondence between Canadian entrepreneurs & Korean intermediary over 2 years	N/A
	Principal Findings & Recommendations: At earliest stage, logistics discussed frequently and products and personal topics, such as compensation, received relatively little mention. Two years later, relative frequency of mention of topics reversed. Correspondence revealed disagreement on issues and great personal strains between collaborators. Venture more market-focused than product focused. Entrepreneurs wrestled with questions of ethics and did not consider their travel to have a high personal cost.				
Transitioning Economies					
Abetti, O'Such, & Porowski, 1992	Transition of Central & Eastern Europe through technological entrepreneurship	N/A	Draws on experiences & research in Ukraine, Republic of Ireland, France, Mexico, Puerto Rico, Poland, & U.S.	Compares data across countries & draws conclusions	N/A
	Principal Findings & Recommendations: Argues that technological entrepreneurship can succeed in Central and Eastern European countries and will greatly contribute to their economic renewal. Western assistance is critical to achieve this success and should be regarded as a profitable investment in long range business development.				
Dyson, 1991	Computer entrepreneurs in Central Europe & Soviet Union	N/A	Draws on many individual & venture examples	N/A	N/A
	Principal Findings & Recommendations: Describes entrepreneurial processes in Central Europe and Soviet Union, highlighting computer entrepreneurs. Details history of Graphisoft, an international new venture, & several other new firms and joint ventures. Describes entry of several U.S. businesses into distribution system of Moscow.				
Hoy, Pivoda, & Machrle, 1992	Competing in Eastern Europe	1 Czechoslovakian venture	Case study of small venture	N/A	N/A
	Principal Findings & Recommendations: Case shows how a tiny venture can absorb two larger state-owned enterprises to become a multi-national competitor. Demonstrates how new venture owners may be able to survive and grow their firms even if they lack adequate resources.				
Lyles, Carter, & Baird, 1994	Partnerships of small firms in a transitioning economy	69 small Hungarian ventures	Structured interview, cross-sectional	Analysis of variance, pairwise comparison of means	Ownership: sole proprietorship, regional partnership, partnership with U.S. firm

Authors, Year	Key Issues	Sample	Research Method	Data Analysis	Dependent Variable
Welfens, 1992	Privatization & FDI in Eastern Europe	N/A	Draws on theory to analyze the role of FDI in the East European transition	N/A	N/A
	Principal Findings & Recommendations: U.S. partnerships did not seem to offer advantages to their Hungarian partners—did not indicate that they had greater access to financial or other resources, a well thought-out strategy, or that they were clear about their implementation process.				
	Principal Findings & Recommendations: Privatization—including new business ventures—are vital for Eastern Europe which needs outward orientation and sustaining capital inflows. FDI is critical for economic growth. New liberal investment policies are required.				
Venture Financing					
Choy, 1990	Comparison of venture financing in 3 East Asian countries & U.S.	N/A	Presents descriptive information	N/A	N/A
	Principal Findings & Recommendations: Compares similarities and differences in the sources of financing (e.g., banks, tontines, self, government, venture capital, etc.) in the U.S., China, Japan, and Taiwan.				
Harrison & Mason, 1991	Cross-cultural characteristics & behavior of informal investors	63 actual & potential U.K. informal investors	Survey method not indicated, makes comparisons to U.S. surveys	Descriptive statistics	N/A
	Principal Findings & Recommendations: U.K. informal investors invest less, operate independently, have high rate of return and capital gain expectations, and are less satisfied overall with performance of their portfolios than are U.S. investors. U.K. informal VC market appears to operate less efficiently, thereby reducing potential contribution to venture financing.				
Hurry, Miller & Bowman, 1992	Comparison of Japanese & U.S. venture capital firms	10 Japanese & 20 U.S. venture capital firms	Faxed questionnaire, cross-sectional	Del statistic	N/A
	Principal Findings & Recommendations: VC industry in Japan described and compared and compared to U.S. No significant differences between stated time horizons. Findings suggest that Japanese and U.S. VC have different motivations. U.S. followed a project strategy and did not conclude venturing with technology transfer. Strategic logic of Japanese investment an implicit call option on new technology, and there was further investment in product development, manufacturing and distribution.				
Landstrom, 1993	Investment risk	52 informal investors in Sweden, U.K., & U.S.	Mailed questionnaire, cross-sectional	Descriptive statistics, cross-sectional comparison of results with other studies	Professionalism, risk levels, degree of involvement
	Principal Findings & Recommendations: Swedish investors were the most professional. Americans took the most risk & were the most highly involved.				
Manigart, 1994	Venture capital firm founding dates	504 VC firm founding dates in U.K., France, & the Netherlands	Secondary data from numerous sources	Event history & event count analyses, maximum likelihood	Time interval between foundings & quarterly number of foundings

Authors, Year	Key Issues	Sample	Research Method	Data Analysis	Dependent Variable
	Principal Findings & Recommendations: Major factor that influences the overall founding rate in each of the three countries is the density of the industry, i.e., number of organizations that already exist in the industry.				
Manigart, Joos, & Vos, 1992	Venture capital risk & return	33 venture capital firms in France, U.K., Ireland, the Netherlands, Belgium, & Spain	Secondary data, comparisons made to Continental sample, longitudinal	Nonparametric Wilcoxon Rank-Sum tests, Hodges-Lehmann estimator	Yearly stock return, SD weekly stock return, excess return
	Principal Findings & Recommendations: VC companies specializing in a specific investment had a higher return, while regional companies had lower return than general companies. Systematic risk of specialized companies is higher than that of general companies. U.K. companies had a significantly higher return than Continental companies.				
Muzyka, Bygrave, Leleux, & Hay, 1993	Financing ventures	291 entrepreneurs of venture-backed companies in Spain, Italy, Sweden, Belgium, France, U.K., Germany, & Netherlands	Mailed questionnaire, cross-sectional	Descriptive statistics	Entrepreneurial financing preferences
	Principal Findings & Recommendations: First preference was retained earnings, then borrowing from banks, financial institutions, and VCs, then selling equity through IPOs, to VCs, financial institutions, another company, and wealthy individuals, in that order. Entrepreneurs disliked informal sources of funding, especially family and friends.				
Muzyka, Birley, Leleux, Rossell, & Bendixen, 1993	Venture capital investment criteria	31 venture capital firms in 10 European countries	Questionnaire delivered personally, cross-sectional	Multi-attribute, pairwise conjoint analysis	Investment decision criteria
	Principal Findings & Recommendations: Human factors are the most important. Several distinct clusters of VCs can be identified by their investment criteria. There are no apparent differences in investment criteria across European VCs.				
Muzyka & Hay, 1993	MBO investors' assessment of opportunity	30 management buy-out fund investors from U.K., France, Germany, & Belgium	Mailed questionnaire, cross-sectional	Descriptive statistics	N/A
	Principal Findings & Recommendations: MBO investors are similar to VCs in terms of the factors utilized in their assessment of opportunities. MBO investors favor a leader who is an effective change agent as opposed to a long-term consensus builder. Favor teams whereby change can be agreed and implemented quickly.				
Roure, Keeley, & Keller, 1992	Cross-cultural venture capital strategies	53 U.S. & 34 European (7 countries) VC funds	Industry statistics, mailed questionnaire, interview	Descriptive statistics, t-tests, regression	IRR & expected IRR
	Principal Findings & Recommendations: U.S. VCs emphasized technology. Europeans emphasized buy-outs and consumer and general industrial products. In most cases VCs react to "local" developments, not to national trends.				

CHAPTER 14

Entrepreneurship in the Not-for-Profit Sector: The State of the Art

ROBERT D. HISRICH, EVERETTE FREEMAN,
ANNE P. STANDLEY, JOHN A. YANKEY,
AND DENNIS R. YOUNG

I F ANY ONE THEME HAS DOMINATED THE MANAGEMENT literature over the past few decades, it is that the environment for organizations (in all sectors) is changing rapidly and that future success and survival depend critically on management's ability to keep pace and adapt to new and turbulent conditions (e.g., Annison, 1993; Vaill, 1991; Senge, 1990; Theobold, 1992; Nadler et al., 1995). It becomes incumbent upon (new or existing) organizations to develop new products and services, modernize their production processes, and/or find new ways of doing things more effectively. Organizations of the future need to be entrepreneurial and innovate in order to survive in the world's hypercompetitive environment.

Entrepreneurial and innovative thinking is no less urgent for the nonprofit sector, which has experienced rapid growth and development over the past three decades and faces its own unprecedented economic and political change. Nowhere is this more true than in the fundraising arena, as sources of funding move substantially away from governmental support and toward sales of services in the marketplace (Salamon, 1992). As charitable fundraising has become much more competitive, corporate funding for nonprofits has become almost indistinguishable from corporate marketing. Moreover, serious ethical lapses in several of the most prestigious national nonprofit organizations have eroded public confidence and prompted calls for stronger standards of public accountability. Ironically, these developments are occurring in an increasingly stringent political environment in which nonprofits will be expected to fill the service voids left by federal government retrenchment and devolution of responsibilities to states and localities. If ever there were a time for entrepreneurialism and innovation to enable nonprofits to address their missions with greater effectiveness, the present era qualifies.

Unfortunately, present understanding of entrepreneurship and innovation in the nonprofit sector is rather thin (Perri, 1993). This aspect has not been a strong focus of research on nonprofit organizations, nor has scholarship on entrepreneurship and innovation devoted much attention to nonprofit organizations.

Innovation and Entrepreneurship

There are widely differing views in the literature on how innovation and entrepreneurship processes are related to one another. Some definitions of entrepreneurship intrinsically incorporate the concept of innovation and others do not. Similarly, some views of innovation see entrepreneurship as a dominating element in the innovation process, while others see it as just one of several variables and not necessarily the most important one.

The classic definition of entrepreneurship, given by Joseph Schumpeter (1949), closely interweaves innovation and entrepreneurship. Schumpeter defined entrepreneurship as the implementation of "new combinations" of the means of production. He identified five types of entrepreneurial activity, including:

❖ Introduction of a new economic good or service

❖ Introduction of a new method of production

❖ Opening of a new market

❖ Conquest of a new source of raw materials

❖ Reorganization of an industry, such as the creation or breaking up of a monopoly

The thrust of Schumpeter's definition of entrepreneurship is the *implementation of change,* which very much parallels the idea of innovation.

Peter Drucker (1985, 19) supports the emphasis on innovation as a defining characteristic of entrepreneurship. He defines innovation as the means by which entrepreneurs exploit change in order to provide a new business or service. Firstenberg (1986, 211) adds to this definition of entrepreneurship, labeling certain organizations as entrepreneurial because they are willing to accept uncertainty and the possibility of failure in order to reap the benefits from innovative change. According to Firstenberg's view of entrepreneurship (shared by Kao, 1991, and others), either entrepreneurship can exist without (successful) innovation or the definition of innovation must include the possibility that change can be unsuccessful.

Other definitions of entrepreneurship give less emphasis to change or innovation and more emphasis to risk-taking and profit-seeking in commercial ventures. For example, Hisrich and Peters (1995), define entrepreneurship as a process of creating something new of value by investing the required time and effort, assuming the associated financial, psychic, and moral risks, and receiving in return monetary reward, personal satisfaction, and independence. This definition emphasizes innovation, effort, risk, and motivation, facets of entrepreneurial activity in both the profit and nonprofit sector. Risk-taking and profit-seeking have actually received as much attention in the nonprofit sector literature than innovation because of the recent thrust by nonprofits to develop commercial sources of income (see Skloot, 1988). Of course, these phenomena are not mutually exclusive; many nonprofit commercial ventures qualify as entrepreneurial and innovative, and some nonprofit innovations are commercial in nature.

Entrepreneurship appears to be a necessary element in innovation, with someone, or some group, championing a new idea and working toward its implementation. Yet, the importance of entrepreneurship to innovation is seen differently by different researchers. Schumpeter (1949) sees the entrepreneur as a dislocational element, disturbing the current economic equilibrium and bringing about wholly new arrangements for production. Kirzner (1979) sees the entrepreneur as more of a discoverer, seeing new possibilities and bringing about more efficient combinations within existing conditions. Other researchers feel other elements may be more important than entrepreneurship for bringing about innovation. Perri (1993) emphasizes public policies and incentives that encourage or inhibit innovation, while Robert and Weiss (1988) and Janov (1994) project alternative management strategies for innovation in organizations. In other words, entrepreneurs innovate under the right conditions and strategies. The nature of those conditions are described by Kao (1991) and by Tropman and Morningstar (1989); the entrepreneur must apply his or her skills to the nature of the task at hand, within an accepting organizational context, and a receptive external environment. Thus, entrepreneurship is a catalytic element and a necessary but not sufficient condition for innovation. As Kao (1991) indicates, entrepreneurs may be seen as the "agency" for innovation, by someone committed to the realization of an idea.

Nonprofit Sector Innovation

There is evidence that entrepreneurship and innovation not only take place in the nonprofit sector but are also stimulated by the sector. Many nonprofit organizations are established explicitly to bring about change. Indeed, social welfare advocacy organizations are designated with their own tax code [501(c)4] for this purpose.

Also, the missions of many foundations and charitable nonprofits are framed in terms of finding solutions to social, health or environmental problems, supporting new means of expression in the arts, or implementing new concepts of service delivery.

However, views differ on whether innovation is a hallmark of the nonprofit sector or, indeed, whether nonprofit organizations are relatively slow to innovate compared with business or government. For example, Perri (1993) reviews the theoretical argument and finds that nonprofits are less innovative than business because innovation is spurred most strongly by financial returns and the profit motive. Nelson (1993) found that the role of nonprofit organizations in industrial innovation depends heavily on context. He cites universities, technical and professional societies, industry trade associations, and free-standing nonprofit research laboratories as contributors to technological innovation. These innovations frequently were spurred by government-sponsored rather than foundation-sponsored research and development.

Other researchers have studied the relative innovativeness of nonprofits versus government. Knapp et al. (1990) see nonprofits as more flexible than government. As such, nonprofits are able to experiment and extend the range of public services to constituencies with low visibility or public priority. However, Schorr (1970) argues that the government has been responsible for major innovations in social services. This is consistent with Nelson's (1993) view that government has taken over from foundations as primary funders of basic scientific research. Even so, Knapp et al. (1990, 207) point out that government often carries out its innovations through the voluntary sector which acts as the "creative arm" of the public sector.

Kramer (1987), reviewing opposing arguments on the degree of innovativeness of nonprofit organizations, notes that one of the oft-cited roles of nonprofits is to perform as *vanguards* whose purpose is to experiment, pioneer, and demonstrate in order to pave the way for government. While recognizing that nonprofits, particularly the larger more bureaucratic organizations, have also been criticized as resistant to change, the author argues that nonprofit organizations are more likely to be trailblazers in their early stages, and the high birth rate of these organizations helps ensure change in the social services. According to Kramer, the larger, more bureaucratic, and professional agencies have been the leading initiators of new programs, even if those programs have mostly extended and improved existing services rather than create entirely new ones. Kramer also cites the natural inclinations of nonprofits to extend their services to particular market segments and constituencies, to serve through advocacy as change agents in public policy, and to undertake small scale, individualized, flexible, and holistic approaches to human needs.

Osborne (1995), studying change in a volunteer bureau in the United Kingdom, stresses the role of serendipity, the political character of the process, the connection of innovation to the life cycle of an organization and to the larger historical context, and the importance of the environment as a stimulant and support to the innovation process within nonprofit organizations.

Hisrich et al. (1996), evaluating 808 applications by nonprofits from 1992 to 1994, found that programmatic and service innovations far outnumber management process or structural innovations, such as the development of new management systems, and new organizations and markets. The innovations in nonprofit organizations almost universally impacted the missions and the clientele served but had a much smaller effect on their management processes. External processes, such as problems in the community or changes in the environment, were more common stimuli of nonprofit innovations than responses to internal processes or problems, suggesting that management innovations require more attention in the future, especially in the quest for resources. The authors also found that risk-taking and persistence were two very important characteristics associated with achieving the more pervasive types of innovation—projects that are new not just for the organizations that implement them but for the communities and industries in which they operate as well. Finally, contrary to popular stereotypes, the results indicated that paid staff play a prominent role promoting innovations in nonprofit organizations compared to other key players such as CEOs and individual product champions.

Nonprofit Entrepreneurship

Even though entrepreneurship is a vital element to innovation in nonprofit organizations, relatively little has been written on nonprofit entrepreneurship. The limited literature on nonprofit entrepreneurship has concentrated on five main areas. First, it provides empirical evidence of entrepreneurial activity in the nonprofit sector. Second, it looks at the motivations that underlie entrepreneurship in the nonprofit sector, in light of the absence of a salient profit motive. Third, the literature focuses on commercial ventures undertaken by nonprofit organizations. Fourth, the literature contributes to economic theories explaining the existence and behavior of nonprofit organizations. Fifth, the skills and capacities that allow nonprofit entrepreneurs to be successful are explored.

Evidence of Nonprofit Entrepreneurship

Drucker (1985) cites examples of innovations in the nonprofit sector, which he ascribes to entrepreneurship, such as:

❖ Creation of the modern university in the late 19th century.

❖ Establishment of new private and metropolitan universities after World War II.

❖ Establishment of the modern hospital and the community hospital in the late 18th century.

❖ Development of specialized health clinics in the early 20th century.

❖ New program developments in a number of specific organizations in the social services, religion, health care, and professional societies.

Young (1985) documents several different forms that nonprofit entrepreneurial ventures can take, such as the establishment of new organizations designed to implement new service concepts, new organizations parented by existing organizations (through mergers or spin-offs), and new program initiatives undertaken within the framework of existing organizations. Brudney and Willis (1995) cite evidence of entrepreneurial behavior by volunteers who received one of President Bush's Daily Point of Light Awards. Overall, numerous examples and case studies of nonprofit entrepreneurship have been documented by Young (1983, 1985, 1990, 1991), Kao (1991), and Drucker (1985).

Several other factors indicate the importance of entrepreneurship as an intrinsic force in the nonprofit sector. The nonprofit sector is a fast-growing segment of the overall economy in the United States. In terms of income and employment, the sector's growth has at least paralleled and often exceeded the growth of government and business over the past two decades (Hodgkinson et al., 1993). This significant growth, underpinned by the commitment of new public and private contributions, suggests the presence of considerable entrepreneurial effort within the sector to transform resources into new operating programs and entities.

Second, 57 percent of existing charitable nonprofit organizations came into existence within the last twenty years (Hodgkinson et al., 1993) and the number of new public charities increased at a rate of 6.5 percent between 1965 and 1990 (Bowen et al., 1994). These statistics reflect many individuals or groups motivated to address social, health, environmental, or other issues because of their dissatisfaction with existing services and awareness of new sources of potential support. The fact that the nonprofit sector exhibits a steady entry of new organizations and is populated largely by young, small organizations reflects its entrepreneurial character. Even though older, larger organizations can also nurture entrepreneurship (Pinchot, 1985, 1996; Kao, 1991; Kanter, 1983), such activity is most frequently associated with smaller, younger organizations.

Motivations for Nonprofit Entrepreneurship

In the business context, the desire for independence and the opportunity to make money are the primary motivations for being an entrepreneur. What takes the place of making money in motivating entrepreneurship in the nonprofit sector? This question can be addressed in terms of three issues:

❖ Making money is not the sole motivator for entrepreneurship, even in the business sector.

❖ Making money does sometimes play a role in nonprofit entrepreneurship.

❖ Other things can motivate nonprofit entrepreneurship.

Motivation for entrepreneurs in the business sector is widely understood. Basically, the primary reasons given by entrepreneurs for starting their business are: need for independence, money, and falling in love with a new idea. McClelland (1973) identified the needs for power and affiliation as sources of entrepreneurial motivation, especially in sectors other than business. In the nonprofit sector, researchers have also studied entrepreneurial motivations. James (1987) found promotion of one's own religious values to be a key source of nonprofit entrepreneurship; people forming educational, social service, and health organizations want to create environments that allow them to transmit their religious values to others or to maintain those values within their own group. Hansmann (1980) identifies the quest for income and desire to lead institutions of high quality as sources of nonprofit entrepreneurial motivation, especially those in education, health care, or social services, where professionals play an important role. Studying a range of nonprofit, governmental, and business ventures in the social services, Young (1983) identified a spectrum of entrepreneurial motivations, including craftsmanship and pride of creative accomplishment, acclaim of professional peers, belief in a cause, search for personal identity, need for autonomy and independence, desire to preserve a cherished organization, need for power or control, and desire for personal wealth. In his scheme of motivations by sector, income-seeking was more heavily associated with entrepreneurship in the business sector, power-seeking was more heavily found in the public sector, and other motivations tended to cluster in the nonprofit sector.

Commercial Ventures

Although the seeking of personal wealth is a minor factor in motivating nonprofit sector entrepreneurship, the role of profits generated by the entrepreneurial activities of nonprofit organizations is nonetheless important. In particular, the undertaking of commercial ventures with the intent of generating financial surpluses that can ultimately contribute to accomplishment of the organization's mission has become an increasingly common nonprofit sector phenomenon (Crimmons and Keil, 1983; Skloot, 1987; Starkweather, 1993). Indeed, such activity has stirred up a storm of controversy in the small business sector over the issue of "unfair competition" (Wellford and Gallagher, 1988; Bennett and DiLorenzo, 1989). The growth of commercial ventures in the nonprofit sector has paralleled the more general usage of fees to finance a variety of nonprofit sector services. Fee income, consisting of conventional service fees as well as other commercial income, accounted for over half the growth of the nonprofit sector between 1977 and 1989 (Salamon, 1992).

The rationale for developing and operating commercial ventures by nonprofit organizations is twofold. First, some commercial activities, such as university sporting events or sales of art reproductions by museums, may contribute directly to the mission and work of the organization. Sporting events are presumably a part of a well-rounded physical education program, while art reproductions help educate people about great works of art. Most nonprofit commercial ventures are related to the organization's mission (Skloot, 1988). Other nonprofit commercial activities are not directly related to the mission but generate profits that can be allocated to support mission-related services. Profits from such "unrelated business" are subject to federal unrelated business income tax (UBIT), which is similar to a corporate profits tax. While relatively little UBIT is actually paid, such collections and the level of unrelated nonprofit commercial activity are increasing (Schiff and Weisbrod, 1991).

Economic Theory of Nonprofits

Motivation for nonprofit entrepreneurship is a key question in developing a theory to explain why nonprofits contribute to important parts of the economy. Most economic theory of the nonprofit sector focuses on "demand," attempting to explain why people want and will pay for the services of nonprofit organizations. However, demand-side theory does not answer the question of how such demand is translated into the actual supply of services. In the business sector, it is assumed that supply will manifest itself in the form of new firms or expansion of existing firms, implicitly driven by profit-seeking entrepreneurs. For the nonprofit sector, James (1987), Hansmann (1980), and Young (1983) have proposed a variety of entrepreneurial motivations to explain the manifestation of supply. Alternatively, Ben-Ner and Van Hoomissen (1993) postulate that coalitions of stakeholders (consumers, donors, sponsors) assume much of the entrepreneurial initiative in nonprofit organizations, motivated by the desire to closely control the quality and character of services they consider important.

Requirements for Success

Many feel that understanding the conditions and skills of entrepreneurship is important to effectively managing nonprofit organizations. Drucker (1985) identified four conditions or organizational "policies" for successful entrepreneurship in what he called "public-service institutions":

❖ A clear definition of mission

❖ A realistic statement of goals

❖ Willingness to question the validity of objectives that are not achieved after repeated attempts

❖ Constant search for innovative opportunities

Firstenberg (1986) focuses more specifically on the style of an organization's management. His ten characteristics are:

1. Coherent aims and values

2. Focus on comparative advantage

3. Intuitive decision-making

4. An adaptive (internal) environment

5. Excellence of execution

6. Staying power

7. Marshaling exceptional talent

8. Finesse with diverse constituencies

9. Having a sense of where the action is

10. Active-positive leadership

Young (1985, 1991) focuses more specifically on the skills and knowledge of the entrepreneurial leader, in the context of an existing organization or in the process of building a new one. These capabilities include:

1. Developing a sense of mission

2. Problem-solving ability

3. Applying creativity and ingenuity

4. Identifying opportunities and good timing

5. Analyzing risks

6. Consensus and team-building

7. Mobilizing resources

8. Persistence

There is a clear nexus between Drucker's, Firstenberg's, and Young's requirements in the areas of mission focus and proactive searching for opportunities. While Drucker's principles more clearly emphasize the role of organizational culture and policy in creating the context for entrepreneurial management, Firstenberg's emphasis is on management style, and Young focuses more on the capacities of entrepreneurs themselves.

Overview and Perspective

The literature on nonprofit sector innovation and entrepreneurship is wide-ranging, scattered in its foci, and relatively thin. Nonetheless, it builds on much wider literatures on innovation and entrepreneurship in the economy as a whole, and reveals a number of salient themes that suggest further exploration and research and can help guide nonprofit managerial practice.

First, the literature makes clear that the concept of innovation revolves around the implementation of new ways of doing things, although it is ambiguous on whether that implementation must have a successful impact in order to qualify as an innovation. Innovation is differentiated from invention on the one hand and imitation on the other. Innovation can also manifest itself in a variety of ways: through new products and services, new processes for producing those outputs, or new organizational arrangements for governing and administering those processes.

Second, the literature suggests that entrepreneurship is an essential element in the innovation process, in the nonprofit sector as much as in the business sector. The literature is ambivalent about whether nonprofit organizations are any more or less innovative than businesses or government, but it is clear that examples and other evidence of nonprofit sector innovation and entrepreneurial ventures abound and, indeed, that innovation is essential to the sector's survival and growth in an environment of turbulent change.

Third, while commercial ventures constitute an important category of entrepreneurial activity in the nonprofit sector, the literature suggests that these ventures are not the essence of nonprofit sector innovation or entrepreneurship. Nor are nonprofit commercial ventures necessarily driven by profit-seeking per se, but rather by desires to contribute directly and indirectly to organizational missions. Overall, nonprofit-sector entrepreneurial ventures are found to assume a variety of forms, commercial and otherwise, and are undertaken for a wide range of personal and organizational reasons.

Finally, the literature offers a number of prescriptions for successful nonprofit-sector entrepreneurship. These prescriptions recognize a variety of individual capacities, organizational variables, and environmental factors that must come together for nonprofit ventures to succeed and for innovation to be accomplished.

Research Needs and Issues

Overall, the literature reveals substantive contributions to knowledge about nonprofit sector entrepreneurship in five areas: the degree and importance of entrepreneurial activity in the nonprofit sector, the motivations for this activity, the role of commercial ventures in the nonprofit sector, the role of entrepreneurship in the supply-side theory of nonprofit organizations, and the requirements for successful nonprofit entrepreneurship. Nonetheless, most of this research just scratches the surface; all of these topical areas constitute important venues for continued future study.

In addition, a number of interesting and interrelated research implications are embedded in our overall discussion of entrepreneurship in nonprofit organizations. The first and perhaps most far-reaching is that the nonprofit sector, as evident from the growth of entrepreneurial efforts within it, has adopted and adapted the ways of business to an important degree. Whereas nonprofit organizations of years ago may have seen themselves as counterweights to the social ills generated by capitalism, and therefore resisted the norms and ways of business, nonprofit organizations today still fight to end social, health, and environmental problems, but by adopting the means and methods of free enterprise. In outlook and operations, nonprofit organizations are adopting the same norms of rationality used by successful businesses (Thompson, 1967). Perhaps the most obvious of these norms is the expectation that entrepreneurship and innovation are critical factors for organizational success. These nonprofit organizations know that they must compete by effectively spawning entrepreneurial and innovative projects and programs.

The growth in graduate-level degree programs in management of nonprofit organizations is but one indication of the extent to which the free enterprise ethos has transformed nonprofit organizations into centers of entrepreneurship and innovation. More research is needed on how nonprofit organizations operationalize the language and world view of free enterprise in their day-to-day affairs. Perhaps some clues to the kind of research questions that should be asked are encrusted on the battered hulls of nonprofit organizations caught in the crosscurrents of fiscal scandal. Is there a limit, for instance, in the degree to which the business ethos can be adopted by nonprofits before ethical problems conspire against the organization?

A second, no less important implication that flows from the research on nonprofit entrepreneurship and innovation is that environmental factors have blurred the once hard and fast lines of demarcation between the spheres of activity of for-profit and nonprofit organizations. Increasingly, the latter are not only embracing the business ethos but adopting its competitive credo. In the face of a stringent economy and shrinking government support, nonprofit organizations are competing with each other and the business sector for scarce private-sector resources. It is unlikely that nonprofit organizations will retreat from their efforts to secure newer funding and revenue sources merely because such efforts upset others. Notwithstanding calls by some small businesses to legislate restrictions on revenue-generating activities of nonprofits, members of nonprofit organizations are starting to see themselves as marketplace players. The proverbial genie is out and is not likely to be rebottled merely because custom and tradition argue for limited entrepreneurial activities on the part of nonprofit organizations. One of the research questions that needs to be addressed is whether nonprofits expand to meet operating expense and mission needs exclusively, or whether expansion takes on a logic all its own once the nonprofit organization embarks upon a course of seeking revenue sources outside its customary streams. Further, it is important to know more about how innovation is used by nonprofit organizations to establish beachheads in formerly unchartered revenue-producing areas. Is innovation itself seen by nonprofit organizations, for example, as a fundraising and marketing tool? Do nonprofit organizations, as the study by Hisrich et al. (1996) suggests, concentrate on externally-directed program innovations simply because they are more marketable? Do nonprofit organization leaders, even though they do not regard commercial ventures as an essential part of their core mission, see risk-taking as an imperative for organizational survival purposes? Finally, to what degree is nonprofit entrepreneurship and innovation stimulated by incursions of the business sector into traditional areas of nonprofit service, such as health care or social services?

A third implication of entrepreneurship and innovation for nonprofit organization research is related to the way researchers identify, or fail to identify, domains of nonprofit sector entrepreneurship. Many nonprofit organizations came into being precisely with the aim of finding solutions to social, health, and environmental problems. If researchers are not sensitive to the plasticity of entrepreneurship and innovation, in the sense that they may appear in the most unlikely places, then there is a real danger that wide forests of innovation, creativity, and risk-taking will be missed as attention is confined to the more common instances of this activity. Given the plasticity of idea formation that results in entrepreneurship and innovation, research needs to carefully ensure that all elements of nonprofit organizations, including their staff, boards, volunteers, boosters, and stakeholders, are studied. In this regard, we need to know more about the role staff members play in nonprofit entrepreneurship. For example, what is the degree to which staff deliberately circumvent or ignore organizational rules and bureaucracy in championing innovative programs? Currently, it is not known how a nonprofit organizational structure fosters innovation or retards it. Nor do we know much about how luck, serendipity, adumbration, and inspiration play a part in nonprofit entrepreneurship and innovation.

Finally, this paper suggests that Schumpeter's notion of entrepreneurship and Drucker's characterization of innovation may be more helpful in understanding what is taking place in nonprofit organizations than might first appear to be the case. Both Schumpeter's and Drucker's generic definitions instruct researchers to rely more on what organizations are actually doing rather than on what we expect to find them doing. In arguing that entrepreneurship entails the implementation of "new combinations" in production, Schumpeter provides researchers with the insight of understanding nonprofit entrepreneurship beyond the bounds of simply a concrete product. The combinations that are ultimately the most innovative in nonprofit organizations may be on the process-side rather than the product-side of the equation. Just as the Japanese have excelled in taking American products and developing new and better processes for producing them (Thurow, 1992), nonprofit organizations may be achieving their greatest entrepreneurial and innovative victories in taking profit-sector ideas and framing them in new and exciting forms of entrepreneurship and innovation. By paying closer attention to Drucker's notion of innovation as a "specific tool" of entrepreneurship, researchers may discover approaches, models, and paradigms nonprofit organizations can use to charter and blaze new trails or to remap entirely old ones.

REFERENCES

Annison, M.H. 1993. *Managing the Whirlwind.* Engelwood, CO: Medical Group Management Association.

Ben-Ner, A., and T. Van Hoomissen. 1993. Nonprofit organizations in the mixed economy: A demand and supply analysis. In A. Ben-Ner, and B. Gui (eds.): *The Nonprofit Sector in the Mixed Economy.* Ann Arbor: University of Michigan Press.

Bennett, J.T., and T.J. DiLorenzo. 1989. *Unfair Competition.* Maryland: Hamilton Press.

Bowen, W.G., T.I. Nygren, S.E. Turner, and E. Duffy. 1994. *The Charitable Nonprofits.* San Francisco: Jossey-Bass.

Brudney, J.L., and K.L. Willis. 1995, The Daily Point of Light Awards: An analysis of recipients and effects. *Journal of Volunteer Administration* (Summer):1-9.

Crimmins, J.C., and M. Keil. 1983. *Enterprise in the Nonprofit Sector.* Washington, DC: Partners for Liveable Places.

Drucker, P.F. 1985. *Innovation and Entrepreneurs.* New York: Harper and Row.

Firstenberg, P.B. 1986. *Managing for Profit in the Nonprofit World.* New York: The Foundation Center.

Hansmann, H.B. 1980. The role of nonprofit enterprise. *Yale Law Journal* 89:835-898.

Hisrich, R.D., E. Freeman, A.P. Standley, J.A. Yankey, and D.R. Young. 1996. Innovations by Nonprofit Organizations: A Study of the Applicants for the Peter F. Drucker Award in Nonprofit Innovation. Discussion paper, Mandel Center for Nonprofit Organizations, Case Western Reserve University.

Hisrich, R.D., and M.P. Peters. 1995. *Entrepreneurship: Starting, Developing and Managing a New Enterprise*. Chicago: Irwin.

Hodgkinson, V.A., and C. Toppe. 1991. A new research and planning tool for managers: The National Taxonomy of Exempt Entities. *Nonprofit Management and Leadership* 1(4):403-414.

Hodgkinson, V.A., M.S. Weitzman, S.M. Noga, and H. Gorski. 1993. *A Portrait of the Independent Sector*. Washington, DC: Independent Sector.

James, E. 1987. The nonprofit sector in comparative perspective. In W.W. Powell (ed.): *The Nonprofit Sector: A Research Handbook*. New Haven, CT: Yale University Press, 397-415.

Janov, J. 1994. *The Inventive Organization*. San Francisco: Jossey-Bass.

Kanter, R.M. 1983. *The Change Masters*. New York: Simon and Schuster.

Kao, J.J. 1991, *The Entrepreneurial Organization*. Englewood Cliffs, NJ: Prentice Hall.

Kirzner, I.M. 1979. *Perception, Opportunity, and Profit*. Chicago: University of Chicago Press.

Knapp, M., E. Robertson, and C. Thomason. 1990. Public money, voluntary action: Whose welfare? In H.K. Anheier and W. Seibel (eds.): *The Third Sector: Comparative Studies of Nonprofit Organizations*. New York: Walter de Gruyter, 183-218

Kramer, R.M. 1987. Voluntary agencies and the personal social services. In Powell, W.W. (ed.): *The Nonprofit Sector: A Research Handbook*. New Haven, CT: Yale University Press, 240-257.

McClelland, D.C. 1973. The two faces of power. In D.C. McClelland and R.S. Steele (eds.): *Human Motivation*. Morris, NJ: General Learning Press.

Nadler, D.D., R.B. Shaw, R.B. Walton, A. Elise, et al. 1995. *Discontinuous Change: Leading Organizational Transformation*. San Francisco: Jossey-Bass .

Nelson, R.R. 1993. Technological innovation: The role of nonprofit organizations. In D.C. Hammack and D.R. Young (eds.): *Nonprofit Organizations in a Market Economy*. San Francisco: Jossey-Bass, 363-377

Nelson, R.R., and S.G. Winter. 1982. *An Evolutionary Theory of Economic Change*. Cambridge, MA: Harvard University Press.

Osborne, S.P. 1995. Don t you just love being in control? Managing innovation and change in a local voluntary agency. Aston Business School, Aston University, draft manuscript.

Perri, 6. 1993. Innovation by nonprofit organizations. *Nonprofit Management and Leadership* 3(4):397-414.

Pinchot, G. 1985. *Intrapreneuring*. New York: Harper and Row.

Pinchot, G. 1996. Creating organizations with many leaders. In F. Hesselbein, M. Goldsmith, and R. Beckhard (eds.): *The Leader of the Future*. San Francisco: Jossey-Bass, 25-39.

Robert, M., and A. Weiss. 1988. *The Innovation Formula*. New York: Ballinger.

Salamon, L.M. 1992. *America's Nonprofit Sector*: New York: The Foundation Center.

Schiff, J., and B.A. Weisbrod. 1991. Competition between for-profit and non-profit organizations in commercial activities. *Annals of Public and Cooperative Economics* 1:62.

Schorr, A.L. 1970. The tasks for volunteerism in the next decade. *Child Welfare* 49:425-434.

Schumpeter, J. 1949. *The Theory of Economic Development.* Cambridge, MA: Harvard University Press.

Senge, P.M. 1990. *The Fifth Discipline.* New York: Doubleday.

Skloot, E. 1987. Enterprise and commerce in nonprofit organizations. In W.W. Powell (ed.): *The Nonprofit Sector: A Research Handbook.* New Haven, CT: Yale University Press, 380-396.

Skloot, E. 1988. *The Nonprofit Entrepreneur.* New York: The Foundation Center.

Starkweather, D.B. 1993. Profit making by nonprofit hospitals. In D.C. Hammack and D.R. Young (eds.): *Nonprofit Organizations in a Market Economy.* San Francisco: Jossey-Bass, 105-137.

Theobold, R. 1992. *Turning the Century.* Indianapolis: Knowledge Systems.

Thompson, J.D. 1967. *Organizations in Action: Social Science Bases of Administrative Theory.* New York: McGraw-Hill.

Thurow, L.C. 1992. *Head to Head: The Coming Economic Battle Among Japan, Europe, and America.* New York: Morrow.

Tropman. J.E., and G. Morningstar. 1989. *Entrepreneurial Systems for the 1990s.* New York: Quorum Books.

Vaill, P.B. 1991. *Managing as a Performing Art.* San Francisco: Jossey-Bass .

Wellford, W.H., and J.G. Gallagher. 1988. *Unfair Competition?* Washington, DC: The National Assembly.

Young, D.R. 1983. *If Not for Profit, for What?* Lexington, MA: D.C. Heath.

Young, D.R. 1985. *Casebook of Management for Nonprofit Organizations.* New York: Haworth Press.

Young, D.R. 1990. Champions of change: Entrepreneurs in social work. In H.H. Weissman (ed.): *Serious Play.* Silver Spring, MD: National Association of Social Workers, 126-135.

Young, D.R. 1991. Providing entrepreneurial leadership. In R.L. Edwards and J.A.Yankey (eds.): *Skills for Effective Human Service Management.* Silver Spring, MD: NASW Press, 62-75.

Young, D.R. 1997 (forthcoming). Nonprofit entrepreneurship," In J.M. Shafritz (ed.): *The International Encyclopedia of Public Policy and Administration.* New York: Henry Holt.

Research Applications, Issues, and Needs

SECTION V

Research Applications, Issues, and Needs

RESEARCH IN THE FIELD OF ENTREPRENEURSHIP HAS been hampered by the lack of longitudinal databases that provide data at the micro, or firm, level. Entrepreneurship researchers examining smaller, rapidly growing firms do not have access to annual reports as do researchers studying larger corporate organizations. Yet this does not mean that the desired data is not available. It is available but not at the same level of detail as that for larger firms. Phillips and Dennis discuss the availability, specifications, and limitations of the public databases that exist primarily through the efforts of the Small Business Administration as well as private databases developed by the National Federation of Independent Businesses, Dun and Bradstreet, and the Ernst and Young Entrepreneur of the Year Database being developed by the National Center for Entrepreneurship Research at the Ewing Marion Kauffman Foundation.

Hoy suggests that if entrepreneurship research is going to have any relevance and make a difference to the interests of stakeholders other than academics, it must be expanded to include public policy decision-makers and practicing entrepreneurs of industry groups. He further suggests that the requirements for academic tenure and promotion be reconsidered to allow for research papers written for broader audience. In response to the question, Have we made a difference? The answer is a qualified yes but there is so much more that could be done.

Aldrich and Baker address a similar issue by asking, Has there been progress in entrepreneurship research? Through an analysis of publications in major academic journals they conclude that research methodology is showing signs of improvement through better research design, larger sample sizes, and more sophisticated analytical techniques.

Finally, Sexton concludes with a summary of the changes in the state of the art in entrepreneurship research over the past several years. He identifies issues, topics, and needs for researchers that will lead the field into the 21st century.

CHAPTER 15

Databases for Small Business Analysis

BRUCE D. PHILLIPS

AND

WILLIAM J. DENNIS, JR.

T HIS CHAPTER REVIEWS SEVERAL MAJOR DATABASES available to analyze the formation, growth, and volatility of small firms. It concludes that there is no "greatest hits" data source for all small firm and entrepreneurship analysis. Each has its assets and liabilities. Following this brief introduction, a general description of individual data sets occurs. Included in the discussion are the variables contained and time period covered as well as public availability.

A few general observations can be made about small business data sets at the outset. Some data sets cover only firm characteristics but not those of the owner(s) and vice versa. With the exceptions noted below, demographic and business data are separated.

Second, most available databases do not include financial data, i.e., balance sheet and income statement information. This is the most sensitive type of information and is rarely available, even in aggregate form. Data on profits are particularly hard to obtain.

Third, it is useful to know wages paid and people hired among firms with employees. Such data are not often present. However, there is progress to report on that front.

Fourth, the two issues of data timeliness (currency) and its dynamics continue to be a major quagmire. While "census type" data will always lag behind three to four years, new data on firm dynamics, especially births and deaths, is becoming more readily available from the private sector. The entries/exit series produced by the Wells Fargo Bank and the National Federation of Independent Business Education

Foundation in cooperation with the Gallup Organization is one example discussed. Job creation by firm size on a current basis as has been noted often can only be measured from dynamic data sets. Yet, census data sets, though new in the sense of different data, lag two to three years.

Fifth, definitional purity, i.e., the loss of meaning in a quest for precision, increases the difficulty of obtaining relevant static data, let alone developing data useful for dynamic analysis. Many data sets are based on antiquated concepts including a firm's legal form of organization.

And sixth, we will remain dependent on the private sector for significant amounts of small business data. While government data sets increasingly recognize the importance of self-employment and business size as relevant variables, budget issues do not bode well for expansion of small business-related data.

Organization of the Chapter

The first part of this chapter discusses the Small Business Administration's (SBA) new census-based Small Business Database. It now extends in aggregate form from 1988 to 1993 and is publicly available. To fill in data on small firm finances, four governmental sources of information will be discussed in Part II of this chapter. These include the 1994 Federal Reserve Survey of Small Firm Finances, a very detailed survey on the sources and uses of funds of 5,000 small firms, and the federal Survey of Consumer Finances. The Census Bureau's 1992–94 Characteristics of Business Owners, the only government source of data on both the characteristics of firms and their owners, will also be discussed. Finally, applicable financial data on small business from IRS's Statistics of Income (SOI) Bulletin and Corporate Sourcebook will be analyzed.

Part III of this chapter discusses several additional federal data sets that contain some small business information, although designed for other purposes. This principally includes an examination of data from the Census Bureau's expanded Current Population Surveys and Labor's National Longitudinal Surveys of Youth.

Part IV introduces private-sector data sources and focuses on NFIB's quarterly small business economic survey which dates to 1973 (monthly to 1986). The series' development will be highlighted, as well as the problems and opportunities created by surveys of association samples.

Part V is devoted to a cooperative venture between private organizations resulting in the Wells Fargo/NFIB Series on Business Entries and Exits. The last part of this chapter includes brief discussions of other private sector series such as those originating in the for-profit Dun and Bradstreet Corporation and the nonprofit Center for Entrepreneurial Leadership at the Ewing Marion Kauffman Foundation.

The chapter concludes with a look into the next century when the primary means of transmitting data will be the Internet and numerous nonfederal data sets will make important contributions to the understanding of small firms.

The Public Sector

SBA's Census-Based Small Business Database

Beginning in late 1991, the Office of Advocacy of the SBA contracted with the Economic Surveys Division (ESD) of the Bureau of the Census to produce linked longitudinal data files on an enterprise basis. These files were based upon a match between two major Census files: the bureau's main mailing list, the Standard Statistical Establishment List (SSEL), and the annually updated Company Organization Survey (COS). COS requires firms with 50 or more employees to list all of the component establishments that they own as of March in each year. The establishment is the main building block of this database, and establishments are classified by the size of the firms that own them. Compared with SBA's earlier efforts with linked Dun and Bradstreet files, the Census files cost about half of what had previously been spent with Dun and Bradstreet and include all industries. The industrial coverage matches that in the Census Bureau's annual *County Business Patterns* publication.

The development of this database should be considered to be an extension of the Census's quinquiennial Enterprise Statistics program. The data has now been annualized, produced at a subnational level, and industrial coverage has been expanded. In addition, longitudinal files are being developed as described below.

As of mid-1996, cross-section files have been produced for years 1988 through 1992 with the 1993 file expected during the summer of 1996. The files are available in hard copy in loose-leaf notebooks, on reproducible floppy disks, and in Lotus files on SBA's computers. Data is usually available at the four-digit level of industrial detail for the United States, and at the two-digit level for states.

Variables Included

Files generally include the number of establishments, firms, payroll/firm, payroll/employee, receipts/firm, and receipts/employee for five major size classes: firms with less than 20 employees and those with 20–99, 100–499, or 500 or more employees. Also included are "rollups" for firms with less than 20 and less than 500 employees. In addition, for states at the one- and two-digit levels, the Census Bureau has also produced tabulations and floppies that provide the data by five-employee increments, i.e., for firms and establishments with 1–4, 5–9, 10–14, 15–19

... and 75–99 employees. The latter tabulations are particularly useful for studying the impacts of specific laws or regulations on firms of different size classes. The tabulations are also available by legal form of organization by state at the one-digit SIC level and also for the 100 largest Metropolitan Statistical Areas (MSAs).

No data are yet available on minority- and women-owned firms. The Census will eventually link in minority-owned businesses (MOB) and women-owned businesses (WOB) with employees into the cross-section files for 1992. This will be for one year only. (The Census Bureau's Center for Economic Studies is developing a linked cross-section file of MOB and WOB for 1987 and 1992.)

The new Census Bureau annual survey of WOB will eventually be incorporated into the SBA data tabulations for firms with employees. Preliminary discussions are also occurring within the government that would allow interagency list sharing of business names and addresses if legislation is changed. Data for 1992 on women-owned firms and Black-owned firms was released early in 1996 and includes information on the number of firms, receipts of firms, firms with employees , industry of firms, and the number of firms in each county with 100 or more women-owned or Black-owned firms. There is no information about the owners of these firms. It should be noted that about 85 percent of WOB and MOB have no employees and that only the 15 percent or so of firms with employees will be part of this database.

The data on women-owned firms for 1992 (including corporations owned by women) was released January 29, 1996. In addition, in cooperation with the Federal Interagency Task Force on Women-Owned Firms, the Census Bureau has begun an annual survey of women-owned firms. The first release of this data is scheduled for 1996.

Time Covered

The Census Bureau has just delivered data files for the 1989–91 and 1990–92 periods. These files measure jobs created by new firm births as well as those created by expansions of existing firms. In addition, the files also provide jobs destroyed by firm deaths and jobs lost by contractions of larger firms. In particular, these files are the first files produced within the U.S. government from which job creation can be studied for all industries (see Berney and Phillips, 1995).

Public Availability

Some of the new data by firm size has already been published in a number of sources. Several appendix tables in *The State of Small Business: A Report of the President* (1993, 1994, 1995) contain some of the data. These reports are available from the Government Printing Office. Other tables from this new database have also been previously published in *The Handbook of Small Business Data: 1994* (GPO, order #045-000-00270-5).

Customized tabulations or copies of the database are available as a general rule. But, there will be a cost and/or time delays due to recent budget cutbacks, and all individual names and addresses are confidential by law. Inquiries may be directed to the Research Programming Branch, Bureau of the Census, U.S. Department of Commerce or Office of Economic Research, Office of Advocacy, Small Business Administration. Both are in Washington, DC.

Studying Small Firm Finances

Federal Reserve Survey of Small Firm Finances

Within the last five years, two major surveys of small firm finances have been conducted by the Federal Reserve Board and the Small Business Administration. These National Surveys of Small Firm finances (NSSBF) have been the most detailed examination to date of the credit needs of small firms as well as their sources and uses of funds (*State of Small Business*, 1991). In each survey, over 5,000 small firms with less than 500 employees provided detailed answers on their uses of banks and bank services, the use of alternative sources of credit, difficulties encountered in borrowing or raising expansion capital, and their level of satisfaction from utilizing each type of service.

The Federal Reserve was also interested in possible adverse effects upon small firms from the increasing number of bank consolidations. Major efforts were made in the 1993–94 survey to include a large proportion of small women-owned and minority-owned firms. However, because of data limitations, firms without employees were not included in the two surveys. Dun and Bradstreet provided the sampling frame. Inquiries should be directed to the Office of Economic Research, Office of Advocacy, Small Business Administration (1441 L Street, Washington, DC 20416) or the Division of Research and Statistics, Federal Reserve Board (20th and C Street, Washington, DC 20551).

Federal Reserve Survey of Consumer Finances

Several times during the past 15 years, the SBA has analyzed the household asset information on those parts of the Consumer Finance Survey (CFS) pertaining to business start-up or ownership. In general, the data from the survey provides percentages of a household's assets, both directly and indirectly, which may be considered part of business ownership. In some instances, these examples of ownership are indirect, such as ownership of mutual funds or common stock. In other cases, ownership may be direct, such as direct investment in a firm through life insurance policies, home equity loans, or other household nontraditional household assets such as an art collection that could be sold with the proceeds reinvested in the firm.

One of the subsamples taken from the CFS is a survey of high-income households with income. For example, in the 1989 survey, 400 respondents had income over $50,000 (Federal Reserve Bulletin, 1989). The 1989 survey, which yielded a SAS tape, is currently being analyzed by the Office of Economic Research of the SBA. One disadvantage of this file is that the survey is one of owners, not firms. Therefore, the CFS contains no way to connect the business assets owned by households with the precise businesses in which they are invested.

When viewed more broadly as a potential income source for nascent entrepreneurs, the CFS may provide one or more indicators of potential entrepreneurship. While there is no clear relationship between the ownership of household assets and the start of a business, it is a subject of further research to determine the extent to which household assets are correlated with direct or indirect future business ownership.

The CFS breaks out the data by current occupation of household head including self-employed. Self-employed constitute about 10 percent out of a population of 3,000 respondents. This break-out provides the best view we have of the financial status of business owners. Unfortunately, the sample size results in the production of population medians and gives little hint of what should be intriguing distributions (Kennickell and Star-McCluer, 1995).

The CFS was replicated by the Federal Reserve Board in 1995. Preliminary tabulations should be available to researchers in summary SAS files during 1996. The series originated at the University of Michigan and was recently taken over by the Federal Reserve. Inquiries can be made with the Division of Research and Statistics, Federal Reserve Board (20th and C Street, Washington, DC 20551).

Quarterly Financial Report of
Manufacturing, Mining and Trade Corporations

Because this data source (abbreviated QFR) applies only to a small sample of corporations (7,800 in manufacturing, 500 in mining, and 2,700 in trade), it is of minimal use to study small, start-up businesses. Two other limitations exist with this Census source: the sample size is very small for firms with assets under $5 million, and many values are estimated. Further, as is the case with most Census data, only aggregate values are shown, and no micro-data is available for use by researchers. However, there is a limited amount of balance sheet and income statement information for larger small business corporations.

Characteristics of Business Owners Survey

The Minority Business Development Agency of the Department of Commerce and SBA's Office of Advocacy contracted with the Census Bureau to produce the

Characteristics of Business Owners (CBO) data for 1987 and again for the 1992–94 period. The CBO is a survey of 125,000 small businesses, roughly divided equally into African-American, Hispanic, Asian-American, women-owned, and nonminority male-owned firms. To be included in the CBO sampling frame, firms needed $500 in sales in each respective year and to have filed a tax return.

The CBO is the only nationally representative source of many of the subjects covered in the survey and includes demographic characteristics of the owner (age, gender, and years of prior experience) as well as characteristics of the firm itself (sales, export status, and franchise status), hours and weeks worked by the business owner, sources of debt and equity capital, and so on. In addition, the CBO asks whether the firm is home-based, the only national source of such information.

In the 1992–94 version, crosstabs can separate part-time business commitments from full-time business endeavors. Sales and employment variables may also be used as cutoffs. A considerable number of questions in the CBO are devoted to defining the size of the market of each respective business. Some of the most useful questions concern the sources of debt and equity capital used to start firms. For example, in 1987, over two-thirds of the firms began with less than $5,000 of owners equity. The percentage of persons using credit cards, finance companies, or home equity loans to start firms has also risen.

The CBO has one major liability. It does not include C-corporations or owners of C-corporations. Hence, the group of small businesses with largest economic impact is systematically eliminated. Their inclusion would almost certainly raise size averages in virtually every noncategorical variable, but their impact on categorical variables is not always so obvious.

IRS Statistics of Income

Each quarter the Statistics of Income division of the Internal Revenue Service publishes the *SOI Bulletin*. This publication contains data for both households and businesses and is an invaluable source of historical information. Data on business firms is generally provided by receipt size class for proprietorships, partnerships, and corporations. Special analyses are also done on a rotating basis to determine how specific classes of firms are using different provisions of the tax code. In addition, for the past 15 years, the IRS has also provided the SBA with unpublished data on nonfarm sole proprietors by gender, cross-classified by industry and size of business receipts. The latter data have proven invaluable in demonstrating the above-average growth of women-owned firms during the past decade. Generally, IRS data lags behind two to three years.

Data on business profits from the IRS are elusive. For sole proprietors and partnerships, only data on net income are available. If the taxpayer has more than one noncorporate business, the data apply to all business income combined. The preferred concept, return on assets or ROI (return on investment), is not obtainable directly from the tax return. However, total deductions for various balance sheet items are provided, as are the number of returns and the number of returns with business receipts.

For small business corporations, data availability is considerably brighter. The IRS's *Source Book for Corporations* contains data for corporations by asset size class and industry. Balance sheet and income statement information is available for corporations in about 15 different asset classes. Rates of return on assets can be calculated from these data as well as the profits of small business (generally subchapter S) corporations. But the greatest detail is only averages by asset size and industry; medians, quartiles, or similar distributions are not generally available. Further, there is no means to tie corporate profits data to owner "take-out" other than indirectly through the officers salary line. The IRS does provide academic researchers a restricted access file for these data.

Before the availability of the other financial data on small firms discussed above, the IRS *Source Book for Corporations* was the only source of data on small business finance. Unfortunately, because of numerous cuts in the budget of the SOI division during the 1980s, the quantity of detail, and especially special studies coming from the SOI division has declined dramatically. Statistics of Income Division, Internal Revenue Service, is the organization that produces these data.

Data on Self-Employed Persons from the Departments of Commerce and Labor

Current Population Survey

The Current Population Survey (CPS) conducted by the Census Bureau is the government's standard monthly survey on population, employment, housing, and so on. Each March it poses an expanded series of questions about self-employed persons as part of its annual supplement. These data are particularly useful because they originate from a sample of about 60,000 households (not all of which are self-employed) and include firm size. The questions include the hours and weeks spent working in the business during the previous year, the income earned, and the demographics of the business owner. Some years the questions in the supplement are more interesting for present purposes than are others. The 1995 CPS included an income supplement. However, prior supplements addressed the provision of employee benefits and related questions about the industry of the firm. For example, the best data available on the provision of employee health insurance by firm size was collected by the CPS and subsequently published by the Employee Benefit Research Institute (EBRI) and SBA (*Employment Based Health Benefits*, 1994; *State of Small Business*, 1994).

One major asset of the data set is that some longitudinal analysis is possible. The survey sample is rotated. Most respondents are in four months, out eight, and back in four. Though the majority of the original sample is gone by the second year, a reasonable number of observations are available for year x and year $x + 1$. (None are available for year $x + 2$.) The result is that we can track people entering and exiting. For example, those data reveal that from 1983 to 1993, 92.5 percent of all self-employed people were employed the prior year (83.9 in self-employment), 1.7 percent were unemployed, and 5.8 percent were out-of-the-labor force (Segal, 1996). The difficulty with these data is that we can track only those people whose primary economic activity for most of the year is self-employment. This implies that many small, start-up businesses are ignored because their owners have not spent adequate time (for definitional purposes) on them. Inquiries should be directed to the Population Division, Bureau of the Census, U.S. Department of Commerce.

National Longitudinal Survey

The Bureau of Labor Statistics' (BLS) National Longitudinal Survey (NLS) is the best available database comparing different cohorts of the population as they shift between self-employment and wage and salary work. In addition, it identifies whether a worker is self-employed and working at home. Pratt (1993) used the NLS to study home-based businesses. The NLS was first conducted in 1968 and reinterviews small cohorts of the original population (about 5,000 randomly selected individuals) 10 years later. Not every cohort is reinterviewed each survey period.

Because this data set does not separate business owners from their firms, an interested researcher cannot tell if a person who remained self-employed 10 years later grew a business or not. Therefore, while the NLS does provide some useful information on shifts between wage and salary work and self-employment, it is not really a suitable data set for studying entrepreneurship. The characteristics of the business formed would have to be added in order to do that.

The Private Sector

Publication and subsequent criticism of The Job Generation Process by Birch (1979) focused attention on the use of private-sector data in conducting small business/entrepreneurship research. Birch developed the report's data from the Dun's Market Identifiers (DMI) file produced and owned by Dun and Bradstreet. At the time, Birch acknowledged a series of shortcomings inherent in the file, a file constructed for credit reporting, not longitudinal business demographic analysis. Various analysts, both agreeing and disagreeing with the tenor of Birch's conclusions, decried the database. Yet, in the end, a powerful current of small business research originat-ed and was largely conducted through use of this private sector data file.

Today, a variety of data collection efforts in the private sector focus on the forma-tion, growth, and volatility of all small firms. The sources are both for-profit compa-nies, e.g., Dun and Bradstreet, and private nonprofits, e.g., National Federation of Independent Business (NFIB). The number of "partnerships" in database develop-ment among organizations in different sectors, e.g., Kauffman Foundation/Ernst and Young, are also increasing. While the private-sector efforts are not intended to sup-plant the federal government in terms of data collection, they do make a necessary contribution and complement public efforts. A major type of data collection activity in the private sector is the trade/business association survey.

Small Business Economic Trends

One of the largest private-sector data collection programs on smaller firms is con-ducted by the National Federation of Independent Business (NFIB). NFIB is an asso-ciation of small business owners, the primary purpose of which is advocacy. The orga-nization has approximately 600,000 members throughout the country with offices in Nashville, TN, Washington, DC, and each of the state capitals. The NFIB Education Foundation is affiliated and headquartered in Washington, DC, and is primarily responsible for the organization's data collection efforts.

NFIB's Small Business Economic Trends, formerly titled the Quarterly Economic Report for Small Business, was created in 1973 as a result of a White House meeting between President Nixon and small business leaders. At the meeting, small business leaders requested regular sessions with senior White House staff to assess the state of small business and its needs. Nixon agreed. However, NFIB President Wilson S. Johnson was concerned that these gatherings not deteriorate into "gripe sessions." He felt that they always required substance, and so developed the idea of a quarter-ly economic survey the results of which would be a regular agenda item. Watergate intervened. The regular meetings never occurred. But the survey was instituted and continues through the present. Today, President Clinton's Council of Economic Advisors and the Federal Reserve are among regular recipients of survey results (at their request), and the latter will soon receive the micro-data.

NFIB first began to collect small business economic data in October 1973. The survey continued on a quarterly basis through January 1986, at which time it became a monthly. NFIB receives about 2,000 responses from the mail survey in "quarterly" months, i.e., January, April, July, and October, and about 750 in the other eight.

The primary assets of the data series are its uniqueness, longevity, currency, and over the last decade, its frequency. Other data sets have been instituted in the last few years emulating the NFIB series, e.g., Dun's 5000 and the Australian Chamber of Commerce and Industry's quarterly economic survey. The NFIB economic data is, therefore, not as unique as it once was. However, the series' 22+-year duration is the longest continuous series of small business performance data. The data continues to be available days, not months or years, after it is collected, and the survey's monthly/quarterly (less-than-annual) nature permits more precision for time-sensitive activity than does annualized numbers.

Population Assessed

Small Business Economic Trends is a private, business association survey. The sampling frame is the 600,000 small business-owner members of the National Federation of Independent Business (NFIB). An initial mailing occurs at the beginning of the month; one reminder follows mid-month. The survey remains in the field about 25 days each month. The response rate averages approximately 30 percent. Both the sampling frame and the response rate raise standard questions about representativeness of the data collected.

The NFIB membership reasonably reflects the small business population as a whole demographically. Survey respondents do as well. However, "reasonable" is a vague term. To be more specific, respondents own modestly larger firms, e.g., 20 percent over 20 employees vis-à-vis 10 percent in the population; over-represent manufacturers and agriculture-related businesses and under-represent services; and, are disproportionately rural and Western—even as they reasonably reflect the population. Small Business Economic Trends carries the industry, size and rural/urban distributions monthly. However, the data files do not contain weights for anyone wishing to weight the sample.

The primary unknown is the self-selection bias associated with business organization membership. Confidential marketing surveys indicate minimal difference in views between NFIB members and the small business owner population on such dimensions as desired business growth, interest in public affairs, business profitability in the last 12 months, readership of newspapers and magazines, and satisfaction with the direction the country is headed. Experiences also appear similar. For example, a recent Gallup poll conducted for NFIB produced a one percentage point difference between the percentage of NFIB members and the population who claimed to have been impacted by the Small Business Administration (Dennis, 1995).

Most survey questions in Small Business Economic Trends are designed to yield trend data rather than level data. For example, responses may be much higher, higher, same, lower, and much lower rather than a blank to provide a number. Trend analysis attacks the potential bias problem, for even if a bias should exist, so long as the bias remains constant over time, the trend is unaffected by it.

The sample creates another problem for users. A new sample is selected each month. Different respondents mean a longitudinal panel of micro-data does not exit. Panels, therefore, must be undertaken with populations, e.g., retailers employing more than 20 people.

Variables Included

Today's NFIB economic survey instrument contains three types of questions: performance, expectation, and demographics. As a general rule, performance and expectation questions are paired. For example, one performance question asks about average price changes experienced in the last three months; a complementary expectations question asks about price changes planned in the next three months. The questionnaire poses paired questions relating to sales, prices, employment, inventory, credit conditions, capital expenditures, and employee compensation. A few are not paired, however. The questionnaire poses questions on expected general business conditions and the climate for small business expansion, expectation questions without parallel performance interrogatories. In contrast, NFIB obtains data on earnings over the last three months and interest rates, but no expectations data on either. Two questions report only the current status: satisfaction with inventory levels and current job openings.

A small number of questions can't be classified by the scheme outlined. These questions ask about the single most important business problem, the rate of interest being paid, the ability to satisfy credit needs, and the type of capital expenditures being made. Demographic questions capture legal status, single-digit SIC, annual gross sales (in classes), employment (in classes), "urban/rural," and state. The questionnaire has remained stable over the years. There have been changes, principally additions, e.g., employee compensation. Thus, most changes imply only a shorter series for affected variables.

Public Availability

The data is available to the public in three forms: the "nets," i.e., the percent favorable minus the percent unfavorable as produced in the monthly Small Business Economic Trends, the percent in each response class to any question(s) over time, and the micro-data for any month. The cost of the data to any user is essentially the cost of preparing a data disk (including time) with the desired information. Requests should be directed to the NFIB Education Foundation in Washington, DC.

Small Business Economic Trends data have two primary research values. The first is to provide a current assessment of the state of the small business economy and to offer small business owner views on what will happen over the next few months. The data were used, for example, to demonstrate that the so-called credit crunch in the late 1980s and early 1990s was very different than the problem continually portrayed in the popular press (Dunkelberg and Dennis, 1992). The second is to explore the relationship of small business to the economy as a whole, and how various parts interact with one another. This research value is expansive. NFIB, for example, uses these data to forecast a number of macro-economic changes including employment and unemployment (Dunkelberg and Dennis, 1986), thereby enhancing small business's credibility as a significant economic sector.

Wells Fargo/NFIB Series on Business Entries and Exits

The Wells Fargo Bank of San Francisco and the NFIB Education Foundation entered a partnership in late 1994 to collect data on business entries and exits. The primary purpose of the project is to estimate the number of business entries (de novo start, purchase, other) and terminations (by closure, sale, transfer, inactivity) on a quarterly basis. The secondary objective was to say something about the people who enter and exit, and the tertiary purpose was to say something about the businesses that "opened" and "closed." This project not only represents a collaborative effort between two organizations, but it involves collection of data from the general population rather than the association membership.

No existing data set provides reasonable estimates of entries and exits or their nature. Without a central registry of businesses (assuming a standard definition of "business" exists) and its accompanying costs, a government agency could not collect them either. The private sector is at liberty to tackle the problem differently.

The basic concept of the Wells Fargo/NFIB Series is to interview a sufficiently large sample of households to be able to reliably estimate the incidence of entry/exit. The corollary is to do so in a cost-efficient manner. Thus, the key to the Wells Fargo/NFIB Series on Business Entries and Exits is employment of the Gallup Organization's omnibus survey. The "omni," in which a series of parties purchase specified survey questions and share demographics, allows NFIB to interview 36,000 adults annually about the business formation/dissolution activity of adults in a household (approximately 72,000 people) at a reasonable cost.

The key assets of the Wells Fargo/NFIB Series are its comprehensiveness and its timeliness. It captures activity found in no other databases in large measure because it doesn't require self-reporting. The series solicits the universe of residents thereby obtaining qualifying behavior whether or not registered elsewhere. Further, differing from the CPS, it is inclusive and not focused on the owner's most important economic activity during the year, and includes personal as well as business data. The series also examines entry and exit closer in time to their actual occurrence than any data yet collected. The primary liability of the series is the limited breadth or depth.

Population Assessed

The sample is drawn from the universe of American households generated by a random-digit-dial technique. NFIB purchases two questions: the first asks every respondent, "In the last six months, have you or has another adult living in your household, alone or with others, started or purchased a business, one with sales or income?" The second asks every respondent, "Are you the owner or part owner of any business that may have become inactive, shut down, sold or transferred in the last six months?" These questions are purposefully designed to capture marginal and part-time activity as well as more substantive organizations with various descriptors, allowing analysts to distinguish between them as desired.

If a respondent provides a positive answer to either or both, the questionnaire poses more detailed queries about the person involved and the business. Thus, the sampling error for the raw entry/exit questions is less than a ±0.5 percent. Since the number of positive respondents to the entry question is about 1,250 and the exit question about 700, the sampling error for any particular characteristic of those entry/exit populations approximates ±2–4 percentage points.

Variables Included

The variables included are prioritized to fulfill the objectives of the project. Those that estimate the entry and exit populations involve: month of entry/exit, form of entry/exit, e.g., start, purchase, number with active partners and number of partners, and multiple entries/exits in a household. Variables related to people entering/exiting include: age, sex, race, immigrant status, education, marital status, employment status 30 days prior to entry and 30 days after exit, hours worked in business, and household income. The third group of variables describe the business: employ people other than the owners, home-based, possession of a business telephone number, and a positive cash flow in last 30 days (exits only). The 1996 edition also included questions on amount of financing used (entries), time needed to raise necessary capital (entries), first month of profitability (entries), and duration of firm (exit) and overall profitability throughout a firm's lifetime (exit).

The set of variables necessary to achieve the first objective will be retained as long as the survey continues. The others are subject to change depending on such factors as general interest, annual variation in the results, and so on.

Availability of the Data

These data are available to researchers for cost-of-data reproduction and attribution of the series sponsors (Wells Fargo/NFIB Education Foundation). However, the data will probably be released from 6 to 12 months after its collection. The first year could take somewhat longer due to the need to produce user documentation. The Gallup Organization maintains the right to review all public release data referencing the company or its name. Researchers may be required to obtain clearance from Gallup or not refer to the company. The data are available from the NFIB Education Foundation (Washington, DC 20024).

Other Private Sources

Data collection can be a profit center for private businesses and nonprofit organizations, though more commonly the function is break-even or ancillary (support) to a primary function. Some firms, however, are in the information business. The most notable in connection with small firms is the for-profit Dun and Bradstreet Corporation. In a different sense, the nonprofit Ewing Marion Kauffman Foundation is an information business as well.

Dun and Bradstreet

Dun and Bradstreet (D&B) still maintains its DMI file, which can be used for research on new and small firms. Its assets and liabilities have been well-documented. The D&B file offers the most contemporaneous, comprehensive, and publicly accessible micro-data in the country. Moreover, the data in the file has been used extensively, and interesting research continues to come from it, e.g., the publications of Cognetics, Inc., in Cambridge, MA. The file is a prime sampling frame, particularly for research involving emerging and larger small firms.

Dun and Bradstreet also produces the New Business Incorporations series and the Business Failure Record. The former provides an actual count of new incorporations by state and quarter. Many have used the series as a proxy for new formations because it is the only series with any longevity that resembles a formations count. However, the desirability of incorporation from the practitioners perspective varies with changes in tax and liability law among other things. Further, most formations are noncorporate. The result is that at best the series is a proxy which must be placed in the current tax and legal contexts.

The Business Failure Record counts the number of firms going out of business and leaving debts by size of debt and state. The file is not necessarily a business bankruptcy record because some firms exit with unpaid debt, but do not formally file for bankruptcy. Unfortunately, D&B's failures are often mistaken for business exits or terminations. But the latter are multiples of the former. Disappearances from the DMI file run about 20 times the number of failures. Inquiries about these data sets should be made of the Economics and Statistics section, Dun and Bradstreet, Wilton, CT.

The Center for Entrepreneurial Leadership
and Ernst and Young Database of Fast-Growth Companies

The National Center for Entrepreneurship Research is a joint venture between Ernst and Young (EY) and the Center for Entrepreneurial Leadership Inc. (CEL) at the Ewing Marion Kauffman Foundation in Kansas City, MO. The Center's database, built around the Ernst and Young Entrepreneur of the Year award recipients, is designed to provide a vehicle for research that will contribute to better understanding of fast-growth firms and to produce findings that enable fast-growth firms to become more successful. Development of the database was launched in 1995, and is expected to become fully operational in March 1997.

The database contains micro-level information on the visions and strategic intentions of entrepreneurs (quantified through content analysis) with longitudinal financial data (balance sheet and income statements) over a three- to five-year period and key financial ratios with industry comparisons provided by Dun and Bradstreet. In addition, each firm's best practices are being recorded in a number of functional areas. By March 1997, the database will include roughly 3,000 firms with median annual sales of about $25 million in roughly 600 SIC codes. Existing data will be updated and an additional 400 to 500 firms will be added annually.

Access to the database for academic, industry, economic development and public policy research will be available on a fee basis. Names and addresses of individual firms will not be released nor will micro-data when there are less than five or fewer firms per cell. Interested researchers should contact Donald Sexton at the Center for Entrepreneurial Leadership Inc. at the Ewing Marion Kauffman Foundation (4900 Oak, Kansas City, MO 64112).

Ad Hoc Data Collection

The data sets previously outlined are time series. With the exception of the CEL/EOYI database, they are not classically longitudinal in the sense that they observe the same firms over time. However, they collect the same (or reasonably same) data at regular intervals. This single characteristic distinguishes the discussed data sets from many in existence. But data sets are often ad hoc, drawn from a single survey or other one time data collection efforts. There is nothing wrong with these sets. Good research can be conducted from them. Further, potential opportunities appear often missed when data sets are cast aside before being fully "milked."

The NFIB Education Foundation among others conducts a variety of ad hoc surveys, mail and telephone, across the NFIB membership and across the population as a whole. Since each has different parameters and subject matter, generalization about them is difficult. For present purposes, the most interesting is New Business in America: The Firms and Their Owners, a three-year longitudinal study of nearly

3,000 new businesses, all NFIB members (Cooper et al., 1990). These data are currently not available in the public domain.

Conclusion

This chapter has been selective in the data sets chosen for discussion. A reasonable argument can be made for the inclusion of others. Certainly, County Business Patterns and Enterprise Statistics on the public side could have been mentioned. The data of Venture Economics, Robert Morris Associates, PIMS, Link Resources, various polling firms and trade associations could have been discussed on the private side. There are also projects like the Panel Study on Income Dynamics (PSID) conducted at the University of Michigan with public and private money.

The notion that choices must be made among a series of data sets, many of which have similar worth, is itself instructive. It underscores the point that small business data sets and other data sets having small business value are highly fragmented. They are located in various places, follow varying formats, employ assorted definitions, possess different foci and are generally unrelated. In particular, few bridges tie the individual to the firm. Both usually appear in not so splendid isolation. Moreover, the utility of even these data sets can rapidly change. Sometimes the mere addition or deletion of a single firm size variable can make an entire data set very helpful or negate its small business value altogether.

This fragmentation is not expected to change much in the immediate future. It may even grow worse. Federal budget cutbacks are a fact of life. The implication is that many existing data series are in jeopardy; expansion of useful series or creating new ones are highly unlikely. Even data collection efforts sponsored by the Federal Government are becoming more difficult. The clearance process now requires a 90-day review (minimum) at the Office of Management and Budget (OMB) and 60-day announcement in the Federal Register.

Efficiencies in some of the available sets can be made. And while efficiencies may not provide more data or even better bridging among data sets, they may increase the utility of what we now possess. Adding C-corporations under a certain size to the CBO would produce far better data with negligible cost implications, for example, but even with greater efficiency researchers will increasingly rely on the private sector and public/private cooperative endeavors for their data.

Researchers must be prepared not only to investigate small business-specific data sets but subject matter data sets as well. These sets may be difficult to locate, but many will contain the critical firm size variable (or at least an establishment size variable). Many will be ad hoc sets and have been mined previously. Researchers must also be prepared to work with the sponsoring organization to achieve the objectives of both. That is not so much a threat to the intellectual integrity of the researcher as it is a serious additional demand on time and attention. Finally, researchers must understand that they are in the data collection business. Differing from colleagues in such disciplines as economics or sociology, those in small business and entrepreneurship rarely have the luxury of large publicly available data sets ripe for manipulation. In Chapter 17 of this book, Aldrich and Baker note the dependence of small business and entrepreneurship research on surveys. The implication is that even now, let alone in the future, researchers must be grounded in practical data collection methods including surveys whether or not they intend to use them.

This chapter has noted many publicly available data sets. Technology and budget considerations, not only in government but in the private sector, are having a pronounced effect on how producers deliver these data. Public access information, including unidentified micro-data, will increasingly be put on the Internet where users can grab and manipulate it. Greater use of the Internet by producers of data enhances researcher awareness of data availability and eliminates everything from the time and cost inherent in making the data request to the time and cost of filling it. The implication, of course, is not only computer literacy from the perspective of users, but greater literacy from the perspective of producers as the people available to answer questions relating to such matters as documentation shrink.

The amount of data on small business and entrepreneurship will increase as we move into the 21st century because people recognize the sector's importance and because the sector is politically popular. The increases will not be as rapid or as coordinated as advocates would like for the reasons cited above. But, we are headed in the right direction, even if that direction is not always straight.

REFERENCES

Berney, R.E., and B.D. Phillips. 1995. Small Business and Job Creation: An Update. Presented at the Conference on the Dynamics of Employment and Industry Evaluation, Mannheim, Germany.

Birch, D.L. 1979. The Job Generation Process. MIT Program on Neighborhood and Regional Change, Cambridge, MA.

Cooper, A.C., W.C. Dunkelberg, C. Woo, and W.J. Dennis, Jr. 1990, *New Business in America: The Owners and Their Firms*. Washington, DC: NFIB Education Foundation.

Dennis, W.J., Jr. 1995. *Small Business and the Future of SBA*, Small Business Matters. Washington, DC: NFIB Education Foundation.

Dunkelberg, W.C., and W.J. Dennis, Jr. 1986. *Small Business Forecasts of National Labor Market Changes: Business Cycle Surveys in the Assessment of Economic Activity*. Aldershot, UK: Gower Publishing Company.

Dunkelberg, W.C., and W.J. Dennis, Jr. 1992. *The Small Business Credit Crunch.* Washington, DC: NFIB Education Foundation.

Employment-Based Health Benefits: 1994. Analysis of the April 1993 Current Population Survey. EBRI Special Report and Issue Brief Number 152.

Financial Characteristics of High-Income Families. 1989. Federal Reserve Bulletin, March.

Kennickell, A.B., and M. Starr-McCluer. 1995. *Changes in Family Finances from 1989 to 1992: Evidence from the Survey of Consumer Finances.* Federal Reserve Bulletin, October, 861-882.

Pratt, J.H. 1993. *Myths and Realities of Working at Home: Characteristics of Home-Based Business Owners and Telecommuters,* Prepared for the Office of Advocacy, Small Business Administration, March.

Segal, L.W. 1996 (forthcoming). Flexible employment: Composition and trends. *Journal of Labor Research.*

State of Small Business: A Report to the President. 1994. Washington, DC: Government Printing Office.

CHAPTER 16

Relevance in Entrepreneurship Research

FRANK HOY

T HE THESAURUS SHOWS "RELEVANT" TO BE A SYNONYM for "applicable." This chapter begs the rhetorical question, Is entrepreneurship research being applied? Would a review of the academic literature on entrepreneurship reveal theories, observations, and prescriptions that address the needs and concerns of practitioners? More directly, if we were to survey practitioners, could they identify any scholars who contributed to their understanding of the entrepreneurial process? Would practitioners trade the last 10 years of advances in another field, say the management of quality, for the advances in entrepreneurship? Would they agree that scholars are researching the right problems—the problems that matter in their day-to-day lives in business?

Each of the three books preceding this one in the state-of-the-art series contains calls for relevance in entrepreneurship research. This chapter reviews those earlier calls, identifies stakeholders for entrepreneurship research, compares recent published research with stakeholder proxies, examines the environment for fostering relevant research, and discusses mechanisms for communicating with stakeholders.

Calls For Relevance

Concerns for relevance appeared at the origin of this series in the first book, *Encyclopedia of Entrepreneurship* (1982). In Scott's foreword and Kent et al.'s preface, the authors emphasize that entrepreneurship research should impact public policy regarding venture initiation. Peterson and Horvath, in their commentary on

Research in the Field of Entrepreneurship, cautioned researchers to avoid the pattern of scholars in other fields "to learn more and more about less and less."

Editors Sexton and Smilor repeated the concern expressed in the *Encyclopedia* in their preface to *The Art and Science of Entrepreneurship* (1986, xvi): "The study of entrepreneurship has a much more important function than the satisfaction of intellectual curiosity. Basic research must lead to applications in industry and in the public as well as the private sector." In their chapter on "Entrepreneurship Research: Direction and Methods," Churchill and Lewis (1986) reiterated the point that research should give attention to significant questions, i.e., those that will be fruitful for both theory and practice. They followed their charge by acknowledging the dilemma that the applied nature of entrepreneurship research could pose a threat to junior scholars. They recognized the propensity of the academic community to denigrate applied studies.

In the third edition in the series, *The State of the Art of Entrepreneurship*, Hughes in his foreword, and Block and Stumpf in their chapter, "Entrepreneurship Education Research: Experience and Challenge," introduce the landmark study by Porter and McKibbin (1988) conducted on behalf of the American Assembly of Collegiate Schools of Business (AACSB). Porter and McKibbin collected data from multiple stakeholders of business education. The impact of their findings on the AACSB and higher education in business is discussed later in this chapter. One observation they made was that most research by business faculty in general had little if any influence on practitioners. Once again, the editors of the book, Sexton and Kasarda in this case, called for research that would be useful for practitioners and policymakers. Churchill echoed the need for research that could be applied by practitioners in his chapter, "Research Issues in Entrepreneurship."

Obviously, the concern for relevance in entrepreneurship research is not new. The recurrence of such calls may indicate that the responses have not been satisfactory. One interesting point to note in the above review is the frequency with which public policymakers are mentioned. In other arenas of business research, appeals to relevance are almost exclusively directed toward the practitioner constituencies. Entrepreneurship scholars apparently recognize multiple stakeholders.

Who Are the Stakeholders?

Clearly, there is wide acceptance of the notion that academic research should have relevance beyond a small network of scholars. Consistent with prior contributors to the state-of-the-art series, this author identified four audiences for entrepreneurship research: colleagues, students, practitioners, and public policy formulators. Katz (1994) also linked stakeholders to prospective communication outlets. This is discussed later in the chapter. The issue being addressed is not exclusively about a belief in relevance, but if in fact it is being achieved. First, consider what relevance means to each stakeholder group.

Communicating research results to faculty is a multifaceted phenomenon. Faculty colleagues read one another's work to advance their knowledge of the field; to contribute to their own research projects; to introduce recent findings to students and practitioners through teaching, training, and consulting; and to evaluate scholarship for tenure and promotion recommendations.

In a globally competitive environment, business faculty in general, and entrepreneurship professors specifically, rely on sound research results to convey useful theories, concepts, and observations to students. Two forces are broadening the definition of student: the acceptance of the notion of lifelong learning and the development of new instructional technologies.

Thus, the border between students and practitioners is no longer clear. Numerous entrepreneurship education programs are characterized by actual enterprise start-ups by students (Mehta, 1996). What has become evident in complex economic environments is that education has value to practitioners. The problem is how to translate and convey the findings of the academy to practical applications.

Public policymakers have traditionally turned to universities for accurate and objective research studies to assist in the formulation of legislation, regulation, and general policy. Examples could be cited from medicine, science, agriculture, engineering, and other fields. The most influential business-related field to date has been economics. Policymakers began to acknowledge the role of small business in the economy and the importance of entrepreneurial strategies for U.S. businesses in the late 1970s (Birch, 1979). Entrepreneurship scholars have the potential of having a major impact on government actions.

The list could be extended to include other stakeholders. University administrators, representatives of the news media, the public at-large in the community being served, countries interested in entrepreneurship as an economic development strategy, and others have stakes in the outcomes of relevant research. The question is, To what degree are the various constituents are being served?

Matching Research to Practice

White House Conferences

In an article published in the *American Journal of Small Business* in 1987, Brockhaus (1987) asked entrepreneurship researchers, "Are we playing the correct game?" He devised an imaginary scenario in which two baseball teams meet to play a championship game. On arriving at the stadium, they discover the field is laid out for football. Undeterred, they arrange a diamond and a mound and engage in vigorous competition. At the conclusion of the game, the spectators are disgruntled and confused—they came to see football. This reaction startles and annoys the players:

> They fret that they were not football players, they were trained to be baseball players and that is all we should be expected to play. Their attitude was that they will continue to play only baseball even if the field is designed for football and the spectators want to see football. Sure, the method of play and results may not be worthwhile to the spectators now but, perhaps, someday they will see the value of our efforts.

Brockhaus raised the question of whether entrepreneurship scholars were demonstrating a similar attitude of arrogance to their practitioner audience by ignoring the priorities of business owners and devoting their efforts to their own interests. He used the top issues from the 1986 White House Conference on Small Business as a proxy for relevancy, i.e., the topics encompassed by the eleven central issues from the conference were assumed to be the most relevant to small business owners and public policymakers at that point in time. Brockhaus compared those eleven items with articles published in three academic journals and papers included in the proceedings from three small business/entrepreneurship conferences. He found only three articles published and three papers presented in 1986 that directly converged with any of the eleven issues. Thirty-two articles and papers were peripherally related to the White House issues. He found no published research for four issues and concluded that although there was evidence of some research activity applicable to the most important concerns of small business owners, major gaps in satisfying practical needs existed.

The Brockhaus study has been partially replicated as one proxy for relevance. This proxy excludes corporate entrepreneurship and only tangentially relates to the process of starting a venture. Nevertheless, attendees at the White House Conference can be assumed to be politically aware and concerned for initiation, survival, growth, and wealth creation and retention of independent businesses. The first White House Conference since 1986 was held in Washington, DC, in June 1995. Eleven issue areas were predefined for the conferees: capital formation, community development, environmental policy, human capital, international trade, main street, procurement, regulation and paperwork, taxation, technology, and unclassified. Based on attendance at breakout sessions and on the number of recommendations adopted, the White House Conference on Small Business Commission (1995) identified four small business policy priorities:

❖ Tax Relief

❖ Regulatory Relief

❖ Access to Capital

❖ Access to Information

In this replication, articles and papers were classified by these priorities rather than by the eleven issue areas from the 1986 Conference.

The same three journals that Brockhaus used were selected as the research sources. It should be noted that the name of the *American Journal of Small Business* was changed in 1989 to *Entrepreneurship Theory and Practice* (ET&P). The name change was accompanied by a change in mission from a journal that attempted to bridge academics and practitioners to one targeted specifically toward a scholarly audience. To ensure adequate inclusion of global research, three international journals were added for the analysis: *Entrepreneurship, Innovation and Change* (EIC), *Entrepreneurship and Regional Development* (ERD), and *Small Business Economics* (SBE). Although the three U.S.-based journals all solicit and publish international articles, the three foreign journals were included to ensure that there was an adequate representation of articles directed at audiences outside of the United States.

Two of the same conference proceedings were used, the Babson College/Kauffman Foundation Entrepreneurship Research Conference (*Frontiers of Entrepreneurship Research*, or FER) and the International Council for Small Business Conference (ICSB). The proceedings from the Academy of Management (AOM) were substituted for those of the Small Business Institute Directors' Association (SBIDA) because of the termination of federal funding for the SBI program, as well as the assumption that Academy of Management presentations are more research-oriented than those occurring at SBIDA meetings. One additional modification to the Brockhaus design was that the review of articles in this chapter covered January 1993 to March 1996, rather than a single year.

The methodology for categorizing the articles and papers shown in Tables 16.1 to 16.3 follows Brockhaus (1987) who, in turn, cited Churchill and Lewis (1986). Table 16.1 on p. 366 contains the count for articles published in the three journals (originally selected by Brockhaus) by White House Conference issue group.

For 1986, Brockhaus tallied eight issue-related articles in these three journals, three of which were classified as directly convergent. Over the most recent three-year period, 31 articles were counted, showing a slight increase to just over 10 per year. The large number of almost convergent articles under the capital issue reflects the published research on formal and informal venture capital, whereas small business owners were expressing concern over availability of financing through banks and

TABLE 16.1
Analysis of White House Conference Issues
by Three U.S.-Based Journals, January 1993 to March 1996

Issue	ET&P	JBV	JSBM	Total
Taxes			1A	1A
Regulation			2A	2A
Capital	1C	1C	4C	6C
		11A	4A	15A
Information	1C			1C
	1A	2A	3A	6A

ET&P = *Entrepreneurship Theory and Practice*
JBV = *Journal of Business Venturing*
JSBM = *Journal of Small Business Management*
A = Almost convergent to core issue
C = Convergent to core issue

TABLE 16.2
Analysis of White House Conference Issues
by Three International Journals, January 1993 to March 1996

Issue	EIC	ERD	SBE	Total
Taxes				
Regulation		1A		1A
Capital			5C	5C
	2A	4A	6A	12A
Information		1C		1C
	1A	4C		5C

EIC = *Entrepreneurship, Innovation and Change* (New York: Plenum)
ERD = *Entrepreneurship and Regional Development* (London: Taylor and Francis)
SBE = *Small Business Economics* (Dordrecht, Holland: Kluwer)

various government incentives and disincentives regarding capital access, accumulation, and use.

Table 16.2 reports the issue-related article counts for three journals based outside the United States.

In these journals, 24 relevant articles were found, or eight per year. It is not surprising that international journals would attend less to White House issues; however, one might reasonably expect that taxes, regulation, capital, and information are of fairly universal importance to practitioners and policymakers. Interestingly, 11 articles in these journals were convergent to the core issues, versus seven in the U.S. journals.

Next, Table 16.3 displays the counts of relevant paper presentations at three academic/professional conferences.

The analysis of Table 16.3 shows a considerable amount of activity at conferences over the three-year period regarding access to capital and to information. Overall, the four White House issues were addressed an average of nearly 34 times each year. In 1986, the *Frontiers of Entrepreneurship Research* contained 11 almost convergent papers. For the 1993–95 period, the *Frontiers* included just over 19 papers per year (58 total), five of which were convergent to core issues.

What other topics were covered by these journals and proceedings? Themes that were addressed in multiple articles and papers in at least three journals and/or pro-

TABLE 16.3
Analysis of White House Conference Issues
by Three Conference Proceedings, 1993 to 1995

Issue	AOM	FER	ICSB	Total
Taxes			2A	2A
Regulation	1C	1C	1C	3C
		1A		1A
Capital	1C	4C	2C	7C
	5A	34A	7A	46A
Information		3C	16C	19C
		15A	8A	23A

AOM = Academy of Management
FER = *Frontiers of Entrepreneurship Research*
ICSB = International Council for Small Business

ceedings include: ethics, marketing, effectiveness, survival/failure, strategic management/planning, international (primarily exporting), health care, franchising, family business, valuation, corporate entrepreneurship, networks, boards of directors, research methods, innovation, personality/psychology, negotiation, culture, quality, technology, strategic alliances/joint ventures, and human resource management. Virtually all these subjects have both applied and basic research dimensions. There was considerable similarity between topics covered by U.S. and international journals and proceedings.

In summary, issues of concern to small business practitioners that are on their agenda for policy formulators were discussed more frequently in research venues in the mid-1990s than in 1986. Not only did the frequency increase within a comparable set of outlets, but also there has been an expansion in the number of outlets for entrepreneurship research, both journals and conferences. Katz (1991) reported only one English-language small business/entrepreneurship journal originating in the 1960s, one in the 1970s, three in the 1980s before 1986, and six more founded after 1986. Thus, there is both greater depth of attention within journals and proceedings and greater breadth of journal and proceedings offerings.

Books and Magazines

The three state-of-the-art volumes that preceded the present book not only called for relevant research, they also included chapters covering applied topics, such as availability and acquisition of capital and information and education issues. Virtually no attention was given to taxation or regulation, however.

A limited review of other research compilations turned up very little applied research. Two publishing houses, JAI Press and North-Holland, have launched research series. The JAI list is almost exclusively devoted to basic research; North-Holland's contains more applied titles. It is truly global in its coverage of material, samples, and authors, containing topics relevant to public policy, although few overlap with the four White House issues.

One other proxy for relevance consists of magazines directed toward the practitioner-entrepreneur. There has been a proliferation of magazines in the past 20 years targeting independent business owners, prospective business owners, owners and managers of high-growth firms, franchisers and franchisees, and others who fall within the entrepreneurship domain. Many of these magazines report on academic research and researchers.

For example, *Inc.* magazine profiled David Birch and other university-based scholars who have specialized in examining the role of new and small businesses in generating jobs. Later, *Inc.* published a list of the top entrepreneurship researchers in the

United States. *Success* magazine reported on "The 25 Best Business Schools for Entrepreneurs." *Nation's Business* magazine often includes academic contributors in its Family Business section.

Although the impact is not clear, this analysis suggests two important findings. First, the volume of academic research focusing on topics of relevance has increased in the past 10 years. Second, information regarding university-based research and education is becoming more widely disseminated through a variety of scholarly and trade media.

An Environment for Relevance

A handicap to achieving relevance in scholarly research has been the lack of incentives in academia. In fact, many reward systems provide disincentives for applied, practical research efforts. Two major factors have contributed to this phenomenon.

First, institutional rankings tend to be a function of scholarly productivity. Rankings are generally a function of reputation. Faculty and administrators external to an institution seldom have measures of teaching or service for the institution. They are more likely to rely on frequency of publication in journals that target academic audiences. The more prestigious journals specialize in basic rather than applied or instructional research. Merit and promotion and tenure policies follow the criteria for institutional rankings and reward publications that are peer-reviewed and read. Such articles and papers are rarely directed toward other constituencies.

Second, career mobility is usually a function of basic research productivity. To be attractive to other universities, faculty must establish their reputations within a field. Again, this is achieved not by teaching or service, but by publishing articles in scholarly journals. The most prestigious journals are virtually exclusively directed at academic audiences.

The field of entrepreneurship has made remarkable advances in academic acceptance in recent years. The advances result largely from the discovery of a huge latent market for entrepreneurship education. Measures of growth for the field include an increase in course offerings from a handful of schools in the mid-1970s to hundreds 20 years later, the number of endowed chairs and professorships funded, and the proliferation of journals (Katz, 1991). The reputations of journals such as the *Journal of Business Venturing* and *Entrepreneurship Theory and Practice* have contributed to peer acceptance. Both of these journals seek to demonstrate to academics in more established fields that entrepreneurship research has rigorous scholarly standards.

Porter and McKibbin (1988) reminded academics that they did not exist in a closed system—that there are other stakeholders who were not being satisfied by research read only by faculty colleagues. In particular, the investigation uncovered the dissatisfaction of corporate executives with business education. The report triggered a major shift in the posture of the American Assembly of Collegiate Schools of Business (AACSB), the foremost accrediting body of business schools in the United States. In 1992, the AACSB adopted new procedures and standards for evaluating accreditation.

Changes by the AACSB of significance to this discussion of relevance include the decision to evaluate the mission statements of business schools. The AACSB requires that mission statements stress quality business education and demand continuous improvement. Schools are then assessed according to their progress toward fulfilling their missions. For some mission-driven schools, this allows the flexibility to emphasize emerging fields, such as entrepreneurship. They can also choose to concentrate on applied or instructional research if such research meets the needs of their constituents better than basic research.

As implied above, another change is the recognition that basic research is not the only type of intellectual contribution that has value. Applied and instructional research are treated equally by the AACSB in the new standards. Schools are expected to identify the amount of emphasis to apply to each category according to their missions. This permits a business school to encourage faculty to engage in applied, practical intellectual contributions if the mission emphasizes teaching.

Hence, two driving forces are creating an environment conducive to increasing the relevance of entrepreneurship research. The first has been the broadening and deepening of the acceptance of entrepreneurship as a discipline worthy of teaching and research. The second is the change in the accrediting process that permits and even encourages flexibility in the provision of incentives for alternative research regimens. This environment supportive of relevance in research allows entrepreneurship scholars to attempt to reach a wider variety of stakeholders.

Reaching Stakeholders

Multiple stakeholders for entrepreneurship research are readily identifiable. In addition, the environment for conducting relevant research has improved. Two issues remain to be resolved by researchers: How do they grasp relevant research topics, and how do they communicate their findings to the stakeholders? In some ways these two issues go hand in hand.

The White House Conference posits one set of issues of concern to small business owners and to policymakers. To provide a twist to much of the foregoing discussion, it can be argued that basic research issues themselves may be relevant to one or more groups of stakeholders. Academia has a societal obligation to conduct investigations that practitioners may criticize as abstract, narrow, or pointless. Academia performs an integrative role for society, one of observing, evaluating, and explaining phenomena. Just as the entrepreneur creates disequilibrium in the marketplace, the entrepreneurship scholar should not be restricted to following trends that have been identified by others. The greatest practical contribution may occur as a result of investigating an issue that has not caught anyone else's attention.

Sources for relevant research issues are, therefore, as varied as the prospective issues themselves. They include the stakeholders, including academic colleagues, who may be impacted by the results of the studies. They should also include novel and unpredictable sources that may currently be outside the bounds of what we define as our domain. Entrepreneurship scholars, perhaps more than most of our peers in other fields, should engage in environmental scanning, explaining both obvious patterns and apparently aberrant behavior. Anthropology, economics, psychology, and sociology have been fertile sources for theories, constructs, and methodologies for entrepreneurship research. Much could be learned from education, engineering, history, and journalism among others, as well.

Although the literature review summarized in this chapter focused on issues identified by practitioners, the journals and proceedings scanned contained articles and papers covering many other topics that have potential relevance for stakeholders. Regardless of the practicality of the information in these articles and papers, they have the potential of being applied only if stakeholders gain exposure to them. In other words, research findings must be in the marketplace if they are to be tested in the marketplace.

Journals and proceedings have already been introduced as mechanisms for reaching the collegial constituency. Textbooks and classrooms are the traditional means of conveying knowledge of the field to students. There are also a number of traditional routes to convey research results to practitioners. These include consulting, training, public speaking, and writing and marketing popular books that translate arcane verbiage for the layperson.

Katz (1994) provided an excellent overview of the relevancy problem, explaining the disaffection of entrepreneurs from academic publications, redefining Hoy's four audiences into "key publics" for entrepreneurship research, and ranking research topics by key publics. Katz then discussed forums for entrepreneurship research, noting that there were virtual null sets for means of communicating academic-to-entrepreneur or academic-to-policymaker.

Katz proposed that advances in technology might offer a solution. He observed an increasing use of the Internet combined with increasing access to electronic and CD-ROM databases by both academics and practitioners. Katz predicted both positive and negative developments. Entrepreneurs who review exchanges between academics will be critical of the use of obscure jargon and the apparent lack of concern for application. Alternatively, electronic media introduce the possibility of interactive learning opportunities for practitioners with academics rather than the traditional reactive modes of books and journals. We are already seeing efforts by elected officials to encourage their constituents to communicate with them via e-mail, which presents opportunities for academics to convey information to policymakers.

What will catch the attention of public policy formulators and their staffs? At any point in time, there are high-visibility, topical issues on which background material can be helpful, such as those identified at the White House Conference. Additionally, there are permanent vested interests in the political environment which relate to entrepreneurship research. The most obvious of these fall under the umbrella of economic development. Examples include the role of venture creation as a job generator, the contributions of small businesses to the balance of trade as exporters, and the impact of taxation and regulation on enterprise survival and growth.

How do academics communicate with policymakers? A typical pattern involves the submission of a proposal for funded research, often in response to a specific request for proposals. The researcher completes the task, writes a report with appropriate disclaimers, then presents the results to the funding agency. The academic researcher tends to be proactive in seeking resources for investigations, but reactive in presenting the results of the studies. More proactive steps are available. At a minimum, the author should ensure that results are clearly communicated, without compromising the integrity of the study. A more aggressive stance would be to supply research results to cognizant officials who have not underwritten the investigation. Yet another approach is active involvement in partisan politics. Such involvement may jeopardize the researcher's reputation for objectivity, but it may facilitate direct influence on a public policymaker.

Conclusions

Primary conclusions regarding the relevance of entrepreneurship research are as follows:

❖ Academic scholars are engaging in research efforts that are applicable to stakeholders, although there continue to be gaps in which the interests of some constituents are not being addressed.

❖ The volume of applied research is increasing.

❖ The number of vehicles through which research can be published or presented is increasing.

❖ Traditional academic media do not reach practitioners or public policymakers.

❖ Alternative media, particularly as a result of telecommunication advances, are available to permit academic-to-practitioner and academic-to-policy-maker communication.

❖ Universities will continue to play a role in basic research, which may, at best, be indirectly applicable to nonacademic stakeholders.

There are some indications that the calls for relevant research originating with the *Encyclopedia of Entrepreneurship* are being heeded. A replication of the 1987 Brockhaus study indicates an increase in the volume of entrepreneurship that can be described as relevant. There is also evidence that public awareness of entrepreneurship education is growing and that researchers are studying more entrepreneurial phenomena.

Despite the volume and visibility of research activity, external stakeholders continue to be uninformed of entrepreneurship research findings or skeptical of the value of the contributions. This suggests that work remains to be done. Two obvious courses of action for entrepreneurship researchers are to use language that communicates clearly to stakeholders and to find new media by which to transmit their findings to a wider spectrum of audiences.

One cautionary note: satisfying one set of constituents (academic colleagues) carries with it some risk of losing relevance to other constituents. Mainstream acceptance of journal publications by academic colleagues is essential to entrepreneurship faculty in receiving positive promotion and tenure decisions. The risk of becoming mainstream is, as stipulated earlier, saying more and more about less and less. The most defensible research designs are narrow and specialized with the investigator able to exercise control over variables. Applied research is more likely to occur in the field, be complex, and lack controls. Additionally, entrepreneurship research, like the entrepreneurial event itself, may violate prior contexts and patterns. It is also more apt to be interdisciplinary, which may preclude publication in discipline-based journals.

Fortunately, the evolving academic environment may favor entrepreneurial studies. The AACSB acknowledgment of the legitimacy of applied research, combined with its support of integrated studies, allows for greater acceptability of relevant research. A continuing flow of relevance through the research pipeline will be a function of faculty members ensuring that doctoral students learn the value of applied research as they complete their apprenticeships. Finally, we all carry an obligation to feed the results of entrepreneurship back to the classroom and avoid the reliance on static texts.

This chapter began by asking whether entrepreneurship research is being applied. The answer is ambiguous. Trend analysis indicates an increase in research publications of practical and applicable research findings. Some evidence also points to a growing awareness of university-based research and educational programs in entrepreneurship. There is less evidence that applied findings are being effectively communicated from the academic arena to policymakers and practitioners. The challenge for the 21st century appears to be for entrepreneurship researchers to be entrepreneurial in communicating their results—to innovate in finding channels that reach their varied constituencies.

REFERENCES

Birch, D.L. 1979. *The Job Generation Process*. Cambridge, MA: MIT Program on Neighborhood and Regional Change.

Block, Z., and S.A. Stumpf. 1992. Entrepreneurship education research: Experience and challenge. In D.L. Sexton and J.D. Kasarda (eds.): *The State of the Art of Entrepreneurship*. Boston: PWS Kent, 17-42.

Brockhaus, R.H., Sr. 1987. Entrepreneurial research: Are we playing the correct game? *American Journal of Small Business* 11(3):43-50.

Churchill, N.C. 1992. Research issues in entrepreneurship. In D.L. Sexton and J.D. Kasarda (eds.): *The State of the Art of Entrepreneurship*. Boston: PWS Kent. 579-646.

Churchill, N.C., and V.L. Lewis. 1986. Entrepreneurship research: Directions and Methods. In D.L. Sexton and R.W. Smilor (eds.): *The Art and Science of Entrepreneurship*. Cambridge, MA: Ballinger, 333-366.

Hughes, J.E. 1992. Foreword. In D.L. Sexton and J.D. Kasarda (eds.): *The State of the Art of Entrepreneurship*. Boston: PWS Kent, xiv-xvi.

Katz, J.A. 1991. The institution and infrastructure of entrepreneurship. *Entrepreneurship Theory & Practice* 15(3):85-102.

Katz, J.A. 1994. Markets for entrepreneurship knowledge: Identifying opportunities and forums for new exchanges of findings from research and practice. In W.D. Bygrave et al. (eds.): *Frontiers of Entrepreneurship Research*. Wellesley, MA: Babson College.

Kent, C.A., D.L. Sexton, and K.H. Vesper (eds.). 1982. *Encyclopedia of Entrepreneurship*. Englewood Cliffs, NJ: Prentice Hall.

Mehta, S.N. 1996. More students start businesses while in school. *Wall Street Journal*, May 6, pp. B1, B7.

Peterson, R., and D. Horvath. 1982. Commentary on research in the field of entrepreneurship. In C.A. Kent, D.L. Sexton, and K.H. Vesper (eds.): *Encyclopedia of Entrepreneurship*. Englewood Cliffs, NJ: Prentice Hall, 374-376.

Porter, L.W., and L.E. McKibbin. 1988. *Management Education and Development: Drift or Thrust into the 21st Century?* New York: McGraw-Hill.

Scott, R.C. 1982. Foreword. In C.A. Kent, D.L. Sexton, and K.H. Vesper (eds.): *Encyclopedia of Entrepreneurship*. Englewood Cliffs, NJ: Prentice Hall, xxvii-xxviii.

Sexton, D.L., and J.D. Kasarda (eds.). 1992. *The State of the Art of Entrepreneurship*. Boston: PWS Kent.

Sexton, D.L., and R.W. Smilor (eds.). 1986. *The Art and Science of Entrepreneurship*. Cambridge, MA: Ballinger Publishing.

White House Conference on Small Business Commission. 1995. Foundation for a new century: A report to the President and Congress. Office of the President of the United States, September. Washington, DC: Government Printing Office.

CHAPTER 17

Blinded by the Cites? Has There Been Progress in Entrepreneurship Research?

HOWARD E. ALDRICH

AND

TED BAKER

A T THE FIRST TWO STATE-OF-THE-ART CONFERENCES ON entrepreneurship, authors were highly critical of entrepreneurship research, faulting it for sloppy thinking and shoddy methods. At the third state-of-the-art book, Aldrich (1992) noted that the field had expanded its repertoire of research designs and analytic techniques, but he concluded his review on an ambiguous note. Rather than directly answering the question of whether entrepreneurship research had made progress, he argued that the answer depended upon one's assumptions about the scientific and normative structure of the field. He posed three viewpoints: a unitary, normal science view, a multiple paradigm view, and a totally pragmatic view. In this chapter the past five years' research is examined using a three-part framework.

Three Views

Three possible views of the norms governing entrepreneurship research are based on different assumptions about what counts for "progress" in the field of entrepreneurship research and how it can be achieved. First, people with a unified or normal science view hold as their ideal the accumulation of empirically-tested hypotheses and well-grounded generalizations, developed through rigorous research designs, quantitative data, and the latest statistical techniques. Based on strong theories, investigators test hypotheses to replicate and confirm previous findings, using negative findings and disconfirmations of previous work as a signal that theories must be modified. Continuity with the past is the order of the day (Aldrich et al., 1994). Units of analysis are carefully chosen to reflect theoretical considerations, rather than by the pragmatics of data collection. Sampling issues are given high priority, as investigators search for the bounds to their empirical generalizations (McKelvey and Aldrich, 1983).

Second, people with a more eclectic view of entrepreneurship research emphasize the importance of diversity in theories and methods. Low and MacMillan (1988, 154), for example, noted the wide variety of disciplines involved in entrepreneurship research. Rather than lamenting disagreements between various subgroups of entrepreneurship researchers, advocates for diversity welcome the invigorating effect of multiple perspectives and methods on research. If a multiple-paradigm perspective was adopted, one would neither expect nor wish for complete convergence in methods. Instead, different subfields would have different standards against which to judge research design and execution, and perhaps even their own journals.

Third, if a more pragmatic approach is adopted, one that focuses on the importance of the issues addressed, the question of research methods assumes a secondary role. From this point of view, methods should be chosen to match researchers' purposes, and these will change as conditions change. In entrepreneurship research, pragmatism may be oriented toward either policy or practitioner concerns. Positive values will be placed on topicality, uniqueness, and usefulness rather than adherence to a confining code of research practices. Indeed, rewards for peculiarity and topical value can create feedback loops that destroy researchers' commitment to normal science norms, promoting greater pursuit of uniqueness rather than continuity (Mone and McKinley, 1993). As the previous reviews are summarized, findings for trends over the past five years will be used as benchmarks against which to evaluate the results.

Previous Reviews

At the first state-of-the-art conference, Paulin et al. (1982) found more formal research on entrepreneurship than they had anticipated, and they also discerned a trend toward more systematic, empirical methods. They were fairly critical of the state of the art, however, arguing that much of the "knowledge" in the field was based on untested or anecdotal wisdom. They called for more diversity in research methods; specifically, they advocated more field studies and experiments, longitudinal studies, and rigorous statistical analyses. Peterson and Horvath (1982) appealed for more cross-national studies, as well as more precise and meaningful definitions of research questions. In contrast, Perryman (1982) defended the imprecision and chaos of the emerging field, arguing that entrepreneurship research was still in its "pre-science" phase.

At the second conference, Wortman (1986) cast a withering glance on the state of the art, and pronounced it decidedly inferior to the research methods being used in other social science fields. Not only did he excoriate entrepreneurship researchers for their weak statistical analyses, but he also advocated a single unifying framework that would integrate entrepreneurship and small business research. At the same conference, Churchill and Lewis (1986) took a more sympathetic view of the field, using a systematic review of Babson Conference papers and 10 academic journals to build empirical generalizations about entrepreneurship research methods. They seconded Perryman's (1982) observation that the field was still in its infancy and hence dependent on exploratory research and simple statistics. The other methods paper at the second conference (Carsrud et al., 1986) reprised Wortman's theme.

In the third state-of-the-art book, Aldrich (1992) replicated Churchill and Lewis's (1986) analysis, and found strong continuity in research methods across all three conferences. Entrepreneurship research was still very much a monomethod field, dependent on mailed surveys and other questionnaire-based techniques, with fairly unsophisticated data analyses. Field-based research designs were notable by their absence.

Beginning in the late 1980s, other voices were added to those of state-of-the-art reviewers calling for more explicit attention to research methods. In 1986, Churchill and Lewis found only six papers—all presented at conferences between 1981 and 1984—that dealt with methodological improvements in the field. In this review of the literature, at least 16 journal articles published between 1987 and 1993 were found that either provided general reviews of methods or advocated a particular remedy to what were seen as methodological deficiencies. The heightened level of self-consciousness about how research is carried out indicated that some investigators were trying to push the field toward a more "normal science" posture, whereas others were resisting attempts at "premature closure."

Bringing the Field up to Date

To maintain continuity with past reviews, the same strategy as our predecessors was used in organizing and defining the field of entrepreneurship research. The Babson College Entrepreneurship Conference is still the premier venue for disseminating unpublished research on entrepreneurship, and all the articles and summaries in the 1990 and 1994 conference volumes were examined.

Aldrich (1992) followed Churchill and Lewis's procedures for choosing the 10 academic journals that published a large number of entrepreneurship articles, and he added the *Journal of Business Venturing* (JBV), which began in 1985. These journals fell naturally into two groups: Group I, which published primarily empirical articles, and Group II, which published primarily conceptual or "think" pieces. The journals listed in Table 17.1 are classified into the two groups, along with the number of articles found in each source. Because the focus is on research methods, Group II journals were eliminated from the analysis, and hence *only articles from Group I journals appear in Tables 17.3 and 17.4 (p. 383 and pp. 385-386, respectively).*

The abstracts of all journals in the ABI/INFORM database were searched, as was done for all three previous conference papers. The same key words used by Aldrich

---

TABLE 17.1
Journals Used in 1990–95 Literature
Search and Number of Articles Found in Each

Babson College Conference
Babson College Conference Proceedings for 1990 and 1994: 188

Group I: Primarily Empirical Articles
Academy of Management Journal [AMJ]
    (all are nonentrepreneurship topics): 111
Administrative Science Quarterly [ASQ]
    (plus 47 nonentrepreneurship topics): 2
American Journal of Small Business [ASB]
    (renamed as *Entrepreneurship: Theory and Practice*): 66
Journal of Small Business Management [JSB]: 45
Journal of Business Venturing [JBV]: 81

Group II: Primarily Conceptual Articles
Academy of Management Review [AMR]: 2
Business Horizons [BHO]: 8
California Management Review [CMR]: 5
Harvard Business Review [HBR]: 19
Journal of Business Strategy [JST]: 1
Journal of Economics and Business [EBB]: 0

(1992): "entrepreneur," "corporate venturing," and "intrapreneur," as well as variations on all three words. There was no search on "small business." The search uncovered 164 articles in the Group I journals. The goal was to include all articles published between 1991 and 1995, but *Entrepreneurship: Theory and Practice* (ETP) did not publish a 1995 issue until after the search was completed, and the *Journal of Business Venturing*'s 1995 volume was not available at the time of the search.

Many authors reviewing entrepreneurship methods have made implicit comparisons to mainstream organization studies journals, and so a specific comparison group of journals was included in the study. The *Administrative Science Quarterly* (ASQ) and the *Academy of Management Journal* (AMJ) are the oldest and most prestigious of the organization and management journals, and so all the empirical articles they published in 1990 and 1995 were examined. *All* articles were coded, regardless of subject matter. As they publish almost no nonempirical articles, these journals provide a good standard of comparison for examining research methods. There was no overlap between the articles found in our Group I search and the articles coded from ASQ and AMJ.

Trends in Methodological Focus

The classification scheme of Churchill and Lewis (1986) was used, as modified by Aldrich (1992), and several new categories were added, as shown in Table 17.2, p. 382. The added categories signify several changes in the field. First, in the 1990s ETP began publishing case studies of entrepreneurial firms as a special section of the journal, evidently as a service to instructors looking for classroom discussion material. Other journals have followed a similar route. Second, literature reviews were added as an acknowledgment of a more disciplined type of conceptual article. Literature reviews are an explicit effort to summarize what other authors have said about a specific topic, rather than an attempt at model building or commentary. Third, the occasional papers on research methods in the 1980s apparently spawned a more concentrated effort by authors in the 1990s to deal with methodological issues, and such papers were separated out from other literature reviews. Fourth, the Babson College Conference organizers have taken note of initiatives by the others and put entrepreneurship education on a more solid empirical footing, and entrepreneurship journals have also begun paying more attention to that topic. To maintain continuity with earlier analyses, literature reviews and methods/entrepreneurship education topics are not included in the percents reported in Table 17.3, on p. 383, and subsequent analyses.

TABLE 17.2
Description of Research Methodology Categories Used by Aldrich (1992) and Updated for 1996

Journalistic (vignette or reportage): Refers generally to organizational or personal histories; case studies without conclusions, generalizations, or hypothesis-building; journalistic reporting of events or circumstances, or about people and/or organizations; a more or less straightforward setting forth of the facts, particularly with regard to new or proposed legislation, government programs, etc. (in the latter case without bringing forth discussion of broader policy issues).

Armchair (observational and contemplative theory building): Either anecdotal or formal theory based on one or more of the following: contemplation, experiential learning, and hypothesized relationships between or among variables.

Survey: Survey sampling of larger populations based on questionnaires, tests, interviews, or a combination thereof.

Public database: Analysis of data from public or private archival sources, e.g., Dun & Bradstreet credit files, and industry databases.

Ethnography (field study): Direct and in-depth observation of phenomena in natural settings, longitudinal in nature.

Computer simulation or modeling: Mathematical theory-building allowing manipulation of variables in a nonexperimental way.

Case study: Either a teaching case, based on interviews and documents, or an intensive but nonethnographic study of a single organization or industry.

Approaches not included in categories above or in Tables 17.3 and 17.4:
Literature review: Review of previous research intended to summarize the state of the art rather than build a new model or theory. (1994 = 11)

Methods topics: A discussion or demonstration of research methods rather than a substantive article on entrepreneurship itself. (1994 = 11)

Entrepreneurship education: Conceptual or empirical article on programs for educating entrepreneurs, or an assessment of such programs. (1994 = 26)

Adapted from Churchill, N.D., and Lewis, V.L. (1986): Entrepreneurship research: Direction and methods. In D.L. Sexton and R. Smilor (eds.): *The Art and Science of Entrepreneurship*. Cambridge, MA: Ballinger, 333–365.

TABLE 17.3
Research Methods Used in
Entrepreneurship Articles from 1981 to 1995

Methodology	1981–84 Journals %	1986 Babson %	1989 Babson %	1985–90 Journals %	1990 Babson %	1994 Babson %	1991–95 Journals %	1990–95 ASQ/AMJ %
Journalistic	15	3	3	12	1	0	5	0
Armchair	54	3	0	28	1	2.5	31	4
Survey	24	78	72	43	81	77	47.5	42
mailed	na	(36)	(42)	(21)	(39)	(40)	(34)	(26)
other	na	(42)	(30)	(22)	(42)	(37)	(13.5)	(16)
Public database	4	9	16	17	13	13	9	43
Ethnography	3	6	9	0	1	1	2.5	3
Simulation	0	1	0	0	0	4	0	8
Case Study	N/A	N/A	N/A	N/A	3	2.5	5	0
Total %	**100**	**100**	**100**	**100**	**100**	**100**	**100**	**100**
Total Number	**(298)**	**(67)**	**(74)**	**(124)**	**(70)**	**(83)**	**(165)**	**(156)**

N/A = Not applicable

How much has changed since the last state of the art conference? Not much, as shown in Table 17.3. Indeed, research design and sources of data have not changed very much over the past 15 years, other than a decisive break with journalistic and armchair methods by the journals after 1985. In contrast to a 69 percent share of journal articles from the 1981–84 period, journalistic and armchair articles made up only a 36 percent share in the most recent period. In keeping with the Babson Conference's mandate, almost no journalistic or armchair papers were accepted in either 1990 or 1994, and both ASQ and AMJ effectively bar such papers.

Despite repeated calls for change, survey research has maintained an almost constant share of Babson Conference papers over the past decade, with a 78 percent share in 1986 and a 77 percent share in 1994. Among the entrepreneurship journals, survey methods also maintained their prominent place, rising only slightly from 43 to 48 percent, after a sharp jump from 1981–84 (when nonempirical methods predominated).

In addition to publishing almost no journalistic and armchair papers, the two general organizations journals included a very large number of empirical papers using publicly available data. Whereas only nine percent of articles published in the entrepreneurship journals used publicly available data, 43 percent of the articles published in ASQ/AMJ did so. With so many papers using data from sources accessible to all investigators, ASQ/AMJ have built a pool of empirical results that facilitates replication and disconfirmation research by other scholars. By contrast, most entrepreneurship researchers still work with proprietary data they have collected themselves, mainly through questionnaires.

Ethnographic research has actually declined in significance at Babson Conferences, and it has fared poorly in the journals, as well. After a modest showing at the 1986 and 1989 Babson meetings, ethnographers took a holiday in the 1990s, with only two reporting at the 1990 and 1994 meetings. Ethnographic studies were also unpopular with both entrepreneurship journals and authors of ASQ/AMJ articles: only about 3 percent of the papers published in either set featured ethnographic research. The continued isolation of ethnography reveals the futility of passionate exhortations to unwilling researchers—commentators have repeatedly urged that more such research be conducted.

Simulations and experiments are another category of methods that reviewers have proposed to counter the field's dependence on surveys, but they have never appeared in any of the entrepreneurship journal articles covered by reviews. Low and MacMillan (1988) noted that experiments were extremely rare—they cited only two successful ones from the 1980s. They have also rarely made appearances at Babson conferences. By contrast, about one in 12 of the papers published in ASQ/AMJ have been simulations or experiments, mostly testing social-psychological hypotheses.

Case studies include accounts of nonethnographic empirical reports on single firms or industries, typically prepared for teaching purposes. A handful of such studies has been presented at Babson conferences and in ETP. The mandates of ASQ/AMJ rule out case studies in this mold.

Trends in Research Design

Research design issues involve not only data collection strategies but also strategies affecting the scope of a research project: what topic to focus on, what populations to study, how to define a sampling frame, and so forth. For the third conference, Aldrich (1992) presented data on nine indicators, which have been replicated and extended for this analysis. For ASQ and two entrepreneurship journals—ETP and JBV—information was also collected on four new indicators that directly address the extent to which investigators are following a normal science strategy. The full coding scheme is available from the authors.

Changes in some aspects of research design have occurred, as shown in Table 17.4, but the continuity between our results and those of the last round is more

TABLE 17.4
Research Design

	1986 Babson %	1989 Babson %	1985–90 Journals %	1990 Babson %	1994 Babson %	1991–95 Journals %	1990–95 ASQ/AMJ %
All Studies: Focus on Personality Traits	18	13	15	20	14	31	5
Research Design							
Explicit longitudinal data collection	*	*	*	9	16	5	25
More than one nation studied	5	6	4	14	16	14	8
Included a nation besides U. S.	33	28	18	31	43	40	18
Identified a homogeneous population	22	16	19	15	29	16	46
single homogeneous population	N/A	N/A	N/A	(9)	(16)	(5)	(38)
multiple homogeneous populations	N/A	N/A	N/A	(6)	(13)	(11)	(8)
Explicitly sampled from an identifiable sampling frame	50	35	62	63	47	62	87
Subnational	N/A	N/A	N/A	(22)	(31)	(35)	(38)
National or international	N/A	N/A	N/A	(41)	(16)	(27)	(49)
Replication							
Not a replication	—	*	*	*	*	14	12
Indirect replication	*	—	*	*	*	74	56
Direct replication	*	*	*	*	*	12	32
Total Percent	*	*	—	*	*	100	100
Total Number	*	*	*	*	*	(62)*	(41)*
Topic Area							
Hypothesis Testing	*	*	*	—	*	48	83
Negative Findings?	*	*	*	*	*	17	17
Reliability Assessment	*	*	*	*	—	31	42
Sample: Response Rate							
0–24	25	29	25	30	35	32	8
25–49	35	38	25	40	31	42	32
50–74	20	17	19	25	19	16	34
75–100	20	17	31	5	15	11	26
Total Percent	100	100	100	100	100	101	100
Total Number	(20)	(24)	(16)	(20)	(26)	(57)	(50)

continued

TABLE 17.4, continued

	1986 Babson %	1989 Babson %	1985–90 Journals %	1990 Babson %	1994 Babson %	1991–95 Journals %	1990–95 ASQ/AMJ %
All Studies: Number of Cases	%	%	%	%	%	%	%
1–4	2	5	7	8	4	11	7
5–24	14	13	9	12	17	6	8
25–99	38	24	44	40	46	21	22
100–249	21	20	23	23	22	31	30
250–999	12	18	14	6	11	25	24
1000+	12	20	3	11	1	7	10
Total Percent	99	100	100	100	101	101	101
Total Number	(56)	(55)	(74)	(65)	(79)	(105)	(138)
All Studies: Statistical Methods	%	%	%	%	%	%	%
None	10	13	1	10	9	17	1
Simple percents or raw numbers	43	23	38	37	19	18	5
Chi-Square	10	2	3	10	6	8	3
T-Tests, ANOVA, factor analysis	10	24	24	25	27	24	10
Ordinary least squares	27	36	28	9	21	17	16
Other regression, disciminant analysis	na	na	na	9	11	14	49
Nonrecursive, event history, or formal network models	na	na	na	0	2	1	8
Other	0	2	5	0	5	2	8
Total Percent	100	100	100	100	100	100	100
Total Number	(51)	(53)	(74)	(59)	(64)	(115)	(150)

N/A = not applicable

*Includes only ETP/JBV and ASQ.

impressive. Only one *topic* was chosen for detailed investigation—the extent to which articles focused on the traits of entrepreneurs versus other themes. Debate over the usefulness of studying entrepreneurial traits has been raging for over a decade (Gartner, 1988, 1989), and a small committed community of researchers continues to publish traits research. At the Babson meetings, personality traits research has fluctuated between 13 and 20 percent of papers presented, with the most recent conference (1994) at 14 percent. Only 15 percent of the entrepreneurship journal articles between 1985 and 1990 emphasized an entrepreneur's personality traits, but between 1991 and 1994, 31 percent of journal articles focused on this theme. ETP had the highest (44 percent) but JBV was not far behind (32 percent), and the JSB was close by (26 percent). In sharp contrast to the entrepreneurship journals, AMJ/ASQ published almost no traits articles—only 5 percent fell into this category.

Less Parochial than Before?

At the first state-of-the-art-conference, calls were issued for more cross-national research, and since then, international participation at Babson conference meetings has steadily increased. Several initiatives over the past decade have expanded international involvement, such as Babson College's holding two of its conferences overseas, and Sue Birley and Ian MacMillan's founding of the Global Entrepreneurship Conference. The fruits of these efforts are apparent in the steady increase in the proportion of papers and articles reporting research on countries other than the United States. For Babson, the percent began at 33 in 1986, dropped to 28 in 1989, but then rose to 31 in 1990 , and climbed to 43 by 1994. Similarly, 18 percent of the journal articles in the 1985–90 period included countries other than the United States, growing to 40 percent in the 1991–95 period. By contrast, AMJ and ASQ are much more parochial journals, with about 82 percent of their articles focusing only on U.S. cases.

As in previous years, a much lower percentage of articles are truly comparative, including more than one nation. In 1986, only 5 percent of the Babson papers were comparative, but by 1995 this percentage had more than tripled, to 16 percent. In the 1985–90 period, only 4 percent of the journal articles were comparative, and again this percentage more than tripled by the 1991–95 period, to 14 percent. Comparative studies made up only about 8 percent of AMJ and ASQ's articles. The gap between the high percentage of international contributions and the relatively low percentage of comparative contributions can be attributed to the slow growth of collaborative relations and alliances between scholars from different nations.

Sampling

In normal science, researchers build empirical generalizations by identifying the scope conditions under which a principle holds (McKelvey and Aldrich, 1983) and collecting data from populations that are homogeneous enough to allow generalization to apply to most of their units. Two interrelated decisions are involved: what population is an appropriate context in which to test an hypothesis, and what sampling frame will generate a representative sample of that population or populations. These decisions clearly affect a third decision, as well: what statistical techniques to use. Most modern statistics are based on the assumption that a representative sample has been drawn from a larger limited population.

State-of-the-art reviews at the first two conferences did not explicitly address sampling and population definition issues, but authors implied that researchers had not been as systematic as they should have been. Many of the studies reviewed were based on convenience or quota samples, rather than being drawn from identifiable sampling frames. In 1990, Aldrich presented evidence showing that 62 percent of the journal articles in 1985–90 used an explicit sampling frame, compared with only 35 percent of the 1989 Babson papers. As shown in Table 17.4 (p. 385–386), no change has occurred in the sampling frames of journal articles since then, whereas Babson conference papers have been inconsistent, rising and falling over the years.

We were interested in whether investigators were attempting to generalize their results to entire nations, rather than limiting their claims to local or regional populations. For Babson, the percent of papers with an identifiable sampling frame dropped from 63 to 47 percent, and the percent with national or international frames dropped from 41 to 16 percent.

For entrepreneurship journals, two comparisons can be made to the Babson conferences, and to AMJ/ASQ articles. First, as we noted, the journals have been very consistent in the percent of articles reporting an explicit sampling frame: 62 percent in each of the two study periods. Within the 1991–95 group, the percent of national/international frames in journals was lower than the 1990 Babson Conference but higher than the 1994 meeting. Second, AMJ/ASQ clearly enforce a different set of standards on their submissions than do the entrepreneurship journals, as not only did 87 percent of their papers report an identifiable sampling frame, but also almost half—49 percent—used a national or international frame. This striking difference means that readers of AMJ/ASQ articles can more easily envision generalizing the results of what they read to a national level than can the readers of entrepreneurship journals. Whether it is reasonable to do so, however, depends on whether investigators identify a reasonably homogeneous population or set of populations.

AMJ and ASQ again stand out in comparison with entrepreneurship journals and Babson Conference papers; 46 percent of their articles identified a homogeneous population, with about 80 percent of such articles focusing on a single population and the rest on multiple homogeneous populations. Using an explicit sampling frame substantially increases the likelihood that a homogeneous population will be identified by AMJ/ASQ authors; with no frame, 24 percent of the articles involved a homogeneous population; with a subnational frame, the percent increased to 47 percent; and with a national or international frame, the percent increased further to 61 percent. Within the entrepreneurship journals, there was no association between the type of frame used and the resulting population. Taken together with the strong emphasis in AMJ/ASQ on using an identifiable sampling frame, these results are another manifestation of the strong normal science norms underlying AMJ/ASQ's editorial strategy.

The contrast with entrepreneurship journals and Babson papers is clear-cut: the percent of entrepreneurship journal articles reporting on homogeneous populations actually fell from 19 percent in the 1985–90 period to 16 percent in the 1991–95 period, whereas Babson's papers have fluctuated between 15 and 29 percent over the past decade. In contrast to AMJ/ASQ papers, Babson papers were about equally divided between single and multiple homogeneous populations, and the small fraction of entrepreneurship journal articles with a homogeneous population was slanted toward multiple populations.

A final sampling issue involves deciding between cross-sectional and longitudinal data collection, taking account of resource constraints and problems of access to data from more than one time point. In previous methodological reviews, almost every author decried the scarcity of longitudinal designs and dynamic statistical analyses. Aldrich (1992) thought he detected some hopeful signs in his review of research between 1985 and 1990, but a closer look at his coding scheme revealed that he had been too generous in crediting investigators with longitudinal designs. Accordingly, the coding of the 1990–95 period, as shown in Table 17.4, was used and asterisks were entered for columns from previous years.

Very few entrepreneurship conference papers or articles used an explicit dynamic design: 9 percent in 1990 and 16 percent in 1994 for Babson, and only 5 percent for entrepreneurship journals in the 1991–95 period. AMJ/ASQ articles, by contrast, were much more likely to use dynamic designs, with one-quarter of all papers making use of longitudinal data sets. The considerable gap between AMJ/ASQ and the entrepreneurship journals *cannot* be fully explained by resource constraints on entrepreneurship investigators because entrepreneurship journal articles are now using samples that are equivalent in size to those in AMJ/ASQ, as noted below. Moreover, entrepreneurship researchers are more likely than AMJ/ASQ authors to use cross-national designs, which undoubtedly involve more logistical and organizational problems than one-nation designs. Instead, the difference in use of longitudinal data may stem from differences in how problems are conceptualized and how much attention is given to the fit between theories of action and the data needed to test such theories.

Replication and Hypothesis Testing

Normal science norms concerning "progress" strongly support four other practices: replicating previous studies before placing much confidence in their results, formulating explicit a priori hypotheses to avoid data-dredging and dust-bowl empiricism, checking the reliability of one's measures whenever possible, and publishing negative or disconfirming results rather than only supportive ones. Woo et al. (1991) demonstrated the value of replication when they found that a common typology—craftsmen versus opportunists—did not stand up to closer scrutiny. These practices are held up as a standard against which to judge research, but they also have the effect of slowing down the introduction of innovative topics. Authors who adopt a more pragmatic, topical orientation may dismiss these practices as stultifying and antithetical to creativity in entrepreneurship research.

Articles in ETP, JBV, and ASQ were coded along these four dimensions. The coding process was revealing because it showed how the norms regarding professional discourse differ across fields. ASQ readers may expect to see precedents clearly listed and hypotheses formally stated, whereas one often has to wade through paragraphs of prose for such information in ETP and JBV.

Most articles in all three journals made some mention of theoretical precedents for their research—86 percent of ETP/JBV and 88 percent of ASQ papers—but ASQ authors were more likely to claim a direct replication of previous work than were ETP/JBV authors. We found two types of direct replications. First, a handful of papers specifically replicated a prior finding by choosing the same population, the same concepts, the same indicators, and examining the same relationships. Second, and more typically, authors attempted to confirm the form of a relationship that was previously observed, such as the pattern of density dependence in founding rates, or a finding that early adopters of an innovation are more central in a network than late adopters. A key criterion was that an author not only cited general precedents for examining a problem but also cited specific empirical generalizations as justification for testing a proposition (again). We found that 32 percent of the ASQ and 12 percent of the ETP/JBV articles fulfilled this criterion.

Authors more frequently used earlier papers when applying an older idea to a new domain, arguing that a concept or principle was important, without citing previous empirical generalizations. The new study may have created hypotheses that don't specifically refer to a past study, using concepts that cover a wide range of previous work, with indicators unique to the new study. About 56 percent of the ASQ and 74 percent of the ETP/JBV papers fell into this category.

Hypothesis-testing practices differed dramatically between the two sets of journals: 83 percent of the ASQ papers contained explicit hypotheses, compared with 48 percent of ETP/JBV papers. In roughly half of the ETP/JBV articles without explicit hypotheses, authors posed questions that were descriptive and did not predict the form or sign of an expected relation. Without clearly specifying hypotheses, authors cannot really know if their results confirm or disconfirm previous findings. In any case, as shown in Table 17.4, very few published papers reported findings that conflicted with the expectations authors laid out in their theoretical introductions. Our criterion for negative findings was that 50 percent or more of the measures of association reported had to be nonsignificant, and only 17 percent of the articles in both sets of journals contained such a pattern. Among articles with explicit hypotheses, 23 percent reported negative findings, compared with only 6 percent of authors who had failed to set out formal expectations (two out of 35 articles). This pattern did not differ significantly between ASQ and ETP/JBV.

Determining whether a study actually obtained negative findings was difficult, a sign that norms surrounding research practice are still in flux, even in the most prestigious journal in organization studies. Even if authors explicitly stated their hypotheses, their results and discussion sections often did not refer back to which hypotheses were confirmed and which were not. Often, authors concluded their papers by ignoring what they had said in their theory review section. Even in ASQ, authors who presented formal, numbered hypotheses sometimes ignored them when discussing their results.

The next assessment of normal science practices was whether authors tested the reliability of at least some of their measures. Reliability was easiest to code when personality traits or other individual characteristics were studied, for two reasons. First, authors tended to adopt measures with previously documented reliability. Second, authors studying traits or using individuals as units of analysis and data collection tended to use multiple-item questionnaires, allowing the collection of multiple indicators, and thus their raw data lent itself to easy manipulation. When organizations were the unit of analysis, authors apparently either assumed that their data were reliable, or ignored this issue. We noticed that when organizational records were used for individuals or organizations, investigators paid almost no attention to their reliability or to the use of multiple indicators.

About 31 percent of the ETP/JBV papers reported reliability checks on at least some of their measures, compared with 42 percent of the ASQ papers. A strong association was found between authors attempting to replicate prior research and doing at least some testing for data reliability. Reliability testing was performed in 7 percent of the nonreplications, 37 percent of the indirect replications, and 50 percent of the direct replications.

Without data from prior years, it cannot be determined whether the patterns uncovered here are a continuation of past practices or points in a long-term trend. The results that have been obtained will encourage some normal science advocates but disappoint others. Almost all authors made some pretense of linking their work to the past, but only a minority of entrepreneurship researchers situated themselves squarely in a stream of empirical generalizations that they intended to replicate. About half of the entrepreneurship papers developed formal expectations or hypotheses, an encouraging sign but one that pales in comparison with ASQ's standard. Few studies disappointed their authors, as over 80 percent reported confirming findings, thus providing few clues as to what to discard for the next round of research projects.

Response Rates and Sample Size

Regardless of whether investigators chose cases from an identifiable sampling frame, many nonetheless treated the resulting target population of respondents or cases as a "sample." They then reported how many cases they obtained information from out of the original target population, enabling them to report a response rate for their efforts. Table 17.4 shows the response rates for all studies using surveys or public databases. Some studies did not report response rates, possibly biasing our figures upward.

As Aldrich (1992) noted, response rates to entrepreneurship surveys have never been very high, and that tradition continued from 1990 to 1995. Response rates for studies presented at Babson conferences have fluctuated somewhat over the past decade and may have become worse. In 1986, 60 percent of the studies reported response rates *below* 50 percent; in 1989, it was 67 percent; in 1990, 70 percent, and in 1994, 66 percent. For the journals, the latest period was a step backward, as 74 percent reported response rates *below* 50 percent, compared with 50 percent in the 1985–90 period. At these levels of response from the target population, serious questions arise about possible sample bias. Only a small number of the studies reported tests for possible sample selection bias.

Response rates for ASQ/AMJ were higher than for the entrepreneurship journals from 1990 to 1995, as 60 percent of their papers reported rates of 50 percent or better. Because no data exists for AMJ/ASQ from the earlier period, it is not known whether this is an improvement. Only 8 percent of the articles reported response rates below 25 percent, compared with about one-third of papers published in the entrepreneurship journals or presented at Babson in recent years.

In calculating the number of cases on which a study was based, surveys in addition to ethnographies and case studies were included to maintain continuity with reviews at previous conferences. At the last state-of-the-art conference, sample sizes were larger in Babson conference papers than in the entrepreneurship journals, and Aldrich (1992) thought he detected a trend toward increasing sample sizes. His predictions were premature, however, at least insofar as Babson is concerned. In 1990, 60 percent of the Babson papers worked with samples *under* 100, and in 1994, the percent actually rose to 67.

In contrast, the number of cases analyzed in journal articles increased substantially between the 1985–90 and 1991–95 periods. In the former, about 60 percent of the studies were based on fewer than 100 cases, and the figure dropped to only 38 percent in the latest period. Indeed, the study size distributions for entrepreneurship journals and AMJ/ASQ are statistically indistinguishable, especially in their tails—both have about the same percentage of very small- and very large-scale studies.

Statistical Methods

Following the lead of reviewers at the two previous conferences, Aldrich (1992) noted that investigators continued to rely heavily on simple descriptive statistics, but he detected a trend toward greater use of significance tests and models assessing the strength of associations between variables. In this chapter, an account is being taken of the evolving nature of analytic techniques, and two new categories are added to the classification scheme: "other regression and discriminant analysis" and "nonre-cursive, event history, or formal network models." These categories will ultimately prove their value when they are used again at the next conference.

If articles in AMJ/ASQ are used as a standard against which to judge the field, then the statistical-sophistication gap noted in earlier critiques is still enormous: 81 percent of the papers in AMJ/ASQ use ordinary least squares or more sophisticated methods to analyze their data, compared with only 34 percent in entrepreneurship journals and 39 percent at the 1994 Babson conference. At the other extreme, only 6 percent of the articles in AMJ/ASQ rely on simple percents or raw numbers, compared with 35 percent in the entrepreneurship journals and 28 percent at the 1994 Babson conference.

If changes from an earlier period are used as a standard against which to judge the present state of the field, then the statistical-sophistication gap may be closing, although progress has been slow. Simple percents, raw numbers, or no numbers at all dropped from 53 percent at the 1986 Babson conference to 28 percent in 1994. In entrepreneurship journals, use of methods such as regression analysis and other methods that explore the form of associations between variables increased from 28 percent in the 1985–90 period to 34 percent in the 1991–95 period. More sophisticated forms of analysis—beyond ordinary least squares—have also appeared, including event history analysis.

Ethnography

Ethnographic or direct field observations allow researchers to uncover the meaning of patterns in social processes and to detect subtle processes and interpret interactions that participants may be unable to articulate in interviews. Unlike mailed surveys or archival records, ethnographic methods allow researchers to pursue intriguing lines of thought they had not considered before entering the field. Themes in the anthropological literature mesh very well with the concerns of entrepreneurship researchers, including the processes of accumulating knowledge and skills and gaining access to resources. Ethnographic work is extremely time-consuming, however, and requires a significant "methodological investment" (Stewart, 1991).

At the third state-of-the-art conference, only 13 true field studies were discovered: 11 from the Babson conferences and two more in the HBR. In the search, only six true field studies on entrepreneurship topics were found: two from Babson and four in JBV. Calls for more field research have been as ubiquitous as the clamor for more longitudinal studies, and with the same consequences: still more calls for action but almost no actual research heeding the calls! Despite repeated affirmations of the value of field work, the number of ethnographic studies found through the search strategy dropped by about half from the last conference. The lack of ethnographic research cannot be attributed to ignorance of its value or the methods for carrying it out, as a large and growing literature exists on such methods. Applications are also visible in other management and organization fields, such as among organizational culture researchers (Frost et al., 1991).

Babson and JBV

Have the Babson College conferences been playing a role as an incubator for papers that are revised and then published in entrepreneurship journals? By nurturing particular types of research, Babson may have contributed to the standardization of research practices in entrepreneurship and created a core community of researchers who can play gatekeeper roles in the profession and enforce its gradually emerging standards.

This question was investigated by asking the 20 researchers most active at Babson from 1990 to 1994 whether they had published their Babson papers. The 20 authors' names appeared 151 times in the Babson Conference Proceedings between 1990 and 1994. The researchers were asked whether their Babson papers had been published—somewhere other than the Babson Proceedings—and where. Fifteen people replied, representing 117 Babson papers. Forty percent of the papers had been published, 6 percent were under review, 6 percent were still in process, and 3 percent were in limbo, with the authors having lost track of them (coauthors may have been working on them). The rest were unpublished and no longer being worked on.

Of the 47 papers that had been published, 14 were in JBV, 10 in books or monographs, three in *Entrepreneurship and Regional Development*, three in the *Journal of Business Research*, and the remainder were scattered over 13 other journals. No baseline exists from which to judge the relative success of these authors, but three points stand out. First, over half of the papers presented have either been published or were still under active revision. These authors have treated the Babson conferences as an opportunity for the first presentation of their ideas, rather than as an end it itself. Second, since its founding in 1985, JBV has become the premier outlet for entrepreneurship research, and it has been the journal these Babson participants have considered first when preparing their work for publication. Third, the diversity of outlets for entrepreneurship research is indicated by the range of 16 journals in which the 47 articles were published, and there are many others that occasionally publish entrepreneurship papers. Diversity enhances the opportunities for specialized or unusual research to find an outlet, but it also complicates the process of developing agreed-upon norms of research practice. JBV's rising prominence in the entrepreneurship journal market may allow it to act as a core arbiter of standards for the field.

Have We Made a Difference?

It has been suggested that reasonable people might adopt one of at least three perspectives—normal science, multiplicity and diversity, or pragmatism—in considering whether entrepreneurship research has made much progress over the past two decades. The perspective adopted in this study suggests what features are important in defining a coherent field of research and focuses attention on whether progress is being made in the features that define coherence. In this section, features that suggest coherence from each of the three perspectives are discussed, and the evidence in favor of progress for people adopting each of the three is reviewed.

Normal Science

Previous reviewers have mainly adopted a normal science view when they examined gains and shortcomings of entrepreneurship research. Because this chapter builds on the past, it adopts a predominantly normal science viewpoint. To recapitulate, coherence, from the normal science perspective, consists in pursuing research that results in the cumulation of findings over time, both within and across individual scholars' work. Cumulation is generated when a group of scholars comes to accept as a worldview the discipline of a research paradigm that defines *both* what are legitimate and interesting questions and what are legitimate methods for attempting to answer them.

Progress from this perspective has been limited, in comparison both with past work and with more general, high-quality organizational research. The entrepreneurship literature has become somewhat more comparative and international, and less likely to engage in purely speculative or purely descriptive work. Statistical sophistication has gotten slightly better—at least at the low end. The work we reviewed is still dominated by survey research, and response rates have not improved.

Empirical articles in entrepreneurship journals are using bigger samples, often as large as those found in the top organizations journals. Entrepreneurship articles are more likely than work in ASQ and AMJ to utilize cross-national data. However, papers in ASQ are more likely to test hypotheses explicitly, and to directly replicate previous work. The top organizations' journals are more likely than the top outlets in entrepreneurship research to publish articles that are statistically sophisticated, use explicit and national or international sampling frames, identify homogeneous populations, and provide dynamic analyses of longitudinal data.

Multiplicity and Diversity

It has been argued that there is no well-developed paradigm creating coherence in entrepreneurship research. Multiple voices, expressing multiple points of view and methods, contribute to the body of work reaching the outlets that were examined. Coherence in a field supporting multiple paradigms suggests the existence of multiple communities of scholars accepting and committed to research worldviews that dictate which questions are interesting and what methods are legitimate. In a normal science view, multiple paradigms might appear to exist either in a somewhat chaotic "pre-paradigmatic" state of development or when a new paradigm is positioned to replace an old one but is waiting out the retirement of those scholars wedded to the old worldview.

Multiple paradigms might be expected in entrepreneurship research because scholars might come to the entrepreneurship field with commitments to their home disciplines, such as strategy, economics, sociology, psychology, and others. The closest evidence found of multiple paradigms was reflected in research that has been labeled "traits" or "not traits." Research focusing on psychological traits of entrepreneurs has been reviewed and sharply criticized in several prominent articles. The authors of these critiques have called for an end to traits research and have tried to cleanly distinguish traits research from other scholarship. However, as has been shown, traits topics are continuing to generate significant numbers of papers, and several authors have published rejections of the earlier critiques. If one measure of a paradigm is the topics it defines as interesting, then one might infer that traits research is generated from a paradigm evolving separately from the paradigm underlying other behavioral and "rates" research. It has also been suggested that traits research is more likely to discuss and evaluate the reliability of its measures and to utilize established psychological measures and scales. If paradigms define what methods are legitimate, one might also infer that a traits paradigm continues to emerge.

However, the evidence for multiple paradigms, beyond "traits versus nontraits" is weak. Within the chorus of multiple voices, nevertheless, there are some signs of coherence at the level of the research community. A substantial core of scholars write papers for Babson year after year, and continue to develop those papers over time. Ideas introduced at Babson find later outlets as journal articles far more frequently than had been imagined. Coherence and progress are also evident in the emergence and improvement of leading entrepreneurship journals. In particular, JBV provides a favored forum for a wide variety of scholars, including one group committed to Babson as an incubator and another group that seems to eschew participation at Babson. ETP has taken on an important role as an outlet for literature reviews and self-reflection by entrepreneurship researchers.

Pragmatism

Little space has been devoted to the issue of pragmatism, since Frank Hoy in Chapter 16 in this book provides a focused examination of the relevance of entrepreneurship research to a variety of stakeholders. We believe that entrepreneurship research has become more relevant to practicing entrepreneurs and policymakers and that there is both need and hope for greater improvements in getting the word out.

Pragmatism is addressed only from the perspective of its effects on the coherence of entrepreneurship research. A great deal of the research reviewed was energized by the belief—debated in some circles but largely accepted among entrepreneurship researchers—that entrepreneurial firms generate an inordinate proportion of job growth in this country, and that they provide a powerful outlet for innovation (see the special issue of *Small Business Economics* in which Harrison [1995] took on his critics). This orientation to macroeconomic effects is frequently implicit but sometimes quite blunt and directive (e.g., Low and MacMillan, 1988).

In normal science, a paradigm helps to structure research by defining what questions are interesting. Pragmatic researchers who focus on the macro-effects and environment of entrepreneurial activities similarly define what is interesting, and thereby lend topical coherence to the field. Such coherence may come at the expense of topics which might be important to audiences less concerned with macroeconomic effects.

One such audience consists of practicing entrepreneurs. Few entrepreneurs can afford the luxury of time spent ruminating on the powerful role of entrepreneurship in the greater economy. In contrast to academic researchers and policymakers, most entrepreneurs need to be closely oriented to the relatively micro-concerns of their own businesses. Researchers who orient their research to macroeconomic policy issues should not expect to find their work of direct practical value to individual business owners.

A Managed or Evolutionary Process?

From each of three perspectives—normal science, multiple paradigms, and pragmatism—a case can be made for researchers' contributions to the coherence of entrepreneurship research and progress over time. Attention to scientific standards, an openness to competing interests and approaches, and a concern with practical relevance all continue to contribute to entrepreneurship research. But from all three perspectives, progress has been quite limited. Judging from normal science standards, entrepreneurship research is still in a very early stage. If no single powerful paradigm exists, then there is even less evidence for multiple coherent points of view. Finally, entrepreneurship research is improving but still of limited topical concern and value to practicing entrepreneurs.

Admonitions to change practice in entrepreneurship research seem to have little effect, regardless of the status of their source. The field lacks the sort of overall coherence that might allow a limited group of leading figures to exert strong intentional direction on the field. Rather, what coherence exists depends on a mixture of legitimate perspectives. Progress comes in scattered bits from a variety of sources and is much closer to being an evolutionary process than one that is managed, or manageable, by leading scholars.

Progress tends to be achieved in young scientific fields without initial consensus on definitions (Vander Werf and Brush, 1989). Progress has tended to come after groups of researchers converge on study of simple, well-defined "entities" or populations. But for us, their most important point is that convergence on what is studied comes because researchers are *attracted* by the initial progress made by early investigators. The convergence is spontaneous rather than forced.

What lesson can be learned from history? Influence comes from exemplary research, not from the propagation of rules or admonitions. The field will be shaped by those who produce research that interests and attracts others to build on their work. This may also provide an antidote to the frustratingly repetitive and ineffective calls we hear to do "more ethnographic work" and more "longitudinal studies." Those who believe they know the path forward need to do such work themselves and who can provide exemplars that attract others to follow.

REFERENCES

Aldrich, H.E. 1992. Methods in our madness? Trends in entrepreneurship research. In D.L. Sexton and J.D. Kasarda (eds.): *The State of the Art in Entrepreneurship Research*. Boston: PWS-Kent, 191-213.

Aldrich, H.E. and G. Wiedenmayer. 1993. From traits to rates: An ecological perspective on organizational foundings. In J. Katz and R.H. Brockhaus (eds.): *Advances in Entrepreneurship, Firm Emergence, and Growth*, vol. 1. Greenwich, CT: JAI Press, 145-195.

Aldrich, H.E., S.W. Fowler, N. Liou , and S.J. Marsh. 1994. Other people's concepts: "Why and how we sustain historical continuity in our field." *Organization* 1(1):65-80.

Carsrud, A.L., K.W. Olm, and G.E. Eddy. 1986. Entrepreneurship: Research in quest of a paradigm. In D.L. Sexton and R. Smilor (eds.): *The Art and Science of Entrepreneurship*. Cambridge, MA: Ballinger, 367-378.

Churchill, N.C., and V.L. Lewis. 1986. Entrepreneurship research: Directions and methods. In D. Sexton and R. Smilor (eds.): *The Art and Science of Entrepreneurship*. Cambridge, MA: Ballinger, 333-365.

Frost, P.J., L.F. Moore, M.R. Louis, C.C. Lundberg, and J. Martin (eds.): 1991. *Reframing Organizational Culture*. Newbury Park, CA: Sage.

Gartner, W.B. 1988. "Who is an entrepreneur?" is the wrong question. *American Journal of Small Business* 12(4):11-32.

Gartner, W.B. 1989. Some suggestions for research on entrepreneurial traits and characteristics. *Entrepreneurship: Theory and Practice* 14(1):27-38.

Harrison, B. 1995. Symposium on Harrison's "lean and mean": What are the questions? *Small Business Economics* 7(5):25-31.

Katz, J.A., R.H. Brockhaus, and G.E. Hills. 1993. Demographic variables in entrepreneurship research. In J. Katz and R. Brochaus (eds.): *Advances in Entrepreneurship, Firm Emergence, and Growth*. Greenwich, CT: JAI. Press, 197-236.

Low, M., and I.C. MacMillan. 1988. Entrepreneurship: Past research and future challenges. *Journal of Management* 14(2):139-161.

McKelvey, B., and H.E. Aldrich. 1983. Applied population science. *Administrative Science Quarterly*, 28(1):101-128.

Mone, M.A., and W. McKinley. 1993. The uniqueness value and its consequences for organization studies. *Journal of Management Inquiry* 2(3):284-296.

Paulin, W.L., R.E. Coffey, and M.E. Spaulding. 1982. Entrepreneurship research: Methods and directions. In C.A. Kent, D.L. Sexton, and K.H. Vesper (eds.): *Encyclopedia of Entrepreneurship*. Englewood Cliffs, NJ: Prentice Hall, 353-373.

Perryman, M.R. 1982. Commentary on research in the field of entrepreneurship. In C.A. Kent, D.L. Sexton, and K.H. Vesper (eds.): *Encyclopedia of Entrepreneurship*. Englewood Cliffs, NJ: Prentice Hall, 377-378.

Peterson, R., and D. Horvath. 1982. Commentary on research in the field of entrepreneurship. In C.A. Kent, D.L. Sexton, and K.H. Vesper (eds.): *Encyclopedia of Entrepreneurship*. Englewood Cliffs, NJ: Prentice Hall, 374-376.

Stewart, A. 1991. A prospectus on the anthropology of entrepreneurship. *Entrepreneurship: Theory and Practice* 16(2):71-92.

Vander Werf, P.A., and C.G. Brush. 1989. Achieving empirical progress in an undefined field. *Entrepreneurship: Theory and Practice* 14(2):45-58.

Woo, C.Y., A.C. Cooper, and W.C. Dunkelberg. 1991. The development and interpretation of entrepreneurial typologies. *Journal of Business Venturing* 6(2):93-114.

Wortman, M.S., Jr. 1986. A unified framework, research typologies, and research prospectuses for the interface between entrepreneurship and small business. In D.L. Sexton and R. Smilor (eds.): *The Art and Science of Entrepreneurship*. Cambridge, MA: Ballinger, 272-332.

CHAPTER 18

Entrepreneurship Research Needs and Issues

DONALD L. SEXTON

All that we know is still infinitely less than all that still remains unknown.
—William Harvey, 1628

IFTEEN YEARS HAVE PASSED SINCE THE FIRST STATE-OF-THE-ART conference and book. It was the intent at the first meeting in 1980 to examine the state of the art at five-year intervals. Each five-year evaluation was to start with a determination of what topics in the previous book were still issues of concern, which no longer represented cutting edge research, and what new or emerging issues needed to be examined. These determinations, then as now, represent the consensus of the leading scholars in the field. A review of the topics and the research over the past 15 years provides an assessment of the field as seen by the direction in which the field is moving, the advancements in the state of the art for continuing topics and the remaining research issues that need to be addressed to increase our knowledge in the field of entrepreneurship.

Advancements in entrepreneurship research, in many ways, have paralleled the importance of entrepreneurship to our nation's economy. Research contributions in specific areas have advanced at an uneven rate. Topics that were considered important at earlier meetings are no longer of interest. This is mostly because the field has moved beyond where it was, and these topics either did not make a contribution to the basic body of knowledge of the field or has been found to be of lesser importance with the discovery of other relative concepts. Their purpose, however, was served as they provided a stepping stone to a more advanced level of understanding.

In 1980, the field was beginning to emerge and what was known at that time represented the newness of the field. Issues of importance included studies related to the characteristics of the entrepreneur and his or her psychology, the social environment, and the environment for entrepreneurship. Other topics addressed included financing the Austrian school of economic thought, the impact of innovation on entrepreneurship, and corporate entrepreneurship.

By the second conference and book in 1985, the field was beginning to become more structured and broader concepts started to appear. The implications, process, and components of growth replaced studies of the entrepreneur. Distinctions were drawn between entrepreneurship and small business on the basis of income generation versus value creation and average or status quo growth versus rapid growth. Also at this time, many of the special interest topics were beginning to be viewed as market specialization rather than components of entrepreneurship.

The third conference and book occurred in 1990 as the field of entrepreneurship began to be recognized for its enormity and importance. Integration of entrepreneurship research with research in other areas was a major topic of examination. International entrepreneurship was being examined, and research in the areas of venture financing and growth were making significant advances.

Concurrent with developments in the academic research of the field was the recognition of entrepreneurship as a major contributor to the economy of the United States. This, in turn, generated more interest, recognition, and appreciation of the academic field of entrepreneurship.

Some areas of interest have remained important over the 15-year period. Financing growth has always been a topic of interest. In this book, however, the topic of harvesting the value created in the firm is addressed for the first time.

Research methodology has also advanced significantly, but the application of more advanced techniques is still not a standard of the research. This could be due, in part, to the variety of disciplines used to train those now on this field of endeavor.

Research methods have always been hampered by the lack of longitudinal databases. New databases currently being developed are expected to overcome this limitation. Further, alliances with public and private organizations are resulting in increased availability of data that can span the time frames required to evaluate the impact of government activities on firms.

The concern for relevance in entrepreneurship research, which has always been an area of concern, is now becoming an even more significant topic. An increased focus on this area comes with the recognition of a broader scope of stakeholders that are interested in new research findings.

The issues that confront researchers of entrepreneurship have changed as the field has emerged. Both the changes in the state-of-the-art research and the growth of entrepreneurship as an important sector in our nation's economy are reflected in this volume. The attitude of entrepreneurship researchers toward their field has changed from one of wonderment in 1980, to excitement in 1985, to an awareness of the magnitude of their tasks in 1990 and is now one of concern over the changes needed to continue the current momentum into the next century.

Many research needs and issues have been recognized and addressed. Others have been recognized but have not yet been resolved, and there are many issues still to be recognized at all. The emphasis of this final chapter in the fourth state-of-the-art book is to summarize the findings of the contributors to each topic and to communicate future research needs or issues that, when resolved, will help the field continue its rapid growth. In essence, the purpose is to delineate a research agenda for the field of entrepreneurship in the year 2000 and beyond.

Overall questions that need to be addressed include:

❖ What value do we bring to companies wrestling with the issues of growth as they compete in the new economy?

❖ How do entrepreneurs rate entrepreneurship research, and how can they benefit from the results?

❖ How can academics, entrepreneurs, and consultants form strategic alliances in such a way that the field of entrepreneurship does not face the possibility of becoming irrelevant in the new economy?

❖ How do we address the issue that, in the new market economy, battles will be decided by competition that occurs long before, or entirely outside, the end-product market?

Is our research keeping pace with the fast-changing issue sets that confront growth-oriented entrepreneurs applying the current best practices known today?

The research needed to propel the field into the 21st century is enormous and varied. Excerpts from the chapters in this book best portray these needs:

With regard to entrepreneurial teams, few topics in entrepreneurship research are so central and also so under-researched. (Cooper and Daily, Chapter 6)

Entrepreneurial teams are at the heart of any new venture. It is also clear that there has been little empirical research examining how teams are formed, how they function, whether they are stable, and how they influence organizational performance. (Cooper and Daily, Chapter 6)

There is no dearth of theories in the domain of organizational mode. The need of the hour is not more theories but high-quality empirical research on the area of mode choice in new business startups. (Venkataraman and Macmillan, Chapter 7)

There is a want for a more complete understanding of the identification, acquisition, and deployment of resources within various ethnic groups. Research is needed to answer the question, Why do ethnic entrepreneurs who have businesses funded through similar processes and have similar resource input experience different outcomes and levels of success? (Butler and Greene, Chapter 12)

The major opportunity for finance students in this field is the exploration of effective methods of valuation of the private firm. This includes the valuation of the investment structured to mitigate risk and reduce the cost of capital. (Brophy, Chapter 1)

Most research has focused on the earlier stages of entrepreneurship, namely, the identification and exploitation of the opportunity. Yet all entrepreneurs must eventually leave the firm. While departing situations will differ, all will face it sooner or later. For some, knowledge of the harvesting process will enhance their after-business life. (Petty, Chapter 4)

Many international research articles are devoid of theory, hypothesis, or even research questions. (McDougall and Oviatt, Chapter 13)

There is a direct relationship between business growth and complexity. Businesses do not follow the same stages of growth. They develop at different rates that require a transition to move to the next level. Growth may affect how an organization relates to its environment by changing the nature of an organization's environment interface. (Covin and Slevin, Chapter 5)

There appears to be no need to create a market for youth entrepreneurship programs. It already exists. The challenge is to meet the existing demand with cost-effective programs and proven benefits. (Kourilsky and Carlson, Chapter 9)

General models for the education of entrepreneurs need to be developed. Greater emphasis should be placed on the development and evaluation of specific pedagogical methods suitable for practicing entrepreneurs. (Young, Chapter 10)

The most promising opportunity for informal venture capital research is expected to flow from efforts in the United States and abroad to create new early-stage equity capital markets for entrepreneurs. (Freear, Sohl, and Wetzel, Chapter 3)

We know very little about the family firms within minority subpopulations, differences of family firms between large-scale and micro-enterprises, and the dynamic change of the life course of the family firm. (Upton and Heck, Chapter 11)

Transition research is needed to address how family business succession differs for family dyads other than father/son and mother/daughter. (Upton and Heck, Chapter 11)

Not-for-profit entrepreneurship is an area that can benefit from most advances in entrepreneurship research. (Hisrich, Freeman, Standley, Yankey, and Young, Chapter 14)

Research in general does not get to the heart of venture capital decision-making, which is how venture capitalists decide whether or not to invest in ventures that get beyond the initial reading of the business plan. (Timmons and Bygrave, Chapter 2)

Clearly, the needs are many. However, entrepreneurship is a dynamic and growing field that will provide ample opportunities for researchers interested in studies that will further the development.

The field will not be advanced unless the quality of research is accurate, reliable, and drawn from well-defined samples with response rates that are of a statistically significant size.

All researchers have the responsibility to provide quality research that will interest others to join our endeavor. Some of the methodological concerns, as expressed by the chapter contributors, include:

Researchers should be cautious in implying causalty in our findings. (Cooper and Daily, Chapter 6)

International entrepreneurship is not an academic endeavor but an academic arena in which many disciplines extend their theories in an attempt to discover and explain facts about entrepreneurship across national borders. (McDougall and Oviatt, Chapter 13)

A collaborative approach to international entrepreneurship would allow the discovery of the most powerful rather than most favorable practices. In addition, bringing more approaches to bear on questions will likely lead to the use of more sophisticated theories. (McDougall and Oviatt, Chapter 14)

It is important for researchers in the field to report the characteristics of the firms being studied. Omitting descriptive statistics that reviewers must have before they can evaluate the work is a trend that should be discouraged. (Timmons and Bygrave, Chapter 2)

Emerging research directions do not focus on the share of net jobs generated by small versus large firms. Researchers have shifted their focus to measuring the economic contributions of firm formation, growth, decline, and death. (Kirchoff and Acs, Chapter 8)

This field has been plagued by unsubstantiated opinions as well as research of such quality that it cannot be extrapolated to a broader base. Following the suggestions and concerns discussed within this book will help stay the myths and gain respectability for the field.

Establishing relevance, for most academic research, is a problem. When the audience is fast-growth entrepreneurs, it is an especially difficult task. Entrepreneurs do not want to be concerned about surveys or biases, nonvalidated test instruments, statistically significant samples, or response rates. The following comments address some of the relevance issues for the field of entrepreneurship research:

In the area of financing growth, research is needed that builds practical models of various types of firms and industries. These models will be of great help in raising the level of economic and financial understanding among entrepreneurs. (Brophy, Chapter 1)

Despite the volume and visibility of research activity, external stakeholders continue to be uninformed of entrepreneurship research findings or are skeptical of the value of these contributions. Researchers need to communicate clearly and effectively as well as find new media and methods to transmit their findings. (Hoy, Chapter 16)

Entrepreneurs of the future will be more inclined to accept and embrace the inevitability of continuous organizational change. They will also be, correspondingly, more proficient at transition management. (Covin and Slevin, Chapter 5)

There are abundant opportunities for venture capital research. However, it seems that the more relevant the research is to the practitioners, the harder it is to conduct. This is due to the fact that venture capitalists are notoriously inaccessible to academic researchers. (Timmons and Bygrave, Chapter 2)

As Hoy points out in Chapter 16, we have stakeholders beyond fellow academicians and students. We must reach out to practicing entrepreneurs and to public policymakers.

As noted by a number of the chapter authors, one of the major impediments has been the lack of access to longitudinal relational databases. The major concerns of the contributors on this topic were:

There is no "greatest hits" data source for small firm analysis. The problem is that most databases 1) do not cover both the characteristics of the firm and the characteristics of the firm owner, 2) do not include balance sheet and income statement financial data, and 3) report data that considerably lags in timelines. In addition, most data sets are highly fragmented, follow varying formats, imply assorted definitions, possess different foci, and are generally unrelated. (Phillips and Dennis, Chapter 15)

There are no directories of business angels and no public records of investment transactions. (Freear, Sohl, and Wetzel, Chapter 3)

We need to create informal venture capital databases that are substantial enough to support vigorous research. (Freear, Sohl, and Wetzel, Chapter 3)

Applied research in the area of family business is impaired by the lack of a well-established national statistical series of high quality and comprehensive data sources. (Upton and Heck, Chapter 11)

Until recently, the only source of business statistical data in the United States was that produced by government agencies. The availability of this data was constrained by federal laws which prevented the release of information about individual firms. Thus, micro-data is nonexistent. (Kirchoff and Acs, Chapter 8)

Existing databases do not allow reliable information of new firms and their founders. (Kirchoff and Acs, Chapter 8)

Fortunately, the overall interest in the field has resulted in a number of new database developments, which will provide for more research opportunities.

In closing, the hope of the chapter contributors and the editors is that this book, like the ones that preceded it, will soon become obsolete as new and more advanced research establishes the field of entrepreneurship research as an academic discipline that will make a difference in the economic development of the United States.

Index